THE NEW MIDDLE AGES

BONNIE WHEELER, *Series Editor*

The New Middle Ages presents transdisciplinary studies of medieval cultures. It includes both scholarly monographs and essay collections.

PUBLISHED BY PALGRAVE:

Women in the Medieval Islamic World: Power, Patronage, and Piety
edited by Gavin R. G. Hambly

The Ethics of Nature in the Middle Ages: On Boccaccio's Poetaphysics
by Gregory B. Stone

Presence and Presentation: Women in the Chinese Literati Tradition
by Sherry J. Mou

The Lost Love Letters of Heloise and Abelard: Perceptions of Dialogue in Twelfth-Century France
by Constant J. Mews

Understanding Scholastic Thought with Foucault
by Philipp W. Rosemann

For Her Good Estate: The Life of Elizabeth de Burgh
by Frances A. Underhill

Constructions of Widowhood and Virginity in the Middle Ages
edited by Cindy L. Carlson and Angela Jane Weisl

Motherhood and Mothering in Anglo-Saxon England
by Mary Dockray-Miller

Listening to Heloise: The Voice of a Twelfth-Century Woman
edited by Bonnie Wheeler

The Postcolonial Middle Ages
edited by Jeffrey Jerome Cohen

Chaucer's Pardoner and Gender Theory
by Robert S. Sturges

Crossing the Bridge: Comparative Essays on Medieval European and Heian Japanese Women Writers
edited by Barbara Stevenson and Cynthia Ho

Engaging Words: The Culture of Reading in the Later Middle Ages
by Laurel Amtower

Robes and Honor: The Medieval World of Investiture
edited by Stewart Gordon

Representing Rape in Medieval and Early Modern Literature
edited by Elizabeth Robertson and Christine M. Rose

Same Sex Love and Desire Among Women in the Middle Ages
edited by Francesca Canadé Sautman and Pamela Sheingorn

Sight and Embodiment in the Middle Ages: Ocular Desires
by Suzannah Biernoff

Listen Daughter: The Speculum virginum and the Formation of Religious Women in the Middle Ages
edited by Constant J. Mews

Science, the Singular, and the Question of Theology
by Richard A. Lee, Jr.

Gender in Debate from the Early Middle Ages to the Renaissance
edited by Thelma S. Fenster and Clare A. Lees

THE TEXTURE OF SOCIETY

MEDIEVAL WOMEN IN THE SOUTHERN LOW COUNTRIES

Edited by

Ellen E. Kittell and Mary A. Suydam

First published 2004 by
PALGRAVE MACMILLAN™
175 Fifth Avenue, New York, N.Y. 10010 and
Houndmills, Basingstoke, Hampshire, England RG21 6XS
Companies and representatives throughout the world

PALGRAVE MACMILLAN is the global academic imprint of the Palgrave Macmillan division of St. Martin's Press, LLC and of Palgrave Macmillan Ltd. Macmillan® is a registered trademark in the United States, United Kingdom and other countries. Palgrave is a registered trademark in the European Union and other countries.

ISBN 0–312–29332–1 hardback

Library of Congress Cataloging-in-Publication Data
    The texture of society : medieval women in the southern Low Countries / edited by Ellen E. Kittell and Mary A. Suydam.
        p. cm.—(The new Middle Ages)
    Includes bibliographical references and index.
        ISBN 0–312–29332–1
        1. Women—Benelux countries—History. 2. Women—History—Middle Ages, 500–1500. 3. Social history—Medieval, 500–1500. I. Kittell, Ellen E. II. Suydam, Mary A., 1951– III. Series.

HQ 1147.B46T49 2004
305.4′09492—dc22   2003058084

A catalogue record for this book is available from the British Library.

Design by Newgen Imaging Systems (P) Ltd., Chennai, India.

First edition: January, 2004
10 9 8 7 6 5 4 3 2 1

Printed in the United States of America.

CONTENTS

LIST OF MAPS, TABLES, AND ILLUSTRATIONS

Maps

Tables

Illustrations

ABOUT THE CONTRIBUTORS

Eric Bousmar is a professor of History at the Facultés universitaires Saint-Louis (Brussels, Belgium), where he mainly teaches historical methodology. He received his Ph. D. in History from the Université catholique de Louvain (Louvain-la-Neuve, Belgium) and also studied Mediaeval Studies at the Katholieke Universiteit Leuven (Louvain, Belgium). His main research interests are culture and society in the Burgundian Netherlands, especially gender issues. He has published a variety of articles and is completing a book on this theme . He also edited with J.-M. Cauchies *Faire bans, edictz et statuz: l'activité législative communale dans l'Occident médiéval* (Brussels, 2001).

Laura D. Gelfand is an Associate Professor of art history at the University of Akron. She received her Ph.D from Case Western Reserve University in 1994. She has published on Margaret of Austria in "The Iconography of Style: Margaret of Austria and the Church of St. Nicolas of Tolentino at Brou" in *Widowhood and Visual Culture in Early Modern Europe*, Allison Levy, ed., Ashgate Press, 2003, pp. 145-159. The forthcoming article "'Y Me Tarde': The Valois, Pilgrimage and the Chartreuse de Champmol" in *The Art and Architecture of Late Medieval Pilgrimage in Northern Europe*, Sarah Blick and Rita Tekippe, eds., Brill Pub., 2004, continues her work on the Chartreuse de Champmol.

Linda Guzzetti graduated in French language and literature at the Università statale, Milan. She received a M.A. and Ph.D in medieval and modern history and Italian literature at the Technische Universitaet, Berlin. She has published articles on the dowry system in Venice and on Venetian women in religious confraternities in late Middle Ages. She currently teaches Italian as a foreign language at the universities of Berlin.

Katrien Heene obtained her Ph.D in Classical Philology in 1993 at Ghent University. She is the author of *The Legacy of Paradise: Woman, Marriage and Motherhood in Carolingian Edifying Literature* (Peter Lang, 1997) and has published several articles on gender topics in medieval Latin texts, in particular saints' lives. Currently she participates in a research project concerning mobility and gender in the late medieval Low Countries.

Ellen E. Kittell is Associate Professor of History at the University of Idaho. She studied with Donald E. Queller at the University of Illinois, and received her PhD in 1983. Author of a number of studies on Flemish medieval bureaucracy, she turned her attention to medieval Flemish women when she encountered a list of local receivers which included at least five women. Curious, she has been investigating further and has authored a number of studies on the subject, among them "Guardianship over Women in Medieval Flanders" and "Women, Audience and Public Acts in Medieval Flanders." She is currently working on a study of women and appellatives.

Mariann Naessens is a Research Assistant of the Fund for Scientific Research – Flanders (Belgium) (F.W.O.) and is affiliated to the University of Leuven, Campus Kortrijk (KULAK). She has an M.A. in history with a major in medieval history from the University of Leuven (Belgium) and has completed her studies in medieval history at the Centre d'Études Supérieures de Civilisation Médiévale (Poitiers, France). She is currently writing her doctoral dissertation, on the theme of Forbidden Sex and Criminalized Sexual Behavior in Late Medieval Urban Flanders. She has published several articles on this topic, regarding the towns of Kortrijk, Bruges and Ghent.

Mary A. Suydam received her Ph.D from the University of California at Santa Barbara in 1993. She has published numerous articles about Hadewijch of Antwerp, and is editor, along with Joanna Ziegler, of *Performance and Transformation: New Approaches to Late Medieval Spirituality* (St. Martin's Press, 1999). She is currently Assistant Professor of Religious Studies at Kenyon College.

Ulrike Wiethaus received her Ph.D in Religious Studies from Temple University and is professor of humanities at Wake Forest University. She is author of *Ecstatic Transformations: Ecstasies and Visions in the Work of Mechthild of Magdeburg and Transpersonal Psychology* (Syracuse, 1995), editor of *Maps of Flesh and Light: The Religious Experience of Women* (Syracuse, 1993), co-editor of *Dear Sister: The Correspondence of Medieval Women* (Philadelphia,1993), and translator of *Agnes Blannbekin: Life and Revelations of a Viennese Beguine* (Cambridge, 2002). She is currently working on a study of alterity in German medieval mystical writing.

Joanna E. Ziegler is Professor of Art History at Holy Cross College. Her last book, *Performance and Transformation: New Approaches to Late Medieval Spirituality*, was edited with Mary Suydam (St Martin's Press, 1999). She is currently finishing a book for Palgrave Macmillan with philosopher Christopher A Dustin, *Practicing Mortality: Art, Philosophy, and Contemplative Seeing*. Professor Ziegler's recent publications explore subjectivity and academic practice via spirituality and creative expression, especially dance.

INTRODUCTION

Ellen E. Kittell and Mary A. Suydam

Our intentions in this volume are three-fold: to focus on the historical experience of medieval women in the region known as the southern Low Countries, to bring the work of European scholars to the attention of the Anglo-American world, and finally, to raise significant conceptual issues. The authors in this volume include a cross-section of European and American scholars who work in the field of women's studies in the history of the southern Low Countries. Until now, some of their work has never been available to the non-Dutch-speaking world. Others have written in English but their work has not been known beyond the small circle of scholars who specialize in this field.

The Southern Low Countries: An Introduction to the Region and Its Culture

If you drew a triangle with one point resting on Paris, another on London, and the third at Cologne, the area covered would represent the region known as the southern Low Countries. Today that section of the continent makes up part of northern France and Belgium, but in the period from the late twelfth through the sixteenth centuries, the region had more of an economic coherence than a political or linguistic one. Overlordship of the region was split variously between the French king, the Holy Roman Emperor, and the Burgundian dukes.[1] The region was not only politically but also linguistically diverse. The Franco-Flemish language line split the county of Flanders along an east–west axis just north of Lille.

Of greater and more immediate impact were the large towns that dotted the countryside. Ghent boasted a population second only to that of Paris, while the populations of Bruges, Ypres, Lille, and Douai (all located within a 40-mile [64 km.] radius of each other) were among the highest in northern Europe, making the region the most urbanized outside of Italy. The southern Low Countries were commercially precocious as well.

The textile industry produced not only large quantities of cloth but also cloth of such exceptional quality that it was highly valued as far away as Novogorod, Russia.[2] Great Italian banking houses, such as the Peruzzi and the Bardi, set up branches in Bruges, while Ghent was known as a major commodities hub and Ypres as a manufacturing center.[3] Merchants and other travelers came to this region from all over northern Europe, either to do business or on their way to someplace else. Commercial and economic activities were so vital that Flemish-speaking children were often boarded out to French-speaking families (and vice versa) in order to acquire the linguistic skills necessary for the success in a multilingual world.[4]

A central feature of this urban landscape was the relatively weak nature of both feudal and episcopal government. In the twelfth and thirteenth centuries, the southern Low Countries were divided into several principalities, theoretically owing fealty to either the French crown or the German emperor. However, such loyalties were fragile; they were vigorously contested by other political powers such as the Burgundian dukes, as well as by the determination of cities to remain as independent as possible. These circumstances meant that local customs varied considerably throughout the region.

Mirroring the political diversity was the episcopal division of the region into five dioceses, none of which coincided with the theoretical boundaries of the principalities. As Walter Simons has noted, all the diocesan sees (with the exception of Liège) "lay at the very edge of the territory they were supposed to supervise."[5] As well, most of these dioceses owed fealty to the German emperor and were thus hostile to the currents of religious reform sweeping through Europe. Such circumstances allowed lay people latitude to experiment and create new religious forms of expression particularly suited to their urban circumstances.

This concatenation of circumstances engendered a very heterogeneous landscape in which distinctions between male and female, religious and lay did not so much define as describe. As the essays included here demonstrate, community norms throughout the region were such that neither gender nor religious affiliation strictly limited anyone to a particular sphere of action. It has been argued that during the central Middle Ages polarized notions of gender associated with learned professions, such as that of lawyer and theologian, became generalized to the population at large.[6] This does not appear to have been the case in the southern Low Countries, for the active commercial life in this region encouraged a high degree of literacy across gender and class lines. Both rich and poor, girls and boys, received basic education that included reading and writing. Although education was not public, it was not uncommon for the city to provide it for free to those parents or guardians who were unable otherwise to afford it.[7]

Despite the comparatively high literacy rate, most affairs were handled orally, either outdoors or in other public sectors.[8] Daily life was played out in an oral–aural space, routinely accessible to the community at large.[9] By the thirteenth century, custom had come to enshrine a clear distrust of anything smacking of the hidden. The difference between homicide and murder, for instance, like the difference between theft and robbery, was conceived essentially in terms of the degree of concealment involved.[10] Moreover, unlike in Italy, people in the southern Low Countries conducted most of their official business publicly, before the aldermen, and not in the privacy of a notary's office.[11] What may have passed for domestic or private affairs in Italian cities effectively remained public business in the southern Low Countries, delaying the conception of a clear dichotomy between two spheres of action.

A high rate of literacy combined with continued orality of public life contributed to the integration of women at almost all levels of the region's society. Women ruled Flanders as countesses for most of the thirteenth century and as duchesses of Brabant in the fourteenth. They were regents for the Hapsburgs in the sixteenth. They could be found in the count's administration,[12] bargaining in the markets of the major towns,[13] baking bread, tanning, retailing, growing wheat, butchering meat, selling cloth, and warping loom threads.[14] This integration is perhaps best exemplified in the custom of identifying an individual, male or female, primarily by their first and last names. While appellatives detailing family associations, particularly in the case of women, were not uncommon, they were by no means applied uniquely as they were, for example, in Genoa and in Venice. Women, like men, were routinely identified not only by familial association, but also by citizenship of a particular community, title, occupation, location, and religious affiliation.[15]

This latter was also more descriptive than defining. The blurring of lines between religious and lay life is perhaps one of the most well-known characteristics of Low Countries daily life, best exemplified by the large number of beguines and beguinages (*begijnhoven*) whose presence distinguished many of the cities in the southern Low Countries.[16] The women of this religious reform movement succeeded in establishing a religious lifestyle in small homes or larger, more organized beguinages, but did not take permanent vows and were not strictly enclosed within a cloister.[17] As emphasized above, secular women's participation in all facets of daily life in Flanders was routine. We would expect such participation to be characteristic also of Flemish women's religious lives, especially beguines and those who began religious lives as beguines.

In fact, the terms "secular" and "religious" create a dichotomy that did not exist for beguines in the southern Low Countries. Because beguines did not live in endowed convents, economic self-sufficiency defined their movement.[18] Like their secular sisters, beguines participated in economic ventures outside their beguinages and bought and sold property. Early rules indicate that beguines were expected to be self-supporting, either from regular rents received, sale of property, or by working (usually in some aspect of the cloth industry).[19] Some rules also stipulated that beguines were expected to assent publically to aldermanic statutes in their area.[20]

Because beguine devotional life took place in urban and communal settings, beguines were much more visible in public than nuns living in monasteries far from town centers. The beguinages of most Flemish cities such as Lier, Gent, Mechelen, Dendermonde, and Antwerp were located in the centers of these towns. Beguines ran schools and infirmaries, conducted their own trade, and attended parish churches.[21]

Thus, unlike nuns, beguines lived in communal spaces within the towns and did not take permanent vows. Unlike lay people, however, beguines were dedicated to a religious way of life so long as they remained beguines—they did not marry and spent much of their days in religious devotion and the care of others. Unlike the Clares in Italy, the beguines could dedicate themselves to a life of poverty and service without being enclosed within convent walls.[22] Many beguines did eventually choose to join convents, but it is important to acknowledge the variety possible in their religious careers.

The blending of religious and secular, along with the lack of specifically gendered spheres of activity, was exemplified in a number of ways over the course of the thirteenth, fourteenth, and fifteenth centuries. These included social opportunities for living alone, for traveling, and for making wills. A legal and social mentality developed that was at least initially flexible in its view of women's capacities.

Community Norms

Caroline Walker Bynum concluded that religious women usually did not conceive of themselves as a distinct, gendered category, although religious men most certainly did.[23] It is impossible to tell how secular southern Low Countries women in the Middle Ages imagined themselves with regard to gender and social categories, given that they did not produce the kinds of writings that religious women did. On the other hand, there are other types of evidence: ordinances, accounts, judicial records, and the whole body of records pertaining to beguines. Authors in this volume utilize these records to construct community norms.

By the thirteenth century, both communes and princes in the southern Low Countries had developed rudimentary systems for handling behavior they deemed unacceptable. It is not surprising, given the ubiquity of women in the social and economic life of the region, that these systems did not usually distinguish between male and female malefactors. In "Reconciliation or Punishment: Women, Community and Malefaction in the Medieval County of Flanders" (chapter 1), Ellen E. Kittell argues that such distinctions, while uncommon in the thirteenth century, were becoming increasingly routine throughout subsequent centuries. This evolution can be attributed to the increasing systematization of legal procedures, particularly that associated with the change of emphasis from negotiation to prosecution. Settling the conflict resulting from the malefaction was the primary focus in the former case, whereas defining transgression and punishing the transgressor was the focus of the latter. Gender played a greater role in such definition and by extension punishment, so it is not surprising that by the late fourteenth century women had come to be linked to certain types of malefactions, notably those associated with domestic behavior.

Women in the southern Low Countries enjoyed a freedom of movement in the thirteenth century that testifies to the degree to which they were not confined to a private sphere. According to Katrien Heene's "Gender and Mobility in the Low Countries: Traveling Women in Thirteenth-Century Exempla and Saints' Lives" (chapter 2) these sources painted a negative picture of female mobility, underlining the catastrophes that could ensue from freedom of movement. There is every reason to believe, however, that these writings were reactive in nature, and that women from many different classes and stations traveled to distant destinations for many reasons. The degree to which one had a capacity to move about freely in one's society could be considered an index of the degree to which a society confined or did not confine a particular group. That there were forces which attempted to curb such freedom of movement does not in and of itself negate its existence. It does, however, suggest that among certain powerful sectors of society, such freedom of movement was considered threatening.

Such undercurrents apparently began to effect fundamental changes in the late Middle Ages and early modern period. Mariann Naessens, in "Judicial Authorities' Views of Women's Roles in Late Medieval Flanders" (chapter 3), continues where Kittell leaves off. She argues that a new morality came into being some time in the late medieval period. For the first time women were punished for cross-dressing in and of itself, and not merely as an extenuating circumstance attendant to adultery. Women were also increasingly penalized for not living up to a preconceived notion of motherhood. Finally, judges in the sixteenth century began to view the business of brothels as the husband's occupation, but considered the social or managerial aspect of the brothel (that is, caring for the inmates) as the purview of women and fined them both accordingly.

For reasons that are not quite clear, social norms in the southern Low Countries in the fifteenth and sixteenth centuries appear to have been coming more in line with those of its neighbors and even with those of the Mediterranean regions. But had they always been that different in the first place? Linda Guzzetti addresses this question in her examination of "Women's Inheritance and Testamentary Practices in Late Fourteenth- and Early Fifteenth-Century Venice and Ghent" (chapter 4). She argues that in Ghent, where marital regimens reflected Flemish customary law, women's inheritance patterns were predicated on a common marital fund; dowries were the exception and not the rule. Moreover, women in Ghent moved easily through the public spaces of that city. In Venice, governed according to Roman law as well as customary law, the dowry system dominated. Yet the commercial aspects of Venetian life mitigated the dowry system, and through the use of testaments women were free to dispose of portions of their capital. What is striking is that in Ghent, by the sixteenth century, the use of the common marital fund had given way to the dowry system.

Although women's roles in the society of the southern Low Countries appear to have entered a period of constriction in the fifteenth and sixteenth centuries, women never lost their essential capacity to move about and work in public spaces. In "Neither Equality nor Radical Oppression: The Elasticity of Women's Roles in the Late Medieval Low Countries" (chapter 5), Eric Bousmar examines marriage and gender roles, the conception of "honest" and "dishonest" men and women, and, finally, courtly subjugation, all through the lens of the holistic perception of the body that was characteristic of the period. He postulates a model of elasticity that explains how women, who had by the fifteenth century become clearly subordinate to their spouses, still retained the capacity to exercise public functions.

Community norms existed in flexible tension with actual practice. It is one thing to assume that they were already in place and that change occurred as women (and men, for that matter) pushed repeatedly in daily practice against the norms that bound them and made them "social." It is another to argue that the establishment, or perhaps more accurately, the definition of particular community norms was an ongoing, organic process, predicated on a fundamentally dualistic exercise—in describing what was acceptable the process also prescribed what was acceptable. The results over time might have been kaleidoscopic in nature, but what remained constant gave a region its character and its flavor. From these essays, it is clear that one constant was the normative participation of women in their society, not necessarily as exceptional appendages to an acceptable "public" entity, a man, but in their own right.

Art and Performance

The essays in part 2 of the volume address the public aesthetic dimensions of life for women. For medieval people in the southern Low Countries, public performance and creative expression did not exist as ends unto themselves, but formed part of the social, political, and economic fabric in which they were interwoven. Events that we consider to be artistic or theatrical in nature may not have been considered as such in this period. We therefore impose an artificial construct, not in order to "read back" artistic performances into the Middle Ages, but to raise issues of interpretation that have heretofore been overlooked and which have relevance for the possibilities open to women in the medieval southern Low Countries.

Although medieval people may not have had our conceptions of "art" and "theater" we do theorize that art and performance were integral to daily life. Mary A. Suydam's essay, "Visionaries in the Public Eye: Beguine Literature as Performance" (chapter 6), argues that beguine texts demonstrate a performance-oriented model of sanctity that is particular to the southern Low Countries. Focus on the performative aspects of beguine piety restores an understanding of beguine agency within society. Suydam argues that aspects of performance are essential to understanding beguine mysticism, but she focuses, not upon beguine performances themselves, but upon the texts that record them. She believes that beguine textuality is fundamentally performative in nature: that it focuses upon the performances of its protagonists and encourages performances in its readers. In this interpretation, sanctity is regarded as a quality that is publically demonstrated and enacted (and can be repeated) rather than passively received and recorded.

Ulrike Wiethaus's essay, "Mystical Sound and Hagiographical Politics in Medieval Lorraine" (Chapter 7), studies the relationship between Marie d'Oignies, a beguine, and her two biographers: Jacques de Vitry, a French bishop, and Thomas de Cantimpré, a Dominican friar. Wiethaus explores Marie's use of singing as a form of sonic mysticism uniquely employed by holy women in the southern Low Countries. She juxtaposes Marie's ecstatic death song with the theological and political agendas evident in her two biographers. She explores several models of holiness—Latinate clerical, regional clerical, and lay regional—to uncover a spiritual matrix of meaning linking religious women, death, mysticism, and music in the southern Low Countries. This sonic mysticism was in turn reinterpreted by her two biographers. Wiethaus's essay clearly demonstrates how phenomena we consider artistic (music) were embedded and contested within its political and social landscape, even beyond the boundaries of the Low Countries.

In "On the Artistic Nature of Elisabeth of Spalbeek's Ecstasy: The Southern Low Countries Do Matter" (chapter 8), Joanna E. Ziegler studies the unusual case of a beguine who dramatically reenacted Christ's passion. According to Ziegler, this kind of ecstatic mysticism is fundamentally artistic in nature and requires us to engage it on visual and artistic terms. Ziegler's essay requires readers to reconsider the assumed dichotomy between spontaneous spirituality and the artifice of artistic performance. She argues that practice and repetition, so integral to artistic performance, are also components of religious performances. Noting that Elisabeth's technique was practiced, dramatic, and visually engaging, Ziegler connects this type of mysticism with the highly theatrical and visual culture of the southern Low Countries. She believes that here flourished an enormously creative model of spiritual practices founded on exceptionally sophisticated visual and artistic principles. For Ziegler, Elisabeth's practice of her enactment of Christ's passion enhances, rather than negates, its spiritual power.

Finally, Laura D. Gelfand's essay, "Regency, Power and Dynastic Visual Memory: Margaret of Austria as Patron and Propagandist" (chapter 9), shows how devotional portrait dyptichs commissioned by the fifteenth-century ruler Margaret of Austria mobilized art to further her dynastic and political claims. Margaret used the visual arts to draw upon the Valois associations incorporated within them to claim her right to govern. Her artistic commissions reflect a clear sense of the relationship between iconography and politics in the southern Low Countries at the end of the Middle Ages.

Challenging Assumptions: Suggestions for Further Research

Incorporating women's history in the southern Low Countries has significant implications for a number of fundamental assumptions currently under debate not only in the scholarly community but in the broader public arena as well. The essays in this collection argue that medieval Flemish women were publicly visible and well integrated into their society. Such a claim is counter to three general assumptions current in medievalist scholarship. First, partly due to the domination of the field by Anglo-American scholars, many historians generalize the experience of medieval England and France—basically rural areas—to the rest of Europe, including urban areas such as the southern Low Countries.[24] This practice ignores the fact that England, for most of European history up to the Industrial Revolution, was as peripheral to the continental historical experience as was Denmark or the Iberian peninsula.

An over-generalizing emphasis upon England's situation also stems from the difficulties that language can pose for other historians. Although it is very common for medievalists to be fluent in English, French, and sometimes German, few American scholars can read Dutch. A recent collection of articles, edited by Linda Mitchell, is a case in point.[25] In this volume, American Louis Haas asks whether women enjoyed public power in medieval cities. His answer for the Low Countries was no. There were a number of problems with this essay, but perhaps the most serious one was that Professor Haas based this conclusion on the work of only two historians, both of them American.[26] He is clearly unfamiliar with the valuable work of a myriad of scholars outside the United States, especially the large body of work available in Dutch-language journals and monographs.

A second assumption that is central to the expectations of Haas and a large number of other scholars is the belief that medieval society was organized around an ongoing public/private dichotomy. In the most gross sense, the concept of separate public and private spheres is based on the belief that women everywhere and throughout history have experienced life primarily from the private, or domestic, sphere. Men, on the other hand, have experienced both public and private life indiscriminately—the separation between the two spheres governs only how women are viewed. There is every indication that this assumption, while not useless, is not the best organizing principle for material from the Middle Ages. The essays in this collection suggest that such a dichotomy only began to appear in Europe toward the end of the Middle Ages.

Two mutually contradictory and debated assumptions involve the advantages and disadvantages for women of "civilization," where "civilization" is defined as the achievement of strong central governments with significant urban centers. One group of scholars have long argued that as medieval Europe became more civilized conditions improved for everyone, including women. The division of medieval history into the Early (or "Dark") and the High Middle Ages is based on this assumption. Warren Hollister's popular *Medieval Europe: A Short History* contends that by the thirteenth century, people lived longer, were safer, and society as a whole was more prosperous.[27] Countering this long-standing view has been a recent trend among some feminist medieval scholars to view civilization itself as inherently patriarchal. Thus, urban prosperity may not work for the benefit of women. Jo Ann McNamara and Suzanne Wemple, for example, have argued that the public power of both early medieval and aristocratic secular and religious women decreased significantly after the twelfth century.[28] McNamara has also suggested that, in some areas during the early Middle Ages, some "frontier outposts" provided more egalitarian possibilities for some women than existed during the Roman period.[29] Conversely, the "passion for ordering," which characterized the twelfth and thirteenth centuries, worked to polarize gender identity to women's detriment.[30]

In particular, McNamara argues that an important component of capitalist gender systems is a "belief in women's financial incompetence."[31] Thus as money economies became prominent women's status everywhere declined as "civilization" advanced in the period after 1000. Two good examples of such decline are the well-attested economic decline of women's monasteries everywhere as well as women's exclusion from the most prominent guilds in England.[32]

Overlooked in this debate has been the situation of women in one of Europe's most urban emerging capitalist societies: the southern Low Countries. Essays in this volume indicate the regular participation of urban women in all aspects of their society. Furthermore, women neither acquired nor lost these roles as civilization advanced. As feminist scholars, we do not necessarily view the triumph of patriarchy as inevitable with the march of civilization. One avenue for future research is the continuity or discontinuity of women's roles between the medieval and the early modern periods.

Each essay in this volume focuses upon a particular slice of Low Countries daily life. Taken together, the essays suggest an emerging theme: that women there were prominent in the economic, social, and religious spheres of their society. These essays, then, represent a contribution to ongoing research and to the debate on the role of women in the medieval southern Low Countries in particular and in Europe in general. It is our hope that readers will begin to take a closer look at the culture of the medieval southern Low Countries, and at the important scholarship on both sides of the Atlantic.

Notes

1. Both French- and Flemish-speaking areas were held by the count of Flanders. French Flanders includes much of Picardy as well as important towns such as Lille and Douai. Flemish Flanders more or less includes the regions around important towns such as Ghent, Bruges, and Ypres. The count, in turn, was a vassal of the king of France for both sections until the first years of the fourteenth century when the king took French Flanders under his direct control. Brabant, Limburg, and the modern-day provinces of Hainaut and Namur were technically held by the Holy Roman Empire. In 1384, Philip, duke of Burgundy, who already held Imperial Flanders, became count of Flanders by right of his wife Margaret. The dukes of Burgundy retained suzerainty over the southern Low Countries until the death of Charles the Bold at the walls of Nancy in 1477. Thereafter French Flanders reverted to the French king while Flemish Flanders and the Imperial territories fell into the hands of the Hapsburg emperors.

2. Henri Pirenne, "Dras d'Ypres à Novgorod au commencement du XIIe siècle," *Revue belge de philologie et d'histoire* 9 (1930), pp. 563–66. Reprinted in O. Mus, ed. *Prisma van Geschiedenis van Ieper* (Ypres: Stadsbestuur, 1974), pp. 356–58.

3. Ypres's economy was so tied up in the manufacture of textiles that when it began to fail in the fourteenth century the city went into a decline from which it did not recover.

4. Hilde De Ridder-Symoens, "Stad en kennis" in *Hart en marge in de laatmiddeleeuwse stedelijke maatschappij/Core and Periphery in Late Medieval Urban Society*, ed. Myriam Carlier, Anke Greve, Walter Prevenier, and Peter Stabel (Leuven-Kessel-Lo (Belgium) and Apeldoorn (The Netherlands): Garant, 1996), pp.136–37.

5. Walter Simons, *The City of Ladies: Beguine Communities in the Medieval Low Countries, 1200–1565* (Philadelphia: University of Pennsylvania, 2001), p.12.

6. Susan Stuard, "The Dominion of Gender: Women's Fortunes in the High Middle Ages," in *Becoming Visible: Women in European History*, ed. Renate Bridenthal, Claudia Koonz, and Susan Stuard, 2nd ed. (Boston: Houghton-Mifflin Company, 1998), p. 130.

7. Hilde De Ridder-Symoens, "Stad en kennis," p. 133.

8. Until the fourteenth century, in fact, "reading" did not mean reading silently to oneself, but, rather, reading aloud to an audience (Paul Saenger, "Silent Reading: Its Impact on Late Medieval Script and Society," *Viator* 13 (1982), p. 412 f.; and Mary Suydam, "Writing Beguines: Ecstatic Performances," *Magistra* 2, no. 1 (Summer, 1996), pp. 137–69).

9. Even when aldermanic sessions took place indoors, free public access was provided (R.C. van Caenegem, *Geschiedenis van het strafprocesrecht in Vlaanderen van de XIe tot de XIVe eeuw* (Brussels: Palais der Academien, 1956), p.88).

10. van Caengem, *Strafprocesrecht*, 87–88. It was very rare, at least until the fourteenth century, for any court case, for example, to be conducted in secret (R.C. van Caenegem, *Geschiedenis van het strafrecht in Vlaanderen van de XIe tot de XIVe eeuw* (Brussels: Palais der Academien, 1954), p. 88).

11. Wills in Genoa, for example, were commonly drawn up either in the notary's office or in the home of the testator, while wills in Douai had to be publicly authenticated in front of the aldermen (Ellen E. Kittell, "Testaments of Two Cities: A Comparative Analysis of the Wills of Medieval Genoa and Douai," *European Review of History* 5, no. 1 (1998), pp. 51–55).

12. Ellen E. Kittell, "Women in the Administration of the Count of Flanders," in *Frau und spätmittelalterlicher alltag* (Vienna: Verlag der Österreichischen Akademie der Wissenschaften, 1986), pp. 487–508.

13. Peter Stabel, "Women at the Market. Gender and Retail in the Towns of Late Medieval Flanders," in *Secretum Scriptorum: Liber alumnorum Walter Prevenier*, ed. Wim Blockmans, Marc Boone, and Thérèse de Hemptinne (Leuven-Kessel-Lo (Belgium) and Apeldoorn (The Netherlands): Garant, 1999), pp. 259–76.

14. Ellen E. Kittell and Kurt Queller, " 'Whether Man or Woman': Gender Inclusivity in the Town Ordinances of Medieval Douai," *Journal of Medieval and Early Modern Studies* 30, no. 1 (Winter, 2000), pp. 98–99.

15. Ellen E. Kittell, "The Construction of Women's Social Identity in Medieval Douai: Evidence from Identifying Epithets," *Journal of Medieval History* 25, no. 3 (1999), pp. 215–27.

16. The southern Low Countries also enjoyed the participation of the mendicant orders—whose members, after all, took urban areas as their special province of activity—to a higher degree than probably any other region outside northern Italy. See Walter Simons, *Stad en apolstolaat. De vestiging van dedelorden in het graafschap Vlaanderen (ca. 1225–ca. 1350)* (Brussels: AWLSK, 1987).

17. Beguines first appeared in the late twelfth century and by 1216 had obtained papal approval for their way of life. Until their condemnation in 1310 they were a widespread religious movement in the Low Countries and central Europe (beguines in the southern Low Countries continued to flourish long after 1310). The standard work in English on beguines has long been Ernest McDonnell, *The Beguines and Beghards in Medieval Culture: With Special Emphasis on the Belgian Scene* (New Brunswick: Octagon Books, 1954). More recently, Walter Simons's *Cities of Ladies: Beguine Communities in the Medieval Low Countries, 1200–1565* (Philadelphia: University of Pennsylvania Press, 2001) provides an updated overview of this movement. See also Simons's "The Beguine Movement in the Southern Low Countries: A Reassessment," *Bulletin de l'institut historique belge de Rome* 59 (1989), pp. 63–105. The origins of the beguine movement continue to be debated. See Carol Neel, "The Origins of the Beguines," in *Sisters and Workers in the Middle Ages*, ed. Judith Bennett et al. (Chicago: University of Chicago Press, 1989), pp. 240–60. But see also Joanna Ziegler, "Secular Canonesses as Antecedent of the Beguines in the southern Low Countries: An Introduction to Some Older Views," *Studies in Medieval and Renaissance History* 13 (1991), pp. 114–35; "Women of the Middle Ages: Some Questions Regarding the Beguines and Devotional Art," *Vox Benedictina* 3, no. 4, pp. 338–57; and *Sculpture of Compassion: The Pietà and the Beguines in the Southern Low Countries, c. 1300–1600* (Brussels: Institut historique belge de Rome, 1992).

18. Early rules for beguinages stipulate that women who had property would give it to the beguinage upon entry. As was the case with convents, wealthy lay people often donated land and buildings. But because beguines had no entry fee, the entrance of poor beguines with little money or land meant that beguines had to work to provide for the welfare of the *hof.*

19. "The Rule of the Beguinage of Mechelen (1286)" states that mistresses of the *Begijnhof* may receive rents from outside the *hof* for the alleviation of poor beguines (F. De Ridder, "De Oudste Statuten van het Mechelse Begijnhof," *Handelingen van de Mechelse kring voor Oudheidkunde* 39 (1934), pp. 18–29). Descriptions of early beguine economic practices are also detailed in Rose-Marijn Quintijn, *Normen en normering van het begijnhoven* (Ghent: Rijksuniversiteit Gent, 1983), pp. 51–56.

20. Florence Koorn, *Begijnhoven in Holland en Zeeland gedurende de Middeleeuwen* (Assen: Van Gorcum, 1981), pp. 80–81.

21. Early Rules for beguinages assume that women will leave the *hof* but regulate the circumstances under which they may do so. For example, the 1246 Rule for beguines in the diocese of Liège lists "going out without permission" (*allene wt te gane plach sonder orloff*) as a serious error (reproduced in L.J.M. Philippen, *De Begijnhoven: Oorsprong, Geschiedenis, Inrichting* (Antwerp: Ch. And H. Courtin, 1918), p. 307). The 1286 Rule of Mechelen states: "This is the desire of the house, that one will [live] communally; that no young or full-grown woman who dwells in the house will go outside the house" (*dit sijn de pointe die thoef beghert, dat men houde ghemeinlike: dat ghene joffrouwe or vrouwe, die woent inden hof, ga buten denhove. . .*). The same Rule also states, "no beguine will go into town without the approval of her housemistress, nor without a companion. . ." (*Negene beghine en sal gaen inde stat orlof hare huus meestersen, noch sonder gesellinne buten der groter poerten vanden hove*). F. DeRidder, "De Oudste Statuten van het Begijnhof van Mechelen," pp. 24, 28. Both Rules assume that women will leave the *hof* but regulate the circumstances.

22. The oft-cited critiques of the beguine movement by contemporary writers obscure the enthusiasm for the movement characteristic of both religious and secular leaders. Such critiques generally centered around questions of unorthodoxy in theology rather than the beguines' participation "in the world." Jacques de Vitry's catalogue of opposition to *mulieres sanctae* cannot be taken as a general guide of medieval criticism, in view of the official recognition of the movement by bishops, popes, and clerical leaders. Neither should the condemnation of beguines after 1310 obscure the wide support for the movement in the thirteenth century. The Bishop of Liège wrote a rule for the beguinages in his diocese, educated writers such as Jacques de Vitry and Thomas de Cantimpré wrote enthusiastic *Vitae* of holy beguines, and the papacy took members of the movement under its protection (McDonnell, *The Beguines and the Beghards in Medieval Culture*, pp. 154–64).

23. Caroline Walker Bynum, " 'And Women His Humanity': Female Imagery in the Religious Writings of the Later Middle Ages," in *Gender and Religion: On the Complexity of Symbols*, ed. Caroline Walker Bynum, Stephen Harrell, and Paula Richman (Boston: Beacon Press, 1986), p. 277.

24. A glance at recent titles demonstrates this point: Roberta Gilchrist's *Gender and Material Culture: The Archaeology of Religious Women* (Routledge, 1994) concentrates primarily upon English convent architecture. More broadly representative is Judith M. Bennett and Amy M. Froide, eds., *Singlewomen in the European Past, 1250–1800* (Philadelphia: University of Pennsylvania Press, 1999), which includes three essays on singlewomen in England, two in France, two in Germany, and two general essays that use Italian sources as comparison. Finally, Joan Ferrante's essay "Public Postures and Private Maneuvers: Roles Medieval Women Play," in *Women and Power in the Middle Ages*, ed. Mary Erler and Maryanne Kowaleski (Athens, Georgia: University of Georgia Press, 1988) is in fact limited to specific English, French, and German medieval literary characters and authors.

25. Linda Mitchell, ed., *Women in Medieval Western European Culture* (New York: Garland, 1999).

26. His explanation for this was that if these two historians could find no evidence of women in public power, no one could. Louis Haas, "Women and Politics in the Urban Milieu," in Mitchell, ed., *Women in Medieval Western European Culture*, pp. 222–23.

27. C. Warren Hollister, *Medieval Europe: A Short History*, 7th edn. (New York: McGraw Hill, 1994).

28. Jo Ann McNamara and Suzanne Wemple, "The Power of Women Through the Family in Medieval Europe, 500–1100," in *Women and Power in the Middle Ages*, ed. Mary Erler and Maryanne Kowaleski (Athens, Georgia: University of Georgia Press, 1988), pp. 83–101.

29. Jo Ann McNamara, *Sisters in Arms: Catholic Nuns Through Two Millennia* (Cambridge, MA: Harvard University Press, 1996). For example, in Ireland "cut loose from the firm administrative structures that underpinned their authority. . .[monastic] women's prayers were on a relatively equal footing with men's, in contrast to the Roman system" (p. 121).

30. McNamara, *Sisters in Arms*, pp. 289–91.

31. McNamara, *Sisters in Arms*, pp. 272–73.

32. McNamara, *Sisters in Arms*, pp. 289–91. See also Ruth Mazo Karras, *Common Women: Prostitution and Sexuality in Medieval England* (New York: Oxford University Press, 1996).

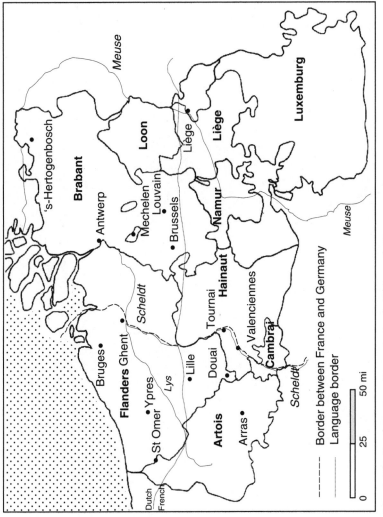

Map 1: The Southern Low Countries in the Thirteenth Century

PART ONE

COMMUNITY NORMS

CHAPTER 1

RECONCILIATION OR PUNISHMENT: WOMEN, COMMUNITY, AND MALEFACTION IN THE MEDIEVAL COUNTY OF FLANDERS

Ellen E. Kittell

Introduction

In 1956 R.C. van Caenegem published the second volume of his monumental work on Flemish medieval criminal law.[1] The two volumes covered almost every conceivable facet of the Flemish criminal justice system except its treatment of women.[2] His very brief discussion of women and malefaction is confined primarily to a section under the rubric "Particular protection of women," in which he mentions that protection—which, in this context, means protection from criminal proceedings[3]—had essentially disappeared by the thirteenth century.[4] He also remarks that when a woman committed a misdeed, the fine was doubled, as it was routine during the Middle Ages for women to pay greater fines for transgressions than did men.[5]

Thirty years later, the French historian A. Porteau-Bitker suggested that, at least for France, this was not the case. She concluded that throughout France women and men, for the most part, received the same treatment at the hands of the law.[6] Beyond using a source or two from Lille, however, she pays no particular attention to Flanders.[7]

This present essay argues that Porteau-Bitker's conclusions are also pertinent for Flanders. Contrary to van Caenegem's contention, there appears to have been few distinctions between female and male malefactors in the Flemish legal system, regardless of community. As prosecutory procedures and their records became more systematized over the course of the fourteenth century, however, the legal system began to distinguish between men and women and to take the first steps toward treating them differently. While the number of crimes women committed does not seem to have changed, women did begin to be associated with specific types, particularly domestic ones.

There are, however, differences between Flanders and France. Since Porteau-Bitker examines only accusatory and inquisitorial procedures, her study focuses exclusively on malefaction as expressed in royal ordinances, city charters, and judicial decisions rendered by seigneurial and royal juris-dictions.[8] The thirteenth- and fourteenth-century Flemish legal system relied for its part far more heavily on negotiation and arbitration backed by local communal authorities than on prosecutorial procedures (whether accusatorial or inquisitorial) managed by comital officials. Moreover, Flemish society does not appear to have been conceptually divided into a public and a private sphere—the former a privileged domain populated primarily if not exclusively by men and the latter a marginalized position to which women would be automatically relegated. Absent such compartmentalizations, there is indeed no particular reason for construing female misdeeds as involving some sort of double transgression.[9]

Women in Flanders

Porteau-Bitker's study is predicated on her use of men's experience as the default point of reference, on the implicit assumption that men's actions are the standard against which women's actions are to be compared. To be sure, this orientation might be justified if there were evidence that the Flemish conceived of public action by definition as located primarily in men. Women were, however, integral to Flemish public life. Louis Haas's recent comment notwithstanding,[10] women can be found at almost all levels of public life to a degree which suggests that if there indeed was any domain of social activity marked off as a "private sphere," it can hardly be defined in terms of women as a marginalized social constituency. First, there exist for at least one Flemish city—Douai—numerous ordinances in which the aldermen were clearly targeting the general public as composed of both men and women. This is attested by their unrelenting use not only of generic gender-inclusive doublets like *hom ne feme* and *borgois ne borgoise* when referring to the citizenry and population at large, but also of myriad specific ones like *taneres ne taneresse* to address the practitioners of particu-lar trades.[11] Among the few ordinances of Douai in the thirteenth century directed specifically to men were those regulating certain events and occa-sions, such as tournaments, dicing, and games of chance, where violence was likely to break out.[12] It could be argued that only men played these games and that is why these ordinances are directed specifically to them, and perhaps further that these ordinances represent a limitation of the actions of women. But there is no evidence that women did not play such games. Given the routine nature of referring to the public as consisting of both men and women, these ordinances, in fact, tell us no more than that the aldermen recognized that men, under certain circumstances, were more likely to be disruptive than were women.[13] Women throughout medieval Flanders, moreover, regularly bore the appellative "citizen."[14] In very few cases was the term *bourgeoise* augmented by familial information; clearly the public status of "citizen" was sufficient.

More generally, women's names constantly appear in public records of towns like Ypres and Ghent unaccompanied either by a man's name or by any other details of her domestic association.[15] On April 20, 1298, for example, Griele Brant was granted her citizenship;[16] on April 17, 1271, the alderman publicly acknowledged that Margrite de Courtrai had discharged her debt to Ernaut Rubert;[17] while on September 17, 1374, Bette Onghebouchs was fined for selling bread that was not of regulation size at the public market.[18] Had women been consigned to a private sphere, appellatives such as "sister of," "daughter of," or "wife of" would have been obligatory, since the hypothesis of a private sphere implies that women have no independent identity outside it. To appear legitimately in the alien arena of public affairs would have required the identifying passport of those sanctioning connections.

Arbitration and Negotiation

Van Caenegem maintains that juridical history in Flanders was determined by essentially political factors, rooted in two different social bonds. One, the feudal and seignorial, bound the subject to the count, and eventually to the state. The other was based instead on a hypothetical voluntary association of community members; it bound the citizen to his community under the direction of the institutions of city government as constituted by that community.[19] Since it is clear that women were citizens, as well as holders of fiefs, they were comprised in both bonds.[20]

In medieval Europe, the Church, the prince, and the commune were all more or less independently developing mechanisms for dealing with the resolution of conflicts. J. Goebel remarks, "even in developed Frankish procedure private arbitration exists side by side with regular judicial proceedings and back of both is the latent threat of feud."[21] Economic and class divisions, as well as distinctions between citizen and noncitizen, could set group against group. Violent upheavals might be ignited in one neighborhood, or among one familial faction, and then spread from there.[22]

Early Germanic custom had encouraged the use of privately arranged arbitrations among the kindreds involved as a means to avoid continual bloodletting.[23] Such arbitration required the "appeasing" or pacification of groups aggrieved by the outrages perpetrated against them by offending parties. As society evolved, so too did the nature of social groupings and the potential for conflict among them. Family and guild remained primary associations, but by the thirteenth century, Flemish urban society had come to be composed of a series of overlapping associations, each of which made demands on residents. Family loyalties competed with loyalties to neighborhood, parish, and perhaps even age cohort.[24] Private arbitrators came to be supplemented and then replaced in many Flemish communes by *paysierders*.[25] These, like other arbitrators, typically strove to resolve a conflict by arriving at a settlement—a *zoen*—that would be acceptable to all parties concerned.[26]

By the mid-thirteenth century, *verzoening* had become formalized as a routine expedient for conflict resolution. Communities did not relish the thought of comital interference, for it suggested a dependence on the count that most cities were at pains to avoid. Towns such as Bruges and Courtrai tried to maintain peace within their walls as part of their claim to autonomy. J. van Herwaarden convincingly argues that, although economic inequality was a fact of life in cities such as Ypres or Furnes, there developed a legal fiction of equality among citizens.[27] This legal fiction, expressed in the ubiquity of the word *zoen* and its variants throughout legal records, bespeaks a culture intent upon fostering mediation and arbitration as the preferred means of keeping the peace—at the expense of appeals to authority. The former implies the intrinsic responsibility of being a citizen, the latter the extrinsic responsibility invested in a transcendent authority—within the medieval context, usually a prince or princely representative. The former finds its most characteristic expression in arbitration under the aegis of city authorities. The latter is linked to the notion of a single authority and is characteristically expressed in the meting out of punishment.

The content of a *zoen* might include agreements to pay fines (usually, but not only to the victimized kin), to go into exile, to make an expiatory pilgrimage, or to carry out some combination of these. David Nicholas claims that a *zoen* was merely "a blood price, not innocent victims' compensation."[28] This definition is problematic, for it ignores that fact that the *zoen* was essentially a process that involved the reconciliation of conflicting parties;[29] the modern Dutch word *verzoening*, in fact, means "reconciliation." Van Herwaarden defines the *zoen* within a broad context comprising *compositio* (the preliminary action of bringing together the conflicting parties) and *pax* (the peaceful resolution that was its intended result).[30] In other words, the *zoen* should be understood as a process that reestablished the sense of moral justice necessary for continued social relationships between members of feuding parties in particular and residents and citizens of a community in general. By the mid-thirteenth century at the latest, the term *verzoening* was imbued with a rich texture of secular and religious connotations, all centered on the concept of reconciliation.[31]

Feud by definition involved all members of conflicting households; its resolution had to as well. The *zoen*, therefore, comprehended obligations undertaken by members of both parties. When violence occurred as a result of cursing and slander, for example, both parties were often sent on pilgrimage.[32] A *zoen*'s motive force was to resolve a dispute by establishing conditions that all parties to a conflict could live with. As in early Germanic custom, enforcing these conditions rested fundamentally, if not formally, with the groups making the agreement. The particular attributes of the individual victims or perpetrators were subsumed in a need to appease the family as a corporate group. Corporate honor and internal group dynamics might motivate other members to exert sufficient pressure on the condemned to obtain her compliance with the obligations to which the whole had agreed. The miscreant's own sense of responsibility to the group, meanwhile, might be relied upon to enforce her compliance with their expectations, even if her sense of personal guilt were not in itself sufficient motivation. Corporateness also implied the capacity and thus the right of the collective to handle its own affairs with minimal outside interference.[33] Focusing on differences that distinguished one member from another would only serve to undermine these dynamics. Negotiation and arbitration enabled them to retain the capacity to police their individual members, thus avoiding outside interference that might challenge their autonomy in the broader social arena.

Scholars agree that most conflicts in Flanders up through the fourteenth century were settled by negotiation and arbitration.[34] Under these circumstances, a woman was perceived more as a member of a *particular* group than as a *female* member of a group or of society at large. Since group affiliation was of greater moment than one's gender, assumptions about women's innate nature do not seem to have influenced criminal law to the point where it automatically typed women with respect to certain crimes.

Infractions and Penalties

Misdeeds committed by women ranged from murder to stabbing a cow, and from receiving stolen goods to encouraging two young men to impersonate a woman.[35] Marie, widow of Oste Scare, gave Cristine, wife of Jean le Brune, a neighbor, a *tourteel* (pastry), which, when she and her child ate it, caused them to become very sick. Although the register notes that Marie was subsequently convicted on April 4, 1337 when she confessed to attempted murder, it regrettably gives no indication why Marie wished Cristine dead.[36] Two unnamed *bourgeoises* of Ypres each received a fine of 60 s. in April 1335 for hitting each other in the face,[37] while Beatrice Duvejonx and her daughter Bette were banned on August 6, 1376 for attacking Griele Lauwers with a stick.[38] On March 19, 1320, Marie de Canigheem received a large fine, 60 l., for vandalism.[39] Apparently resenting that her house had been sold, Marie had avenged herself by destroying as much of it as she could before she was stopped.

These represent a few cases for which we have detailed information. Flemish judicial records are not plentiful before the mid-fourteenth century. Evidence of malefaction from the thirteenth and early fourteenth centuries can be much more commonly found in city and baillivial accounts, which routinely noted fines perpetrators paid to the city and indemnities they paid to each other. The brief notation, such as *Lisa Alards: 10 l. contra Gilkinum Barbificem*,[40] for example, mark disputes among people and not between people and the city. Thomas Kuehn suggests that throughout medieval Europe lawsuits were sometimes used to force settlements.[41] Entries in city accounts, such as those of Ypres for the years 1268, 1280, and 1281 testify to this practice.[42]

Conflicts between women and men as well as between two women were not uncommon. There also does not seem to be any significant distinction in the amounts either gender paid. The accounts of Ypres, for example, mention four occasions in which women paid the highest amount attested for the period (11 l. 10 s.), in each case to a man.[43] At least twice, however, women appear to have obtained 10 l. against men.[44] Many of the culpable (regardless of gender) paid as little as 5 s., but the most common amount was 3 l. One man even paid 3 l. to his mother.[45] Men did not receive substantially higher sums from women than from men, nor vice versa. Nor did the amounts women obtained from other women differ from the amounts that men won either from men or from women, or, of course, women from men. To the clerk responsible for constructing the financial record the judicial aspect of these transactions was probably of almost no interest. What was important to him was that money had been exchanged between two parties. The city's ultimate responsibility was for the enforcement of all arbitrated decisions. That very enforcement might, when tabulated in an account, be reduced to its bare monetary essentials, as in *Lisa Alards: 10 l. contra Gilkinum Barbificem.*

In Flanders, as in most of the rest of Europe, murder, rape, and arson were the major capital crimes. These initially involved execution, but over the course of the twelfth and thirteenth centuries, they usually came to entail a fine of 60 l. or more, or permanent banishment.[46] When execution was mandated, men were usually hung or beheaded and women were usually buried alive.[47] The threat of execution, however, was much more common than its incidence. It became routine in many condemnations as a kind of sanction of last resort, intended to secure compliance with an order for banishment or with some other punishment.[48]

Fines and exile were by far the most usual response to both these and lesser malefactions.[49] Banishment was a very public and oral process,[50] and as such could be expected to deter other potential malefactors. More practically, making the identities of the condemned persons public knowledge prevented other citizens from accidentally, through ignorance, aiding and abetting them. In addition it rid the community of proven disturbers of the peace more cheaply than imprisonment could have. Exile was a serious matter. It was understood that an exile found in the community before the expiration of term of banishment not only was liable to execution, but could also be attacked with impunity.[51]

There are, in fact, very few records of women suffering the death penalty.[52] Responsibility for carrying out such a sentence rested with the bailiffs, and their records duly note such occasions.[53] The 1374 account of Olivier de le Stenbrugghe, bailiff of Ghent, details, for example, the costs of executing five women.[54] This is the largest number found at any one time, but there are no details in the account beyond such things as the cost of wood, straw, shackles, cords, and material (11 l. 6 s.),[55] the cost of bringing the women from Waes to Ghent (6 l.),[56] the cost of priests to whom the women made their confession (25 s.),[57] and the cost of the executioner (10 l.)[58] to indicate why these women were being executed.

The misdeed had to be fairly extreme to warrant sentence of death. Two women who were condemned to it had murdered their husbands. In 1306, together with her maid and a young nonresident man, an unnamed woman murdered her husband. She and the maid were buried alive while the young man was hung.[59] Of more interest is the case of Margaret le Meide. One night in 1263, Margaret le Meide murdered her husband, Michel Tourhout.[60] Margaret was a woman of property,[61] a member of the upper classes; both she and her husband were from prominent Yprois families.[62] What makes this case interesting is not that Margaret murdered her husband, but that riots between the two families broke out in the city the very next day. The riots were so severe that the city found itself unable to quell them, and had to call in the countess. Madame le Meide was tried, found guilty, and executed. In addition, Thierry le Meide and Clais Mons were required to go on pilgrimage overseas.[63] Thierry was the brother of Margaret le Meide, and it was determined that the conflict would best achieve lasting resolution if several of Margaret's kin, including her brother, were ordered to go on pilgrimage. Since they were in no way formally considered to be accessories to Margaret le Meide's act, the command to go on pilgrimage could not be considered punishment for the crime.[64]

It could be argued that Margaret was executed because the man she murdered was her husband, and that she had thus in fact committed the more serious crime of wifely betrayal, as such a crime was construed in nearby England.[65] Flemish custom, however, does not seem to have viewed the marital relationship as anything warranting special consideration on behalf of either spouse. In fact, the Flemish evidence clearly indicates that marital status may well have played no role in the assessment or judgment of murderous action, one way or another, for either spouse. In 1335, a man from St. Disier attacked his wife with a knife. He was fined 60 l. for his action, the amount that separated major from lesser crimes. The man appealed to the aldermen of Ypres,[66] claiming that he owed nothing because his victim was merely his wife. The aldermen rejected his argument and the penalty held. They argued that the city's charter stipulated that whoever attacked another with a knife was penalized 60 l.[67]

There is evidence from Douai that suggests a similar point of view. In the last half of the thirteenth century, Douai's aldermen set down guidelines for the punishment of those who murdered its citizens. Three copies of this *ban* still exist from that period. The first merely states *Et kicunke ociroit borgois de cest vile. . .*[68] The second copy, which is dated 1257, expands this dictate slightly: *Et ki onques ociroit borgois ne borgoise, ne fil de borgois u de borgoise. . .*[69] The third copy, dated approximately 1275, goes even further, extending the gender-inclusive provision ("whether man or woman") from victim to perpetrator: *On fait ban ke kiconques, fus hom u feme de ceste vile u deforain ocirioit borgois u borgoise. . .*[70] The fact that there was no special provision made in any of these ordinances for any possible spousal relationship between victim and perpetrator should probably be taken at face value. There is no other formal or informal evidence that the aldermen did not really mean what they said. As the case from Ypres makes clear, neither the gender of the victim nor that of the perpetrator nor any special relationship between the two was of any consequence whatsoever.[71]

A further case, also from Ypres, suggests that there was little difference between the law and its application. On November 12, 1399, Griele de Rivet was exiled forever from Ypres for the murder of John Slotelkin.[72] This was exactly the same punishment Lotin Velle received the same year for the murder of Jaque Bru and William Moutier.[73] At first glance it appears that Lotin Velle was punished for the murder of two men, but the fact that the name *Jaque* was not exclusively given to males makes, in this context, a nice point.[74] This case also illustrates the community's preference for exile over bloody punishment.

The le Meide case illustrates the mixture of prosecution with arbitration. The primary impetus behind the response to Margaret le Meide's action as well as behind the Douaisian ordinances was perhaps not so much desire to modify individual behavior by applying a punitive corrective (to the particular individual) or providing an example (to other, like-minded individuals), but rather the more fundamental goal of redressing the balance in a manner that involved both reconciliation and punishment. The presence of material detailing judicial events across a range of diverse municipal records testifies to the intertwining of both processes. City accounts register fines and other payments used to terminate negotiated or arbitrated conflicts between residents. Aldermanic records list instances of conflict resolution, both those handed down by the aldermen and those achieved through the *paysierders*, while other sources trace the development of customary law.[75] Prosecution was not always easily distinguishable from arbitration. Such lack of clear distinction between the two seems to have served the city well—the malefactor was punished, but at the same time, the feuding parties were appeased.

Men and women were usually treated similarly throughout the county when it came to the disciplining of less serious infractions. All who participated in the perpetration of a given type of harmful action usually paid the same fine. Anyone found guilty of selling "foreign" (non-Ypres) fish in Ypres, for example, paid 20 s.[76] Women in Ghent in 1305 were charged fines as low as 5 s. and as high as 60 s. by the city authorities at about the same rate as were men.[77] In 1336, Kateline Canke, Bette Gypening, and Sare de Zuevenselle of Courtrai paid 5 s. for *mavaisement boureer draps*, exactly the same others paid for the same infraction.[78] In 1268, Michael, son of Yft Scotes, was fined 3 l. for "bad meat."[79] In 1281, thirteen years later, the magistrates fined Grieta of Courtrai the same amount for the same misdemeanor.[80] This practice becomes particularly clear from a glance at almost any community's baillivial accounts up through 1336. They are almost all organized fairly simply, primarily by location.[81] Each section is subdivided into subsections, the first usually being fines and fees for contravention of a community's *keure* (customary law). In Ghent, for example, the 1305 account of bailiff Thièri le Brabantre begins *Dedens le vile de Gant: De ban brisier de le cervoise. . . .D'amendes jugiés par arbitres jurées. . .De ban brisier des herens* and so forth.[82] Under each heading is a list of those who paid the fee or fine, recorded in what appears to be random order.[83] The accounts of bailiffs from other communities follow a similar pattern.[84] These accounts provide visual testimony to the social reality that men and women were, at this level of misdeed, indistinguishable from each other.[85]

Communities routinely handed out the same terms of exile for both female and male malefactors. In the last years of the thirteenth century Ypres issued a special ordinance concerning individuals banished from the city. This ordinance makes it clear that men and women would receive the same punishment for harboring or maintaining fugitives of any gender.[86] The ordinance also makes it clear that such fugitives could be of any gender, and that being female was no guarantee either of preferential or of harsher treatment. Banishment was gender-neutral. By 1319 it had even become common for anyone who had been banished to pay 60 s. to commute that sentence, regardless of the length of the initial sentence (or gender of the perpetrator).[87] One paid 60 s. whether one had been banned for one year or for seven. The amount might also remain unaffected by the nature of the crime. Agnes le Yredemakkigghe, who was banned for one year for keeping a house of ill-repute, paid the same amount (60 s.) as did Coppin Stier, who had been banned for the same number of years for attacking and wounding Hannot le Damhoudre in public.[88] This lack of differentiation may well have resulted from the communities' emphasis on arbitration and reconciliation. Within this conceptual framework, the fact of the misdeed was evidently more important than its type or the characteristics of its perpetrator.[89]

The Shift Toward Prosecutions

Once rudimentary organization had been achieved, however, it created opportunities for further standardization. This in turn threw the nature of the malefaction and characteristics of its perpetrator, including gender, into relief. During the second half of the fourteenth century, prosecutions increased and arbitration and negotiation became less frequent. Increased prosecution resulted in the construction of a typology of crimes and, correspondingly, a change in the type of crimes for which women were prosecuted. Although the number of crimes women committed does not seem to have altered substantially, the kinds for which they were prosecuted does. The change of focus from settlement by arbitration to prosecution, and the corresponding shift of emphasis from reconciliation to punishment, could well have been a response to the disasters plaguing Europe in the fourteenth century; of particular importance was the economic downturn, from which cities such as Ypres never recovered. Also of considerable significance was the accession of Louis of Male as count of Flanders in 1346. His reign is notable for the extension of comital power and administration through the mechanisms of the evolving state apparatus, in which offices such as that of the general receiver, the chancellor, and the sovereign bailiff played a major role.[90] Hitherto, the right to deal with wrongdoing had been determined in a relatively ad hoc fashion. Over the course of the century, however, the count's chief judicial officer—first the general receiver and then the sovereign bailiff—acquired responsibility for the commutation of a large variety of sentences.[91] The commutations that fell under his jurisdiction at this time ran from larceny (which cost Griele Schoedemaker twenty-three years in exile) to "unreasonable behavior" (which cost

Gillekin Lichtvoet three years in exile).[92] By 1369 the number of judicial fines that had become the responsibility of the general receiver had grown to such an extent that they were taken out of his general account and listed in a special, separate one.[93] Systematization and standardization of legal procedure infected the towns as well, and permitted aldermen to gain more control of the regulation of conflicts. The consequent eclipse of arbitration enabled them for the first time to become involved in affairs that were heretofore chiefly managed by families.[94]

The records detailing judicial events in fourteenth-century Flanders reveal a change in the type of malefactions for which women were held accountable. This was due primarily to the shift from the general to the specific in the accounting of the punitive fines paid for malefactions.[95] The most common infraction for which women had been fined in the first half of the century was *mellee*, a rather vague term meaning "conflict," "fray," "free-for-all," or "tussle."[96] Their names also appear in the lists of penalties for economic violations. Irregularities in the selling of fish, wheat, or bread, and in the measuring of the item being sold had resulted in large and small fines, depending upon the seriousness of the transgression.[97] Other rubrics under which women's names appear as having paid penalties were equally vague, including transgressions of the community's *keure*, complaints, inquiries, and conflicts raised between citizens, and fines and fees.[98] Most baillivial accounts consist primarily of rubrics under which are listed the names of those who paid the fines and fees. Details of the circumstances concerning the event that resulted in the penalty are very rare. It was much more common for accounts of bailiffs to specify the circumstances surrounding expenses than those involving income.[99] Clearly, personal characteristics of those making punitive payments and even the reasons behind such payments were considered of little significance.

This would account for the fact that in the first half of the fourteenth century women appear in baillivial records only three times (less than 1 percent of all female misdeeds) for theft or larceny.[100] In the second half of the fourteenth century, women throughout the county were punished for theft and larceny two and a half times that often.[101] To be sure, it is possible that, given the economic and social conditions of the time, women did indeed steal and rob at a higher rate in the second half of the century than in the first. It is much more likely, however, that such nefarious activity in the first half of the fourteenth century was subsumed under one of the undifferentiated rubrics mentioned earlier. Similarly, baillivial accounts list almost no women penalized specifically for actionable language in the first half of the century, while a good 7 percent of the punitive fines they paid in the second half are explicitly associated with this transgression.[102] The likelihood is not that women had been more well behaved in the first half of the century, but again, as in the case of theft, that actionable language had been subsumed under a more general rubric, most probably *mellee*.

Increasing standardization allowed for greater specification in recording not only the types of crime but also the conditions under which they took place. Instead of lists introduced only by a brief rubric, as in the first half of the century, accounts from the second half of the century consist primarily of entries in paragraph form. Entries under the rubric of fines (*boeten*) in the 1374 account of the bailiff of Dam, for example, are in paragraph form instead of the traditional list.[103] One only needs to flip through the pages of the accounts of the bailiff of Ghent for the years 1365 through 1376, edited and published by David Nicholas and Walter Prevenier, to note the absence of the simple lists characteristic of an earlier age.[104] Rubrics themselves were often much more detailed. In the baillivial account of Ghent for the period January 8 to May 7, 1375 one finds, for example, "Fines paid in the amount of 11 1/2 l. for knocking people to the ground with a blow or a sharp implement, of which 6 l. 13 s. 4 d. is due to my lord, 3 l. 6 s. 8 d. to the viscount, 15 s. to the plaintiff, 5 s. to the city, and 10 s. to the comital representative."[105] The information found in the rubric was often not enough, for items detailed not only the name of the person who paid the fine and the amount, but also specific aspects of the malefaction for which the person was penalized.[106]

Although this process gives nod to the traditional notion of malefaction as originating out of conflict between two people,[107] the emphasis was shifting from reconciliation to prosecution. The rubric quoted above is notable for the number of officials who have claim to the fine; the person who registered the original complaint is third in a list of five who have a right to part of it. The other four received their portion by right of being officials, not because they were personally injured in the conflict.[108] The weight, in terms of both personnel and of the portion of the fine that goes to a particular official, is clearly on the judicial apparatus responsible for the process. If this had been arbitration, the point would have been to appease the wronged person and his family, not to remunerate the local, regional, and comital authorities.

These two elements, the eclipse of arbitration by prosecution and the standardization of records and accounts, tended to foster the development of a typology of malefaction and of malefactor. Wrongdoing was no longer determined primarily by the presence of conflict but rather by prosecutors. This is most clearly seen in cases where it is evident that an attack had taken place, but because the victim made no complaint, the attacker was set free. That such cases even made it into the baillivial records is an indication of the process whereby accusation would come slowly to be replaced by indictment, leaving the victim—and thus the need for arbitration or negotiation—completely out of the compensatory process. When groups sponsored accusations of attack, the victim was less likely to be in the spotlight of proof or accusation. Once the malefactor instead of the fact of the disruption caused by the malefaction became important, not only did the accused stand alone, so did the accuser. This might explain the presence of cases in the second half of the fourteenth century where the victim refused to press charges. There are virtually no such cases in the accounts prior to the middle of the fourteenth century; such attacks were likely to have been handled under the general rubric of *mellee*. There were a number of them in the second half of the fourteenth century.[109]

As conflict resolution gave way to prosecution, prosecutors began to acquire the responsibility and thus the capacity for deciding what constituted crime and what characterized a criminal. It was up to them, for example, to decide what distinguished receiving stolen goods from theft itself; arbitrators would be only peripherally interested in such a distinction. Whereas in the first half of the century women and men were jumbled together in the category of *mellee*, prosecutors over the course of the fourteenth century developed a typology of violent acts that included actionable language, pulling of hair, threatening to hit with a fist, hitting with a fist (wounding), hitting with a stick (without wounding), hitting with a stick (wounding), attack by day, attack by night, and so forth.[110] By the middle to late fourteenth century, women were being prosecuted more for certain of these, notably actionable language, pulling hair, and threatening to deck their adversary, than for others. In Ghent, for example, actionable language made up 15 percent of the malefactions for which women paid fines, while attacking with a stick made up only 5 percent.[111] In Furnes, the most common infraction for which women paid fines was pulling hair.[112]

It is in the records of the second half of the fourteenth century that women are first listed as paying fines for malefactions of a more specific and thus new type. These consisted of behaviors that disrupted family relationships sanctioned by custom and upheld by authorities, who, of course, included those prosecuting the action in the first place. Punishable misbehaviors of this sort consisted of mishandling or misleading children, living with another woman's spouse, being led astray, running away with unacceptable men, and helping other women to run away with unacceptable men, among others.[113] To be sure, courts punished men for some infractions of this sort as well. Both Jake Moens and Griele sLappers, for example, in 1375 were held accountable for helping Coppin Thuman's wife run off with another man, and Pieter Piel was assessed 59 s. for pulling Calle sReingiaerts by the hair.[114] While behavioral infractions such as these do not make up much more than 3 percent of the malefactions for which women were fined over the course of the second half of the fourteenth century, they allowed for the possibility, which previous records did not, of judging miscreants on the basis of personal characteristics such as gender.

Some gender bias is suggested by the increased prosecutions for actionable language in Ypres. Actionable language comprises only about 4 percent of the infractions of which women were accused in Ypres in the first half of the century.[115] By the end of the fourteenth century, the proportion had increased four-fold.[116] Data for Ghent clearly show a similar development.[117] Who was to determine what was actionable? In the first half of the century, objectionable words were rarely sufficient on their own to justify prosecution. Since it is highly unlikely that the incidence of screaming threats and hurling verbal insults was so low in the early fourteenth century as not to warrant reaction, it is likely that such actions were subsumed under the ever-useful rubric of *mellee*, or considered to be part of a greater disturbance. In Ypres, a woman simply listed as Sobrin was fined 60 s. not only for actionable words but also for illegal entry.[118] By the end of the fourteenth century, women were being hauled before the court for actionable words alone.[119] This might well be the result of a tightening of security and an increasing intolerance for actions that might escalate into physical violence. Be that as it may, in choosing to prosecute women more vigorously for this particular misdemeanor, magistrates were either planting the idea of female verbal irresponsibility in the minds of the general population, or they were reinforcing it.

The separation of language from the larger conflict (and its consequent development as a specific punishable infraction) is part of the evolution of conflict from something to be resolved (with reconciliation of the conflicting parties) to something to be punished (with correction of the offending parties) by the authorities. As we have seen, order was perceived, until the fourteenth century, as dependent on the regulation of relationships among groups. The management of malefaction involved the various groups who were disrupted by a particular action; the focus was thus on reconciliation of the whole. After the mid-fourteenth century, conflicts appear increasingly to have been reduced to quarrels between individuals, one or both of whom could then be punished separately. Baillivial records are full of entries succinctly detailing quarrels between individuals. In Bruges in 1369, Gilles de Makelare de Scheerre was fined 11 l. for quarreling with Cateline van den Houc,[120] while Grace Aleyden was similarly fined in 1373 in Dam.[121] In Furnes, Beate Boids and in Courtrai, Jhans Merstaertes's wife paid fines for their quarrels with others,[122] while in Ghent and in Quatre Métiers, we find the likes of Lijsbette sBlox and Margriete, Jehan Blankaerts's widow, doing the same.[123]

The wording of the accounts traces this development. Entries in the city accounts of Ypres, as we have seen, had noted such quarrels simply as "X contra Y."[124] Such entries clearly mark disputes among people and not between people and the city or the count. In the records of other communities, such as Bruges, Furnes, Ghent, and Quatre Métiers, altercations and other such disturbances appear to have been subsumed indiscriminately under the rubric of *mellee*.[125] The lack of distinction among misdeeds underlines the arbitral nature of justice, even when resolution entailed judgment. The change that had set in by the second half of the fourteenth century is evident from the rubric in the 1367 account of the bailiff of Bruges: "Fines for Quarrels."[126] Moreover, no longer were those fined merely listed; rather each incident enjoyed a whole paragraph to itself.[127] The expansion in detail and the corresponding diminution in ambivalence points to an increase in efficiency in the judicial proceeding itself, a consequence, no doubt, of the standardization that characterized records of the second half of the fourteenth century.[128] Altercations that earlier would probably have been settled by negotiation or arbitration because they were seen as located in the associated groups had now, because they were perceived as located in the separate individuals, become punishable offenses.

Conclusion

Central to the concept of crime is the judgment that a particular action is somehow injurious to society. The act that is committed, however, does not comprise the whole of a malefaction. The other major component is the person who perpetrated it. Although the infraction itself is usually the primary focus of judgment or resolution, the perpetrator is rarely treated as irrelevant.[129] On the one hand, peculiar characteristics of the doer can come to outweigh the nature and the fact of the infraction. On the other, the peculiar characteristics of the misdeed can come to outweigh the importance of certain characteristics of the doer. In some cases, the simple preservation of law and order pushed the perpetrator into the background by foregrounding the action and its potential for disruption. It was thus possible for the identity of the transgressor to be routinely subordinated not to the type of transgression, but to its fact. Gender-specific characteristics, for example, played a distinctly secondary role in the settling of conflicts in thirteenth- and early fourteenth-century Flanders; this is clearly manifested in the baillivial accounts of the first half of the fourteenth century. It was the specific activities of particular groups, and not necessarily of individual men and women, that needed to be constrained. The focus was more on social disruption than on social offense. As a consequence, even in cases involving prosecution, women in Flanders seem usually to have received neither more nor less severe treatment than did men for similar misdoings.[130]

The emphasis on conflict resolution through a process of arbitration remained dominant throughout the thirteenth century and began to wane only in the fourteenth. The archival collections reflect this. Many of the early fourteenth-century collections possess rudimentary organization, while others, such as the series of decisions edited by Pelsmaeker, have only elementary internal order. The lack of organization within the records themselves may well also have reflected a lack of uniformity in the judicial process itself. Limited uniformity, in turn, could well have hindered the construction, formal or informal, of any typology of malefactions and of malefactors. Prosecution, focused as it was on the action as offense and the actor as offender, encouraged such a construction, and the standardization found after the middle of the fourteenth century reflects associated efficiency.

Although city authorities still arbitrated conflicts in the late fourteenth century, cases had increasingly come to be settled by an appeal to authority. What resulted were prosecutions made by an official such as a bailiff on the basis of authority vested in him by the count, an authority not founded on communal traditions. Transgressions that in the thirteenth century had been treated as sources of conflicts, by the late fourteenth century were coming to be viewed as infractions, a concept that implied the application of statutory as opposed to customary law. The fact that in 1380, for example, the bailiff of Ypres was also a *docteur es décrès*[131] indicates that prosecution according to law, requiring knowledge that could only be mastered in the new universities (which were not open to women[132]) was of at least as much importance as arbitration according to custom, knowledge of which was, after all, open to anyone. In the thirteenth century, the emphasis of justice was on the indemnification of the injured parties, not on the punishment of the injuring one. Offensive language, in order to be actionable, for example, must be located in a specific individual. Thirteenth- and early fourteenth-century documents record almost no fines, penalties, or resolutions of conflicts involving unacceptable words, primarily because shrieking obscenities, roundly cursing, and verbally abusing one's enemy remained undifferentiated from the disturbance as a whole. By the late fourteenth century, however, communities routinely fined individuals specifically for language deemed objectionable. This change in focus necessitated the use of evidence and the proof of guilt—in short the definition of the malefaction and of the malefactor. What was important was that the transgressor be punished. When the focus thus shifted to defining the crime and punishing the misdoer, particular crimes were much more likely to be linked with a particular type of person or with a particular personal characteristic. These characteristics were then able to take on lives of their own; they could in principle transcend any specific disruptive incident. This made linking the characteristic to the malefactor much easier. Once this happened, particular characteristics of the perpetrator, including gender, could force the doer to emerge from the group, her identity no longer principally embedded in her associations.

From the increasing association of women with a given malefaction, moreover, it was but a short step to the identification of that crime as peculiarly female. Connecting a particular type of malefaction with women encouraged the increasing separation of transgressions on the basis of a gender bias, where such bias had formerly been only of minor significance. The focus on conflict resolution using arbitration, after all, involved satisfying groups, appeasing aggrieved factions, and restoring equilibrium. Separation, in fact, encouraged the establishment of an identifiable female criminal sphere. If the implicit recognition of such a sphere of activity was not in itself symptomatic of a constriction in women's participation in society, it at least exerted influence of a sort that was conducive to such constriction.

Notes

1. R.C. van Caenegem, *Geschiedenis van het strafprocesrecht in Vlaanderen van de Xie tot de XIVe eeuw* (Brussels: Palais der Academiën, 1956). The first volume, *Geschiedenis van het strafrecht in Vlaanderen van de XIe tot de XIVe eeuw* (Brussels: Palais der Academiën), had appeared two years earlier, in 1954.

2. An analogy could be drawn with research into heart attacks, most of which was for years carried out almost exclusively on male subjects, with any observations about the cardiac health of women being extrapolated from this evidence.

3. Or in other words, "gender-as-extenuating-circumstance."

4. *Bijzondere bescherming van de vrouwen* (van Caenegem, *Strafrecht*, p. 66).

5. van Caenegem, *Strafrecht*, p. 66, n. 4. The problem is that for proof of this he cites Ph. Wielant's *Corte instructie omme jonge practisenen in materie criminele diende in Vlanderen* (published by A. Orts (*Vlaamsche bibliophilen* 3ᵉ reeks, nur 15), Ghent, 1872), which was published between 1503 and 1519. Other historians have very little to add to van Caenegem's analysis. Female misdeeds, for example, are of only marginal concern to David Nicholas in his "Crime and Punishment in Fourteenth-Century Ghent;" he seems astonished to find them there at all (*Revue belge de philologie et d'histoire* 48 (1970), p. 303 and 1161). This surprise is in line with Nicholas's assumption that women were permanently under male guardianship (David Nicholas, *The Domestic Life of a Medieval City: Women, Children and the Family in Fourteenth-Century Ghent* (Lincoln: University of Nebraska Press, 1985), pp. 18, 24–25), and therefore alien to the "public" sphere of criminal law. For his view of criminal law as public, see Nicholas, "Crime and Punishment," p. 290. For an argument that male guardianship over women was in fact a quite restricted phenomenon, see E. Kittell "Guardianship Over Women in Medieval Flanders: A Reappraisal," *Journal of Social History* 31, no. 4 (Summer, 1998), pp. 897–930.

6. A. Porteau-Bitker, "Criminalité et délinquance féminines dans le droit pénal des XIII et XIVe siècles," *Revue d'histoire de droit de français et d'étrangé* 58 (1980), pp. 14–15.

7. She specifically cites evidence from *Le livre Roisin. Coutumier lillois de la fin du XIIIᵉ siècle* (Paris: Les Éditions Domat-Montchrestien, 1932), particularly item 167 (Porteau-Bitker, p. 53, n. 236).

8. A. Porteau-Bitker, p. 16, n. 9, pp. 17–18.

9. The first transgression, given such a conceptual framework, would be their presence in the public sphere at all; the second would involve the particular malefaction. Perhaps this is the theoretical basis for the notion that fines were doubled if a woman committed a particular crime.

10. Louis Haas, "Women and Politics in the Urban Milieu" in *Women in Medieval European Culture*, ed. Linda Mitchell (New York: Garland Press, 1999), p. 223. Haas's is a rather Ameri-centric focus: he bases his conclusions exclusively on only two American historians of Flanders, David Nicholas and Martha Howell. Nicholas's work on Ghent, *The Domestic life of a Medieval City*, is seriously flawed, however (Kittell, "Guardianship Over Women," p. 897). Howell's work focuses chiefly on Leiden (*Women, Production, and Patriarchy in Late Medieval Cities* (Chicago: University of Chicago Press, 1986)) and on Douai in the early modern period (*The Marriage Exchange* (Chicago: University of Chicago Press, 1998)); the conclusions that she reaches are therefore on the whole not indicative of the situation in medieval Flanders. More importantly, however, Haas completely ignores the whole body of work by Belgian historians.

11. The general public was represented by specifically gender-inclusive doublets, by the impersonal "whoever," or the plural, none of which pinpoints the "public" as exclusively or even predominantly male. It appears that the doublet form was common in the thirteenth century, that the plural enjoyed increasing favor throughout most of the fourteenth century, and that finally, in the late fourteenth and fifteenth centuries, earlier forms were largely supplanted by the masculine singular (E. Kittell and K. Queller, " 'Whether Man or Woman': Gender Inclusivity in the Town Ordinances of Medieval Douai," *The Journal of Medieval and Early Modern Studies* 30, no. 1 (Winter, 2000), pp. 63–100. Gender-inclusive doublets are found in the records of other communities in the county as well, for example, *De nulz cas criminel ne doit estre le grans maiiers en terre de Sainct-Amand rechus a loi a l'encontre de bourgeois ou bourgeoise. . .*(van Caenegem, *Strafprocesrecht* (Brussels, 1956) p. 21, n. 2).

12. Georges Espinas, *La vie urbaine de Douai au moyen âge* (Paris: Libraires des Archives Nationales et de la Société de l'Écoles des Chartes, 1913), p. 3:138–40 #196–200. On such occasions, the ordinances employ forms like *fils, garçons*, and *valet*, which are unmistakably male. For example, see *fiels de bourgois*: ca. 1231 (Espinas, *La vie urbaine*, p. 3:112 #163ABC item 1); for *garçons* see ca.1250 (ibid., p. 3:189 #253 item 3).

13. Given the formulaic construction of these ordinances, we have a case where men, it could be argued, and not women, functioned as the Other.

14. *"Jehane Des Favereus, bourgoise de Douay"* (Espinas, *La vie urbaine*, pp. 488–89 #1311); *"Aelis de Zuinarde, borghoise de Gant"* (Ghent, Rijksarchief. Fonds Gaillard #517); Theo Luykx, *De grafelijke financiële bestuurinstellingen en het grafelijk patrimonium in Vlaanderen tijdens de regering van Margareta van Constantinopel (1244–1278)* (Brussels: Palais der Academiën, 1961), p. 452 #122; *"Beatris Steurtebier, bourgoise d'Ypre"* (G. des Marez, *La lettre de foire á Ypres au XIIIe siècle* (Brussels: H. Lamertin, 1900), pp. 125–26 #31); *"Kerstienne Wightart, borgoise de Bourbourg"* (Ignace de Coussemaker, *Un cartulaire de l'abbaye de Notre-Dame de Bourbourg (1104–1793)* (Lille, 1877–78), p. 1:199 #207); *"Cecile Heldebolle, bourgeoise de leur ville [Courtrai]"* (C. Mussely and E. Molitor, *Cartulaire de l'ancienne église collégiale á Notre-Dame à Courtrai* (Ghent: Imprimerie et Lithographie C. Annoot-Braeckman, Marché aux grains, 1880), p. 232 #1, #260).

15. Sixty-five percent of the women who appear in Ypres's records in the period from the late thirteenth to the late fourteenth century lack any appellative at all. Data for this number comes from Brussels, Algemeen Rijksarchief, and Rekenkamer. Rolrekening (hereafter RR) #1696–1718; G. des Marez and E. de Sagher, *Comptes de la ville d'Ypres (1267–1329)*, 2 vols. (Brussels: Libraire Kiessling et Cie, P. Imbreghts, successeur, 1900–13); G. des Marez, *La lettre de foire à Ypres au XIIIe siècle* (Brussels: H. Lamertin, 1901); G. des Marez, *Le droit privé a Ypres au XIIIme siècle* (Braine-L'Alleud: René Berger, 1927); E. Feys and A. Nélis, *Les cartulaires de la Prevôté de Saint-Martin à Ypres* (Bruges: A. de Zuttere–van Kersschaven, Val des Roses, 1880); I.L.A. Diegerick, *Inventaire analytique et chronologique des chartes et documents apparetenant aux archives de la ville d'Ypres*, vols. I, II (Bruges: Vandecasteele-Werbrouch, 1853, 1854); *Registre aux sentences des échevins d'Ypres*, in *Coutumes des pays et comté de Flandre*, ed. Prosper de Pelsmaeker (Brussels: J. Goemaere, 1914); L. Gilliodts-van Severen, ed., *Sources et développement de la coutume d'Ypres*, in *Coutumes des pays et comté de Flandre* (Brussels: J. Goemaere, 1908).

The lack of appellative should not be taken as a sign that a woman was single, that is, she had never been married or was widowed. See E. Kittell, "The Construction of Women's Social Identity in Medieval Douai: Evidence from Identifying Epithets," *Journal of Medieval History* vol. 25 (1998), pp. 215–27.

16. Des Marez et de Sagher, *Comptes*, 1:121 #10.

17. Des Marez, *La lettre de foire*, pp. 131–32 #38.

18. RR #1711.

19. van Caenegem, *Strafrecht*, pp. 12–24.

20. See Kittell, "Guardianship Over Women," pp. 897–930.

21. J. Goebel, *Felony and Misdemeanor. A Study in the History of Criminal Law* (Philadelphia: University of Pennsylvania Press, 1976), p. 21.

22. As Guido Ruggiero has remarked, "Society, the groups within it, and the people who constitute it have been perceived as ordered by many things. . . but with amazing consistency, these ordering principles have been threatened by passion. . ." (*Binding Passions* (Oxford: Oxford University Press,

1993), p. 11). Perhaps the most famous city feud in Flanders was that which took place between the Borluuts and the van Sinte-Baafs in Ghent. The liveliest account is that of Wim Blockmans, *En middeleeuwse vendetta. Gent 1300* (Houten: de Haan, 1987).

23. Goebel, *Felony and Misdemeanor,* p. 21.

24. There has been almost no work done on liminal groups, for example, adolescents, in Flemish cities. It is likely, however, that they did exist, and that they were somewhat comparable to those in other cities such as Florence. See Richard C. Trexler, *The Children of Renaissance Florence,* vol. I of *Power and Dependence in Renaissance Florence* (Binghamton, New York: Medieval and Renaissance Texts and Studies, 1993), pp. 54–112.

25. van Caenegem, *Strafrecht,* p. 304, n. 2. These were the officials who came to be responsible for negotiating, or if necessary, arbitrating peace between feuding clans or other groups. The Dutch word is based on the French *paiseur,* which, in turn, is from the old French, *apaisier,* which means to restore peace. For a succinct overview of the process, see Nicholas, "Crime and Punishment," p. 1148.

26. Resolutions achieved by arbitration or negotiation were often considered legal only after being promulgated in formal court proceedings (Nicholas, "Crime and Punishment," p. 1148). Cases found in legal records of court officials, therefore, were not necessarily the result of prosecutorial process alone.

27. J. van Herwaarden, *Opgelegde bedvaarten* (Amsterdam: van Gorcum, 1978), pp. 12–13.

28. David Nicholas, *Domestic Life,* pp. 199–201. He continues: "It compensated the males of the clan for the loss of one of themselves, not the nuclear family for the loss of a breadwinner." This does not take into account that the *zoen* was not something levied on individuals; rather its maintenance was the responsibility of the whole group.

29. It is, however, understandable that he reached this conclusion, given that he appears not to have consulted either van Cauwenbergh or van Herwaarden.

30. . . .*de zoen als geheel met compositio et pax* (van Herwaarden, *Opgelegde bedevaarten,* p. 19). Note also the sense of "putting together" implied in *compositio. Pax* in this context is not to be confused with *vrede,* in the sense of "truce" or "temporary cessation of hostility," which must be the first step in the process of *verzoening.* The word *zoen* is etymologically cognate with the old Friesian *sone,* which means "kiss," as in "kiss of peace" (P.A.F. van Veen with Nocline van der Sijs, *Etymologish woordenboek* (Utrecht and Antwerp: van Dale Lexicografie, 1993), p. 838).

31. van Caenegem, *Strafrecht,* pp. 290–92.

32. Nicholas, David, "Crime and Punishment," pp. 1160–61. Women were not the only ones sent on pilgrimage to make amends for vile language and insults. On at least twenty-four occasions between 1331 and 1394, men from Ypres were ordered to go on pilgrimage for using "horrible words" or "ugly remarks." (. . .*pour les mesprisure et les horribles mos.* . .(Pelsmaeker, *Registre aux sentences,* p. 301 #779) . . .*et dist moult vilaine et horible parolles*

sour eux...(ibid., p. 317 #863. See also pp. 5–6 #375; p. 258 #409; p. 308 #820; p. 313 #839; p. 337 #966; and p. 338 #968.)

33. Susan Reynolds, *Fiefs and Vassals* (Oxford: Oxford University Press, 1994), p. 4.

34. Only roughly 10% of the cases in Flanders went through a prosecutory process run by authorities such as the bailiff or the aldermen (R.C. van Caenegem, *Strafrecht*, pp. 320–23). David Nicholas also cites this figure, but has reservations about how van Caenegem arrived at these statistics (David Nicholas, "Crime and Punishment", p. 314 and note 4).

35. On October 22, 1322, Lisebette sHonts received a fine of 3 l. . . .*pour se qu'elle bouta une vake d'un coutel* (Pelsmaeker, *Registre aux sentences*, p. 265 #480). On February 1, 1318, Matte de Bestedigghe and Griele de Steenackere were banned. . .*de mokes achater et rechevoir* (ibid., p. 255 #382). On September 22, 1334, Crestine sGraven. . .*est banie iij ans, sour le fosse, iij lieues de le ville où le conté s'estent, pour che que elle ennorta ij garchons de pourtraire une femme contre droit et pour fauseté* (ibid., p. 269 #520). For the reaction to women cross-dressing as men, see chapter 3 by Marianne Naessens "Judicial Authorities' Views of Women's Roles in the Late Medieval Southern Low Countries" in this volume.

36. Pelsmaeker, *Registere aux sentences,* p. 283 #607.

37. Gilliodts-van Severen, p. 132 #181.

38. . . .*pour ce qu'il frirent le dicte Grielle. . .*(Pelsmaeker, p. 323 #881).

39. *Pelsmaeker*, p. 255, #607.

40. Des Marez and de Sagher, *Comptes*, 1:11. As mentioned earlier, arbitrated decisions were usually considered valid only after being formally promulgated in court.

41. Thomas Kuehn, *Law, Family, and Women. Toward a Legal Anthropology of Renaissance Italy* (Chicago: University of Chicago Press, 1991), p. 19. He also notes that in Renaissance Florence, guild courts were known to handle cases "in an arbitral manner to avoid coming to conclusive, resentment-raising sentences" (p. 21.) Formal court proceedings were also the hallmark of cases decided by judgment. Under these circumstances, distinctions between arbitration and judgment tended to be blurred.

42. These are among the earliest still extant.

43. On August 8,1268, Staskinus Valke received this sum against Marota Ingelberti Cane. On November 20, 1280, Griela Nose paid a similar sum to Marchus Decanus. On June 18, 1281, Coppinus Claigbard received 11 1/2 l. from John de Perwere's wife, while on September 24 of that year, Meulinus Madoul and Hakinus de Befslare obtained a similar sum from Trisa de Vivario (Des Marez and de Sagher, *Comptes*, 1:11; 1:53; 1:60; 1:67).

44. On June 27, 1268, Lisa Alards won a judgment of 10 l. from Gillekin Barbificus, while on October 23, 1280, Machtilde de Staoele was awarded 10 l. from Henricus de Plassce (Des Marez and de Sagher, *Comptes*, 1:11; 1:51).

45. November 6, 1280: *Petrus Scarlaken: 3 l. contra ejus matrem* (Des Marez and de Sagher, *Comptes*, 1:52).

46. For banishment, see van Caenegem, *Strafrecht*, pp. 137–56.

47. van Caenegem, *Strafrecht*, pp. 157–68. Strangling (*sur le hart*) and living burial (*sur le fosse*) seemed to be the most common forms of execution.
48. For example: *Crestine sGravens et banie iij ans, sour le fosse* (Pelsmaeker, *Registre aux sentences*, p. 269 #520); *Matte de Bestedigghe, Griele de Steenackere, cascune est bannie, sour le fosse*...(ibid., p. 255 #382).
49. Nicholas, "Crime and Punishment," pp. 328–29. According to van Caenegem, exile as a response to malefaction originated in the Flemish cities and reached its height in the thirteenth and fourteenth centuries (van Caenegem, *Strafrecht*, p. 153).
50. *Het strafproces is in Vlaanderen in de behandelde periode wezenlijk mondeling gebleven*...*Het ganse proces, in al zijn delen, moet in het openbaar plaats hebben* (van Caenegem, *Strafprocesrecht*, p. 88).
51. Nicholas, "Crime and Punishment," p. 329.
52. This should not be seen as unusual. Not only does it appear that women did not commit murders in any noticeable numbers, but also that Flemish society had an aversion to what van Caenegem calls "bloody punishment" (van Caenegem, *Strafrecht*, p. 200; Nicholas, "Crime and Punishment," p. 327.)
53. Executions were expensive. Their cost was usually listed after the final reckoning in a bailiff's account. The fact that very few such listings are found in bailiffs' accounts before the middle of the fourteenth century suggests first, that they were not common before then, and thus that alternative means—for example, negotiation or arbitration—had been the routine way of dealing with such capital crimes. Second and concomitantly, comital interference in such local affairs must not have become common until then. For examples, see the baillivial accounts conserved at the Algemene Rijksarchief in Brussels, RR #920–#1718.
54. Lijsbette Pijlysers, Amele sMuelneeren, Kalle sLathouwers, Marie van Gheeraerdsberghe, and Meerin van der Haghe (David Nicholas and Walter Prevenier, eds, *Gentse stads- en baljuwsrekeningen (1365–1376)* (Brussels: Palais der Academiën, 1999), p. 346, lns. 21–22).
55. *van houte. van stroe, van ketenen, van crammen ende van stoffen, 11 lb. 6 s.* (Nicholas and Prevenier, eds., *Gentse stads-*, p. 346, ln. 23).
56. ...*hij de wijfs haelde te Vrasene int land van Waes ende deed se bringhen met eenen waghene te Ghend* (ibid., p. 346, ln. 24–25).
57. *Item den priesters, van biechtene 25 s.* (ibid., p. 346, ln. 28).
58. ...*den Coc gheghceven 10 lb.* (ibid., p. 346, ln. 22).
59. van Caenegem, *Strafrecht*, p. 163, n. 2.
60. Lille, Archives départmentales du Nord, B 1561 n. 249 f. 73 #1477. (Hereafter Nord.)
61. In March 1267, Countess Margaret gave the abbess and convent of van-du-Ciel in Diksmuide a house and lands that had formerly belonged to Margaret le Meide (Nord, B 1561 n. 249 f. 73 #1477). On October 25, 1268, Countess Margaret sold Henry of Thorout a number of *rentes* that had been forfeit upon Margaret's death (Nord, B. 1561 n. 65 f. 24–24v #1538).
62. Nord, B1561 n. 120 f. 37v–38 #1364; van Caenegem, *Strafrecht*, pp. 340–42 #4.

63. Nord, B1561 n. 120 f. 37v–38 #1364; van Caenegem, *Strafrecht*, pp. 340–41 #4.

64. . . .*ke Thieris le Meidem jure sour sains a mil homes ke il ne fu mie coupables de la mort celi Michiel*. . .; similarly for Clais Mons:. . .*nemie pour cou ke nous lencoupons de riens de le mort celui Michiel, mais pour bien de pais*. (Nord, B1561 n. 120 f. 37v–38 #1364; van Caenegem, *Strafrecht*, pp. 340–41 #4.) As Nicholas puts it, "But the responsibility of the innocent relatives not to assume the guilt of their kinsman, but to take all actions necessary to prevent a feud, was paramount" (Nicholas, "Crime and Punishment," p. 1155).

65. F. Pollack and F. Maitland, *The History of English Law* (Cambridge: Cambridge University Press, 1968) 2:485.

66. St. Disier was within the jurisdiction of that city (Gilliodts-van Severen, *Sources et développment* p. 61).

67. Ibid., pp. 115–116 #146.

68. Espinas, *La vie urbaine*, 3:123 #172A "And whosoever should kill a citizen of this town. . ."

69. Espinas, *La vie urbaine*, 3:123 #172B[1]. "And whosoever should kill a citizen [m] or citizen [f] or the son of a citizen [m] or citizen [f]. . ."

70. Espinas, *La vie urbaine*, 3:123 #172B[2]: ". . . that whosoever, be it man or woman of this town or from foreign parts, should kill a citizen [m] or citizen [f]. . ."

71. What may have made more of a difference in the case of Margaret le Meide was that the murder appears to have been committed under cover of night.

72. Pelsmaeker, *Registre aux sentences*, p. 264 #469.

73. Ibid., p. 264 #468.

74. It is perfectly clear from the will of Jaque de France, for example, that the testator is female (Douai. Archives de la ville, Fonds FF 862, November 1308). "Jaque" can be short for both "Jakemon" and "Jaqueline."

75. Pelsmaeker, *Registres aux sentences; Sources et développment de la coutume d'Ypres*, in *Coutumes des pays et comté de Flandre*, ed. L. Gilliodts–van Severen (Brussels: J. Goemaere, 1908).

76. Des Marez and de Sagher, *Comptes*, 1:3.

77. *D'amendes jugiés par arbitres jurées*: Women received fines of 5 s. about twice as often as they received fines of 20 s., 40 s., or 60 s. Men, in fact, received fines of 5 s. about half a percent more often than did women. The difference is insignificant. (J. Vuylsteke, *Gentsche stads- en baluwsrekening 1280–1336* (Ghent: Imprimerie F. Meyer-van Loo, 1900) (hereafter GSB), p. 11).

78. "Badly padded cloth" (RR #1054).

79. Or beef: *Michael filius Yft Scotes: 3 l. de mala vacca* (Des Marez and de Sagher, *Comptes*, 1:7).

80. *Grieta de Curtraco: 3 l. de male carne posita in pastillis* (ibid., 1:67).

81. *En le ville daudenarde*, for example (RR #920).

82. "Inside the city of Ghent;" "infractions concerning the brewing of beer;" "Fines judged by arbitrators;" "infractions concerning herring" (Vuylsteke, GSB, 1:11–14).

83. Under *D'amendes jugiés par arbitres jurées*, for example, names are organized neither by amount, by gender, nor even alphabetically by name:

Éverars le Bake,	20 s.
Le vève Simon de Hemsrode	40 s.
Mergriete uten Kelnere,	60 s.
Willaumes Blancars,	60 s.
Fobekins,	30 s.
Weitins Inghel,	5 s.
Le mère Weitin Inghel,	5 s.

and so forth (ibid., 1:11).

84. See, for example, the account of the bailiff of Audenarde (RR #920), Bruges (RR #999), Courtrai (RR #1043), Furnes (RR #1304), and Ypres (RR #1696).

85. This is generally true, the use of appellatives like "wife" (or "widow, daughter, mother of X") notwithstanding. The use in bailiff's records of unrelated appellatives (occupation, locational, religious affiliation, or class status as represented by some sort of title) or no appellative whatsoever never dropped below 50 percent throughout the period 1290 to 1336. In the accounts of the bailiff of Audenarde, for example, 75 percent of women listed therein lack any sort of appellative (RR #920). In Bruges, in 1331, the proportion was around 70 percent (RR #1009), in Courtrai in 1305, about the same (RR #1043), in Dam in 1307 it was approximately 65 percent (RR #1099) and in Ypres in 1336, it was close to 100 percent (RR #1708). I am currently researching the use and significance of appellatives.

86. *Item, il est ordeneit par les piersonnes de seure dis ke quiconques bourgois or bourgoise hierbiergeroient ou soustenroient homme u femme qui fuissent banis d'Ypre a ensient en leur hosteil* (Gilliodts-van Severen, *Sources et développment*, p. 41 #27 n. 4). Both the ordinance and its use of doublets such as *bourgois/bourgoise* and *homme/femme* is very reminiscent of the practice common in Douai.

87. Des Marez and de Sagher, *Comptes*, 2:78–79. It is difficult to tell exactly when this practice became standard. In 1314, commutations ranged from 6 s. to 40 s. (ibid., 1:459–60). In 1315, 1316, and 1317, there were no commutations, perhaps because of the disruptions caused by famine, typhoid, and plague in those years (ibid., 1:505 (*Rappel de ban, néant*) 1:556, 2:1).

88. *Item, le 22 jour de may, Angnes le Yredemakigghe acquist se loy d'un ban, dont elle fu bannie 1 an, de tenir mais ostel, et paia 60 s.* (ibid., 2:277); *Item, le diemenche velle saint Lussie, Coppin Stier acquist se loy d'un ban, dont il fu bannis 1 an, de ce que il feri Hannot de Damhoudres, en presense de wardeurs des marceclier en l'ocoison delle loy, et paia 60 s.* (ibid., 2:277). Had he attacked Hannot at night or in secret, his term of exile would probably have been markedly higher, although the amount he needed to pay to commute his exile may not.

89. Just as in bailiffs' accounts of the early fourteenth century, the fact of payment was more important than noting what the payment was made for. In the January 1306 account of the bailiff of Bruges and the June 1307 account of the bailiff of Courtrai, for example, the fact of payment is merely listed.

There is no rubric under which the action was categorized, nor any explanation as to why in particular that payment was made (RR #1001, #1050).

90. That the cities periodically revolted during his reign was probably more a sign of his success than of his failure in these endeavors. For the impact of the reign of Louis of Male, see Blockmans, Wim, "De vorming van en politieke unie (veertiende-zestiende eeuw)," in *Geschiedenis van der Nederlanden*, ed. J.C.H. Blom and E. Lamberts (Rijswijk: Nijgh and van Ditmar, 1993), pp. 45–117; David Nicholas, *Medieval Flanders*, (London and New York: Longman, 1992) pp. 209–316; Walter Prevenier and Wim Blockmans, *The Promised Lands: The Low Countries under Burgundian Rule, 1369–1530* (Philadelphia: University of Pennsylvania Press, 1999); Ellen Kittell, *From Ad Hoc to Routine. A Case Study in Medieval Bureaucracy* (Philadelphia: University of Pennsylvania Press, 1991), pp. 170–95.

91. Kittell, *From Ad Hoc to Routine*, p. 181.

92. RR #838.

93. RR #838.

94. Robert Jacob, *Les époux, le seigneur et la cité* (Brussels: Faculté universitaires Saint-Louis, 1990), p. 235. In 1376, Ypres, for example, banished Cresitenne Priems forever from the city for larceny (Pelsmaeker, *Registre aux sentences*, p. 323 #883). In the thirteenth century, the person or group from whom she stole the items would have been much more involved in the resolution of the resultant conflict between the family of the perpetrator and their own.

95. By the mid-fourteenth century, it had become very common for sentences of exile to be commuted by monetary payments. So common was this practice that a new account, detailing such payments, came into being in 1369 (RR #838).

96. Women are listed under this rubric in the baillivial records of most of the Flemish communities. Twenty-seven percent of the fines women paid were, in fact, listed under the undifferentiated rubric of *mellee* (Bruges (RR #999, #1009), Dam (RR #1099, #1100–103) Furnes (RR #1306, #1308–10, #1313, #1315, #1317), Ypres (RR #1682, #1697, #1698), Quatre Métiers (RR #1481).

97. Irregularity in the selling of fish was one of the most common activities for which women in both Audenaarde and Ghent were fined (RR #931, Vuylsteke, 1:9, 12, 27), while women in Dam often paid penalties for false measurements (RR #1100, #1101, #1103, #1104).

98. Vuylsteke, GSB, 1:11–16.

99. The 1305 account of the bailiff of Ghent is representative of this practice (ibid., 1:11–16). It is relatively short—it takes up no more than five and a half pages in Vuylsteke's printed version—and is divided into income and expenses. The former is further divided into that collected in the city of Ghent (*Dedens le vile de Gant*) and that from the Vieuxbourg (*C'est en le Viuborch*). The revenue section consists almost exclusively of lists of people who paid some sort of penalty or fine; the subsection *De mellee* has by far the longest list. The *date*, or list of baillivial expenses, is much more detailed

than the section on income. Although it begins with a list of payments for the wages of various baillivial personnel, the majority of the section consists of itemized entries detailing the conditions surrounding a particular payment the bailiff made.

100. In 1305 and in 1331 in Bruges (RR #999, #1009) and in Ghent in 1307 (Vuylsteke, GSB,1:40). The percentages are based on total incidence of women's malefaction in baillivial records.

101. Twenty-seven times or 2.5 percent (Audenarde, 1379 (RR #957); Furnes, 1373 (RR #1323), 1375 (RR #1327), 1376 (RR #1328, #1329, #1330) 1377 (RR #1331); Ghent, 1367 (Nicholas and Prevenier, *Gentse stads-*, p. 190, ln. 1), 1372 (ibid., p. 207, ln. 32; p. #222, ln. 50), 1373 (ibid., p. 238, ln. 10; p. 245, ln. 7), 1374 (ibid., p. 293, ln. 12; p. 321, ln. 4; p. 327, ln. 3; p. 363, ln. 5), 1375 (ibid., p. 373, ln. 14; p. 376, ln. 20; p. 393, ln. 8; p. 396, ln. 1; p. 402, ln. 43; p. 404, ln. 26; p. 404, ln. 29).

102. Seventy-nine of the 1103 times women are listed in baillivial records as paying fines 7 percent were for actionable language, primarily in Ghent (for example, Nicholas and Prevenier, *Gentse stads-*, p. 261, ln. 42) and Ypres (for example, Pelsmaeker, *Registre aux sentences*, p. 278).

103. RR #1108. For another example of an account made up primarily of paragraphs instead of lists, see the account of the bailiff of Courtrai for the same year (RR #1064).

104. Nicholas and Prevenier, *Gentse stads-*, pp. 185–443.

105. *Ghewijsde boeten van 11 1/2 lb. van den lieden ter eerden te slane of te stekene, daeraf ghebuert minen heere 6 lb. 13 s. 4 d., den borchgrave 3 l. 6 s. 8 d., de claghere 15 s., der poert 5 s., ende den scoutheete 10 s* (ibid., p. 379). Here we see the bailiff splitting his comments between the actual infraction and the distribution of the fine once it was paid. Financial considerations were obviously as important as considerations of law and order. Not all rubrics even within the same account were that explicit. They primarily mark the location being accounted for, as in "Received from fines of 60 l., of which the city of Ghent received 3 lb" (*Ontfaen van boeten van 60 lb., daeraf ghebuerd der stede van Ghend 3. lb.*) (ibid., p. 365).

106. *van dat Griele Buckaerts ter eerden slouch Betten sVisschers, ontfaen 6 lb. 13 s. 4 d.* (ibid., p. 379).

107. As represented by reference to the plaintiff's portion (*de claghere 15 s.*) in the example given in note 105 earlier.

108. It could be argued that in theory they represent the various communities who suffered from the fact of the conflict. After all, the organizing principle of the baillivial records was locational and not typological in nature. This may well be an artifact of the notion that malefactions were fundamentally conflicts within a community, and the payment of these sums may well have reflected the right of a community, in the person of its major official, to collect compensation for the disruption conflicts engendered. By the middle to late fourteenth century, however, it is likely that neither the population nor the officials themselves saw these payments as anything more than payment to the local and regional authority as part of the prosecutory action.

109. In approximately 1373, in Ghent: Aechtkine, Clays Brielmans daughter (Nicholas and Prevenier, *Gentse stads-*, pp. 291–92, ln. 50; 1). In 1375, in Ghent: Betkine Kerfs (ibid., p. 381, ln. 20); Kalle Croex (ibid., p. 396, ln. 390); Jans wive van der Bracman (attacked by Kalle Hays Brielmans) (ibid., p. 394, ln. 40–41). In 1376, in Ghent: Adelijssen van Crabbinghen (ibid., p. 446, ln. 20). On September 22, 1376, in Furnes: Machtelt Lotijns, (RR #1330). By 1380, in Ghent, even judgments in which neither party lodged a complaint came before the city arbitrators (Nicholas, "Crime and Punishment," p. 298), and thus began to look more like prosecution and less like arbitration.

110. Actionable language: Nicholas and Prevenier, *Gentse stads-*, p. 316, ln. 1; pulling hair: Furnes: RR #1323; threaten with a fist: Nicholas and Prevenier, *Gentse stads-*, p. 243, ln. 36; hit with a fist (wound): Dam, RR#1108; hit with a stick (without wound): Nicholas and Prevenier, *Gentse stads-*, p. 378, ln. 11; hit with a stick (wound): ibid., p. 225, ln. 25; attack by day: Ypres, RR #1715; attack by night: Nicholas and Prevenier, *Gentse stads-*, p. 329, ln. 11.

111. Ibid., pp.185–463

112. *Haropene* (possibly a constriction of *haare rupfen*). Almost 16 percent of the penalties women paid between 1364 and 1377 were for this misbehavior (RR #1321–31).

113. Misleading or mishandling children: Nicholas and Prevenier, *Gentse stads-*, p. 265, ln. 26; p. #229, ln. 39; p. #221, ln. 11; ibid., p. 221, ln. 31. Living with another women's spouse: Bruges, RR #1010. Being led astray: Furnes, RR #1327; Nicholas and Prevenier, *Gentse stads-*, p. 228, ln. 5; p. 229, ln. 21–22; p. 315, ln. 20. Running away with unacceptable men: ibid., p. 277, ln. 8; p. 334, ln. 46. Helping another woman to run away with an unacceptable man: Furnes, RR #1324.

114. Furnes, RR #1324.

115. Gilliodts–van Severen, *Sources et développment*, p. 97 #101.

116. Pelsmaeker, *Registre aux sentences*, p. 167, 278, 304–305, 331.

117. David Nicholas, *The Domestic Life of a Medieval City*, p. 20.

118. Gilliodts–van Severen, *Sources et développment*, p. 97 #101.

119. Pelsmaeker, *Registre aux sentences*, pp. 167, 278, 304–305, 331.

120. This was listed under the rubric of *Boeten van twist van xi l.* (Bruges: RR #1010).

121. She apparently socked a man named Hase with her fist (Dam, RR #1107).

122. Furnes, RR #1325; Courtrai, RR #1064.

123. In 1372 (Nicholas and Prevenier, *Gentse stads-*, p. 240, ln. 48); and 1379 (Quatre Métiers: RR #1482) respectively.

124. As in *Lisa Alards: 10 l. contra Gilkinum Barbificem* (Des Marez and de Sagher, *Comptes*, 1:11).

125. Bruges, RR #1009; Furnes, RR #1306; Ghent, Vuylsteke, GSB, p. 39; Quatre Métiers: RR #1481.

126. *Boeten uten twiste van lx l.*; *Boeten van twiste van xi l.*; *Boeten van twiste van iii l.* (Bruges: RR #1010).

127. For example, the case in Dam, in 1373. Under the rubric of *Boeten van twist van 3 l.* we find Kateline Heyaerds, *die soe slouch meter vuyst en Machtilt Hughe s'Karels wedewe* (". . .who hit Mactilt, widow of Hughe Karel, with her fist. . .") (Dam, RR #1107).

128. Kittell, *From Ad Hoc to Routine*, pp. 81–86.

129. Even more rarely does the malefaction itself disappear from some consideration, although it is not unheard of for characteristics of the perpetrator to diminish the significance of the malefaction to the point of simply being something done wrong. What then becomes of paramount importance is that this particular person committed the act.

130. These findings are similar to those of Porteau-Bitker.

131. Pelsmaeker, *Registre aux sentences*, p. iv.

132. For the detrimental effects of the influx of university graduates on the conditions of women, see Susan Stuard, "The Dominion of Gender or How Women Fared in the High Middle Ages," in *Becoming Visible: Women in European History*, ed. Renate Bridenthal, Susan Stuard, and Merry Wiesner, 3rd edition (Boston: Houghton-Mifflin, 1998), pp. 129–50.

CHAPTER 2

GENDER AND MOBILITY IN THE LOW COUNTRIES: TRAVELING WOMEN IN THIRTEENTH-CENTURY EXEMPLA AND SAINTS' LIVES

Katrien Heene

In recent years it has become clear that medieval society was in many respects much more mobile than has been supposed, both socially and in terms of movements in space.[1] In fact the roads were crowded with traveling people: merchants traveled around to sell their goods, pilgrims sought salvation and cures at local and international sanctuaries, mendicant friars traveled for their pastoral activities, students moved from one university to another and sovereigns shifted between their various residences.[2] In particular much scholarly attention has been devoted to pilgrimage as a juridical, religious, and anthropological phenomenon.[3] As far as women are concerned, it is said that they made up one-fourth to one-third of medieval pilgrims in general and even half of those visiting local places of pilgrimage.[4] Yet, generally speaking, little research has been done on the possibilities for women to travel. Often it seems to be assumed *a priori* that they had little opportunities for it. Only recently, for example, Jean Verdon states: "It is normal. . .that women, more than men, were confined to the place were they lived, at least when they did not emigrate to get married."[5]

This chapter summarizes the first results of my research on the scholarly discourse concerning women and travel as expressed in late medieval Latin narrative and didactic texts from the Low Countries.[6] This investigation is conducted within the framework of the Itineraria-project.[7] Its main sources are proverbs, sermons, exempla, didactic and moral treatises as well as saints' lives and miracle collections.[8] The central aim of my inquiry is to analyze the representation of traveling from a gender perspective[9] as well as to find out whether relevant norms were explicitly or implicitly established. If norms existed, it is also important to know to what extent they were gender-specific and whether they actually affected women's freedom of movement.[10] How they were motivated or rationalized is another important issue.[11] Which contemporary ideas about masculinity and femininity were brought up in this context?[12] Did satire or moral disgrace, for example, play a role? What about misogynistic discourses?[13]

From the secondary literature it also appears that at least Mediterranean authors strongly wanted to curtail the freedom of movement of women, regardless of their age or civil status.[14] Assuming there were similar restrictions in the Low Countries, I also propose to find out how such restrictions were sidestepped and which alternatives were suggested and/or applied.[15] It is a known fact that critical remarks concerning the moral dangers that threatened women taking part in international pilgrimages already occurred as early as the fourth century.[16] Yet, according to Patricia Halpin, "virtual mobility," for example the use of texts and objects concerning Christ's life, became an alternative for English women who wanted to visit the Holy Land from the eleventh century onward.[17]

The Historical Output of Exempla and Saints' Lives

Before turning to the texts I want to highlight the specific advantages and limitations for historical research of exempla and saints' lives on which this chapter focuses. Since their authors as well as their primary audience were clerics schooled in Latin, the texts clearly are androcentric, clerical, and elitist.[18] These aspects, however, are somewhat eased by the fact that exempla and saints' lives also aimed at a broader audience as well as by the fact that they testify about ordinary men and women's daily life. Didactic and narrative texts could indeed be descriptive as well as prescriptive and reactive. They tell us about the authors' attitudes toward many aspects of actual life and toward the prevailing norms as well as about opinions they tried to promote in an explicit or implicit way.[19] Exempla, for instance, were an important rhetorical component of sermons[20] and didactic works. With these short edifying stories the authors wanted to capture their audience's attention as well as to illustrate an abstract truth or norm in a concrete way.[21] They are, as Hervé Martin beautifully calls them, "une sorte de grand livre du quotidien."[22] Even when the depictions of exempla are not accurate, they do express "the concerns and preoccupations" of the time, as Ruth Karras notes concerning literary texts, and they constitute a valuable source for the opinions with which the authors' contemporaries were regularly confronted.[23] Saints' lives were essentially written to promote or launch a cult but they also contain information on day-to-day life, as well as on ecclesiastical standards of the period in which they were redacted. Hagiographers indeed attempted to create a realistic frame for the spectacular deeds and miraculous events they wanted to propagate. Thus they could exemplify norms of sanctity in their description of the saint him/herself or illustrate virtues and vices in the behavior of other people, such as persons involved in miracles.[24]

Pilgrimage and Other Pious Journeys

In the exempla we only find explicit norms for traveling religious, not for lay or semireligious persons. Thus the Dominican Thomas de Cantimpré devotes several chapters to restrictions on the mobility of priors and conventuals. Examples include the conventual's obligation to leave the convent only on the prior's order and never alone[25] or, in the case of priors, to have at least compelling reasons to go into the "dangerous world" and to be protected by prayers.[26] In this context meeting women can be seen as a threat to monastic chastity.[27] Lay travelers and pilgrims appear when the authors want to give concrete examples of all kinds of other religious issues by means of the travelers' fortunes: for example, the machinations of the devil,[28] the assistance Mary gives to her worshippers,[29] or the importance of confession.[30] The journey *par excellence* brought up in this context is the *peregrinatio maior*, the pilgrimage to Jerusalem, Rome, Santiago de Compostela, or Mont St. Michel.[31] Piously taking part in such an expensive,[32] physically difficult, and dangerous expedition is considered to be of important spiritual merit, a means to atone for one's sins and to mortify "the flesh."[33] Dying along the way or on the final destination is sometimes seen as a special bliss.[34] The participants depicted in these voluntary pilgrimages are as a rule pious lay men.[35] Women are mainly associated with local pilgrimages which they are said to undertake for all kinds of devotional reasons:[36] for example, to obtain miracles or to give thanks for their occurrence. Hagiographical texts describe many of the same motives for women of all social classes. Caesarius of Heisterbach, for example, describes how Margareta, countess of Gelre, went on a pilgrimage to Cologne to thank Saint Engelbert for helping her with a difficult birth.[37] The author of the *vita Godefredi Pachomii* says that the saint's mother undertook an annual pilgrimage from Leuven to Herent on the day of the feast of the Annunciation or of the Assumption to commend herself and her children to the Holy Virgin while offering money and prayers.[38]

Although scholars think women were commonly dissuaded from making long-distance journeys,[39] several texts mention adult women setting out on such travels. In some cases this was not a matter of free choice: two exempla, for instance, describe women undertaking a penitential pilgrimage to Rome, which was imposed on them by their confessor.[40] Yet, the wife of a usurer from Liège, according to Caesarius of Heisterbach, would have traveled to Rome voluntarily to obtain permission from the pope to have her husband buried in the local cemetery.[41] In the saints' lives, especially highborn women undertook journeys and pilgrimages to distant destinations. Countess Oda of Heinsberg, for example, visited Saint Gerlacus of Houthem during his lifetime from far away (de remotis partibus) in order to offer him the land around his cell.[42]

The ascetic and penitential dimension of voluntary long-distance pilgrimage is also stressed in the vitae. Thomas de Cantimpré, in the supplement to the life of Marie d'Oignies, depicts a noble lady who is of her own free will starting on a pilgrimage to Jerusalem, walking barefoot, and tied up with an iron chain, in order to do penance.[43] The author of the vita Fretherici illustrates how a pilgrimage can also be undertaken for altruistic reasons.[44] He recounts that a twelfth-century woman called Gertrud accompanied her brother-in-law, Count Asego, on a pilgrimage to Jerusalem (comitem se obtulit laboris et itineris). Asego would have been advised to do so by Saint Frethericus in order to atone for his sins.[45]

It is well known that people exploited the special status of the pilgrim in order to be able to move more freely.[46] Étienne de Bourbon mentions the Waldensian heretics who wandered around preaching and who used the attire and the distinguishing marks of the pilgrims (habitum et signaculi peregrini) as disguise. He also tells of a heretic woman who brought her daughter to a heretic community and who told her neighbors instead that she had taken the child on a pilgrimage and that it died on the way.[47]

Mobility and Chastity

In the "fabliaux" and the "nouvelles" pilgrimage was considered to be the opportunity par excellence for women to travel as well as the perfect cover for sexual escapades.[48] We find no trace of the latter opinion in the exempla or in the vitae; but Jacques de Vitry mentions a husband who used a pilgrimage as an excuse to get away from his nagging wife.[49] In some saints' lives, however, the link between female mobility and chastity is depicted from a quite different perspective. For a canon like Frederic "wandering about" (circuiens per vicos et plateas) is a positive activity because it is a necessary condition for his pastoral activities.[50] In the vita of Aleydis of Schaarbeek, on the other hand, it is said that, as a young girl, the future saint, although she was very pretty, did not go into the streets, as Dinah once did (non. . .in plateas est egressa). She preferred to stay home following the example of Mary.[51] Dinah, whom Thomas de Cantimpré (TC lb 2 c3, 4 p. 103)) presents as a counter-example for the cloistered religious aspiring to go on pilgrimage, was raped by Sychem, the king's son, when she had left home "to visit the girls of her region" (Genesis 34, 1–3). The example of Dinah was already used by Jerome to warn young women to remain at home, away from the dangers of the public sphere. In the twelfth century Dinah's misfortunes also appeared as an argument for the active claustration of women. To a thirteenth-century literate audience, mentioning her might, in the light of this tradition, automatically suggest the danger of being raped or seduced.[52] Staying at home rather than running around (*discursus, vagari*) was indeed also the contemporary ideal for pious young girls.[53] Hagiographical texts make clear that neither ecclesiastics nor laymen liked girls and women roaming the streets even for religious motives.[54] Margareta of Ypres's confessor, for instance, often obliged the saint to return home, when she had escaped from her mother and aunts' custody to go begging.[55] Ida of Leuven was thought to have gone mad and was put in chains by her relatives for wandering about in shabby clothes.[56] These women were part of the voluntary-poverty movement, but in contrast to the male members of the mendicant orders they were not allowed actively to "follow the naked Christ naked."[57] The urge to restrict semireligious women's freedom of movement also appears in an exemplum of Thomas de Cantimpré: he mentions that in the year 1226 the beguines of Nivelles got a rash on the limbs that were the most involved in their sins. In the case of those who had being walking around excessively (*contra immoderatum discursum*) their feet or shinbones were affected until cured by Saint Gertrude.[58] An exemplum from the section on confession in Caesarius of Heisterbach's *Dialogus Miraculorum* illustrates the idea that the chastity of beautiful, young girls should be especially well protected. Caesarius relates that a priest from Bonn, before leaving the house, locked up his daughter to protect her against the seduction attempts of young men, in particular the local canons.[59]

According to Petrus of Dacia, the biographer of Christina of Stommelen, the saint herself was aware of possible dangers threatening the chastity of young girls who leave the safety of their homes. When he recounts that the saint, as a young girl, fled from Stommelen to Cologne accompanied by another woman in order to join the beguines, he also mentions that Christina feared that her companion would betray her and bring her to "a dishonourable place where something shameful might happen to her."[60] I did not encounter explicit hints to the association of women who roam the streets with whoredom,[61] but Thomas de Cantimpré in the *vita Iohannis* does mention a woman being brought to the saint by her relatives in order to cure her of roaming about (*vagari*).[62]

The Ever-Present Danger of Rape

I have already referred to rape, a gender-specific danger that threatens women, especially when traveling alone.[63] Focusing as they do mainly on male travelers, the exempla pay little attention to it.[64] The hagiographers, however, are less silent on this topic. Johannes, the *magister scholarium* of Stommelen, for instance, tells us that demons brought Christina to a wood notorious for its robbers. He describes how Christina persuaded them to be remorseful and cites the robbers' detailed survey of their victims: not only have they killed many clerics, merchants, travelers, and pilgrims but also girls and women after having raped them.[65] In Lutgard of Tongeren's *vita*, Thomas de Cantimpré also illustrates the risk of rape for female travelers. He recounts how the saint, when she was returning home at night after a visit to her sister, was attacked and nearly raped by a rejected suitor. Fortunately she escaped and, accompanied by an angel, reached the house of her foster mother. The suitor's servants were persuaded that the rape really took place and spread the tidings of the assault.[66] Thomas states that the locals treated Lutgart with suspicion but that she was able to rid herself of shame with Christ's help.[67] This remark clearly alludes to the belief, found among lay persons as well as ecclesiastics, that women were often (at least partly) responsible for being raped.[68]

Other Obstacles for Travelers

The authors of both exempla and *vitae* also refer to other obstacles, natural as well as human, which both male and female travelers experienced.[69] Traveling was in many respects a difficult and hazardous undertaking; therefore travelers with the same destinations often joined together.[70] By describing the misfortunes of the lonely (male) traveler, these texts illustrate that it is not wise to travel alone.[71] Desolate forests are considered to be especially dangerous places because they are populated with demons, robbers, (devilish) seductresses, and rapists.[72] One of the devil's wiles to threaten the traveler's chastity involves taking the shape of a person of the opposite sex.[73] He and his demons also often annoy pilgrims, for example, by trying to misguide them or to make them quarrel.[74] Even in lodging houses not only the travelers' chastity or money but even their lives can be in danger.[75]

Considering all the possible dangers it is seen as a major advantage that travelers can count on supernatural aid, usually in exchange for pious gestures or invocations.[76] A nice example of both dangers and possible remedies is the story Thomas de Cantimpré tells about two Brabant virgins who got lost on the way from Nivelles to Lillois.[77] Upon noticing that they found themselves near a forest, the women began weeping. At that very moment, however, a beautiful young man appeared dressed in white. After asking their destination, he silently showed them the way.[78] The supernatural help for saints is even more spectacular. According to Jacques de Vitry, for example, Marie d'Oignies enjoyed extraordinary protection when she undertook her annual pilgrimage from Oignies to Heignes. Although the road was twisting and woody Marie never lost the way because she was guided by a light;[79] angels held her when she returned exhausted by fasting and vigils; on rainy days stars stopped the rain and prevented her from becoming wet.[80] After her death travelers successfully invoked Marie in their prayers. In the supplement to her *vita*, Thomas de Cantimpré recounts that Marie saved Jacques de Vitry himself during a storm while sailing from Palestine to Rome.[81] Saint Gerlacus, once a penitential pilgrim himself, was also said to watch over the health of the horses of those Saint Jacob pilgrims who had made a vow to him.[82]

Conclusion

The information available in the thirteenth-century exempla and saints' lives on traveling women is fragmentary, especially as far as concrete details about social class, distances, lodging, or attire. The authors were clearly influenced by their own religious status and gender as well as that of their primary audience. They focused much attention on (norms for) male religious travelers and on spiritual motives for traveling, in particular pilgrimage. From their androcentric point of view, women were more often seen as a moral threat for traveling men than vice versa. Although the stories did suggest in various ways that rape was one of the main risks for traveling women, they were not explicitly forbidden to travel, neither for this nor for other reasons.[83] What's more, the authors, when representing daily life, depicted different types of adult women traveling for various reasons and even to distant destinations. In spite of the fact that traveling women were taken for granted, the authors clearly thought it preferable that women—especially pious, young, and/or beautiful ones—stayed at home as much as possible. The underlying motive to curtail these women's freedom of movement seems to have been to help them to protect their virtue and more particularly their virginity and chastity, thus avoiding disgrace for themselves as well as for their families. Whether the authors thought that the women involved needed this protection because they were physically and/or morally more fragile or because they were more prone to sin is not explicitly stated.[84] It is important to reiterate, however, that, even though authors of thirteenth-century exempla and saints' lives may have wanted to restrict women's mobility, their desires did not in fact prevent women from traveling, because these same sources assumed that they did so.

Notes

1. For mobility as a broad and neutral term for "long distance travels as well as all other forms of moving within a social context," see Geert Berings,

"Transport en communicatie in de middeleeuwen," in *Reizen en reizigers in Brabant*, ed. Fernand van Hemelrijck (Brussels: KUB. Centrum voor Brabantse geschiedenis, 1993), p. 9; and Ernst Schubert, *Fahrendes Volk im Mittelalter* (Bielefeld:Verlag für Regionalgeschichte, 1995), p. 29.

2. See, for example, Berings, "Transport en communicatie," pp. 11–26, and Schubert, *Fahrendes Volk*, pp. 29–65.

3. Basic studies include Pierre-André Sigal, *Les marcheurs de Dieu. Pèlerinages et pèlerins au Moyen Age* (Paris: Colin, 1974); Jonathan Sumption, *Pilgrimage:An Image of Mediaeval Religion* (London: Faber and Faber, 1975); Victor and Edith Turner, *Image and Pilgrimage in Christian Culture: Anthropological Perspectives* (New York: Columbia University Press, 1978); Étienne van Cauwenberghe, *Les pèlerinages expiatoires et judiciaires dans le droit communal de la Belgique au moyen âge* (Louvain: Etablissements Ceuterick, 1922) and Jan van Herwaarden, *Opgelegde bedevaarten. Een studie over de praktijk van opleggen van bedevaarten (met name in de stedelijke rechtspraktijk) in de Nederlanden gedurende de late middeleeuwen (ca 1300–ca 1550)* (Assen: van Gorcum, 1978). For a definition of pilgrimage as "movement through space to a site designated as especially holy or privileged," see Susan Morrison, *Women Pilgrims in Late Medieval England. Private Piety as Public Performance* (London: Routledge, 2000), p. 83.

4. See Norbert Ohler, *The Medieval Traveller*, trans. Caroline Hillier (Woodbridge: Boydell and Brewer, 1989), p. 187; Ludwig Schmugge, "Kollektive und Individuelle Motivstrukturen im Mittelalterlichen Pilgerwesen," in *Migration in der Feudalgesellschaft*, ed. Gerard Jaritz and Albert Müller (Frankfurt am Main: Campus, 1988), p. 267.

5. "Il est normal. . .que les femmes restent, encore plus que les hommes, confinées dans leur lieu d'habitation—à moins qu'elles n'émigrent pour se marier" Jean Verdon, *Voyager au Moyen Age* (Paris: Perrin, 1998), p. 11.

6. The text corpus was mainly chosen using the provenance of the authors from the Low Countries as a selective criterion, but I also analyze a number of texts, which although redacted by Parisian college graduates, most certainly circulated in this region. See, for instance, the exempla collection of Étienne de Bourbon as well as the *Dialogus miraculorum* and the *Libri miraculorum* of Caesarius of Heisterbach (+1240). The exempla of Caesarius of Heisterbach provide interesting material for studying women's daily life. See Helga Schüppert, "Frauenbild und Frauenalltag in der Predigtliteratur," in *Frau und Spätmittelalterlicher Alltag* (Wien: Verlag der Österreichischen Akademie der Wissenschaften, 1986), p. 126.

7. This project is the result of a scientific collaboration, sponsored by the Belgian and the Dutch Funds for Scientific Research FWO and NOW, between the University of Ghent (promotor: T. de Hemptinne) and the University of Groningen (promotor: D. De Boer). It aims to trace actual female mobility, not only in the Low Countries and the Rhineland (the region of Cologne) during the Late Middle Ages (1200–1500) but also its representation in scholarly sources and the prevailing norms. Special attention will be paid to travels within the framework of pilgrimage and court life.

8. Debra Birch, *Pilgrimage to Rome in the Middle Ages. Continuity and Change* (Woodbridge: Boydell and Brewer, 1998), pp. 8–22, points out that the many potential sources for studying pilgrimage often contain only chance references to rich and socially important pilgrims or to important pilgrimage centers.

9. Traveling men mainly function as a point of comparison, except when they are involved in female (travel) affairs or when their adventures give information on traveling in general. This restriction is due to the fact that we want to avoid paying too much attention to specific categories of male travelers about whom much research has already been done, such as the wandering scholars or the mendicant friars. The impact of contemporary ideas about masculinity on their and other men's travels for the moment also lies outside the scope of this project. On the importance of studying the social roles of men and women as well as their interaction combined with a sometimes frustrating need to "find the women first," see Elisabeth van Houts, *Medieval Memories. Men, Women and the Past, 700–1300* (Harlow: Longman, 2001), pp. 2–3.

10. In this respect an inquiry into women's mobility also implies investigating the relation between gender and space, specifically the attitude toward women's mobility outside the house, in public space. On the connotation of marginality for those who transgress the authorized borders, see Barbara Hanawalt, "At the Margins of Women's Space in Medieval Europe," in *Matrons and Marginal Women in Medieval Society*, ed. Robert R. Edwards and Vickie Ziegler (Woodbridge: Boydell and Brewer, 1995), pp. 1–17. On the role of spatial segregation in the construction of female sexuality, see Roberta Gilchrist, *Gender and Material Culture. The Archaeology of Religious Women* (London: Routledge, 1994), pp. 150 and 168–69. On pilgrimage, gender, and space, see Morrison, *Women Pilgrims*, pp. 83–93.

11. On different types of motivations for appropriate behavior, see Theo Meder, "Gepast gedrag. Ethiek en ethische motivatie in de 'Boeken van Zeden,' " in Joris Reynaert, *Wat is Wijsheid? Lekenethiek in de Middelnederlandse letterkunde* (Amsterdam: Prometheus, 1994), pp. 90–99.

12. For a recent study on medieval ideas about gender, see Jacqueline Murray, "Thinking about Gender: The Diversity of Medieval Perspectives," in *Power of the Weak: Studies on Medieval Women*, ed. Jennifer Carpenter and Sally-Beth Maclean (Urbana: University of Illinois Press: 1995), pp. 1–26.

13. For medieval theological and philosophical ideas about women, see, for instance, Marie-Thérèse d'Alverny, "Comment les théologiens et les philosophes voient la femme," in *Cahiers de civilisation médiévale* 20 (1977), pp. 15–39, and Prudence Allen, *The Concept of Woman: The Aristotelian Revolution 750 BC–AD 1250* (Montréal: Eden Press, 1985), pp. 218–478. For misogynistic clichés in medieval literature as well as responses to them, see Alcuin Blamires, *Woman Defamed and Woman Defended. An Anthology of Medieval Texts* (Oxford: Clarendon, 1992), pp. 83–302.

14. See, for example, Geneviève Hasenohr, "La vie quotidienne de la femme vue par l'eglise: l'enseignement des 'Journées Chrétiennes' de la fin du

Moyen-Age," in *Frau und Spätmittelalterlicher Alltag* (Wien: Verlag der Österreichischen Akademie der Wissenschaften, 1986), pp. 61–62. According to Ruth Karras, *Common Women. Prostitution and Sexuality in Medieval England* (New York: Oxford University Press, 1996), p. 135, the attitude in late medieval England would have been less strict than in contemporary Mediterranean countries.

15. We know that there was always some criticism of pilgrimage as an institution especially when religious persons were involved. See Giles Constable, "Opposition to Pilgrimage in the Middle Ages," *Studia Gratiana* 19 (1976), pp. 125–46.

16. See Sigal, *Les marcheurs*, pp. 43–44; idem., "Les différents types de pèlerinage au Moyen Age," in *Wallfahrt kennt keine Grenzen*, ed. Gerda Möhler and Lenz Kriss-Rettenbeck (München-Zürich: Schnell und Steiner, 1984), p. 83, and Jan van Herwaarden, "Pilgrimages and Social Prestige. Some Reflections on a Theme," in *Wallfahrt und Alltag im Mittelalter und früher Neuzeit*, ed. Gerard Jaritz and Barbara Shuh (Wien: Österreichischen Akademie der Wissenschaften, 1992), pp. 25–79.

17. See Patricia Halpin, "Anglo-Saxon Women and Pilgrimage," in *Anglo-Norman Studies XIX. Proceedings of the Battle Conference 1996*, ed. Christopher Harper-Bill (Woodbridge: Boydell Press, 1997), pp.100–101 and 110–22. For late medieval alternatives, see, for instance, Ferdinand Rapp, "Neue Formen der Spiritualität im Spätmittelalter," in *Spiritualität des Pilgerns. Kontinuität und Wandel*, ed. Klaus Herbers and Robert Plötz (Tübingen: Narr, 1993), pp. 55–56.

18. As far as we know there were no female authors writing in Latin in the period and region under scrutiny.

19. On the different levels of information in sermons, see Schüppert, "Frauenbild und Frauenalltag," p. 129. I think the information on daily life is in particular trustworthy when it is incidental to the norm or dogma the author wants to illustrate.

20. For the mixed audience of preachers, see Hervé Martin, *Le métier de prédicateur en France Septentrionale à la fin de Moyen Age (1350–1520)* (Paris: Cerf, 1988), p. 557.

21. For a definition of an exemplum, see Claude Brémond and Jacques Le Goff, *L'exemplum* (Turnhout: Brepols, 1982), pp. 36–38; for its historical significance, pp. 79–84. On the presence of aspects of daily life as well as of ecclesiastical norms in exempla, see Jaap van Moolenbroek, *Mirakels historisch. De exempels van Caesarius van Heisterbach over Nederland en de Nederlanders* (Hilversum:Verloren, 1999), p. 317. Jacques Berlioz and Marie-Anne Polo de Beaulieu, "Exempla: A Discussion and a Case Study," in *Medieval Women and the Sources of Medieval History*, ed. Joel Rosenthal (Athens: University of Georgia Press, 1990), pp. 37–43, describes the value of exempla as a source for women's history. On the importance of credibility in exempla, see Martin, *Le métier de prédicateur*, pp. 512–515.

22. See Martin, *Le métier de prédicateur*, p. 517.

23. See Karras, *Common Women*, pp. 88–89 and 105–106 and, analogously, Berlioz and Polo de Beaulieu, "Exempla: A Discussion and a Case Study," p. 43.

24. See Jane Schulenburg, "Saints' Lives as a Source for the History of Women, 500–1100," in *Medieval Women and the Sources of Medieval History*, ed. Joel Rosenthal (Athens: University of Georgia Press, 1990), pp. 303–304, and Katrien Heene, *The Legacy of Paradise: Marriage, Motherhood and Woman in Carolingian Edifying Literature* (Frankfurt am Main: Lang, 1997), pp. 12–13. On the permanent mixture of admirable and imitable elements in medieval hagiography, see André Vauchez, "Saints admirables et saints imitables: les fonctions de l'hagiographie ont-elles changés aux derniers siècles du Moyen Âge?" in *Les fonctions des saints dans le monde occidental (IIIe–XIIIe siècle)* (Rome: Ecole française de Rome, 1991), pp. 161–72.

25. See Thomas de Cantimpré, *Miraculorum et exemplorum memorabilium sui temporis libri duo*, ed. Georgius Colvenerius (Douai: Belleri, 1597) (hereafter TC), liber 2 capitulum 11, 2 (hereafter lb and c) (pp. 152–54 of the edition). The need for formal permission is concretely illustrated in the vita Ivettae c 88–89 (ASS Ian. I (1643), pp. 879–80 and in Caesarius of Heisterbach; see Alfons Hilka, *Die Wundergeschichte des Caesarius von Heisterbach. Die beiden ersten bücher des Libri VIII miraculorum* (Bonn: Hanstein, 1937), lb 1 c 18 (pp. 40–41) (hereafter LM). For the dangers of traveling alone, see TC lb 2 c 11, 2 (pp. 153–54): *Credo solis, id est sine socio foris ambulantibus, mille infortunia, et plura quam credi potest, saepius occurrisse*. See also later, note 71.

26. See TC lb 1 c 12, 3 (p. 41); lb 1 c 18, 1 (pp. 52–54); lb 1 c 19, 1–3 (pp. 56–57).

27. See TC lb 2 c 11, 2 (pp. 152–54): *ubicunque femine sunt, invicem vestram pudicitiam custodite* and *nec socius socium debet deserere, maxime in colloquio mulieris, nisi alter alterum, videat colloquentem*. For women as a moral threat in the exempla in general, see, for instance, Karras, *Common Women*, pp. 106–111.

28. See, for instance, Caesarius of Heisterbach, *Dialogus miraculorum* (hereafter DM), in *Caesarii Heisterbacensis monachi ordinis cisterciensis Dialogus miraculorum*, ed. Josephus Strange (Köln: Verlag von J.M. Heberle, 1851), dist. 5, c 38 (lb 1, p. 324): *Pro Christo et pro peccatis suis peregrinari volentes retrahunt*. For concrete examples, see later, notes 74–75.

29. DM dist. 7, c 38 (lb 2, pp. 53–54).

30. See LM lb 1 c 29 (p. 54) and Étienne de Bourbon, *Tractatus de diversis materiis praedicabilibus, ordinatis in septem partes*, ed. Albert Lecoy de la Marche (Paris: Librairie Renouard, 1877) (hereafter EdB), c 183 (p. 160).

31. Jerusalem: TC lb 1 c 25, 5 (p. 85); TC lb 2 c 40, 3 (pp. 328–29); TC lb 2 c 40, 4 (pp. 329–30); TC lb 2 c 43, 32 (p. 426); DM dist. 10, c 9 (lb 2, pp. 218–19); DM dist. 12, c 9 (lb 2, p. 323). Rome: DM dist. 5, c 37 (lb 1, p. 321); TC lb 1 c 12, 2–3 (pp. 40–41); TC lb 2 c 29, 15 (pp. 240–43); EdB c 167 (p. 144). Santiago: Goswin Frenken, *Die Exempla des Jacob von Vitry. Ein Beitrag zur Geschichte der Erzählungsliteratur des Mittelalter* (Munich: C.H. Beck, 1914) (hereafter JdV (Frenken)), c 64 (pp. 128–29); Thomas Crane, *The Exempla or Illustrative Stories from the Sermones Vulgares of Jacques de Vitry. Edited with Introduction, Analysis and Notes* (hereafter JdV(Crane))

(London: Produits Roche, 1890), c 205 (pp. 85–86); LM lb 2 c 27 (p. 108); DM dist. 5, c 39 (lb 1, p. 324); DM dist. 8, c 58 (lb 2, pp. 130–31). Mont St. Michel: JdV (Frenken) c 104 (p. 48); EdB c 114 (p. 99). On the pilgrimage phenomenon as a source for metaphors and exempla, see Martin, *Le métier de prédicateur*, p. 418.

32. The social class of the long-distance pilgrims is often omitted, although their wealth sometimes comes up; see JdV (Crane) c 205 (pp. 85–86) (*dives*); DM dist. 5, c 39 (lb 1, p. 324) (*cives Colonienses, divites et honesti*). Taking into account the expenses involved in a similar expedition, one can assume that—except when acting as someone's substitute in exchange for money—these pilgrims indeed as a rule belonged to the social elite. See also Martin, *Le métier de prédicateur*, pp. 418–419.

33. EdB c 92 (p. 167): *Sextus titulus pertinens ad satisfacionem et carnis macerationem* and EdB c 187 (p. 163): *labores corporis*. Étienne de Bourbon (EdB c 192–97 (pp. 167–74)) describes seven norms and six motives for a dignified pilgrimage. For comments on this passage, see the article by Jacques Berlioz, "Pèlerinage et pénitence dans le recueil d'exempla d'Étienne de Bourbon (OP + vers 1261)," in *La faute, le repression et le pardon. Philologie et histoire jusqu'à 1610* (Paris: Comité des travaux historiques et scientifiques, 1984), pp. 399–412. TC lb 2 c 3, 4 (p. 103) also mentions the mortifying dimension of pilgrimage (*in absolutionem peccaminum labores peregrinationis*) without however considering it a justified reason for a monk to break his vow of enclosure. On the incompatibility of monastic enclosure and pilgrimage in the twelfth century, see Giles Constable, "Monachisme et pèlerinage au Moyen Âge," *Revue Historique* 258 (1977), pp. 21–22. On the importance of the penitential value of pilgrimage in the thirteenth century, see Carlo Delcorno, "Gli ordini mendicanti e il pellegrinagio," in *Romei e Gubilei. Il pellegrinaggio medievale a San Pietro (350–1350)*, ed. Mario D'Onofrio (Milano: Electa, 1999), pp. 229–31. For the money spent by a usurer from Trier during his pilgrimage to Santiago being returned to him by the saint on his deathbed, see LM lb 2 c 27 (p. 108). On God's special affection for pilgrims, see for instance, JdV (Crane) c 104 (p. 48); c 132 (p. 59); c 133 (p. 59). On the inconveniences of traveling, see also *vita Christinae* (ASS Iun. IV (1707), lb 5 c 9 (p. 411) and c 29 (p. 419).

34. TC lb 1 c 25, 5 (p. 85).

35. From Frederic Tubach, *Index exemplorum. A Handbook of Medieval Religious Tales* (Helsinki: Academia Scientiarum Fennica, 1981) (s.v. Pilgrim, Pilgrimage), it is also evident that the paradigmatic (long-distance) pilgrim is male. For a concrete example, see DM dist. 4, c 22 (lb 1, p. 293). In fabliaux the travel motive is often only a means to launch the action. See Marie-Thérèse Lorcin, "Les voyages ne forment que la jeunesse ou le voyage et l'étranger dans les fabliaux," *Sénéfiance* 2 (1976), p. 453 and *Façons de sentir et de penser: les fabliaux français* (Paris: Champion, 1979), p. 19. A husband's pilgrimage can also be used as a reason for telling an amusing story concerning his wife. For an example, see JdV (Crane) c 205 (pp. 85–86) and c 236 (pp. 98–99).

36. For devotion in general, see TC lb 2 c 29, 15 (p. 241); for the recovery of a child, see DM dist. 6, c 22 (lb 1, p. 375); for the spiritual welfare of a spouse,

see DM dist. 12, c 7 (lb 2, p. 323); for the cure of a disease, see EdB c 110 (pp. 97–98). For comments on the impact of gender on the distance of a pilgrimage, see Roland Finucane, *Miracles and Pilgrims. Popular Beliefs in Medieval England* (Basingstoke: MacMillan, 1977), pp. 166–69 and 184.

37. Vita et miracula Engelberti c 10, Fritz Zschaeck, "Leben, Leiden und Wunder des Heiligen Engelbert," in *Die Wundergeschichten des Caesarius von Heisterbach* III, ed. Alfons Hilka (Bonn: Hanstein, 1937), pp. 289–90. On this passage, see also van Moolenbroek, *Mirakels historisch*, pp. 291–94.

38. Vita Godefridi Pachomii c 2 (*Analecta Bollandiana* 14 (1895), p. 265) *in peregrinatione ibat.* When one takes into account that these two places are only three kilometres away from each other, this passage suggests that intention is much more important than distance for pilgrimages. On this opinion in general, see van Herwaarden, "Pilgrimages," pp. 65–66. It is possible that this line of reasoning applies in particular to women, but this remains to be shown.

39. See, for instance, van Herwaarden, "Pilgrimages," pp. 76–78.

40. See TC lb 2 c 29, 15 (pp. 240–43) where a German nun, who was impregnated by her father and who had afterward drowned her newborn child, is sent to Rome to gain absolution from the pope. See also EdB c 456 (p. 394) where the former mistress of a noble man is accompanied by her confessor on a penitential pilgrimage to Rome. In general on pilgrimage imposed as a penance by ecclesiastical authorities, see Sigal, *Les marcheurs*, pp. 17–19 and van Herwaarden, *Opgelegde bedevaarten*, pp. 29–47.

41. DM dist. 12, c 24 (lb 2, p. 335). On the impact of social class on the distance of pilgrimages, see, for instance, Morrison, *Women Pilgrims*, p. 2 and Finucane, *Miracles and Pilgrims*, pp. 186–87. For the travels of noble women being considered as part of the "domestic arena," see Hanawalt, "At the Margins," p. 11.

42. Vita Gerlaci c 13 (Corneille Kneepkens, "Erasmus Ghoyee, Divi Gerlaci vita et miracula," in *De kluizenaar in de eik. Gerlach van Houthem en zijn verering*, ed. Anneke Mulder-Bakker (Hilversum: Verloren, 1995), p. 170. See also vita Mariae lb 2 c 106 (ASS Iun. IV (1707), p. 665, where a Cistercian nun, the former spouse of the count of Leuven, comes from Cologne to Oignies to see the saint's corpse before she is buried.

43. Vita Mariae, supplementum c 18 (ASS Iun. IV (1707), p. 673): *in Lotharingiae partibus nobilissimam feminam vidi, quae miro ardore spiritus cruce suscepta, usque in terram sanctam Jerusalem, vinculo ferreo cincta, carensque vehiculis, nudis etiam pedibus ambulavit.* On self-chastisement and gender in twelfth- and thirteenth-century Latin saints' lives from the Low Countries, see Katrien Heene, "Deliberate Self-Harm and Gender in Medieval Saints' Lives," *Hagiographica* 6 (1999), pp. 1–21.

44. Vita Fretherici c 31 (Aemilius Wybrands, *Gesta abbatum orti S. Marie* (Leeuwarden: Kuipers, 1879), pp. 35–36). On different types of self-chastisement as a means to help people in distress especially to obtain the remission of sins of the living as well as the dead's liberation from purgatory, in general see *Dictionnaire de Spiritualité* 1 (1937), s.v. Ascèse, pp. 969–87.

For the visiting of holy places (*loca sanctorum*) by the living as an aid for the deceased in purgatory, see EdB c 31 (p. 38) and DM dist. 12, c 7 (lb 2, pp. 322–23).

45. According to Wybrands, *Gesta abbatum*, pp. 35–36 (n. 2) this would be the oldest Dutch case of a pilgrimage to Jerusalem imposed as ecclesiastical penance. On this passage, without however mentioning the presence of Gertrud, see van Herwaarden, *Opgelegde bedevaarten*, p. 37.

46. See, for instance, Sigal, *Les marcheurs*, p. 143; and Norbert Ohler, "Überlegungen zum Rechtlichen Status Mittelalterlicher Reisende," *Columbeis* 5 (1993), pp. 59–60.

47. EdB c 342 (p. 293): *per villas discurrentes et domos penetrantes et in plateis predicantes* and EdB c 340 (p. 289). DM dist. 6, c 25 (lb 1, pp. 377–78) mentions a thief disguised as pilgrim as well as a real pilgrim falsely accused of theft.

48. See Lorcin, *Les voyages*, pp. 464–65 and van Herwaarden, "Pilgrimages," p. 78. This theme also occurs in English secular texts. See Morrison, *Women Pilgrims*, pp. 112–116.

49. JdV (Frenken) c 64 (pp. 128–29).

50. See vita Fretherici c 35 (p. 29). Nor is it shameful for the Dominicans to be called *gyrovagi*, see TC lb 2 c 3, 4 (p. 103).

51. Vita Aleydis c 2 (ASS Iun. II (1698), p. 477): *Fuit igitur praedicta Domina, a primevae aetatis initio, omnium aspectui amabilis et gratiosa, tamen non more Dinae, aliarum feminarum pulchritudinem minus caute indagantis, in plateas est egressa, sed more Dei genetricis, intra cubiculum commorantis gratiamque nutrientis, domi semper est morata.* Analogously but without a reference to Dinah or Mary, see vita Idae de Nivella c 1 (Chrysostomus Henriquez, *Quinque prudentes virgines* (Antwerp: Ioannem Cnobbaert, 1630), p. 200). For women adorning themselves when planning to go outside, see JdV (Crane) c 273 (p. 114).

52. According to some medieval interpreters Dinah had provoked her rape. See Joy Schroeder, "The Rape of Dinah: Luther's Interpretation of a Biblical Narrative," *Sixteenth Century Journal* 28 (1997), pp. 776–80 and Barbara Newman, "Flaws in the Golden Bowl: Gender and Spiritual Formation in the Twelfth Century," *Traditio* 45 (1989–90), p. 119. Thomas de Cantimpré mentions that Dinah was indeed violently raped but that afterwards she was nevertheless seduced by the flatteries of Sychem and Hemor, see TC lb 2 c 3, 4 (p. 103).

53. See vita Idae de Lewis c 7 (ASS Oct. XIII (1883), p. 109): *discursus nescia, plurimumque constans et stabilis, et omnino, tranquillaque residens et quieta, seque in huiusce modi adeo mirabiliter exercebat, ut eam iam possent asserere morum conversio. . .claustro non saeculo substitutam.*

54. For critical remarks from ecclesiastics on wandering and begging beguines and for the attempts to cloister them, see Peter Dinzelbacher, *Mittelalterliche Frauenmystik* (Paderborn: Schöningh, 1993), pp. 37–38, 50, and 57–58. For the ever present "danger of female indecency," see Hanawalt, "At the Margins," p. 3.

55. Franciscus Choquetius, *Sancti Belgi Ordinis Praedicatorum*, Vita Margaretae c 22 (Douai: Belleri, 1618), p. 170: *Matrem et materteras quandoque fugit, ut mendicaret, sed saepe iussu dicti patris sui redire et manere cum matre est coacta.*

56. Vita Idae de Lovanio lb1 c 18 (ASS April. II (1675), p. 163): *per vicos et plateas. . .coepit ambulando procedere. . .velut amens et fatua. . .*and c 19 (163): *vilis et abiecta. . .incessisset; tandem a propinquis cognita, et non ficte sed veraciter ab his insana pariter et phrenetica reputata,. . .ter uno die ligata, ter loris fortibus et vinculis est astricta.* On this and similar passsages concerning madness in vitae and exempla, see my article "Was Medieval Madness Gendered? A Case Study on Deviant Behaviour in the Twelfth and Thirteenth century," in *Charles V in Context: The Making of a European Identity,* ed. Marc Boone and Marysa Demoor (Brussels: VUB-Press, 2003), pp. 207–36.

57. In general, see James Brundage, "Enclosure of Nuns: the Decretal Periculoso and its Commentators," *Journal of Medieval History* 20 (1994), pp. 151–52. Marie d' Oignies also wanted to lead a mendicant life but according to her biographer, Jacques de Vitry, her friends persuaded her to stay home (vita Mariae lb 2 c 45, p. 648): *Unde quadam die fugere proposuit, ut inter extraneos ignota et despecta ostiatim mendicaret, ut nudum Christum nuda sequeretur. . .vix multis suorum amicorum lacrymis potuit retineri. Cum iam suis valedixisset, et iter in tali habitu, cum sacculo suo et scypho, paupercula Christi arripere vellet.* This could of course be a stylization on Jacques's part. The hagiographer also mentions that Marie could hardly be restrained from taking part in the crusade against the Albigensians (vita Mariae lb 2 c 82 (p. 658): *Unde tantum huius peregrinationis concepit ardorem, quod vix retineri posset, si sine scandalo proximorum aliquo modo it peragere valeret. Cumque quasi ridendo ab ea quaereremus quid illic si pervenisset faceret; saltem aiebat illa, Dominum meum honorarem).* For comments on the poverty movement in the vita Mariae, see Iris Geyer, *Maria von Oignies. Ein hochmittelalterliche Mystikerin zwischen Ketzerei und Rechtgläubigkeit* (Frankfurt am Main: Lang, 1992), pp. 118–23, 136, 138.

58. TC lb 2 c 51, 12 (p. 395): *Proinde circa annum incarnationis Dominici MCCXXVI, res mirabilis accidit in oppido Nivellensi. In hac urbe, ut pluribus adhuc viventibus notum est, mulierum devotarum, quae Beghinae dicuntur, nunc late diffusa per orbem religiositas inchoavit. Harum perplures quae magis spirituales erant igne sacro acriter sunt accensae, et hoc in membris tantum in quibus magis peccaverant postquam ad agnitionem venerant veritatis. Aliae in lingua, contra ingluviem vel loquacitatem, aliae in auribus, contra susurrium: aliae in manu, contra opus illicitum vel contactum: aliae in pede vel tibia, contra immoderatum discursum. . .etet hoc per tempus, secundum magis aut minus quod peccatis et negligentiis fuerant irretitae.*

59. Dialogus Miraculorum dist. 3, c 8 (lb 1, p. 121). The priest's protective measures were in vain because his daughter was eventually seduced by an *incubus,* a male demon, an event that ultimately made her go insane. For female confinement, see DM dist. 11, c 29 (lb 2, p. 294), where a canon shuts up a beautiful widow with whom he has fallen in love. EdB c 456 (p. 394) mentions a repentant whore being locked up by her confessor to prevent her from relapsing.

60. Vita Christinae lb 1 c 4 (p. 276): *cum quadam femina venit Coloniam, et quia inexperta erat, et naturaliter verecunda, plurimum in via timet, ne ductrix sua eam proderet, et ad aliquem locum infamem duceret, ubi ei aliqua confusio vel infamia posset invenire.* On female procurers, see Karras, *Common Women,* pp. 62–63.

61. For the association between being in the streets, especially at night, and whoredom, see Karras, *Common Women*, pp. 70–71 and 111. Analogously for walking alone in a forest, see Annelies van Gijsen, "Love and Marriage: Fictional Perspectives," in *Showing Status: Representation of Social Positions in the Middle Ages*, ed. Wim Blockmans and Anton Janse (Turnhout: Brepols, 1999), pp. 250–53.

62. See v. Iohannis lb 2 c 20 (*Revue d'Histoire Ecclésiastique* 76 (1981), p. 303). Caesarius (DM dist. 11, c 59 (lb 2, pp. 310–311)) links up the *puella luxuriosa, vaga, saecularis* with love magic. It is possible that both these passages echo the *mulier garrula et vaga* from the Proverbs (Proverbs 7:10–12),·the noisy, whorish woman who cannot stay home but wanders around the streets.

63. For a thirteenth-century "nouvelle" describing the rape of a married, noble female pilgrim, see Dietmar Rieger, "Le motif de viol dans la littérature de la France médiévale entre norme courtoise et réalité courtoise," *Cahiers de civilisation médiévale* 31 (1988), p. 266.

64. In an exemplum of Étienne de Bourbon the devil, in the shape of a young man, tries to rape a girl in a forest. He disappears when the girl starts shouting "Ave, Maria" (EdB c 108 (pp. 96–97)).

65. *Vita Christinae* lb 4 c131–38 (pp. 388–390): *sacerdotes. . .in hac silva manibus nostris interfecimus,. . .clericos. . .occidimus, centum puellas et matronas, violenter corruptas, postea mortificavimus; mulieres etiam impraegnatas occidimus: de reliquis vero hominibus, mercatoribus, viatoribus, et peregrinis, a nobis interfectis, non est numerus: hos omnes ablatis rebus occidimus, nec cuidam quantumque supplicant pepercimus.* See also ibid. lb 4 c 138 (p. 390). Christina persuades the men to turn themselves in. Although they are lynched without having had the opportunity to confess, according to the author, they will go to purgatory because of their remorse and faith (lb 4 c 139 (p. 391)).

66. *Vita Liutgardis* c 6–7 (ASS Iun. III (1701), p. 237): *Accidit quod Lutgardis, a sorore sua per nuntios accersita, iter arriperet: cui iuvenis obvius cum turba satellitum eam rapere nitebatur. Mox puella, equo quo sedebat exiliens, a manibus se iuvenis violenter extorsit, et tota nocte fugiens, per ignota silvarum, Angelico ductu, ad domum nutricis mane pervenit. Quam ut nutrix vidit, suspicata raptum, dixit: Numquid te iuvenis ille hac nocte violenter oppressit? Cui illa: Non, inquit. Nec mirum si nutrix hoc suspicabatur, ut diximus: Servi enim eius, ut viderunt praecendenti vespere iuvenem super se cum manu valida venientem, fugerunt; et ut in talibus mos est, inclamaverunt iuvenem ut raptorem. Et ille voce clamantium pavefactus, cessavit a persecutione virginis et aufugit. Occasione igitur huius clamore et fugae, in suspicionem hominum innocens puella devenit.*

67. Ibid., c 7 (p. 238): *Concursu ergo populi curiosius conglomerata, ibi immenso coepit erubescentiae pondere fatigari, statimque Christum reduxit ad mentem, et fortiter animo imperans, mox velum a facie manu iniecta dimovit. . .in revelatione faciei eius confusa populi multitudo discessit.*

68. See Rieger, "Le motif de viol," p. 255. On similar ideas in John Bromyard and other theologians, see Karras, *Common Women*, p. 109.

69. In general see, for example, Sigal, *Les marcheurs*, pp. 66–67 and Verdon, *Voyager*, pp. 53–87. Storm: see for example vita Iohannis lb 2 c 7 (pp. 282–83); privateers: DM dist. 7, (lb 2 c 38, pp. 53–54); murderers: JdV (Crane) c 104 (p. 48); robbers: JDV (Crane) c 56 (p. 27) *cantabit vacuus coram latrone viator*, EdB c 258 (p. 219). For travelers becoming the victims of false accusations of theft, see DM dist. 6, c 25 (lb1, pp. 377–78) and DM dist. 8, c 58 (lb 2, p. 130). Christina of Stommelen worried a lot about the troubles Peter of Dacia could encounter on his travels, see vita Christinae lb 2 c 58 (pp. 318–319): *de aura et molestia viae, et prolixitate et infortunio, de hospitio et receptione hospitum.*

70. See Ohler, "Überlegungen," pp. 59–60. The texts indeed mention these types of groups, see, for instance, EdB c 114 (p. 99) and vita Fretherici c 31 (p. 37). In particular the religious are said to travel with a (devout) companion: vita Iulianae (ASS April. I (1675) pp. 435–75), lb 1 c 36–38 (pp. 455–56) and TC lb 2 c 44, 10 (p. 434) cited in note 78. Thomas de Cantimpré (TC lb 2 c 57, 36 (pp. 471–72)) explicitly warns the brothers not to move too far away from each other during travels. He stresses the possible threat to their chastity.

71. DM dist. 5, lb 1 c 51 (p. 335) and DM dist. 5, lb 1 c 55 (pp. 337–38). EdB c 113 (p. 35) refers to the importance of good companions since robbers prefer to attack lonely pilgrims. When Christina is being threatened by a demon in the shape of a bull, a man who sees her running around like a mad woman, asks why she wandering about all by herself: *Quid est, o bona puella, quod sic sola vagando discurritis* (vita Christinae lb 4 c 53 (pp. 360–61)).

72. See Ohler, "Überlegungen," p. 55 and Verdon, *Voyager*, p. 62. For concrete examples, see, for instance, EdB c 30 (p. 37) (demons); c 79 (p. 75) (fallen angels); c 108 (pp. 96–97) (devil as rapist); JdV (Crane) c 104 (p. 48) (robbers-murderers).

73. See, for instance, DM dist. 5, c 51 (lb 1, p. 335); DM dist. 7, c 16 (lb 2, p. 18) and vita Arnulfi c 26 (ASS Iun. V (1709), (p. 622) where the saint, upon entering a wood, meets three beautiful women who offer themselves to him. The saint, however, scares them off by making the sign of the cross. In the vita Christinae lb 3 c 59–60 (pp. 341–42) the devil not only takes the shape of all kinds of wild animals but also of a beautiful young man. For men as a threat to the honor of wives and daughters in municipal regulations, see Jan van Herwaarden, "Graaf Floris V en het reizen in zijn dagen," in *Handel en Wandel in de Dertiende Eeuw*, ed. Detlev Ellmers (Amsterdam: De Bataafsche Leeuw, 1986), p. 14.

74. *De diabolo, qui visus est seminare discordiam inter duos peregrinos amicos* (DM dist. 5, c 39 (lb 1, p. 324)). On the devil trying to prevent the accomplishment of a pilgrimage vow, see DM dist. 5, c 42 (lb 1, pp. 326–27). See also TC lb 2 c 57, 35 (p. 471) where a demon accompanies a friar in the shape of his companion until they arrive in a village. The remaining friar is afraid to enter a house on his own but luckily his real companion turns up. Saints of both sexes are pictured as being bothered by demons while traveling. See, for instance, vita Gerlaci c 6 (p. 156); c 6 (p. 158); c 12 (pp. 168–170) and vita Ivettae c 18 (p. 866).

75. In the vita Iohannis lb 2 c 6 (pp. 281–82) a merchant is murdered in a guesthouse (*in hospitio*). In DM dist. 4 c 100 (lb 1, p. 271) a Cistercian convert is seduced at night by the servant of his host. For a swindling innkeeper, see JdV (Crane) c 310 (p. 130).

76. For scaring away demons, see vita Gerlaci c 12 (pp. 168–70) (showing the Cross); vita Ivettae c 18 (p. 866) (invocation of Christ's name and making the sign of the Cross) and DM dist. 5 c 55 (lb 1, p. 338) (reciting psalms). For prayers to Mary in order to calm a storm, see DM dist.7 c 38 (lb 2, pp. 53–54). One can also pray for someone else's sake, see TC lb 1 c 12, 2–3 (pp. 39–41). In the latter exemplum, which illustrates the need to care for the well-being of one's superior, a knight is said to travel without troubles as long as a poor man prays for him in exchange for food. The exemplum concludes as follows: *Discant. . .subditi praelatum suum foris ad negocia procedentem precibus tueri, et cordis compassione iuvare*. Christina of Stommelen also prayed for the safety of Peter of Dacia (vita Christinae lb 2 c 58 (pp. 318–319) and lb 3 c 15 (pp. 326–27). On spiritual remedies for travelers in general, see Verdon, *Voyager*, 87–92. Pious people can also be miraculously transferred: see DM dist.10 c 9 (lb 2, pp. 218–219); EdB c 152 (pp. 129–31) and Tubach, *Index exemplorum*, n. 3791. For the devil being involved in miraculous moves, see DM dist. 5 c 37 (lb 1, pp. 321–22) and DM dist. 5 c 56 (lb 1, pp. 338–340); DM dist. 8 c 95 (lb 2, p. 131).

77. For travelers getting lost, see EdB c 180 (pp. 157–58); JdV (Frenken) c 3 (pp. 95–97). In the latter exemplum the monks who got lost found a lodging in a convent inhabited by demons, but they managed to escape unharmed.

78. This exemplum is part of the section "on the happiness of pious souls" (*de felicitate et gaudio sanctarum animarum*) (TC lb 2 c 54, 10 (pp. 434–35). TC lb2 c 54, 11 (pp. 435–36) describes how an angel in pilgrim's attire comforts and helps two Dominican friars who are worrying where they will get a meal. See also JdV (Frenken) c 4 (p. 98) where an angel directs a pious layman to a lodginghouse run by Mary and Jesus. Taking into account that medieval people were accustomed to pray for the help of angels, the presence of a guiding angel certainly is not solely a literary device. See Ohler, *Medieval Traveller*, p. 132 and "Überlegungen," p. 48.

79. Vita Mariae lb 1 c 28 (p. 643): *Solebat autem causa peregrinationis et orationis fere singulis annis ecclesiam B. Mariae de Heignis visitare. . .cumque una sola comitante ancilla … viam, quae valde distorta est et nemorosa, nescirent; lumine quodam eam praecedente viamque ostendente, numquam errabat.*

80. Vita Mariae lb 1 c 28 (p. 643). For comments on this passage in the framework of the antiheretical character of the life, see Geyer, *Maria von Oignies*, pp. 140–42. For holy persons miraculously stopping rain showers or avoiding getting wet, see Charles Loomis, *White Magic. An Introduction to the Folklore of Christian Legend* (Medieval Academy of America: Cambridge, Massachusetts, 1937), p. 39 and vita Mariae, suppl. c 8 (pp. 669–670).

81. See vita Mariae, suppl. c 20–21 (p. 673).

82. See miracula Gerlaci c 24 (p. 204), and Caesarius (DM dist. 8 c 58 (lb 2, pp. 130–131)) for a well-known exemplum (Tubach, *Index exemplorum*, note 3785), which describes how saint Jacob saved a pilgrim who was wrongfully hanged, by supporting the man's feet until his father arrived.

83. We have not encountered virtual alternatives to traveling in the sources we examined up to now. For mental pilgrimage in an exemplum out of the *Alphabetum narrationum* of Arnoldus of Liège (late thirteenth century), see Marie-Anne Polo de Beaulieu, "Modèles et contre-modèles du pèlerin dans la littérature exemplaire du Moyen Age," in *L'image du pèlerin au Moyen Age et sous l'Ancien Régime*, ed. Pierre-André Sigal (Gramat: Association des amis de Rocamadour, 1994), p. 152.

84. We encounter the latter type of misogynistic arguments in the framework of the propagation of enclosure. See Brundage, "Enclosure of Nuns," pp. 147 and 152.

CHAPTER 3

JUDICIAL AUTHORITIES' VIEWS OF WOMEN'S ROLES IN LATE MEDIEVAL FLANDERS

Mariann Naessens

"Contrary to the virtue of all women. . . ." This is how the judicial authorities of Bruges described and judged the practices of Glaudyne Malengin in 1510.[1] It was a strong moral judgment on cross-dressing. Glaudyne was banished from the town and from the county of Flanders, "because for a considerable amount of time she walked around dressed as a man, contrary to the virtue of all women."[2] Although very brief, this phrase reveals a clear opinion about the practices of not only the individual concerned but also the entire female sex.

In a number of other judgments, the judicial authorities—wittingly or unwittingly—revealed their opinions on the role of women in society. In this chapter, we will investigate whether it is possible to reconstruct female identity as it was perceived by the judges. In order to do so, we will analyse penalized sexual behavior. First, we will focus on the unusually sharp moral condemnation of female cross-dressing. The question of female honor and virtue will be raised and answered at the end of this chapter. In crimes against the family—among which are infanticide and procuring one's own daughters—the (moral) responsibility of both the parents and especially the mother is investigated. With respect to prostitution, the unbalanced sex-ratio of convicted brothel-keepers raises the question to what degree men and women in that profession were held legally responsible. Finally, the almost complete absence of female adulterers in the judicial statistics reveals unequal treatment of men and women, caused by sex-specific notions of honor. The results of these four (sub)inquiries might enable us partly to reconstruct the underlying ideal of women held by the judges. What was, according to them, an honorable or virtuous woman? How was she supposed to behave within the marriage and within the family?

Because of the close connection between the aforementioned crimes and the field of sex and family, these crimes and the sentences the perpetrators received may prove to be useful sources of information about this particular aspect of female identity—albeit about this aspect only. Our conclusions will offer only a fragmentary view on women, but late medieval society considered the sexuality of women to be an essential part of female nature.

The Flemish towns of Bruges and Ghent in the late medieval period (1470–1550) serve as test cases for these issues. These towns still played a dominant role in the late medieval Flemish economy: Bruges as a commercial centre, Ghent as a major producer of cloth. With over 40,000 inhabitants each at that time, they were the largest towns of Flanders. Their late medieval judicial archives have been partially preserved and form the basis of the present research.

Our view of the judges' opinion about the place of women in society is almost exclusively based on judicial evidence dating from the end of the fifteenth and the beginning of the sixteenth centuries. Earlier sources were consulted as well, but our search there did not produce any relevant results. The great increase in sources at the end of the fifteenth century may be a possible cause. Indeed, from that time onward, legal administration improved, which resulted in a more rational registration and a better preservation of the relevant documents. As a result, ever more detailed sources have become available. However, the sudden appearance of judicial decisions on essentially moral issues was probably the result of a change of judicial focus. Recent historiography on medieval prostitution commonly mentions the changing notion of morality. For example, Peter Schüster, who investigated municipal brothels in Germany, argues that the system of morality experienced a shift around 1500.[3] L.L.Otis, also, notices "the dramatic transformation in morals which took place at the end of the fifteenth and throughout the sixteenth centuries" in Languedoc (France).[4] While discussing prostitution and the increasing number of regulations imposed on this activity, such historians also observe a growing attention to the *problem* of adultery. From there, it is only a small step to family. It has been argued that, at that time, the protection of the family had become a priority.[5]

This so-called new morality has been discussed at great length for the Low Countries, mainly by Dutch authors who based their research on literary and iconographical sources. Using different methods and studying various kinds of sources, they all came to the same conclusion: apart from the imposition of ever-stricter sexual standards, a new sensibility to marriage and family came into being around 1500. This new sensibility stressed a more rigid dichotomy between the public and the private spheres.[6]

The authority of the husband was emphasized, and one could speak about the birth of the modern housewife: the wife was subordinated to her husband and was assigned only domestic and pedagogical tasks.[7] She was expelled from public life into the private sphere, and was supposed to devote herself there to domestic tasks. According to the aforementioned literary and art historians, the tradition of a relative independence for women was interrupted.

Through the years, this view of the ideal woman developed into a consistent system of values that was expressed in late medieval art and literature; there, it was held up as a mirror to women. These, however, are representational sources, and the question remains whether—and to what extent—this ideal was expressed in real life. The study of legal records will allow us to check whether the evolution found in literature and iconography can also be observed in everyday life. The central issues dealt with in this chapter are: first, the concepts of female virtue and of the role of women that can be found in our judicial sources dating from the end of the fifteenth and the beginning of the sixteenth centuries, and second, their similarity to the insights gleaned from literary and art-historical research. In other words, do we find the same ideal image and, if so, should we—in the light of the aforementioned evolution—consider it as being evidence of a new era, rather than a typically (late) medieval concept?

Transvestism

On September 28, 1502, Nase de Poorter, dressed in men's clothes, was pilloried on the Burg in Bruges.[8] Afterward, she was dressed in women's clothes and banished from the county of Flanders for the period of one year. Before she was convicted she had already lived a rather eventful life. She had married sixteen years earlier, but had stayed with her husband for no more than a year. She had given up her well-regulated life in order to roam the country. The source mentions outright that, since that time, she had "run wild and lived in an adulterous relationship."[9] Four years before she was convicted, she had met with a priest who had come under her spell, and they had left together. Nase dressed as a man and posed as the priest's brother "in order to be better able to continue living her bad and perverted life and to avoid being recognized, reproved or corrected."[10] Together, they moved from Oostkamp to Louvain, from Louvain to Lille and, finally, from Lille to Bruges. "Until she was arrested, nobody suspected that she was not a man."[11] Indeed, it was suggested that her cross-dressing and the continuous moving around had only one purpose, namely to obscure her illicit relationship with the priest. Finally, she was convicted "because she was a married woman and walked around dressed as a man."[12]

3.1   Transvestism; from Adriaen van de Venne's Album (1626); British Museum.

The second case is that of the said Glaudyne Malengin. She was a hardened thief who dressed as a man.[13] She was convicted in Bruges twice. The reports of the aldermen mention explicitly that her transvestism helped her successfully to carry out her criminal activities. She had been member of a gang of thieves for some time when she suddenly decided to dress as a man. In other words, her cross-dressing was just an additional aspect of her deviant and socially maladjusted behavior. Even when she was convicted and banished for the first time, she threw off the women's clothes she had received from the court, and put on men's clothes once more.

The two women were not only guilty of transvestism; Nase committed adultery and Glaudyne was a thief. However, this does not mean that the other crimes took precedence over the charge of cross-dressing, despite the claim by Dekker and van de Pol, authors of one of the rare studies written about the subject of transvestism. They argue that the penalty was primarily defined by the seriousness of the other crimes, even though the cross-dressing was certainly considered to be an aggravating circumstance, "an indication of their depravity."[14] However, in the cases of Nase and Glaudyne, there is clear evidence that transvestism in itself was targeted by the judicial authorities. In the reports of the aldermen concerning the case of Glaudyne Malengin, the cross-dressing is mentioned first, and a moral condemnation accompanies it; only then are the thefts reported: "because, for some time, she has walked around dressed as a man, contrary to the virtue of all women, and because she had associated with some men who stole and committed several thefts, whom she assisted and on the loot of which thefts she lived. . ."[15] The bailiff's account does not even mention the thefts committed by her: he gets paid "for having pilloried Glaudyne Malengin because she was walking around dressed in men's clothes."[16] The case of Nase de Poorter is very similar; here, the bailiff's account reads: "for having pilloried Donaze Poorters, because she was married and had the audacity to walk around in a man's guise."[17] Her adultery is only implicit in the mention of her married status, but the fact of cross-dressing is explicit. Even more revealing is the penalty: Nase as well as Glaudyne are to be bound to the pillory, dressed in men's clothes, and both of them are to be banished, dressed in a woman's dress. In the Middle Ages, judges— and society as a whole—had a marked preference for symbolic "mirroring punishments," penalties allegorically reflecting the reprehensible behavior they sought to remedy.[18] In these cases, the penalty clearly refers to the women's practice of cross-dressing. According to this theory, these two women were, first and foremost, convicted for transvestism.

But why was female cross-dressing considered to be so reprehensible? Why did the courts feel the need to have these women scaffolded, exposed, and disgraced in front of the entire urban community, and, finally, expelled from it? Against what ideal view on women, held by the judges, did these women sin?

The judges used the word *eerbaerhede*, translated as "virtue," "honesty," or "honor," to justify their judgment.[19] They argued that these two women acted *contrary to the virtue of all women* by acting the way they did. Further in this essay, we will see how the concept of honor influenced the judicial practice. What was at stake here was not the honor associated with knights and gentlemen, but rather a personal notion of honor.[20] This honor originated from public recognition. *Ohne Öffentlichkeit gibt es keine Ehre*: without publicness, there is no honor.[21] In other words: all honor is public honor. Honor equalled social judgment and, as such, it was made and broken by society. As a result, historical research into the concept of honor often focuses on cases of defamation brought to trial. Honor could be wounded by defamation, insults or slander. These slanders are invaluable tools for a historian who is trying to find out what was regarded as honorable at the time. The offender made sure to choose the most effective insults. In order to do so, he had to refer to the violation of generally established norms. By way of inverse reasoning, these norms can be discovered. However, one has to remain careful.[22]

It is striking that, through the centuries and throughout Europe, an insult to a woman would almost always consist of her being called a whore.

On first sight, one could conclude that a woman's sexual behavior was constitutive for her honor. However, many scholars have stressed the fact that sexual behavior was only one component of female honor. Sex-related slander was so prominent because it was often symbolically used; when a woman was called a prostitute this negative term was in no way limited exclusively to the sexual aspect. Instead, the word prostitute was used with a multitude of connotations that encompassed the entire spectrum of roles attributed to women. As a result, the insult "prostitute" clearly implied a negative judgment of such women in all the roles they were supposed to fulfil.[23] In other words, the slur of prostitution symbolically indicated the violation of other social taboos and—to be more precise—the failure to live up to role expectations.[24] The insult "whore" did not necessarily imply paid sex. It was a code word to indicate that a woman's honor had been tainted by behaving contrary to the established role patterns.[25] It is therefore important to stress that female honor cannot be limited to sexual honor. Honorable conduct essentially depended on the fulfillment of a role, in a way the community considered to be adequate.[26] It is clear that (female) transvestites tried to escape the role that had been imposed on them by God, nature, and society. What that role might have been in the later Middle Ages, and what was considered honorable behavior are the questions that inform the rest of this essay.

Crimes Against the Family

The examples mentioned in the previous section are early manifestations and convictions of female transvestism brought before a secular court.[27] According to Dekker and van de Pol, the earliest examples from neighboring countries date from ca. 1535 in France, 1544 in Germany, 1550 in the Netherlands, and 1642 in England.[28] Since only a very small part of the judicial archives has been studied, we assume that further research will advance the date of these first attestations. However, this does not change the fact that the cases known for Bruges are considerably older than those from surrounding countries: 1502 for the case of Nase de Poorter, 1510 for Glaudyne Malengin. Moreover, the Flemish judgments contain a clear moral condemnation of the crimes, which is not present in the other countries.

In Bruges, the first convictions for, and moral rejections of, transvestism coincide with the appearance in the first half of the sixteenth century of other similar judicial positions with regard to the place of women and the way they were supposed to behave. The opinions that were expressed there may help us to further define and refine the concept of female virtue that we have thus far reconstructed from the judgments concerning transvestism. Bruges is the only town in Flanders where this kind of discourse can be found, because it is the only place for which we have registers with extensive sentences pronounced by the aldermen.[29]

These clearly reveal opinions judges held with regard to the role of women in society. Already in 1510, prostituting one's own daughters had been described as "contrary to all laws and going against all decency and against every mother's nature."[30] Along similar lines, it was written, "according to the law and also to God and nature, every mother must do the very best she can to raise her children in honor and virtue, and not set them a bad example or let them come to shame in any way."[31] It is noteworthy that there are references to (written) law, to divine law and to the law of nature.[32] They are not extensive citations from law books, but merely notations, used by the judges to stress the fact that in this case, not just local law was violated, but universal rules, applicable everywhere and to everyone. In this way, the sentence was made much more forceful. References to written law were common in medieval judgments; divine law, on the other hand, was rarely invoked, and it is only in these very specific cases of procuring one's own daughters that the sources refer to the law of nature. Only in one other case did we find another reference to natural law, that concerning the behavior of children toward their parents.[33]

The attention paid to the mother's role in the judicial records is conspicuous, not only when the repression of procuration is concerned, but also in cases of infanticide. In 1528, the judges explicitly expressed their views on motherhood in a judgment concerning the abandonment of a child. Tanne Muelencar was ordered "to accept her forementioned child, to feed and to keep it, as a mother must and should do, according to (the laws of) God and Nature."[34] In 1543, the concept of motherly love was used for the first time in the conviction of an infanticide; the judges specified that the murder had taken place "without showing any motherly love."[35] A mother's care and love for her children were thus described as being natural and honorable. As a consequence, they were imposed as a standard on the whole of female society.

It is interesting to compare this discourse with that concerning the fathers role in similar matters.[36] Can it be a coincidence that there is no judgment concerning child abandonment, infanticide, or procuration that mentions the father? This silence is significant; the father is never held accountable. The harrowing case of Maye of Ypres provides a clear example. Her husband abandoned her only two months after their marriage. Maye learned that he had gone to Bruges and followed him there. She did not succeed in locating him, but she stayed in Bruges nevertheless. In order to provide for her and for her child, she prostituted herself ("has abandoned her body and has had conversation in the flesh with whomever desired it from her").[37] Eventually, she even abandoned her child, "contrary to the law of God and nature."[38] The authorities, however, were completely unsympathetic; no extenuating circumstances were offered. According to the judges' silence, the father had no part in the responsibility for the child.

Did the judges make any statements at all about the role of the father? It is not easy to find an equally clearly stated description for fatherhood. However, there are some indirect indications about a man's role. In convictions for male adultery, it was often considered an aggravating circumstance if the man had left his wife and his children in poverty. This was the case with Danneel Bollaert, who had "left his lawfully wedded wife in great poverty and misery, with six children."[39] Another man was punished for "abandoning and leaving his lawfully wedded wife alone, in great poverty and misery and spending everything he earned and could lay his hands on with the said woman."[40] It appears to be rather stereotypical. Time and again in sixteenth-century judgments the man charged with adultery is reproached for having left his wife in poverty. The judges always seem to start from the assumption that the family had no or insufficient financial means to carry on after the man had left. In other words, it was the man's job to provide for his family.

The degree to which this belief had been established becomes clear from a Ghent case from 1540. It concerns a man who was seriously injured in a work-related accident. The man asked to be compensated, arguing that—as a result of his accident—he would not be able to work for weeks, and "would be unable to provide for his wife and children, as he used to do."[41] This is the reason why he enumerates all the earnings he had before the accident, "all the yearly earnings and profits of which he, his wife and children had been deprived because of the said accident, as a result of which they had to live in great poverty, on alms they received from good people."[42] The fact that the financial argument was worked out in such detail indicates that the man in question was convinced that it might help to persuade the judges. This would only be the case if the idea was firmly established that it was first and foremost the man, far more than the woman, who had to provide for the family.[43] Therefore, it cannot be denied that these sentences show a certain division of tasks within the family; the man was supposed to provide for his family, the woman had the care of the children.[44]

Keeping a Brothel

Until now, research has been restricted to some rare cases of transvestism, infanticide, child abandonment, and procuring. These cases shocked society and provoked quite strong reactions. However, the everyday, almost systematic repression of brothel-keeping and adultery at the end of the fifteenth and beginning of the sixteenth centuries also proves to be quite interesting. Although the sources offer very little substantial information—putting only the most essential elements in more or less regular, recurring categories—through quantitative analysis of the data it is possible to glean from these sources something about the view on women held by late medieval judges.

As to brothel-keeping, the situation in Ghent is particularly suitable for study because of the very interesting conflict of two kinds of sources: the *ballincboek* (Book of Exiles), a register in which the aldermen noted all the banishments they pronounced, and the bailiff's accounts, in which this official registered all the collected fines.[45] The comparison of these two sources results in an important hypothesis. In the Book of Exiles[46] women dominate the sex ratio to a large degree: 80 percent of all convicted brothel-keepers were women compared to only 20 percent of men. However, in the bailiff's accounts[47] primarily men—70 percent—were denounced for keeping a brothel (Table 3.1). And yet the sources are almost contemporary. The Book of Exiles was preserved until the year 1537, but the number of entries dropped from 1520 onward. In the bailiff's accounts, fines for prostitution were first registered in 1515. This small difference in time cannot sufficiently explain the great difference in contents. So how do we explain this remarkable difference?

To answer this question we have to look at the sources in greater detail (Table 3.2). The vast majority—76 percent—of the 152 women in the Book of Exiles who were convicted for keeping a brothel were single women. The rest were married women who were banished together with their husbands. Only a very small percentage of judgments (6 percent) concerned married women whose partner was not convicted. For the convicted men an entirely different picture emerges. Here, single men were the minority (30 percent). The great majority consisted of married men, convicted

Table 3.1   Sex ratio of brothel-keepers in Ghent

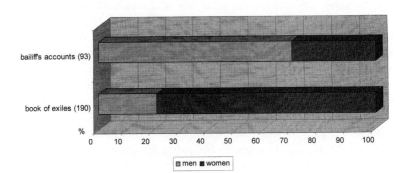

Table 3.2   Marital status of brothel-keepers in Ghent

	Book of Exiles		Bailiff's accounts	
	Absolute figures	%	Absolute figures	%
Men				
single	12	30		
married	0	0	No information	
couple	28	70		
total	40	100	65	100
Women				
single	115	76	23	82
married	9	6	5	18
couple	28	18	0	0
total	152	100	28	100

together with their wives, who comprised 70 percent of all cases. Thus, the Book of Exiles primarily contains names of single women and married couples.

However, in the bailiff's accounts we find a completely different situation. Convicted women formed a minority (28 women, 65 men). They were single or married (only 5), but the latter were never sentenced together with their husbands. In contrast to the Book of Exiles the bailiff's accounts make no mention of any couples. Unfortunately, we have no information about the marital status of the men. From the study of some individual cases and from a comparison with the international literature on the subject it is possible to formulate an interesting hypothesis about marital status and the legal responsibility of the brothel-keepers. For example, in 1501 and 1512, Kalle Dappers, together with her husband, Cornelis Danckaert, was banished from Ghent for keeping a brothel. In 1526, according to the bailiff's accounts, only her husband was fined after a similar charge. In another case Jehanne Danckaerts, a single woman, was expelled from town in 1512 for keeping a brothel. In 1519, she was fined for the same reason, and as a result, she was registered in the bailiff's accounts. In 1525, she was once more banished. However, in the meantime, she married Jan Clemme. From that moment Jehanne disappears from the sources. Until his marriage, her husband had never been connected with brothel-keeping. However, he was sentenced to a fine for this activity in 1528. In another example in 1516 and 1517, Jozyne vanden Berghe, a single woman, paid a fine for brothel-keeping. In 1519, she was a married woman and together with her husband, Lievin, she was banished for brothel-keeping. Jozyne was never again sentenced or fined. Her husband, on the other hand, paid a fine for keeping a brothel twice, in 1521 and 1522.

It is clear that, whereas the Book of Exiles indicates that a couple was sentenced, the bailiff's accounts only mention the name of the husband, even when it is obvious that the woman had been actively involved in the business for much longer than her husband. Women who were registered in the Book of Exiles (and also in the bailiff's accounts) more than once disappeared from the bailiff's accounts as soon as they got married. Afterward, only the names of their husbands were registered. Not once do the bailiff's accounts record a simultaneous conviction of both husband and wife. The man probably represented the couple in the (financial) dealings with the bailiff concerning brothel-keeping.

Ruth Mazo Karras argued that, with regard to the beginning of the sixteenth century, "it is likely that women are in fact underrepresented in the records. Because of the way medieval courts viewed the legal responsibility of women, if a married couple committed an offense, often only the husband was charged. If a married woman committed an offense on her own, her husband still might be the one charged for it."[48] From this, she drew far-reaching conclusions about the legal view of women: "Even if the law considered women more likely to be involved in this particular trade, it still did not accord married women an unusual degree of individual responsibility."[49] This position seems grossly exaggerated with regard to the situation in Flanders. Married women were indeed held responsible: they were banished from the towns. Only when a monetary fine was involved was the husband alone addressed. This argues not for a restricted legal responsibility for (married) women, but, instead, for restricted financial responsibility. This is logical, since, according to the customary law of Ghent, a husband was lord and master of the marital goods: "that, according to the customary law of this town, in his marriage, a man is lord of all the movables and the acquired property, belonging to him and his wife. . .according to the above-mentioned custom, all said movable goods are within the power of, at the disposal of and within the will of the said man."[50]

It is clear that, in the bailiff's accounts, many married women are hidden behind the names of convicted men. Nevertheless, it was the madam who represented the brothel to the outside world. She is always the one depicted in representations of brothels and stews, next to her girls and their customers (figure 3.2). She was charged with the care of the prostitutes, and, as a consequence, the judicial authorities held her responsible for possible abuse within her brothel. When a virgin was raped in a brothel, for instance, it was the madam, and not the husband, who was convicted for it. For example, Gillyne van Dessendonct was banished "because she has lodged a man and permitted him to come with a young virgin, (a man) who has done his very best to know the said virgin carnally, against her will, and also (because she) has accommodated a married woman, who had sex there and lost her

3.2　Brothel scene; woodcut from *De Verloren Sone*, printed in 1540 in Antwerp by Willem Vorsterman; British Library BL Shelfmark number: c 34 h 7.

honor."[51] Only female brothel-keepers were convicted for seducing virtuous daughters and introducing them to prostitution: "Coline sDonckers for having taken with her a young girl to place her in the brothel."[52]

Thus, in dealings with the authorities the wife assumed moral responsibility for the brothel while her husband handled the financial side of the enterprise (in Karras's terms men are owners and women are managers). In conclusion, the same division of tasks between man and woman detailed earlier in this chapter—woman as caregiver, man as provider—are repeated concerning prostitution in Ghent.

However, can this explain why so few unmarried women were sentenced to pay a fine? In the Book of Exiles, single women represented 60 percent of all convictions, three times the number of convicted men. In the bailiff's accounts, only 25 percent were single women—three times less than men. Single female brothel-keepers may figure so prominently in the Book of Exiles because brothel-keeping was a possible fin-de-carrière activity for prostitutes.[53] However, if this is the case, then why don't they occur just as frequently in the bailiff's accounts? Were unmarried women, like their married counterparts, also considered to be fiscally irresponsible or incapable? Or did the authorities prefer to banish the single female brothel-keepers? If so, since being banished was a harsher punishment than a fine, single women were more severely punished than men. In fact, their banishment was not solely due to brothel-keeping, but because it was more strictly forbidden for women to run a brothel than men. A useful comparison outside Flanders was the London suburb of Southwark, where regulations required all stewholders to be men. Their wives could work with them, but, officially, no unmarried woman could keep a stewhouse.[54] In Ghent no such regulations have been found but the officials may have held the same opinions: an unmarried woman could not run a brothel. This is only a very tentative hypothesis.

Adultery

What insights into the position of women can be gathered from the repression of adultery? We have very few qualitative data at our disposal for the Flemish towns investigated here. More than 90 percent of all convictions for adultery at the end of the fifteenth and beginning of the sixteenth centuries were registered under the heading of "adultery" or some other vague description such as "men living with women other than their lawfully wedded wives" (or vice versa) or "men/women misbehaving within their marriage." At the height of the repression of adultery—between ca. 1510 and 1540—convictions can only be found under such headings.[55] The greatest disadvantage is the lack of additional information: only the name of the offender is given and there is no mention of his/her partner in crime. Nonetheless we can form some hypotheses from quantitative analysis of the data.

When cases concern adultery it is clear that women are almost absent from the legal records. Adulteresses are rare both in the registers of the aldermen and in the bailiff's accounts in Ghent as well as in Bruges or Ypres, and even in the documents of the ecclesiastical courts.[56] The man–woman ratio of the convicted persons is about 80/20 in all the judicial sources of these towns or of other institutions (Table 3.3).

Table 3.3   Sex ratio of adulterers

	Men		Women		Totals
	Absolute figures	%	Absolute figures	%	
Bruges 1459–1537	75	80	19	20	94
Ghent 1300–1555	298	76	92	24	390
Ypres 1300–1555	57	83	12	17	69
Church 15th cent.	388	79	101	21	489
	818	79	224	21	1042

This predominance of men can partially be explained by the assumption that men actually committed adultery more often than women. Myriam Carlier has deduced this from the civil status of the parents of illegitimate children, which indicates that far more married men than women had illicit children.[57] Still, this cannot explain the overwhelmingly high percentage of men. There are several cases of men being punished for adultery with married women. By definition these women also committed adultery, but their names are absent from the sources. Therefore, it is far more likely that the disproportion is the result of a different view about male and female adultery. This view, however, is not explicit in legal texts; indeed, these sources do not distinguish between the sexes.[58] Yet the belief that male adultery had to be punished more systematically than female adultery would explain such pronounced differences.

Contemporary literary and iconographic sources usually offer more relevant information about such beliefs than the rather concise judicial sources. First we will examine the representation of the "criminal offence" of adultery in the *Practice and Manual of Criminal Cases (Practycke ende handbouck in criminele zaeken)* by Joos de Damhouder (1551).[59] The author intended a practical handbook and manual for jurists without the benefit of a university education. It offers a thorough study of procedural and substantive criminal law of his time and is illustrated with fifty-seven woodcuts depicting different crimes and punishments. In this juridical treatise, adultery is represented by a woman who receives her lover within the conjugal bed (figure 3.3). Numerous other medieval representations portray, time and again, the adultress and her lover. Contrary to the evidence of legal records, the literature of that time also represents adultery as an exclusively female offense. For example, the theme of the cuckold was very popular in the Middle Ages.[60] The story of *De cnape van Dordrecht* ("The Young Man from Dordrecht") is illustrative.[61] This fabliau tells us about a young man who makes a living by making love to married women in exchange for money. The young man is handsome, rich, and generous, and he leads a good-for-nothing's life of ease in Dordrecht. His extravagant behavior arouses the suspicion of the keepers of public order, the bailiff's helpers. In vain, they watch his movements in order to find out how he earns his living. When the bailiff approaches the young man about the subject, he at first refuses to believe that someone can actually make a living by offering women love for money. However, the bailiff witnesses the young man fix a date with an old and crippled woman. After this, the bailiff no longer puts the slightest obstacle in the young man's way. Eventually, during a family gathering, he tells about the young man. Without delay, his wife sends her chambermaid in search of this young man. That same night, while her husband makes his rounds, she seizes the opportunity and avails herself of the young man's services. But when dawn breaks and her husband's return is imminent, she cannot

145   Van adulterie of ouerſpel.

3.3   Adultery; woodcut from Joos de Damhouder, *Practycke ende handbouck in criminele zaeken* (printed in 1551), Library of the University of Ghent (Jur. 932, p. 145).

pay him, so he refuses to leave her bed. As a result, he is still with her when her husband, the bailiff, returns. The latter immediately understands the situation and pays the young man, dismissing him with these revealing words: "I beg of you: do not disgrace me in this region."[62]

The events described in the story—the activities of male gigolos—can also be found in the contemporary judicial sources.[63] However, the story's importance lies in the portrayal of emotions that the author's public could recognize.[64] In this regard, the end of the story is especially interesting: resignedly, the bailiff pays for his wife's adultery and begs the young man not to disgrace him in the entire region. "The bailiff spoke: 'Do not disgrace me, this I beg of you, in this country. XX pounds I will give you, but never in my life did I giving money hurt me so.' "[65] Since they were caught in the act, the husband was entitled to stab to death the adulterer: "the laws permit the man to kill—without committing a crime by doing so—the adulterer he finds with his wife."[66] Being the bailiff, he also had the right to arrest them both (cases in which a single man is convicted for having committed adultery with a married woman are known). But none of this happens. The bailiff prefers a cover-up to shame and possible disgrace.

By committing adultery, a woman not only brought shame upon herself but also upon her husband.[67] Indeed, a man's honor was partially defined by his wife's chastity.[68] Adulterous wives cuckolded their husbands[69] and—in so doing—robbed them of their manliness and their honor. We have stated that honor—and its loss—had everything to do with society; the general opinion of it determined a person's reputation. As a result, individual behavior was partially defined by the fear of society's censure. Consequently, furtiveness and secrecy were important elements in stories concerning adultery.[70]

The literary theme of the cuckold, and the related concepts of honor and disgrace, can easily be recognized in judicial reality. The concept of shame is used in its literal sense in the rare convictions of women on grounds of adultery. In those cases the verdict explicitly states that the woman committed adultery with another person, "leaving her lawfully wedded husband in great disgrace and desolation."[71] When a man committed adultery, on the other hand, the idea of disgrace was omitted; instead, the following expression was used: "leaving his wife alone in great poverty and misery."[72]

The fact that female adultery did indeed bring disgrace to a man is also clear from other judicial statements. Frequently, cases concerning insults were taken to court. To call someone a cuckold seems to have been very popular. Examples can be found in the *civiele sentencien* of Bruges: Laureyns vander Kercke "had had the audacity, one night in the previous month of November, to come knocking on the house of an important burgher, a craftsman of this town, saying and shouting in a very loud voice, and against all truth, that his wife was an overfucked whore, that he had seen her lying and misbehaving upon a bridge."[73] The fact that this reproach was taken to court indicates that it was hurtful to a man, whether it was true or not. Indeed, honor was a public commodity, shaped by the outside world, by neighbors' gossip and talk. Honor that had been tainted in public (by gossip) had to be publicly restored (in court). In a society in which individual and personal honor was defined by others the "negotiation of honor" could only function in public.[74]

This perception of honor and disgrace with regard to adultery explains the apparent conflict between iconography and literature on the one hand—where the woman is portrayed as being adulterous and unfaithful—and the judicial sources on the other hand—in which female adultery is practically absent. The numerous allusions to female adultery can be interpreted as warnings about the grave dangers of dishonor. The small number of convictions, on the other hand, can be explained by the fact that it was in a man's best interest not to expose his wife's infidelity. Brundage tells us, "it was customary in many places for adulteresses to be dealt with privately by their husbands or families, while the man was turned over to the courts." [75] The notions of male honor and disgrace were strong enough to make a person look for a solution without involving the court. In other words infrajudicial procedures were used to discipline a woman's adultery. As in literature, the element of secrecy is also paramount. Because these cases were not taken to court, and consequently were not recorded in judicial sources, it is not easy to find information about these procedures. [76] However, such cases occasionally come to light, as in the following example:

> The said bailiff and the men of the law brought charges against the lady, the wife of Pierre le Duutsche, because—notwithstanding her married state and notwithstanding the fact that she should live well and honestly according to her said state with her said husband, she lives, on the contrary, a dishonest and evil life, and notwithstanding the fact that four or five agreements were made by the parents and friends of both sides, between herself and the said husband, and peace (was made) between them, and each of them promised never again to live their life as before, still she persisted in her said evil way of life. . .[77]

It is clearly indicated here that the family and friends of both parties had previously and on more than one occasion entered into an agreement with the intent of disciplining the woman. The court had only been involved when these informal procedures repeatedly had failed to achieve the intended result. The frequent application of this kind of solution probably explains the very low number of cases of female adultery in judicial sources. [78] This also means that female adultery will always be underrepresented.

But why was it so disgraceful for a man that his wife was unfaithful to him? This question is not easily answered. There is no extensive discourse on honor in the sources. Fortunately, other avenues of interpretation developed in anthropology can prove useful. For example, Peter Burke's study on honor in early modern Italy points out the striking similarities between early Italian notions of honor and a number of twentieth-century Mediterranean cultures. In the latter, the *cornuto's* (cuckold's) disgrace is many-sided: the adultery of his wife not only raises suspicion about his capacity to subject and monopolize her, but also about his sexual competence. [79] (Figure 3.4.)

The same pattern can be found in Low Countries history. The shame associated with adultery resulted primarily from the adulterous woman's

3.4   Cornuto; from Joris Hoefnaghel, *Patientia, 24 politieke emblemata* (1569); collection of the municipal library of Rouen, ms. Leber 2916, fol. 23.

defiance of her husband's authority. In Flemish customary law the husband is the lord and master, the wife is obliged to honor and serve him. The most tangible expression of this authority can be seen in a husband's right to correct his wife because she has the obligation to obey him: it is said, "a man who beats his wife commits no crime, even if she's wounded, when he does so to punish her, to correct her, to instruct her, or to make her obedient. . ."[80] When a woman committed adultery, this was proof of the fact that the husband had failed to control and discipline his wife to a sufficient degree to make her remain faithful to him; in other words, that he was a weakling. In this respect, the disgrace of the deceived husband is very similar to that of the henpecked husband.[81] Both types of man risked becoming an object of derision within the community, and both had a good chance of becoming the target of *charivari*, a kind of playful popular tribunal, a ritual sanctioning of deviant behavior and, as such, an instrument for communal social control.[82] The punishment was, first and foremost, intended to ridicule the offender and his reprehensible behavior in order to disgrace him. This indicates that public opinion expected the man to be the boss. The cuckold's loss of honor resulted from the fact that he was not able to control his wife.

Second, probably also at the root of this loss of honor was the man's supposed inability to satisfy his wife's sexual needs, thus causing her to seek her pleasures elsewhere. A husband's inability or inadequacy was in a way responsible for his wife's adultery. German Shrove Tuesday plays offer this kind of argument.[83] Martin Dinges states it as a fact[84] and Brundage mentions, "common belief held that a wife's adultery was often due to her husband's sexual shortcomings, which may also have made men reluctant to press charges."[85] We have not yet found this argument explicitly stated in the Flemish judicial sources, but there is no reason to believe that the situation was different here. It seems safe to say that judicial sources may also— albeit implicitly—offer a view on men and manliness.

By now, it is clear how perceptions of honor and dishonor and of the role of men and women influenced judicial practice. This explains the underrepresentation of women in the records of the repression of adultery in urban Flanders.

Conclusion

For the *crime* of transvestism, women were punished for all to see in order to restore that female honor which their actions had violated. With regard to brothel-keeping, women were held responsible and so they were banished by the judicial authorities. In adultery cases women were almost absent because they were not brought into public court. Because male honor was involved, they were dealt with privately, that is, in an infrajudicial way.

What does all this say about the role of women in late medieval Flemish society? It seems clear to us that they were in a subordinate position. Whenever financial dealings with the judicial authorities were concerned, their husbands took over. When a man's honor was at stake a woman's crimes were dealt with privately.

In conclusion we can say that the honorable thing for a wife to do was to remain faithful to her husband and to obey him as her lord and master. Only then would his authority remain unquestioned and would he escape becoming the object of derision. Fidelity and subordination were the two essential constitutive elements of female honor. Shortcomings in either area led to dishonorable conduct.[86]

By now, it is evident that the judicial authorities defended the same social norms in their verdicts as are to be found in contemporary literary and iconographical sources. Moreover, their views fit in completely with the new morality of that period. These late medieval sources already show signs of a new state of affairs, one that came into existence during the transitional period between the Middle Ages and modernity, and which therefore is not entirely representative for all of the medieval period. Hopefully, further research will pinpoint more accurately when this evolution started in Flanders, and describe how this new morality differed from the old. It is our opinion that the transition consisted first and foremost in a change of emphasis; existing ideas were reinforced by stressing them.

In this chapter, only a single aspect of female identity was studied, namely her role in family life; her economic activities were not taken into account. As far as can be concluded at this early research stage, within the limited sphere of the family women were expected to behave in a particular fashion. Challenging this expectation was highly dishonorable. Therefore the virtue or honor of a Flemish woman living in the first half of the sixteenth century consisted of living up to the role society had dictated to her: obeying her husband, taking care of the children and the housekeeping, always in a subordinate position, all without questioning male prerogatives.

Notes

1. Bruges, Stadsarchief (hereafter SAB), MS Series 192 (*Verluydboek*), no. 1 fol. 59r (1510).
2. *. . . omme dat zoe zekeren goeden tyd gheghaen heift in mans habyte, contrarye der eerbaerhede van allen vrauwen* (SAB, MS Series 192, no. 1 fol. 59r).
3. Peter Schüster, *Das Frauenhaus: städtische Bordelle in Deutschland (1350–1600)* (Paderborn: Schöningh, 1992), p. 155.
4. Leah Lydia Otis, *Prostitution in Medieval Society: The History of an Urban Institution in Languedoc* (Chicago: University of Chicago Press, 1985), p. 108.
5. A survey and summary of this research tradition, with references to recent research, can be found in Peter Spierenburg, *De verbroken betovering. Mentaliteit en cultuur in preïndustrieel Europa* (Hilversum: Verloren, 1998), pp. 315–57.
6. Herman Pleij, *De sneeuwpoppen van 1511: literatuur en stadscultuur tussen middeleeuwen en moderne tijd* (Amsterdam: Meulenhoff, 1988), pp. 259–87 and 321–56; Pieter Spierenburg, *De verbroken betovering*, pp. 259–60 and 263–66; T. Brandenbarg, "De moeder- en maagschapcultus in de Nederlanden omstreeks 1500. De Annadevotie als symptoom van veranderde opvattingen over huwelijk en gezin" in *Vijf eeuwen gezinsleven. Liefde, huwelijk en opvoeding in Nederland*, ed. H. Peeters, L. Dresen-Coenders, and T. Brandenbarg (Nijmegen: uitgeverij SUN, 1988), pp. 100 and 103; and L. Dresen-Coenders, "De machtsbalans tussen man en vrouw in het vroeg-moderne gezin" also in *Vijf eeuwen gezinsleven*, pp. 67 and 81.

7. On the hierarchy within marriage, see Spierenburg, *De verbroken betovering*, pp. 263–66; on the birth of the modern housewife see Pleij, *De sneeuwpoppen*, pp. 278–87.

8. SAB, MS Series 192, no. 1 fol. 34r (1502).

9. . . .*in 't wilde gheloopen ende in overspele gheleift* (SAB, MS Series 192, no. 1 fol. 34r).

10. . . .*om haer quaet ende dommelic leven noch bet te vulbringhene ende ten fyne dat zoe daer inne niet bekent, berespt, noch ghecorrigiert en worde* (SAB, MS Series 192, no. 1 fol. 34r).

11. . . .*zodat men tot hueren vanghene anders niet gheweten en heift dan zoe een mans persoon was* (SAB, MS Series 192, no. 1 fol. 34r).

12. . . .*a cause qu'elle estoit mariee et se avance d'aler en guyse d'homme* (Brussels, Algemeen Rijksarchief (hereafter ARA), MS Auditor's Office no. 13783 fol. 47r).

13. SAB, MS Series 192, no. 1 fol. 59r.

14. Rudolf Dekker and Lotte van de Pol, *Vrouwen in mannenkleren. De geschiedenis van een tegendraadse traditie. Europa 1500–1800* (Amsterdam: Uitgeverij Wereldbibliotheek, 1989), p. 102; available in English as *The Tradition of Female Transvestism in Early Modern Europe* (London: Macmillan, 1989).

15. . . .*dat zoe zekeren goeden tyd gheghaen heift in mans habyte, contrarye der eerbaerhede van allen vrauwen ende dat zoe conversacie ghehad heift met diverschen ghesellen die hemlieden onderwonden hebben met stelene ende diverse dieften, daer toe zoe ghehulpich heift gheweist ende up zulc aes gheleift.* . .(SAB, MS Series 192, no. 1 fol. 59r.)

16. . . .*pour avoir eschavoté Glaudyne Malengin, pour ce qu'elle alloit en habyt d'homme* (Brussels, ARA, MS Auditor's Office no. 13783 fol. 94v).

17. . . .*a cause qu'elle estoit mariee et se avance d'aler en guyse d'homme* (Brussels, ARA, MS Auditor's Office no. 13783 fol. 94v).

18. L. Th. Maes, *Vijf eeuwen stedelijk strafrecht. Bijdrage tot de rechts- en cultuurgeschiedenis der Nederlanden* (Antwerp: De Sikkel, 1947), p. 375.

19. Within the historiographic tradition concerning the subject, there is some doubt with regard to terminology. The term "honor" is most frequently used (as is also the case in this chapter); however, some authors are wary of using this word and prefer the terms "honesty" or "virtue" instead. The insights concerning "honor" presented in this chapter are the tentative result of an initial exploration into a very extensive and complex field of research. Unfortunately, few studies exist taking a clear position on the role of honor in the assessment of sexual offences in Flanders.

20. *der allgemein menschlichen Ehre jedes Subjektes* (Martin Dinges, "Die Ehre als Thema der Stadtgeschichte. Eine Semantik im Übergang vom Ancien Régime zur Moderne," in *Verletzte Ehre: Ehrkonflikte in Gesellschaften des Mittelalters und der Frühen Neuzeit*, ed. Klaus Schreiner and Gerd Schwerhoff (Köln: Böhlau, 1995), p. 435).

21. Ibid., p. 423. Research into the concept of "honor" is mainly a German tradition, crossing from the fields of sociology and historical anthropology into history. With regard to this topic, the research of Martin Dinges is authoritative.

22. Martin Dinges, "Weiblichkeit in Männlichkeitsritualen? Zu weiblichen Taktiken im Ehrenhandel im Paris im 18. Jahrhundert," *Francia. Forschungen zur westeuropäischen Geschichte* 18 (1991), p. 86.

23. Das Negativsymbol 'Prostituierte' verweist damit bei der Beleidigung von Frauen keineswegs nur auf Sex. Vielmehr muß unter dieser Oberfläche die nun freigelegte ganze Vielfalt von Rollenerwartungen an Frauen mitbedacht werden, wenn die putain auftaucht. Daraus wird denn auch ersichtlich, wieso die Beleidigung als Prostituierte so universal Frauenrollen negativ kodieren kann (ibid., p. 89).

24. der Vielschichtigkeit des Prostitutionsvorwurfs als Symbol für die Verletzung gesellschaftlicher Tabus ("the multi-layeredness of the accusation of prostitution as a symbol of the injury to social taboos"), (ibid., p. 88). See also the contributions by M.-T. Leuker and H. Roodenburg in the theme issue of the *Volkskundig bulletin* 18 (1992): Annemieke Keunen and Herman Roodenburg, eds., *Schimpen en schelden. Eer en belediging in Nederland, ca. 1600–ca. 1850* (Amsterdam: Koninklijke Nederlandse akademie van wetenschappen. P. J. Meertens-instituut voor dialectologie, volkskunde en naamkunde, 1992), especially pp. 318 and 421.

25. Spierenburg, *Verbroken betovering*, p. 280.

26. Myriam Carlier, "Paternity in Late Medieval Flanders," in *Secretum Scriptorum. Liber alumnorum Walter Prevenier*, ed. Wim Blockmans, Marc Boone, and Thérèse de Hemptinne (Leuven/Apeldoorn: Garant, 1999), p. 257.

27. James Brundage also points out the increasing attention paid by the ecclesiastical courts to the phenomenon of transvestism during the sixteenth and seventeenth centuries (James A. Brundage, *Law, Sex, and Christian Society in Medieval Europe* (Chicago/London: The University of Chicago Press, 1987), p. 571).

28. Dekker en van de Pol, *Vrouwen in mannenkleren*, p. 14.

29. The *Verluydboek* list registered the confessions (verluyden) of the criminals and the sentences they received. They have been preserved from 1490 onward; the years 1490–1555 are being studied here. The *Civiele Sentencien* (civil sentences) contain the sentences in civil cases that were pronounced by the aldermen in solemn public session. We can make use of this type of source from 1490 onward. Earlier registers are preserved, but they have a different content.

30. . . .contrarye allen rechten ende naertelicke jeghens alle heerbaerhede ende jeghens de natuerlichede van elker moedre (SAB, MS Series 192, no. 1 fol. 54r (1510).

31. . . .naer rechte ende ooc van gods ende nature weghe alle moeders ghehouden zijn huerlieder uterste besten ende vermoghen te doene omme huerlieder kinderen ter eere ende ter duecht te bringhene zonder hemlieden quaet exemple te ghevene ofte te laten commene in scanden in eenegher manieren (SAB, MS Series 157, 1528–34 fol. 160r and 162r (1530)).

32. "Written law" can be defined as the sum of Roman and Canon Law. "Divine law" is constituted by God's commandments as found in the Bible. "Natural law" is very hard to define. The medieval tradition concerning the concept of natural law is diverse and ambiguous; whole books have been

written on the subject. In an attempt to define the concept to at least some degree, I would like to suggest the following: natural law consists of the guidelines for man's individual and social conduct, guidelines derived from nature, that is, the natural order of God's creation, and therefore applicable everywhere and to everyone. (Brundage, *Law, Sex, and Christian Society*, passim; Harold J. Johnson, ed., *The Medieval Tradition of Natural Law. Studies in Medieval Culture* 22, (Kalamazoo: Medieval Institute, 1987), pp. 1–2). We do not find a well-considered use of the concept of natural law in the sixteenth-century Brugeois judgments. In his treatise on criminal law Wielant used the concept without actually defining it. What the aldermen wanted to express was that universal rules had been violated, thus justifying harsh action. In other words, they used the concept of natural law to stress their arguments. Many thanks to Prof. Dr. Jos Monballyu for his help on this subject.

33. "According to the laws of God and nature, every man must render every honor and dignity to his father and mother" (. . .*hoe al eist zo dat van gods rechts ende natueren weghe elc mensche sculdich es ende behoort vadere ende moedere alle eere ende weerdichede te doene*) (SAB, MS Series 157, 1520–28 fol. 162r (1523)).

34. . . .*haer voorseide kyndt te anveerden, voedene ende onderhoudene, alzo een moedere van gods ende natueren weghe sculdich es ende behoort te doene* (SAB, MS Series 192, no. 1 fol. 200v (1528)).

35. . . .*zonder eeneghe moederlicke liefde te tooghene* (SAB, MS Series 192, no. 2 fol. 108v (1540)).

36. The husband's role as a father has only seldom been the subject of detailed study. Myriam Carlier offers a short survey of the literature on the subject in her article on "Paternity in Late Medieval Flanders," pp. 235–37.

37. . . .*heift huer lichame gheabandonneirt ende vleesschelicke conversatie ghenomen met elc diet an huer begheerde* (SAB, MS Series 192, no. 2 fol. 61v (1540)).

38. . . .*contrarie gods wet ende van nature* (SAB, MS Series 192, no. 2 fol. 61v).

39. . . .*heift zyn ghetraude wyf laten zitten in grooter armoede ende miserie met zes kinderen* (SAB, MS Series 192, no. 1 fol. 223v (1531)).

40. . . .*abandonnerende ende latende tzelve zijn ghetrauwet wijff alleene zitten in grooter aermoede ende ketivichede ende verteerende al dat hij wan ende ghecryghen conste metter voorseide andere vrauwe* (SAB, MS Series 157, 1528–34, fol. 161v (1530)).

41. . . .*zonder zyne huusvrauwe ende kinderen den cost ende nootdurst te connen ofte moghen winnen, also hij te vooren placht te doene* (SAG, MS Series 231bis, no. 1 fol 158r (1542)).

42. . . .*van al welcke jaerlicxsche winninghe ende proffyten hy, zijne huusvrauwe ende kinderen bijden voornomde myncke ghepriveert waeren nemaer leven moesten in groote miserie bijden aelmoesene vanden goede lieden* (SAG, MS Series 231bis, no. 1 fol 158r).

43. This does not mean that women did not participate in economic life; there is sufficient evidence to the contrary. However, there is also a consensus among historians that women "generally failed to achieve success in high-status jobs. . .Instead they were very numerous in underpaid or marginal

stages in manufacturing and trading processes." (Peter Stabel, "Women at the Market. Gender and Retail in the Towns of Late Medieval Flanders" in *Secretum Scriptorum. Liber alumnorum Walter Prevenier*, ed. Wim Blockmans, Marc Boone, and Thérèse de Hemptinne (Kessel-Lo, Louvain, Apeldoorn: Garant, 1999), p. 262; see also the literature cited there.)

44. Myriam Carlier, "Paternity in Late Medieval Flanders," pp. 245 and 250.

45. In order to ensure justice, the *schepenen* (aldermen), the representatives of the city, and the *baljuw* (bailiff), the representative of the count of Flanders, cooperated. The *schepenen* were the judges, the bailiff had to carry out their sentences. The *schepenen* wrote their sentences down in registers. The fines that were collected and the corporal and capital punishments that were carried out are recorded in the accounts of the bailiff.

46. SAG, MS Series 212 (1472–1537).

47. Studied for the years 1300–1555; especially interesting from ca. 1500 onward.

48. Ruth Mazo Karras, *Common Women: Prostitution and Sexuality in Medieval England* (New York: Oxford University Press, 1996), p. 44. See also Brundage, *Law, Sex, and Christian Society*, p. 519: "Several authorities maintained that when a woman committed adultery, her husband was at fault and should be punished as much or more than she was. . ."

49. Karras, *Common Women*, p. 44.

50. . . .*dat naer de costume deser stede een man in huwelicke zynde es heere van allen den meublen ende concquesten goede hem ende zijnder huusvrauwe toebehoorende,. . . volghende de voorseide usancie daerbij alle de zelve meublen ende cateylicke goedinghen zijn inde macht cohertie ende wille vanden zelven man* (SAG, MS Series 231bis, no. 1 fol. 138v (1542)). See also Marianne Danneel, "Gender and the Life Course in the Late Medieval Flemish Town" in *Secretum Scriptorum*, p. 231.

51. . . .*omme dat se ghelogiert ende ghedoeght heeft eenen man persoen te commene met eender jongher maeght die aldaer zijn vermueghen ende beste ghedaen heeft omme de selve maeght jeghens hueren danc ende wille vleesschelic te bekennene ende oec eenen ghehude vrauwe gheheerbercht die aldaer also bekent gheweest ende huere eere verloren heeft* (SAG, MS Series 212, fol. 171r. (1514)).

52. *Coline Sdonckers pour ce quelle avoit emmenee une josne pucelle pour le mectre au bourdeau* (ARA, MS Auditor's Office no. 14551 fol. 9r. (1492)).

53. Guy Dupont, *Maagdenverleidsters, hoeren en speculanten. Prostitutie in Brugge tijdens de Bourgondische periode (1385–1515)*.Vlaamse Historische Studies 10 (Bruges: Marc van de Wiele, 1996), p. 108.

54. Karras, *Common Women*, p. 44.

55. Results based on data from the bailiff's accounts (ARA, MS Auditor's Office no. 13783–784).

56. Cases mentioned in: Monique Vleeschouwers-van Melkebeek, *Computus sigilliferi curie Tornacensis 1429–1481* (Brussels: Koninklijke Academie van België, 1995), an edition of the fifteenth-century accounts of the ecclesiastical courts of Tournai that were preserved.

57. Carlier, "Paternity in Late Medieval Flanders," p. 240.

58. In the Ghent *Voorgeboden* (the town regulations), for instance, adultery is mentioned only in the vaguest of terms. Wielant, a fifteenth-century jurist who wrote down the prevailing law of his time, unwittingly stressed female adultery. Philips Wielant, *Corte instructie in materie criminele*, ed. Jos Monballyu (Brussels: Koninklijke Academie van België, 1995), pp. 215–219.

59. Joos de Damhouder, *Practycke ende handbouck in criminele zaeke*, ed. Jozef Dauwe and Jos Monballyu, Anastatic reprint of the edition of 1555 (Roeselare: Den Wijngaert, 1981).

60. Carlier, "Paternity in Late Medieval Flanders," p. 240.

61. *De cnape van Dordrecht* is a fourteenth-century fabliau, a short and funny story in verse. French and German versions also exist (*Le foteor* and *Bürgermeister und Königssohn*), but this version of the story probably is of Dutch origin. It has been recorded in the Brabant van Hulthem-manuscript (*ca. 1410*), however, and because the text is adaptable to many situations, it probably was also known in Flanders. (Dini Hogenelst, "Sproken in de stad: horen zien en zwijgen" and Fred Lodder, "Corrupte baljuws en overspelige echtgenotes. Over het beoogde publiek van drie boerden" in Herman Pleij et al., *Op belofte van profijt. Stadsliteratuur en burgermoraal in de Nederlandse letterkunde van de middeleeuwen*. Nederlandse literatuur en cultuur in de middeleeuwen IV (Amsterdam: Prometheus, 1991), pp. 166–83 and 217–27.

62. Freely adapted from the text edition in Ludo Jongen, *Van papen en hoeren, van ridders en boeren: tien middeleeuwse moppen* (Hilversum: Verloren, 1995), pp. 46–49. For the Middle Dutch version, see Bart Besamusca and Erwin Mantingh, "Vanden cnape van Dordrecht" in *Klein kapitaal uit het handschrift-Van Hulthem. Zeventien teksten uit Hs. Brussel, K.B., 15.589–623 uitgegeven en ingeleid door neerlandici, verbonden aan tien universiteiten in Nederland en België*. Medieval Studies and Sources 33 (Hilversum: Verloren, 1992), pp. 104–112.

63. "Hubrecht vander Eecke has admitted and confessed. . .that he has had sexual conversation with a married woman and that, for this, he was paid a pair of stockings, a pair of socks and about ten pence in coins. . ." (*Hubrecht vander Eecke heeft verkendt ende verleden. . .dat hy ten diverschen stonden vleeschelicke conversatie ghehadt heift met een ghehuwede vrauwe ende te dier causen van huer ontfaen ende te loone ghehadt een paer coussens, een paer halve coussens ende ontrent x stuvers in ghelde. . .*) (SAB, MS Series 192, no. 2 fol. 23v (1539)).

64. A.M.J. van Buuren, "Eer en schande in enkele laat-Middelnederlandse literaire teksten" and Maria-Theresia Leuker and Herman Roodenburg, "Overspel, eer en schande in de zeventiende eeuw" in *Soete minne en helsche boosheit: seksuele voorstellingen in Nederland 1300–1850*, ed. Gert Hekma and Herman Roodenburg (Nijmegen: SUN, 1988), pp. 41 and 74.

65. *De baeliu sprac: Doet mi ghene scande, des biddic u, in desen lande. XX pond salic u gheven, maer noit en gavic in mijn leven gelt dat mi dede soe wee.* (verses 151–55).

66. *De rechten permitteeren den man doot te slaene zonder mesdoen, den adulterin die hy vint met zyn wive. . .*(Wielant, *Corte instructie in materie criminele*, p. 216). Natalie Zemon Davis, *Fiction in the Archives. Pardon Tales and Their Tellers in Sixteenth-Century France* (Stanford: Stanford University Press, 1987), pp. 95–99, draws

attention to the fact that male murderers pleaded as an extenuating circumstance the fact that their wife's adultery caused the bloodshed; their honor could only be restored by killing the unfaithful wife and/or her lover.

67. Carlier, "Paternity in Late Medieval Flanders," p. 240.

68. Martin Dinges, "Ehre und Geschlecht in der Frühen Neuzeit," in *Ehrkonzepte in der Frühen Neuzeit. Identitäten und Abgrenzungen*, ed. Sibylle Backmann (Berlin: Academie Verlag, 1998), p. 133.

69. In Dutch the word *gehoornde* (cuckold) refers to the *hoorns* (horns) of a (male) goat, the only animal that allows other males to approach his mate (A.M.J. van Buuren, "Eer en schande," p. 62). On stage and in other visual representations, the cuckold is literally horned (see figure 3.4: representation of a *charivari*).

70. A.M.J. van Buuren, "Eer en schande," pp. 40–41.

71. . . .*latende haren ghetrauden man alleene zitten in grooter scande ende desolatie* (SAB, MS Series 157, 1520–28 fol. 157v (1523)).

72. . . .*latende zijn wijf alleene zitten in grooter aermoede ende miserie* (SAB, MS Series 157, 1520–28 fol. 163r (1523)).

73. . . .*hadde hem vervoordert up eenen avondt in de maendt van november lestleden te commen cloppende voor een goet poorters huus ambochtsman van deser stede, zegghende ende roupende overluut contrarie der waerheyt dat zyn wyf een duernaeyde hoere was, dat hij huer hadde ghezien ligghen, huer mesdraghende up een brugghe* (SAB, MS Series 157, 1528–34 fol. 209r (1531)).

74. M.T. Leuker, "Schelmen, hoeren, eerdieven en lastertongen. Smaad en belediging in zeventiende-eeuwse kluchten en blijspelen" in *Schimpen en Schelden*, ed. Annemieke Keunen and Herman Roodenburg, p. 318.

75. Brundage, *Law, Sex, and Christian Society*, p. 519.

76. Cf. Susan Dwyer Amussen, *An Ordered Society. Gender and Class in Early Modern England* (Oxford: Blackwell, 1988), p. 131.

77. *De damoiselle la femme de Pierre le Duutsche, laquelle fu calengie par ledit escoutette et ceulz de la loy, a cause que combien quelle estoit en estat de mariage et que par ce elle se devuoit bien et honnestement gouverner en sondit estat avec sondit mary; neantmoins au contraire, elle mena et vescu ung deshonneste et vylaine vie, et non obstandt que de ce furent faiz par les parens et amis des deux costés entre elle et sondit mary de quatre a cincq acors et paix entre eulz et lesquelz et chacun deulz elle promist de jamais faire ne mener telle vie comme paravant, elle neantmoins demoura persister en sadite vilaine vie. . .*(ARA, Auditor's Office, MS no. 13780 fol. 70v. (1476)).

78. Raoul Charles van Caenegem says that approximately 70 percent of all judicial cases were settled in this informal way (*Geschiedenis van het strafrecht in Vlaanderen van de XIe tot de XIVe eeuw* (Brussels: Koninklijke Vlaamse academie voor wetenschappen, letteren en schone kunsten van België, 1954), p. 322).

79. Anton Blok, "Eer en de fysieke persoon," *Tijdschrift voor sociale geschiedenis* 18 (1980), p. 216.

80. *Een vader die zynen zone slaet, [. . .] of een man zyn wyf, [. . .] die en injurieren niet, al eist ooc met weede of met wonde, evenverre dat zyt doen omme te castydene,*

te corigierne, of te bet te instrueerne of leerene, of obedient te makene (Wielant, *Practycke criminele*, p. 274). In Aardenbourg, a small prosperous city near Bruges, this right of correction was made more explicit: "A man may beat and wound his wife, cut her from bottom to top and warm his feet in her blood; he commits no crime if he sews her back together and if she survives" (*een man mach zyn wyf slaen ende steken, upsniden, splitten van beneden tote boven ende waermen zyn voeten in haer bloet, ende naeyse weder toe, zonder verbuerte jeghen den heere, up dat zoe levende blijft*). Quoted in John Gilissen, "La femme dans l'ancien droit belge," in *Recueils de la Société Jean Bodin pour l'histoire comparative des institutions* 12 (Brussels: 1962), pp. 290–91.

81. Amussen notes that the wife who beat her husband and the wife who was unfaithful, were closely connected in popular consciousness (*An Ordered Society*, p. 118).

82. Gerard Rooijakkers, "Ten geleide. Charivaresk gedrag als maatschappelijk ritueel," in *Charivari in de Nederlanden. Rituele sancties op deviant gedrag*, ed. Gerard Rooijakkers and Tiny Romme, *Volkskundig bulletin* 15 (1989), p. 253.

83. With many thanks to Katja Scheel (KULeuven, Department of German Literature) for this information. These plays were carnival comedies, performed on the evening before Lent; in them, the world was turned upside down in order to reinforce social values.

84. Dinges, "Ehre und Geschlecht," p. 132: "Accordingly, one may assume that the wish to harm her male companion often was the only reason for assaulting a woman's sexual honour. Having been cuckolded, such a man would lose his honour, since he was apparently unable to satisfy his own wife" (*Dementsprechend kann man davon ausgehen, daß oft die Sexualehre von Frauen nur angegriffen wurde, um dadurch den mit ihr lebenden Mann zu treffen. Der sollte als Hahnrei seine Ehre verlieren, weil er angeblich die eigene Frau nicht befriedigen konnte*).

85. Brundage, *Law, Sex, and Christian Society*, p. 386.

86. Dinges, "Ehre und Geschlecht," p. 113; B. Ann Tlusty, "Crossing Gender Boundaries: Women as Drunkards in Early Modern Augsburg" in *Ehrkonzepte in der Frühen Neuzeit*, ed. Backmann et al., p. 197.

CHAPTER 4

WOMEN'S INHERITANCE AND TESTAMENTARY PRACTICES IN LATE FOURTEENTH- AND EARLY FIFTEENTH-CENTURY VENICE AND GHENT

Linda Guzzetti

Introduction

This chapter compares the social and legal conditions of women in Ghent and Venice in the late fourteenth and early fifteenth century, with regard to property rights, inheritance rules, property relationships between the spouses, and testamentary dispositions. Testaments encode many of these issues, and an examination of testamentary practice in the two cities provides valuable information both on these legal instruments and on women's social and legal conditions.[1]

Historians have used comparisons for many purposes, among others to concretize general concepts or to explain the historicity of phenomena that may appear natural from a local point of view. For comparisons they have often chosen phenomena that are similar to each other and representative in their category.[2] In particular, comparisons of cities have a tradition both in medieval and in modern history.[3]

Any comparative work involving Venice is encumbered by the claim of this city to be a special case. The city's fame, out of which the Venetian myth developed, dates already from the Middle Ages and was kept alive by the scholars after the fall of the Republic. The frequent comparison of Venice with Florence can but fortify the uniqueness of Venice. On the one hand, after having been common in political and economical history in previous decades, such comparisons are now ongoing in gender studies too.[4] On the

other hand, there exist few studies comparing Venice with any city outside
of Italy, particularly for the period of the late Middle Ages.[5]

In the present study I challenge the idea of the atypicality of the legal
condition of Venetian women and of their use of testaments. Therefore it is
necessary to compare Venice with other contemporary European cities.
Ghent provides a suitable option, although not the only possible one: like
Venice, it was a large, commercial, industrial city and a supraregional center.

Such a comparison raises the question whether Roman law was less
favorable for the social and personal possibilities of women than were customary laws of the regions of oral law.[6] Although generally this question is
answered positively, it is nonetheless advisable to make distinctions within
each particular legal matter and, more importantly, within the framework
of the different developments of Roman law itself. As we shall see, some
legal issues, which were of great meaning for women, such as the restitution of the dowry upon their husbands' death, or the inheritance claims of
daughters, were regulated differently in the Justinianian codification, in the
ius commune and in the Venetian *ius proprium*.[7] At the same time, in Flanders
the provisions of the *keuren* varied considerably from one city to the other,
for instance concerning the legal capacity of married women.

The testamentary provisions for the salvation of one's soul were strik-
ingly similar, which confirms the homogeneity of religious praxis at the
end of the Middle Ages. One major distinction between the two cities in
testamentary praxis, however, was the amount of the estate any testator
could dispose of. In Ghent this amount was strictly limited. In Venice testamentary freedom was much greater. In both cities women could make
wills without permission of their spouse, father, or other male relative. For
modern readers it is fascinating to notice how women in that time made
use of the possibilities that different law systems offered—or left open—to
them. This does not mean that they had a conscious will to take independent decisions as women. They just followed the line of least resistance and
found socially accepted spaces in which to act.

Flanders and Italy: Legal Systems

Comparing the situations of women north and south of the Alps has
become a common reference scheme.[8] In particular, scholars have been
attracted by the differences and similarities between northern Italy and
Flanders—two of the most developed commercial and industrial areas
in fourteenth-century Europe. Papers given at a congress held in Ghent in
January 2000, for example, focused on comparing households in Italy and in
northwestern Europe, especially in Flanders, northern France, and England.[9]
A central issue of this congress was whether family structures may explain

some significant differences concerning the social conditions of women in these two areas. It was emphasized that patrilineality was the main feature of Italian families from the upper social groups in the late Middle Ages and early modern times. Families were understood as diachronic lines of men, in which women had no specific place, although they were necessary to produce the next generation. This was not, however, the structure of the families of the Italian working class, both artisans and laborers; for them, the conjugal family was the center of consumption and of production. The succession of generations was not, in fact, stressed because there was little wealth to transmit. On the contrary, in Flanders, in all social groups the conjugal family had a central place in the social organization and the transmission of property. Each child had inheritance rights from both father and mother, and, to a great extent, sons and daughters were treated equally. Wives, being co-proprietors of the marital fund, had much say in family matters. But in Flanders the patrilinear elements in the family structure grew in importance, at least among the elite, during the late Middle Ages.[10]

In Italian cities, laws and customs had developed out of the Roman law of the late empire to form *iura propria* ("laws peculiar to a particular place"). Most local laws strongly diverged from the Justinianian codification in issues like dowry or inheritance rights of women. This was not the case in Venice, which remained close to it.[11] Since the twelfth century, with the renaissance of Roman law, university-trained jurists attempted to harmonize local laws with the Roman law as it had been codified by Justinian. They built a legal system, called *ius commune*, based on treatises and commentaries and on legal opinions solicited by city courts. In many Italian cities, but not in Venice, the *ius commune* was accepted as a complement for the matters in which *ius proprium* was insufficient.[12]

In Flanders, customary law was of German origin, and the influence of Roman private law was not significant before the sixteenth century.[13] The *keuren* of most cities were written down only in the sixteenth or seventeenth century. For example, the homologated text of the *keure* of Ghent is from 1563, a relatively early date.[14] In Ghent, as in other towns, there exists also a version issued during the preparation of the homologated text, known under the name of *Cahier primitif.* Even if the texts of the *keuren* are late, the acts testifying of their use and the charters issued by the counts and countesses of Flanders or by the local administrations demonstrate that the provisions had been valid in the previous centuries.

Both Venice and Ghent were self-governing, although Ghent was technically under the rule of the count of Flanders, while Venice was an independent city-state. In the late Middle Ages women were mostly excluded from the places where political decisions were made, first of all from the councils—the typical ruling organisms of self-governing cities—but a woman could be countess, duchess, or empress. This had happened in Flanders almost continuously during the thirteenth century.[15] This fact has considerable significance for women's social possibilities. As Ellen Kittell has shown, women, both within and without the *familia* of the countess, occasionally held administrative places in the thirteenth century and even in the fourteenth.[16] Nothing similar occurred in Venice.

Women's Property Rights

In both cities women controlled a part of the existing wealth, which, of course, was a prerequisite for making testaments. Each city, however, had its own property system. As was typical of the Mediterranean area, the largest proportion of the estate of married and widowed women in Venice consisted of their dowries. According to the dowry system, women could not dispose of their dotal assets during marriage, that is, they were prohibited from investing, alienating, giving, or exchanging them.[17] These goods were said to have the purpose of providing for the necessities of the household (*providere ad onera matrimonii*) and for those of the widow after the husband's death. Husbands had no need of their wives' consent and could dispose of the dowry as they liked, but they were obliged to restore it at the end of marriage.[18]

The *ius commune*, like the Venetian statutes and those of virtually all Italian cities, ordained that widowed women were entitled to reacquire their dowries completely upon the deaths of their husbands.[19] But Venetian law had dotal provisions differing from those of most other Italian cities in the cases where the wife predeceased the husband. According to Venetian law, the legal heirs of married women inherited all their dotal and non-dotal assets. In contrast, most Italian local laws asserted that the husbands could claim the whole dowry of his predeceased wife or at least part of it.[20]

The inheritance claims of women in Venice also differed from those in other Italian cities. In Venice, daughters inherited from their deceased mothers equally with sons.[21] Daughters were also the heirs of their fathers, where these had no sons; in most Italian cities the preferred heirs were males from the kin of the deceased. In Venice, the daughters of men who died leaving both sons and daughters were entitled to receive a dowry from the estate of their fathers, if they had not yet received any, although the sons received the bulk of the estate. This last provision meant that in Venice, as generally in the areas of the dowry system, the dowry had become the only part of their father's estate that daughters were entitled to inherit, what jurists called *exclusio propter dotem*.[22]

The local laws of Italian cities had changed from the Justinianian code, which provided for the equality of inheritance rights for sons and daughters.[23] In Venice the *exclusio propter dotem* was attenuated, because daughters were heirs of the mothers in any case and of the fathers if there were no sons. Moreover, bequests from fathers to daughters who had already received a dowry were very common.[24] Under favorable circumstances, then, Venetian law allowed some women to gain considerable wealth.[25]

In the late Middle Ages Venetian women—either married or unmarried—needed no men to confirm their legal acts. As we have seen, women could not dispose of their dowries while married. But, even being married, they could still dispose of non-dotal assets: "If a woman under the authority of her husband (i.e. a married woman) made any legal act on the basis of her dowry, this has no value. . .But she can pledge and alienate all other goods she owns, also without the consent of her husband, as she likes."[26] If they did so, they acted on their own, unlike in other Italian cities, such as Florence, where guardians, called *mundualdi*, oversaw women's legal acts.[27] When making testaments Venetian women, even if married, could dispose of their whole estate. In the later period of the Venetian republic, jurists explained this provision, unusual in the dowry system, by the fact that the testament would go into execution after the end of marriage when the wife was no longer under the power of the husband.[28]

The almost complete equality of inheritance claims of all children, independently of sex and marital status, so typical in Flemish *keuren*, applied also in Ghent. A difference was made only between legitimate and illegitimate children.[29] The structure of marriage property in Ghent was characterized by the existence of a common marital fund.[30] According to the *keure* of Ghent, all movable goods taken by the spouses into the marriage, together with the goods acquired or inherited during marriage, constituted their common fund, which was managed by the husband.[31]

The provision for a common spouses' fund was always present in the Flemish *keuren*, but the forms of its administration were different. For example, the *keure* of Bruges presented an almost symmetrical condition: the spouses could not dispose of the common fund *deen zonder dandere, ende ghesaemder handt* ("the one without the other, and without common agreement"). But even in Bruges the symmetry was not exact, as the next paragraph prohibited wives—with the exception of tradeswomen—from making contracts or debts without the consent of their husbands. The reverse—that is, the consent of wives for husbands willing to make debts—did not appear.[32] Movable goods, which were put in the common fund, generally included real estate, and the *keuren* defined which goods were considered movable. In Ghent, houses in town, but not the ground, belonged to this category.[33] The immovable and fiefs did not become part of the common marriage fund, but remained property of each spouse and were called *propres*.

The *keure* of Ghent provided that the husband had no need for his wife's consent when he wished to alienate goods belonging to the marital fund.[34] All legal acts of married women, however, had to be confirmed by the husband's consent,[35] which was usually manifested through the presence of both of them at the aldermen's court. Therefore, married women in Ghent did not take part in the decisions concerning the common goods during marriage, in spite of being coproprietor of the marital fund and heir of half. Nonetheless, while husbands were permitted to administer their wives' own goods, they were prohibited from alienating them without their wives' express consent. The *keure* mentioned that in the past it had happened that husbands had disposed of their wives' own goods as they liked and prohibited it for the future.[36]

In Ghent's *keure* the emphasis changed according to the articles. On the one hand, in the second article of the section dealing with spouses, married women were said to be "in the power of their husbands" (*in de macht van huerlieder mans*).[37] On the other hand, the third article in the same section states that husband and wife, through marriage, each enjoyed a joint and legal (*ghemeene ende gherecht*) right in half of the movable assets of the other as well in the immovables acquired during marriage. An article in the *Cahier primitif* provided that the goods inherited during marriage could be sold by the spouses in common agreement (*by huerlieder beede consente*).[38] Therefore in this case, the Ghent's *keure* expected the selling or changing of property to happen by consent of both spouses. Nonetheless the homologated version no longer mentioned the mutual agreement. It simply stated that property entering the common fund through exchange took on the same legal nature as the one that had been exchanged for it. The dropping of the mention of the common agreement was probably due to the fact that the legal nature of the property was at stake here.[39]

The legal capacity of Ghent's married women was further augmented by the fact that wives could apply in court for permission to act on their own, if their husbands did not defend their interests against third parties.[40] Finally, the *keure* of Ghent provided that wives did not need permission of their husbands to draw up both last wills and *post obit* donations.[41]

Marianne Danneel examines the subordination of married women in Ghent with regard to the decisions of their husbands in the administration of common goods.[42] Danneel stresses that the fact that husbands alienated even their wives' own goods without their permission was particularly dramatic when husbands were in debt. Furthermore, as wives were not permitted to prosecute their husbands in court except for marital separation, they could not defend themselves legally against such encroachments. Through this provision Danneel explains the absence of court acts regarding the misuse of the wives' estate.

Usually, in the registers of the *scepenen van ghedeele* (one of the two courts of aldermen of the city), married women were often mentioned as accompanied by their "legal husbands and tutors" (*haren wetteliken man ende vocht*). But we also find cases in which a man appeared in court with his wife without such a formula, as it was the case for Jacop Wiericke with Jueren Coolmans, when they acknowledged a general receipt to Jacop's brother.[43] Since in some acts no indication of the marital status of the women was given, it is possible that some of them were in fact married.

Jonfrou Kateline represents an example of a married woman accompanied in court by her husband. She and her son, Pieter Boudin the younger, appeared on October 5, 1392 in front of the aldermen to conclude a dispute by mutual agreement and in accord with a previous sentence of the aldermen.[44] *Jonfrou* Kateline, who was the widow of Pieter Boudin, was accompanied by Cornelis van Heethoute, named as her husband and tutor. Her inheritance from her former husband would become part of the new couple's marital fund, administered by her new husband.

Acts like this show that married women in Ghent were limited in their legal capacity to the advantage of their husbands, but Danneel's judgment, that Gentnaar wives were legally incapable (*rechtsonbekwam*), seems to me too absolute[45] because their legal limitations depended on the kind of property and the nature of its possession, and they all ended with the end of marriage. I argue that elements both of subordination and of equality characterized the legal status of Gentnaar married women, and that through these elements of subordination their legal situation was made similar to that of married women living in areas of a dowry system.

In some acts, the aldermen specified that a woman in Ghent was "her own tutor" (*haers selves wiif siinde*) a formula similar to that used for men (*siin selves man siinde*), when she came of age and was permitted to govern herself and her estate. For example the formula *haer selves wiif siinde* was used in 1401 for Jehane van Daer when the aldermen declared her able to leave the tutelage of her mother and that of a man from her father's kin.[46] Since women could leave tutelage also through marriage, aldermen made such declarations ending the tutelage of orphan children (*uutvochdei*) more often for men than for women.[47] Occasionally this formula was used also in other acts, for instance for Marie sDrayers, a widow, who appeared in the aldermen's court because of the inheritance of her brother.[48]

Venetian and Gentnaar legal provisions completely diverged from each other with regard to the inheritance claims of the surviving spouse. In Flanders the conjugal family was the unit of inheritance transmission. According to Ghent's *keure* the surviving spouse was heir to half the marital fund, to be divided with the legal heirs of the dead spouse, who could be common children, children from previous marriages, or kin of the dead spouse. Furthermore, the surviving spouse had the use or the income both from the half of the movable goods on which the heirs had the property and from the half of the *propres* of the deceased.[49] Over the course of the late Middle Ages—at least among the well off—practice changed the *keure* to the disadvantage of the surviving spouse. Since the fifteenth century, many spouses agreed in their marriage contracts that the widow would receive only a fixed amount, called conventional dower, from the part of the estate of the deceased husband that she did not inherit. If such a contract did not exist, she would receive the half of the whole income, called therefore customary dower.[50] Moreover, at the end of the Middle Ages also in Flanders, the dowry began to be substituted for the rights a wife had in the common fund, but only in the upper echelons of society. Thereafter, the dowry limited the coproprietorial rights of wives.[51]

If a Venetian died intestate, her or his children were automatically the legal heirs. If there were no children, the father or other members of the deceased's kin inherited. Without testament, Venetian spouses did not inherit from each other at all.[52] Some Italian statutes even forbade husbands to leave bequests to their wives or limited their amount.[53] In Venice, however, there were no such limitations, and Venetian husbands' wills were often generous to their wives as were some wives to their husbands.[54] During marriage presents between spouses were not permitted. If the husband had given something to his wife, its value was deducted from the amount the widow was entitled to receive by the dowry restitution.[55] Thus, for spouses, a testament was the only instrument to transfer any property to each other. The prohibition of reciprocal presents between the spouses was common in the Italian cities, while in Flanders this point was regulated differently from city to city.[56] In Ghent, for example, spouses could not make presents to each other during marriage.[57] These provisions were intended to prevent spouses from deviating from the *keure* or from their contracts in the course of marriage, because it was feared that such changes, perhaps done under the influence of mutual love, would disadvantage their kin.

Provisions for One's Death: Testaments and Donations

For the past twenty years, testaments have been used to study the late Middle Ages. Although testamentary provisions concerned only those aspects of people's lives connected with their estates and with the salvation of their souls, scholars of social and religious history have been able to examine them as expressions of mentalities.[58] They have also been studied as examples of the choices single persons could make, for they allowed testators to express one's wishes and to act in the first person. Wills gave the testator the chance to provide for the moment of death and the time afterward: *den onsekere tiit des dooit te vorsiene met testamentarische ordinanche*, as it was expressed in many of Ghent's testaments.[59] A basic theme of the *arengae*[60] in medieval testaments concerned both the insecurity of the moment of death and the surety of its coming, expressed with the Latin formula: *nihil certius quam mors nihil incertius quam hora mortis* ("nothing is surer than death and nothing is less sure than the time of death"). This formula was repeated both in Ghent and in Venice, in Latin and in the vernacular.[61] Furthermore, wills gave testators the opportunity to act as a part of the community of the living and of the dead.[62] Testators provided for Masses for their own souls after death and for those of dead relatives. The living, receiving the testators' worldly goods, were expected to keep their remembrance on earth.

In Ghent and Venice testaments and other provisions in the case of death were subject to different rules. Testaments were unknown in Flanders before the thirteenth century. They came into use for religious purposes, and were considered valid without many of the formal requirements of Roman law and without the institution of heirs.[63] Flemish *keuren* restricted the possibility of disposing of one's estate to a greater degree than did Roman law.[64] In Ghent, testators could not dispose of more than one-third of the estate. Second, one could not appoint as heir just anyone, but only those allowed by customs governing inheritance. One could also not make provisions that advantaged one heir and disadvantaged others.[65] Third, by their testaments married people could not interfere with the legal claims of their spouses deriving both from the *keure* and from the marriage contracts, unless the other spouse agreed.[66]

In spite of these limitations, testaments, as well as *post obit* donations, became popular in Flanders at the end of the Middle Ages, not only because of their religious aim, but also because they permitted testators to bequeath goods to different relatives, friends, servants, and—quite important—to natural children.[67] Since in Flanders nobody was "bastard by the mother's side," women had no need to provide separately for their own illegitimate children, but they could make wills for other illegitimate relatives, like grandchildren, nieces, or nephews.[68] Mergriete van Husse, for instance, made a donation of £6 *grossi tornenses* to each of her brother's two natural children, stating that the bequest was to go to the surviving child if one of them died without heirs.[69] Also common in Flanders were bequests to underage siblings with the proviso—derived from the *pupillaris substitutio* of Roman law—that the legacy would go to the surviving beneficiary.

Under Roman law, common throughout Italy, testators enjoyed great liberty and could dispose of almost their whole estate. This provision was valid also in the Venetian law system. It had only the limitation that—except in the case of disinheritance—the heirs had a legal claim to the *particula*, corresponding to one-third of what they would have received without testament, and similar to the *legitima portio* in Roman law.[70] Stanley Chojnacki has emphasized the importance of making a testament for

Venetian women.[71] He shows that noble women were able to influence their family affairs; since they could change their last wills as long as they lived, they had an effective means of pressure at their disposal. Married women from Ghent could not make the same use of the testament, as they were limited by the one-third clause. In Venice, there were no limitations on the part of their estates women could dispose of by testament, although such limitations on women's testamentary rights were common elsewhere in Italy.[72] Widowed women in both cities had less need to employ such instruments of influence since they could decide how to dispose of their assets during their lifetimes.

Married women in Ghent needed no permission from their husbands to make their last will. For instance, Kerstine Kollins, designated as Pieters van Verneberghe *wettelike wiif* (legal wife), made a donation to the illegitimate son of her brother without the consent of her husband.[73] Mergrit Ghelliaerts, wife of Jans van Reelft, similarly made a donation to the daughter of her sister.[74] Sometimes, Gentnaar husbands gave their wives the consent for a testament or donation, probably because as coproprietor of the marital fund they had to agree to the use of those goods in the wives' last wills. For instance, Kateline van Lucuene made gifts to two nephews who were friars, with the permission both of her husband and of the person named as her heir, who, having the same family name as herself and her two nephews, probably was another member of her kin.[75] The testament of Kateline van Wansvelde was made with the permission of her husband, Lievin Backer, who was also one of her testamentary executors.[76] Her testament consisted only of pious legacies for the amount of about £10 *grossi tornenses*. If she had to use a part of the marital fund to achieve this sum, her husband had to agree, and his role as executor was congruent with the use of common goods for her soul. Aliise Viisen too had the permission of her husband, and in her testament appears the formula that the legacies had to be distributed without expenses or damage to her husband (*sonder den cost of last van Philip haren man*).[77] This kind of permission derives from the *laudatio parentum* (assent of the kinsmen) through which, in the early Middle Ages, the relatives of a person living under German law accepted the alienation—through testament or otherwise—of the real estate on which they had inheritance claims.[78]

A set of differences between the two cities concerned the place where and circumstances under which testaments were made and became legally valid.[79] Fourteenth-century Venetian testaments, like those in twelfth- and thirteenth-century Genoa, were usually authenticated by a notary. While in earlier times a testament was almost always dictated to him (*noncupativum testamentum*), in the fourteenth century it also became common to write a preliminary version on a piece of paper (*cedula*) and to hand it to the notary (*holographicum testamentum*).[80] In both cases the testament was issued essentially in private and made public through the notary. The testator had no need to appear publicly. Testators in Ghent, on the other hand, generally appeared in front of the council of the aldermen when they wanted to make their last will.[81] Attending a meeting of the aldermen was more public than either calling a notary to one's home or visiting him, often in the same parish where one lived.[82] In Ghent the aldermen occasionally remarked that a testator had previously written a note, but even in this case she or he went to the town council. For example, Aechte Sletsaerd (Slatsaerd) appeared on two different days in front of the aldermen and each time brought them one *cedule*, the first containing a donation and the second her last will. Both were reported "word by word" in the register of the aldermen.[83] Thus speaking in front of the aldermen certified the authenticity of a testament in Ghent. In Venice the first version—spoken or written—had a preliminary character, and only the final version, which the notary wrote down in his register after the death of the testator, was authentic.[84]

In Ghent it was also common to provide for *post obit* donations (*ghiften, donationes propter mortem*). In Roman law the difference between a testament and a gift was significant, but in Flanders it was less neat.[85] Flemish testaments often comprised lists of donations, whereas a gift concerned a single donation. Both testaments and gifts had to be distributed before the legal heirs took possession of the estate. Whereas testaments were always revocable, gifts mostly were not. Whereas most testaments entailed the use of executors, the granting of *post obit* gifts did not. Therefore it must have been a duty of the heirs to give them to the beneficiaries. Gifts almost always consisted of cash or money rents, as did many testamentary bequests, although these could also consist of other valuable objects such as cloth.

In Ghent gifts and testaments were probably considered as similar legal instruments. The aldermen joined both terms in the same formula, together with the more general expression "last will," when they wrote that the testator has given and gives *in gherechter ghiften in quitinghen van haren ziele in vuermen van testamente ende utersten wille*.[86] For example, Mergriete Wedenghen's testament, in which this formula was used, consisted of a list of gifts to religious institutions and persons and included no appointment of executors.[87] The aldermen introduced the list of gifts of Machtilt van den Eerenthoutte with the formula "in form of testament and last will such gifts as here next is declared."[88] Else van Velseke made a *post obit* donation of three pounds of *grossi tornenses* to the Augustinian brother Gillisse van Hulst for the purpose of providing for her soul.[89] To provide for the salvation of one's soul through pious legacies was the aim of these three last instruments, and probably it did not make much difference which legal form—testament, last will, donation—was chosen.

In both cities testators had to be of healthy mind (*sana mente*), as Roman law required, but the attitudes toward physical health were different.[90] AlthoughVenetian notaries recorded the physical condition of testators, this had no influence on the validity of their testaments. In the countries of written law it had been usual, at the time of the renaissance of the testament in the high Middle Ages, to make it on the deathbed, as it was seen as a part of the preparation for death together with confession of the sins and the last communion. Only in the late Middle Ages did making testaments while still in good health become popular.

In Flanders the opposite was the case. Flemish *keuren* were suspicious of deathbed wills, because they believed that the fear of death could result in irrational decisions. Some Flemish *keuren* specified that a valid testament required a testator to be able to walk or to ride as far as the church or the center of the town.[91] Most fourteenth- and early fifteenth-century testaments from Ghent specified that the testator could stand and walk (*staende, ghaende*). But eventually practices changed; at the beginning of the fifteenth century, some testatrices had two or three aldermen dispatched to their homes to hear their wills and report them to the aldermanic assembly.[92] In these testaments the formula that they could stand and walk did not appear. Although it was not noted that they were ill, this could have been the case. There were also other possibilities. Lisbette Ghiselbrecht, for example, called two "hereditary men" in front of whom she made her testament, and about a month later when they reported it to the aldermen, they did not mention her state of health.[93]

Who Made Testaments

In both Venice and Ghent, women and men drew up wills. In Venice, the presence of a large number of notaries in the city who drew up all private acts helped the diffusion of testaments throughout all levels of society.[94] In Ghent, on the other hand, testaments were common only among the well-to-do.[95] Moreover, in Ghent, women made their last wills less often than men, although for the period studied here this cannot be confirmed by precise figures. For the second half of the fifteenth century, Vincent Goussey counted twenty-three testaments of men, sixteen of women, and four of couples of spouses in the archival section *staten van goed*. He does not give any figures for *post obit* donations.[96] In fourteenth-century Venice women made testaments more often than men, and more women made several testaments in the course of their lives.[97] If they drew up their first will when pregnant and did not die in childbirth, they often remade the testament when the composition of their families changed.

Unfortunately we cannot compare the marital status of theVenetian and Gentnaar testatrices, because of the way women were denominated in the acts of the two cities. Venetian women were most commonly identified in the records by their first names, followed by some specification. The most usual of these was their marital status, that is wife or widow, and the name of the husband. On this basis I have calculated that about 55 percent of the testatrices were married, 35 percent were widows, and the remaining number were probably unmarried.[98] Obviously, these data do not correspond to the whole society, but they do show that in Venice married women too made use of their legal rights. These figures are significant when compared with those of other cities in which married women had a limited testamentary disposition of their goods. For example, in Florence only 10 percent of the testatrices were married.[99]

The records from Ghent often denote women merely by their first and second names, in other words, without direct reference to any husband, living or dead. When in the course of the act it was specified with whom the woman in question was married or when wife and husband made an act together, we notice that spouses often used different family names.

Testamentary Executors

Testamentary executors did not exist in antiquity, but in the Middle Ages they became important for they were charged with holding the testator's estate and dividing it among the beneficiaries. While in Ghent they had to distribute no more than one-third of the estate, in Venice the executors took possession of a testator's whole estate, and the universal heirs as well as all the other beneficiaries would receive their share from them.

An important duty of the executors was to provide for testators' souls through pious legacies. Therefore executors were also called *elemosinarii*, distributors of charities. Most executors of women's testaments in Ghent were priests, while priests were uncommon in Venice as testamentary executors. They comprised, in the last quarter of the fourteenth century, only 2.7 percent of all executors of women's testaments.[100] In both Ghent and Venice executors were rarely members of the religious orders. In Venice, they were prohibited from doing so, although in other parts of Italy they were among the most commonly chosen.[101]

Indeed, in the fourteenth century 40–45 percent of the executors of Venetian testators were women.[102] Women were not only executors almost as frequently as men, but they were also often in charge of pious legacies. Testators who trusted the bequests for their souls to one or more specific persons inside the wider group of their executors (*commissaria*), mostly chose women.[103]

Female executors were the exception in Ghent. There does not appear to have been a legal reason for this exclusion, for the *keure* of the city set no gender limitations. Instead, the lack of female executors may well have been connected to testamentary goals for the salvation of the soul. In other words, since women did not administer sacraments, they appeared to have been unsuitable as executors. Some testators did, however, appoint women to be their executors. For instance, Lisbette Sriike chose as executors not only a priest and another man, but also two women: Kateline Stoermaers and Mergriet Boels, who was the mistress of Hoeyen, one of the beguinages of Ghent.[104] Mergriet Boels was undoubtedly chosen because of her position, as the testatrix left several bequests to this beguinage and to its hospital. Concerning the other executrix, we learn only that she was the beneficiary of two silver spoons, besides a cup weighing a mark silver (*zelverinen scalen 1 marc weghende*) that was given to each executor.[105]

Remembering Friends, Relatives, and Servants

Generally, testaments do not reveal the dimensions of each testator's estate, but Venetian testaments give more hints than do the wills of Ghent. Moreover, since legal heirs were not mentioned in testaments in Ghent, we often do not know if a testator had children or not. On the contrary it was unusual for a Venetian testator not to mention his or her children, if he or she had any.

Some Venetian testators in the fourteenth century made no pious legacies, instead using the testament primarily as a secular instrument.[106] In Ghent, this was not the case, although there were testaments like that of Aeghte van den Berghen, in which the central issue was providing legacies to various people. She made bequests to eleven persons, apparently none of whom was related to her, while she made only four pious legacies.[107]

According to Roman law, the appointment of heirs was the main purpose of the testament. Heirs received all that was not distributed to the beneficiaries of legacies, which was expected to be the bulk of the estate. In Venetian testaments we almost always find the final formula outlining the disposal of the *residuum*, all goods that had not been disposed of in the testament. But in some testaments of women the destination of the *residuum* was evidently a secondary issue, and the *residuum* itself just a portion of the estate. Such testatrices distributed large bequests to their children and next of kin, and designated what was left for the salvation of their souls.

The *keure* of Ghent prohibited bequests to heirs. Each person could be either beneficiary or heir, but not both.[108] Therefore, children were seldom beneficiaries either of their mothers' testaments or of their *post obit* gifts. But through a suitable gift it was possible to exclude a child from inheritance. This occurred if a child was a friar or a nun and therefore not permitted to be an heir, but able to receive legacies, such as life rents.[109] Lisbette van Huusse left her daughter Soetine van Andwerpen, nun in the Gasthuus, a life rent of

£1 *grossi tornenses* per year, with the condition that she would receive no goods by the division of her estate.[110] But the same action could also be taken for children who did not live in a convent. For instance Lisbette van de Moure ende van der Coudeberg, a rich noble woman, bequeathed precious objects to one daughter, *vrouwe* van Neufuille, and real property to another daughter, Katerine *vrouwe* van Oosterhout; the latter was prohibited from taking part in the division of the estate of the testatrix.[111]

In Ghent, many testators left legacies to nieces, nephews, and grandchildren, who would have not been heirs if there were children. Even if the testator had died without issue, such relatives were second behind the parents and siblings of the testator. But as beneficiaries we find also other relatives; Marie Damdt, for instance, left £2 *grossi* to her mother.[112]

Some of the nieces, nephews, and grandchildren who inherited may have been young adults who would need the gifts to set up a new household. These donations came to function in the same way as Venetian bequests of funds for dowries did. But differences are also evident. Recipients in Ghent were women and men who would bring such bequests to a common marital fund, while the Venetian recipients of contributions to their dowries were always women who would give their entire dowries to their husbands. Moreover, since the thirteenth century (south of the Alps) a dowry had become a necessary condition for women to marry, so that dowry bequests to needy women—related and unrelated—were one of the most popular pious legacies. In Flanders, with no such requirement, legacies for marriages were not considered pious legacies.

For young beneficiaries of legacies or donations, expressions like *kint, kinde*, or diminutives of the first names were used. For instance *Adekine van Pollaer Lysbeten vorseid broeder dochter* ("Adekine van Pollaer, daughter of the brother of the mentioned Lysbeten"), who received a gift from the spouses Jhan Samoens Scheppere and Lysbette van Pollaer, was probably a child.[113] But other Gentnaar nieces and nephews who received bequests were adults from whom the testatrices expected help in their old age. Amelberghe van Brambrueghe gave the full property of all the present and future goods for the rest of her life to her niece Katelinen van Brambrueghe and her husband Mases Wouters. In exchange Amelberghe would receive a full assistance until her death.[114]

In late fourteenth-century Venice, beneficiaries of legacies for dowries included relatives and nonrelatives. Among relatives, daughters constituted more than half, and the rest consisted of nieces, granddaughters, and some sisters. Among nonrelatives, a recognizable group consisted of servants; many others were described as daughters of somebody, presumably friends or neighbors. Legacies for dowries could vary in value, small ones approximating the charitable contributions bequeathed to poor girls for marriage. For instance

Giacomella, Antonia, and Catarucia, daughters of Franceschina, received gifts expressly for their dowries, the first one four ducats and the other two a chemise each.[115]

Servants were frequent beneficiaries of legacies, and in this way they sometimes also received their wages.[116] This does not mean that the expressions of thankfulness their mistresses coupled with such legacies were false, since gratitude and payment could go together. In Venice, we find mistresses who bequeathed generous legacies to their servants as well as servants who appointed their mistresses as testamentary executors or even legatees.[117] Both in Venice and in Ghent, the designation "who lives with me" was used. It often referred to servants, but it could also include other members of the household. Not all servants lived in the households of their masters or mistresses, and in Ghent they often changed masters. But in other cases a deep relationship could reflect the past, the present, and a hope for the future. In the testament of Lisbette Ghiselbrecht, Kateline van der Muelen, who received some pieces of cloth, was named as "who used to stay with me" (*die vortijds met mi plach te wonenen*).[118] Costanza, widow of Francesco Bedoloto, bequeathed 20 ducats to Caterina, *que mecum moratur* ("who stays with me"), under the condition that she would still be with her at the time of her death (*si ipsa mecum morabitur tempore mei obitus*), a condition sometimes found in legacies to servants.[119] Bequests to younger or illegitimate relatives as well as to servants fulfilled the wish to be generous to persons to whom testatrices felt obliged or whom they wished to help.

Pious Legacies

The large number of religious and charitable institutions in Ghent and Venice offered testators a wide choice of beneficiaries. Most Venetian women bequeathed pious legacies to numerous religious institutions, as they hoped to be remembered in the prayers of as many people as possible. As wise merchants did not commit their whole property to one ship, the salvation of one's soul should not depend on only one religious institution or person. Many Venetian male testators probably thought likewise. Although some wealthy men did specifically list their pious legacies, most men put only general provisions in their testaments, leaving to their executors the decisions on details. In Ghent, detailed specification of pious legacies was common to testators of both sexes.

At the beginning of Gentnaar testaments—as in contemporary testaments elsewhere in Europe—we find almost regularly the formula that the soul of the testator was committed to God, the Virgin Mary and all the saints of the celestial court. Fourteenth-century Venetian testaments also tended to begin with pious rather than with secular provisions.

After committing their souls to God, testators from Ghent committed their bodies to a church, often to their parish church, and asked their executors to pay their debts. Afterward they started listing their pious bequests. The first bequests were mostly for specific persons and institutions connected with their burial church, for example, for the table of the Holy Ghost, for the confessor and other parish priests, for the upper and the under sacristan, for the local brotherhood (called "our lady"), for a daily prayer (*quotidianus*), and so on.[120] Venetian testatrices less regularly mentioned the burial church. As parish churches were responsible for the burial of their flock, they probably expected to be buried there if they did not specify otherwise.

In the late Middle Ages, Masses became the most popular means for the salvation of one's soul.[121] Even if everybody could expect to have them ordered by relatives and friends after one's death, both in Venice and in Ghent, testaments were nonetheless full of precise dispositions about where, when, by whom, and for how much money Masses had to be celebrated. A specific priest was often appointed for the Masses. This was done in order to have a trusted person ensuring regular celebration and to provide him with a wage; regular Masses, after all, constituted a significant part of the income of priests.

In Venice, a series of thirty Masses—known as Saint Gregory Masses—was one of the most common dispositions. They had to be celebrated one per day for the first month after death; in the last quarter of the fourteenth century their usual price was 1 ducat, a rather low price compared to most other dispositions for the soul. In Ghent ordering a series of thirty Masses was also popular, but they were usually called just "soul masses," and sometimes there were thirty-three.[122] Several testatrices from Ghent wanted the thirty Masses to be celebrated on the day of their death, before their bodies were taken to the grave.[123] In the late Middle Ages, the hours immediately after death were regarded as crucial. This was the moment when the soul had to go through God's trial and needed particular support. Later, Masses and prayers had the function of shortening the soul's stay in the purgatory, while on earth they kept alive the person's memory.

The celebration of Masses at fixed intervals after death, traditionally on the seventh and thirtieth day, was no longer common in fourteenth-century Ghent and Venice, although Masses celebrated at one-year intervals on the death day, called *anniversaria*, were still popular. Daily Masses for one year were an expensive, but still-common pattern. In order to have daily Masses said until the end of time, it was necessary to assign the income of some properties for their perpetual celebration.[124]

Male mendicant orders in Ghent were popular recipients of pious legacies. Some testators from Ghent made bequests of the same sum to all four mendicant orders, while others concentrated their legacies either on the Franciscans or on the Dominicans. In Venice too both patterns were common.

Beguinages had a more important role than female convents in numerous Flemish cities, Ghent included.[125] The beguinages of Ghent were also charitable institutions which took care of the sick and received bequests specifically for their *fermerie* (hospital). In Venice there were several old and prestigious Benedictine convents for women, but they lost popularity in the course of the fourteenth century. A few new institutions attracted more legacies, such as the convents of the sisters of the mendicant orders.[126] In Venice there was nothing comparable to the Flemish beguinages, although some women led religious lives outside convents in connection with the third Franciscan or Dominican orders.[127] Other Venetian women found religious engagement in the *scuole piccole* (confraternities), where they could be members and also officials.[128] In both cities, women who had been engaged in life in religious activities wished to continue this association after death through the investment of a part of their estates. Rich and powerful women could show for the last time their generosity to the religious institutions created or depending on them or their families, as the testament of Lisbette van de Moure ende van der Coudeberg shows.[129]

Obviously, care of the poor and the sick was important in both cities. In Ghent many testatrices made pious legacies to the lepers who lived outside the town in the fields (called *acker sieck* or "field sick"). Hermits too were among the beneficiaries of pious legacies in Ghent and Venice, but the term designated a number of different kinds of persons who lived a holy life, either alone or in small groups. Among the poor, we find the "shamed-face" poor, those who had fallen below their social state and were ashamed to go around asking for charity. They were called in Venice *poveri vergognosi* and in Ghent *huusarmen*. They were the objects of charity for the well-to-do who were probably afraid of the same fate. In Venice there were several hospitals that assisted the poor and the sick and received bequests consisting of sums of money or of food and cloth. In the late fourteenth century the highest number of legacies bequeathed to a single hospital was designated for San Lazzaro, situated on a small island in the lagoon. A meal for the poor and the religious was provided for in both cities, often on the burial day, and was called *pietancia*.

Some testators who could afford it wanted to have their burial accompanied by light as contrasted to the perpetual darkness of death. Margriete van der Cleve, a widow, ordered four torches weighing two stones of wax each.[130] After using the torches at the funeral it was usual to leave some of them to the church in which one would be buried. Margriete van der Cleve did likewise and also ordered five more torches to be given to other churches. Some testators in fourteenth-century Venice wished to have light and many people at their burials. Those who wanted to have a great last appearance required special huge candles, called *dopieri*. For instance, Caterucia, daughter of Andrea da Mosto and widow of Marco Cavazza, bequeathed a comparably high sum, 40 ducats, for what was considered suitable for a honorable burial, that is, "priests, *dopieri* and any costs for my funeral."[131] Other testatrices were willing to avoid those empty vanities and asked that no *dopieri* be burned at their burials. Lucia called Blanca, widow of Benedetto Morosini, for example, wanted her executors to call to her funeral only the priests of her parish church and not to have other *dopieri* than those burning at the Mass.[132]

Conclusion

In the Middle Ages legal provisions put women in a disadvantaged condition all over Europe, but they diverged strongly according to location, even inside the same area. Throughout the Middle Ages, spouses in Ghent preserved the traditional common marital fund based on Germanic law.[133] To be sure, the marital fund, a legacy of Lombard rule, dominated the marriage regimen in most of Italy up to the eleventh century. In the twelfth century with the reappearance of the dowry system, some Italian cities went so far as to prohibit marital presents in order to encourage the use of the dowry.[134] This was not, however, the case in Venice, where the dowry remained the main form of marriage settlement through the medieval centuries and where the presents of bridegrooms to brides had never been either dominant nor prohibited.

The social disadvantages of women were not everywhere the same, and both in Venice and in Ghent they were mitigated by the fact that women did not need to have tutors for their legal acts. To explain the comparatively favorable social condition of women in the two cities we must turn to economic factors.[135] Both cities were characterized by strong commercial and productive growth in the high Middle Ages. In Venice, the high demand for capital in the twelfth and thirteenth centuries brought about the removal of obstacles to free investment, including a few associated with the legal condition of women. Merchants in search of investors, for example, considered themselves lucky to be able to collect the capital of widows without their relatives' permission, and local law allowed it. This did not happen with married women's dowries because the interests of men as husbands proved stronger than those as investors. Therefore, married women's ability to act on their own was limited; their dowries were in possession of their husbands and they could invest only their non-dotal assets.

The Venetian variety of Roman law and the Gentnaar variety of Flemish *keuren* had some similar effects for women, in spite of their many differences.

In both cities unmarried adult and widowed women had free disposition both of themselves and of their estate, but this was based on different economical supports—the restitution of the dowry in Venice and the inheritance rights on the marital fund in Ghent. Married women were limited in their legal capacity in both cities, but compared to the Venetians, married women in Ghent had the advantage of having inheritance claims on their husband's estate. Furthermore in Venice the inheritance rules preferred male descendants, ascendants, and collaterals, a provision unknown in Ghent.

In both cities women engaged in commercial activity, made contracts for selling, alienating, or buying goods or real estate, were appointed legal guardians and made testaments. In particular, the charters of power of attorney show a link between the commercial development of the cities and the increase in women's social possibilities. Both in Venice and in Ghent wives of men who were abroad for a period—still a common event in commercial cities in the late Middle Ages—often received the powers of attorney from their husbands, both general (for all businesses), or special (for a single business).[136]

In Ghent women moved easily in the public spaces of the city; many appeared in the aldermanic courts, and some even worked in the count's administration. In Venice women were less present in the public spaces than in Ghent. They were not, however, confined to their neighborhoods, since many of them were testamentary executors, members or officials of religious confraternities, or had powers of attorney—all roles putting them in touch with notaries, churches, courts, and the administrative offices of the city.[137]

Acts made by women are numerous also in other developed European cities such as Cologne or London.[138] The fact that they are absent or less numerous in cities like Florence shows that economic development alone cannot explain the range of the property rights and social possibilities of women. The interlacing of legal traditions, mentalities, and the socioeconomic developments and their influence on the lives of women were complex and cannot be reduced to a formula of direct dependence. Nonetheless, for the two cases studied here, a convergence of economic development with a comparatively favorable social situation for women can be asserted.

In both cities the use of testaments demonstrates the will of many women to make their own decisions concerning their soul's salvation and the disposal of their earthly goods. In Ghent women as well as men took advantage of the chance of disposing of a part of their estates by testaments and donations primarily to provide for their souls, but also to bequeath specific goods to persons who, according to the inheritance rules, would have not received them. In Venice, testaments gave more opportunities for influencing the disposition of one's estate than in Ghent, and women exploited these opportunities more often than did men. An unexpected difference between the two cities was that Venetian women were often testamentary executors, appointed both by testators as by testatrices, while female executors were rare in Ghent. In both cities women bequeathed a part of their estate to religious institutions in which they had been directly engaged, such as their own parishes or the beguinages in Ghent and the confraternities in Venice.

The comparison of the conditions of women in Venice and Ghent has shown both similarities and differences, the latter being more expected than the former. The provisions of the Ghent's *keure* that strongly limited the possibilities of choice of married women and their influence on the marital fund, made the legal and social condition of Gentnaar wives not so different from that of married women in Venice. If the situation of Venetian women has been often described as atypical, it is probably because it has usually been compared with that of Florentine and other Italian women. In comparison with another large European city it loses its uniqueness. In the great variety of legal regulations characterizing the end of the Middle Ages, the peculiarities both of the Venetian *ius proprium* and of the Ghent's *keure* concerning women demonstrate the possible combinations of the disadvantages and advantages women could enjoy within the constraints of social and legal disabilities attached to their sex.

Notes

1. The law collections of the two cities can be found in the following editions: *Coutume de la ville de Gand*, ed. Albert Eugène Ghedolf (Brussels: 1868) (*Coutumes de pays et comté de Flandre. Ville de Gand 1*); hereafter: *Coutume Gand*. The references will be to the homologated version of 1563, except when otherwise specified. For Venice, see *Statuti veneziani di Jacopo Tiepolo del 1242 e le loro glosse*, A cura di Roberto Cessi (Venice: Memorie del regio istituto veneto di scienze, lettere ed arti, 1938); hereafter: *Statuta veneta*. Testaments can be found for Ghent in Ghent's Stadarchief, registers of the *staten van goed* (hereafter SAG); for Venice in the Archivio di Stato di Venezia, section Archivio Notarile, Testamenti. The information on Venetian testaments is supported by my *Venezianische Vermächtnisse. Die soziale und wirtschaftliche Situation von Frauen im Spiegel spätmittelalterlicher Testamente*, Ergebnisse der Frauenforschung 50 (Stuttgart-Weimar: Metzler, 1998).

2. Marc Bloch has analyzed comparison as a method for historical research in "Pour une histoire comparée des sociétés europeennes" in *Mélanges historiques* (1928) (Paris: S.E.V.P.E.N., 1963), vol. 1, pp. 16–40. For recent discussions see Alette Olin Hill and Boyd H. Hill, Jr., "Marc Bloch and

Comparative History," *American Historical Review* 85 (1980), pp. 828–57, and Hartmut Atsma and André Burguière, *Marc Bloch aujourd'hui. Histoire comparée et sciences sociales* (Paris: École des Hautes Etudes en Sciences Sociales, 1990).

3. See the publications of the Institut für vergleichende Städtegeschichte in Münster.

4. *Florence and Venice: Comparations and Relations. Acts of Two Conferences at Villa I Tatti, 1976–1977,* The Harvard University Center for Italian Renaissance Studies 55 (Florence: La nuova Italia, 1979); John K. Hyde "Some Uses of Literacy in Venice and Florence in the Thirteenth and Fourteenth Centuries," *Transactions of the Royal Historical Society* 29 (1979), pp. 109–28; Gene Brucker, "Tales of Two Cities: Florence and Venice in the Renaissance," *American Historical Review* 88 (1983), pp. 599–616; Anthony Molho, "Tre città-stato i loro debiti pubblici. Quesiti e ipotesi sulla storia di Firenze, Genova, Venezia," in *Italia 1350–1450: tra crisi trasformazione, sviluppo. 13. Convegno di studi, 1991* (Pistoia: Centro italiano di studi di storia ed arte, 1993), pp. 185–215. For a recent collection of essays questioning Venetian history and historiography, but not making use of comparisons, see *Venice Reconsidered. The History and Civilization of an Italian City-State 1297–1797,* ed. John Martin and Dennis Romano (Baltimore: Johns Hopkins University Press, 2000).

5. Alexander Francis Cowan, *The Urban Patriciate: Lübeck and Venice, 1500–1700* (Köln: Böhlau, 1986) is the exception.

6. Customary laws were the almost unique legal sources overall in Europe before the twelfth century. In Flanders customary laws were based on Germanic law and were called *coutumes* or, in Dutch, *keuren.* Hereafter we will use the latter form. John Gilissen *La coutume.* Typologie des sources du Moyen Age occidental 41 (Turnhout: Brepols, 1982).

7. In the sixth century under the eastern Roman emperor Justinian, Roman law was collected and codified in the *Corpus Iuris Civilis.* However, this code was applied nowhere in early medieval western Europe and became a legal source only with the twelfth-century renaissance of Roman law. Oral, uncodified forms of Roman law developed into local customary laws (*iura propria*) in the southern regions of western Europe. On the *ius commune,* see below p. 81.

8. Christiane Klapisch-Zuber, "La famille médiévale," in *Histoire de la population française.* Vol. 1: *Des origines à la Renaissance,* ed. J. Dupâquier et al. (Paris: Quadrige/PUF, 1988), pp. 468–71. Ellen E. Kittell, "Testaments of Two Cities: A Comparative Analysis of the Wills of Medieval Genoa and Douai," *European Review of History* 5 (1998), p. 47. Martha C. Howell, *The Marriage Exchange. Property, Social Place and Gender in Cities of the Low Countries, 1300–1550* (Chicago: University of Chicago Press, 1998), pp. 196–228.

9. *The Household in Late Medieval Cities. Italy and Northwestern Europe Compared.* Proceedings of the International Conference, Ghent, January 21–22, 2000, ed. Myriam Carlier, Studies in Urban Social, Economic and Political History of the Medieval and Early Modern Low Countries 12 (Apeldoorn: Garant, 2001).

10. Régine LeJan, "Conclusions," in *The Household in Late Medieval Cities*. For Douai see Robert Jacob, *Les époux, le seigneur et la cité. Coutume et pratiques matrimoniales des bourgeois et paysans de France du Nord au moyen age* (Brussels: Facultés Universitaires Saint-Louis, 1990), pp. 233–40; Howell, *The Marriage Exchange*, pp. 124–43.

11. Andrea Padovani, "La politica del diritto," in *Storia di Venezia*, vol. 2: *L'età del Comune*. A cura di Giorgio Cracco e Gherardo Ortalli (Roma: Istituto della Enciclopedia Italiana e Fondazione Giorgio Cini, 1995), pp. 303–29. Fernanda Sorelli, *Donne a Venezia nel Medioevo secoli XII–XIV*, Lezioni 17 (Perugia: Università di Perugia, dipartimento di scienze storiche, 2000), pp. 5–6.

12. Thomas Kuehn, "Law, schools of," in *Dictionary of the Middle Ages*, ed. J.R. Strayer (New York: Scribner, 1986), vol. 7, pp. 512–517.

13. Philippe Godding, *Le droit privé dans les Pays bas meridionaux du 12e au 18e siècle* (Brussels: Palais des Academies, 1987), p. 143, item 192.

14. Gilissen, *La coutume*, p. 92. A homologated text is one ratified by the king.

15. Joanna of Constantinople ruled from 1204 to 1244. She was followed by her sister, Margaret, who technically ruled from 1244 to 1278, when she abdicated in favor of her son, Guy of Dampierre. There is some doubt as to whether Margaret really ever handed over the reigns to Guy while she still lived. She died in 1280.

16. Ellen E. Kittell, "Women in the Administration of the Count of Flanders," in *Frau und spätmittelalterlicher Alltag*, Veröffentlichungen des Instituts für mittelalterliche Realienkunde Österreichs 9 (Wien: Österreichische Akademie der Wissenschaften, 1986), pp. 487–508.

17. Diane Owen Hughes, "From Brideprice to Dowry in Mediterranean Europe," *Journal of Family History* 3 (1978), pp. 262–96. Stanley Chojnacki, "Patrician Women in Early Renaissance Venice," *Renaissance Studies* 21 (1974), pp. 176–203; reprinted in Stanley Chojnacki, *Women and Men in Renaissance Venice. Twelve Essays on Patrician Society* (Baltimore: Johns Hopkins University Press, 2000), pp. 115–31. Stanley Chojnacki, "Dowries and Kinsmen in early Renaissance Venice," *Journal of Interdisciplinary History* 5 (1975), pp. 571–600; reprinted in *Women and Men*, pp. 132–52. Christiane Klapisch-Zuber, "Le complexe de Griselda. Dot et dons de mariage au Quattrocento," *Mélanges de l'École française de Rome (Moyen Age, Temps moderns)* 94 (1982), pp. 7–44. Sorelli, *Donne a Venezia*, p. 15.

18. On the right of husbands to dispose freely of the dowry during marriage, see Francesco Ercole, "L'istituto dotale nella pratica e nella legislazione statutaria dell'Italia superiore," *Rivista italiana per le scienze giuridiche*, 46 (1910), pp. 177–78. On the obligation to restore the dowry to the widow, see Ercole, "L'istituto dotale," p. 222.

19. Statuta veneta, Liber I: 39, 54–56. Manlio Bellomo, "Dote," in *Enciclopedia del diritto*. A cura di Francesco Calasso, vol. 14 (Milano: Giuffrè, 1965), pp. 8–32.

20. For the Florentine regulation of this issue see Julius Kirshner, "*Maritus lucretur dotem uxoris sue premortue* in Late Medieval Florence," *Zeitschrift der Savigny-Stiftung für Rechtsgeschichte* 108 (1991), Kan. Abt. 77: 111–55.

21. Statuta veneta, Liber IV: 24–27.

22. *Exclusio propter dotem* (exclusion because of dowry) meant that daughters having received a dowry were excluded from any further hereditary claim on their fathers' estates. This legal principle, which was general in Italy despite contradicting the Justinianian code, was due to the influence of Lombard law. See Thomas Kuehn, "Inheritance," in *Dictionary of the Middle Ages*, ed. J.R. Strayer (New York: Scribner, 1985), vol. 6, p. 458.

23. Corpus Iuris Civilis, Institutiones 3.1.1,6,15.

24. Stanley Chojnacki, "Patrician Women in Early Renaissance Venice," *Renaissance Studies* 21 (1974), reprinted in Chojnacki, *Women and Men*, p. 123. Legacies from fathers to their already endowed daughters were also common in Florence and probably elsewhere.

25. For sixteenth-century examples of convergence of dowries, inheritances, and legacies on making some widows singularly rich, see Anna Bellavitis, "Dot et richesse des femmes au XVI siècle," *CLIO: histoire, femmes et sociétés* 7 (1998), pp. 93–97, and Anna Bellavitis, *Identité, mariage, mobilité sociale. Citoyennes et citoyens à Venise au XVIe siècle* (Paris-Rome: École française de Rome, 2001), pp. 224–30. For fourteenth-century examples of wealthy women see Guzzetti, *Venezianische Vermächtnisse*, pp. 115–116.

26. *Si mulier in potestate viri aliquam cartam fecerit contra repromissam suam, nihil valeat. . .Sed de omnibus bonis, que ipsa possidet, etiam sine consensu viri facere possit et securitatem et alienationem, sicut sibi placuerit.* Statuta veneta, Liber 1: 39.

27. Guido Rossi, "Statut juridique de la femme dans l' histoire du droit italien (époques médiévale et moderne)," *Recueils de la Société Jean Bodin*, vol. 12: *La femme* (Brussels: Éditions de la Librairie Encyclopédique, 1962), p. 126. Thomas Kuehn, "*Cum consensu mundualdi*: Legal Guardianship of Women in Quattrocento Florence," *Viator* 13 (1982), pp. 309–33, reprinted in Kuehn, *Law, Family and Women: Toward a Legal Anthropology of Renaissance Italy* (Chicago: University of Chicago Press, 1991), pp. 212–37.

28. Marco Ferro, *Dizionario del diritto comune e veneto.* (Venezia: Modesto Fenzo, 1778–1781), and also (Venezia: A. Santini e figlio, 1845–47), vol. 5, p. 127.

29. Coutume Gand, rubrica XXVI, 8–11.

30. Coutume Gand, rubrica XX; Godding, *Le droit privé*, p. 273.

31. *De man vermach te disponerene by vercoopinghe, transporte of andere contracten tusschen levende ende ooc by ghiften metter waermer handt, van de ghemeenen goeden, meublen ofte ghereputeert voor meuble ende ooc van conquesten immeuble, 't zynder gheliesten, zonder consent van zynen wyfve, uutghedaen gheconquesteerde leenen daer 't wyf ter erfven commen es* (Coutume Gand, rubrica XX, 1).

32. *Van den rechten ende toebehoorten van ghehuwede lieden ende van de ghemeenheede van dien, 2, Coutumes de la ville de Bruges*, ed. L. Gilliodts-van Severen (Brussels: Goemaere, 1874–75). *Cahier primitif de la coutume de Bruges*, p. 158.

33. See notes 30 and 31; *meublen ofte ghereputeert voor meuble* ("movable or reputed as movable").

34. See note 30.

35. *Ghehuwede vrauwen zyn in de macht van huerlieder mans, in zulcker wys dat se gheen contracten, kennessen of verbanden tusschen levende en vermoghen te makene*

niet meer voor wette dan anders, buuten de wetene ende consente van huere mans,
uutghedaen openbaere coopvrauwen, huerlieder coopmanschepe angaende ende
anderssins niet, die daer mede hemlieden ende heure mans verbinden moghen
(Coutume Gand, rubrica XX, 2).

36. Coutume Gand, rubrica XX, 5–6, 18; Godding, *Le droit privé*, pp. 296–97.

37. Coutume Gand, rubrica XX, 2.

38. Coutume Gand, cahier primitif, rubrica V, 13.

39. Coutume Gand, rubrica XX, 14.

40. Coutume Gand, rubrica XX, 11.

41. Coutume Gand, rubrica XX, 18.

42. Marianne Danneel, *Weduwen en wezen in het laat-middeleeuwse Gent*, Studies in Urban Social Economic and Political History of the Medieval and Modern Low Countries 3 (Leuven-Appeldoorn: Garant, 1995), pp. 332–44.

43. SAG, reeks 330, reg. 9, f. 2 verso, 2nd act, 12/13/1389.

44. SAG, reeks 330, reg. 9, f. 5 recto, 1st act. We do not know the content of the aldermen's sentence, but very likely it concerned Pieter Boudin senior's estate.

45. Danneel, *Weduwen en wezen*, p. 332.

46. SAG, reeks 330, reg. 12, f. 54 recto, 5th act, 11/25/1401.

47. Coutume Gand, rubrica XXI, 10; Danneel, pp. 166–69.

48. SAG, reeks 330, reg. 9, f. 266 verso, 3rd act, 10/02/1392.

49. Coutume Gand, rubrica XXV, 1–9; Godding, *Le droit privé*, pp. 273–74.

50. Coutume Gand, rubrica XXV, 1. Danneel, *Weduwen en wezen*, pp. 254–56.

51. See note 10.

52. Ferro, *Dizionario del diritto*, vol. 7, p. 139; vol. 10, p. 205.

53. Manlio Bellomo, *Ricerche sui rapporti patrimoniali tra coniugi. Contributo alla storia della famiglia medievale* (Milano: Giuffrè, 1961), pp. 5–25. In Milan, husbands often disregarded the provision prohibiting them to leave their wives no more than a quarter of their estate (Laura Deleidi, "Donne milanesi nella prima metà del Cinquecento: la memoria degli atti notarili," *Società e storia* 64 (1994), p. 282).

54. Guzzetti, *Venezianische Vermächtnisse*, p. 149.

55. Ferro, *Dizionario del diritto*, vol. 4, pp. 2–3.

56. Jacob, *Les époux, le seigneur*, pp. 41–47.

57. Coutume Gand, rubrica XX: 21–22; Danneel, *Weduwen en wezen*, p. 337.

58. The study of mentalities through testaments is associated with the Annales school. See Pierre Chaunu, *La mort à Paris, XVIe, XVIIe, XVIIIe siècles* (Paris: Fayard, 1978); Jacques Chiffoleau, *La comptabilité de l'au delà. Les hommes, la mort et la religion dans la region d'Avignon à la fin du Moyen Age* (Roma: École française de Rome, 1980); Michel Vovelle, *Piété baroque et déchristianisation en Provence au XVIIIe siècle* (Paris: Éditions du Seuil, 1973). For the study of individuals through testaments see Attilio Bartoli Langeli, "Nota introduttiva," in *Nolens intestatus decedere. Il testamento come fonte della storia religiosa e sociale*, Archivi dell'Umbria, 7 (Perugia: Umbra Coop, 1985), IX–XVII.

59. "To provide for the unsure time of death with a testamentary disposition." For instance Lisbette van de Moure ende van der Coudeberg used this formula (see note 110).

60. *Arenga* was the introductory part of a medieval charter expressing a general justification for the decision contained in the charter itself.

61. In Flemish we find sentences like *aensiende ende merkende dat negheene dinc zekerre es dan de doet ende met onzekere dan de wiile van haere.*

62. Otto Gerhard Oexle, "Memoria als Kultur," in *Memoria als Kultur*, ed. Otto G. Oexle (Göttingen: Vandenhoeck & Ruprecht, 1995), pp. 33–41. *Memoria. Der geschichtliche Zeugniswert des liturgischen Gedenkens im Mittelalter*, ed. Karl Schmid and Joachim Wollasch (München: Fink, 1984).

63. Coutume Gand, rubrica XXVIII, 1–2, 6.

64. Philippe Godding, "Dans quelle mesure pouvait-on disposer de ses biens par testament dans les anciens Pays-Bas méridionaux," *Tijdschrift voor rechtsgeschiedenis* 50 (1982), p. 284; Godding, *Le droit privé*, p. 380.

65. Coutume Gand, rubrica XXVII; 2, XXVIII, 1.

66. Coutume Gand, XX, 27; Godding, *Le droit privé*, p. 81.

67. Godding, *Le droit privé*, p. 381. Myriam Carlier, *Kinderen van de minne? Bastaarden in het vijftiende-eeuwse Vlaanderen.*Verhandelingen van de Koninklijke Vlaamse Academie van België voor Wetenschappen en Kunsten, 3 (Brussels: Paleis der Academiën, 2001).

68. Coutume Gand, rubrica XXVI, 11.

69. SAG reeks 330, reg. 12, f. 13 verso, 3rd act, 09/28/1400.

70. Statuta veneta, Liber IV: 35; Corpus Iuris Civilis, Institutiones 2.28.6–7, Novellae 18.1.

71. Chojnacki, "Patrician women," reprinted in *Women and Men*, pp. 115–31; Chojnacki, "Dowries and Kinsmen," reprinted in *Women and Men*, pp. 132–52.

72. Antonio Pertile, *Storia del diritto italiano dalla caduta dell'impero romano alla codificazione.* vol. 4: *Storia del diritto privato* (Torino: Unione Tipografico-Editrice, 1874; reprinted Bologna: Forni, 1965–66), pp. 21–22; Chojnacki, "Dowries and Kinsmen," reprinted in *Women and Men*, p. 140; Samuel Kline Cohn, *The Cult of Remembrance and the Black Death, Six Renaissance Cities in Central Italy* (Baltimore: Johns Hopkins University Press, 1992), pp. 198–99; Isabelle Chabot, "Risorse e diritti patrimoniali," in *Lavoro delle donne*, ed. Angela Groppi (Roma-Bari: Laterza, 1996), p. 64.

73. SAG, reeks 330, reg. 12, f. 37 verso, 2nd act, 11/25/1400.

74. SAG, reeks 330, reg. 12, f. 1 verso, 1st act, 08/15/1400.

75. SAG, reeks 330, reg. 12, f. 8 verso, 2nd act, 09/03/1400.

76. SAG, reeks 330, reg. 12, f. 263 recto, 4th act, 10/11/1402. In the register the text of this testament is crossed out.

77. SAG, reeks 330, reg. 12, f. 10 verso, 9th act, 09/25/1400.

78. "Testament," in *Lexikon des Mittelalters*, ed. G. Avella-Widhalm, L. Lutz, R. Matte et al. (Munich: Artemis-Verlag, 1999), vol. 8, p. 565; J.F. Niermeyer, *Mediae latinitatis lexicon minus* (Leiden: Brill, 1960–76), p. 587.

79. Ellen Kittell has developed this issue comparing testaments from Douai and Genoa in "Testaments of Two Cities," pp. 51–54.

80. "Testament," in *Lexikon des Mittelalters*, vol. 8, p. 564.

81. In the Flemish cities in the fourteenth century there were several authorities—other than aldermen—who could validate a testament: Church

authorities, who had mostly validated testaments in the thirteenth century, the *erfachtige lieden* ("hereditary men") and the notaries, who were not yet numerous; Godding, *Le droit prive*, p. 87. For the *erfachtige lieden* see Philippe Lardinois, "Symptomen van een middeleeuwse clan: de erfachtige lieden te Gent in de 1e helft van de 14e eeuw," *Handelingen der Maatschapij voor Geschiednis en Oudheidkunde te Gent*, n.r. 31 (1977), pp. 65–76.

82. Kittell, "Testaments," pp. 51–53; Guzzetti, *Venezianische Vermächtnisse*, p. 23.

83. SAG, reeks 330, reg. 7, f. 89 recto, 9th act, 04/11/1382 and f. 89 verso, 5th act, 04/09/1382.

84. Since the second half of the fourteenth century, an increasing number of women in Venice made use of the possibility of writing the preliminary note in their own hand. Before the sixteenth century, writing the *cedula* for their testaments was the way some women chose to protect themselves from the undesired influences of their husbands or kin on their decisions. Federica Ambrosini, "*De mia manu propria*. Donna, scrittura e prassi testamentaria nella Venezia del Cinquecento," in *Non uno itinere. Studi storici offerti dagli allievi a Federico Seneca* (Venezia: Stamperia, 1993), pp. 33–54. Linda Guzzetti, "Donne e scrittura a Venezia nel Trecento," *Archivio veneto*, 5. serie, 152–87 (1999), pp. 5–31.

85. Philippe Godding, "La pratique testamentaire en Flandre au 13e siècle," *Tijdschrift voor rechtsgeschiedenis* 58 (1990), p. 284.

86. "In righteous gifts in salvation of her soul in form of testament and last will."

87. SAG, reeks 330, reg. 12, f. 8 verso, 1st act, 09/14/1400.

88. *In vuermen van testament ende utersten willen alsulke ghifte als hier naer verklaeerd staen.* SAG, reeks 330, reg. 12, f. 310 recto, 4th act, 07/17/1403.

89. SAG, reeks 330, reg. 12, f. 2 recto, 6th act, 08/17/1400.

90. "Testament," in *Lexikon des Mittelalters*, vol.8, p. 565. Guzzetti, *Venezianische Vermächtnisse*, p. 68.

91. Godding, *Le droit privé*, p. 385. For Douai see Jacob, *Les époux, le seigneur*, p. 131.

92. Aeghte van den Berghe, SAG, reeks 330, reg. 12, f. 57 verso, 3rd act, 01/14/1401. Eleene Leeuwaerts, SAG, reeks 330, reg. 14, f. 194 (= XXVI) recto, 1st act, 01/29/1410.

93. SAG, reeks 330, reg. 12, f. 11 verso, 1st act, 09/13/1400. Like other women mentioned, Lisbette Ghiselbrecht appointed her husband, Vincent van der Zickelen, and two other men as executors of her testament without stating if she had obtained his permission for her testament.

94. Furthermore, in Venice most notaries were parish priests with whom the inhabitants were constantly in touch. Attilio Bartoli Langeli, "Documentazione e notariato," in *Storia di Venezia*, vol. 1: *Origini—Età ducale*. A cura di Lellia Cracco Ruggini et al (Roma: Istituto dell' enciclopedia italiana e Fondazione Giorgio Cini, 1991), vol. 1, pp. 847–64.

95. Marc Boone notes that an inventory of the estate (*staat van goed*) was not done by the court of the aldermen for all inhabitants of Ghent who died with underage children, but only for the wealthy citizens. Boone also notes that, in the fifteenth century, unqualified workers could not afford the prices

for parchment and registration. As testaments were written in the same registers, the price must have been similar; Marc Boone, "De Gentse staten van goed als bron voor de kennis van de materiele cultuur: mogelijkheden en beperkingen (late middeleeuwen—vroege moderne tijden," in *Bronne voor de geschiedenis van de materiele cultuur: staten van goeden en testamenten, Handelingen van de studiedag te Brussel, 24-10-1986,* ed. Frank Daelemans, Archiev—en Bibliotheekwezen in Belgie, extranummer 25, deel 2 (Brussels: [s.n.], 1988), pp. 56–59).

96. Vincent Goussey, *Leven met de dood in de Late Middeleeuwen (1450–1482). Het Gentse testament en andere aktentypes waarin de overdracht van het vermogen over de dood heen wordt anngeraakt* (Universiteit van Gent, unpublished thesis, 1994–95), vol. 2, pp. 5–6. Also in the list of testaments of the first half of the fifteenth century drawn up by Chantal Fontana, women were less numerous than men (*Het belang van testamentaire schenkingen op sociaal, financieel-materieel en financieel vlak in het middeleeuwse Gent (1400–1450)* (Universiteit van Gent, unpublished thesis, 1993)).

97. Bianca Betto, "Linee di politica matrimomiale nella nobiltà veneziana fino al XV secolo. Alcune note genealogiche e l'esempio della famiglia Mocenigo," *Archivio storico italiano,* p. 139 (1981), p. 47. Stanley Chojnacki, " 'The Most Serious Duty': Motherhood, Gender and Patrician Culture in Renaissance Venice," in *Refiguring Woman. Perspectives on Gender and Italian Renaissance,* ed. Marilyn Migiel and Juliana Schiesari (Ithaca, N.Y.: Cornell University Press, 1991), p. 145, note 36. Dennis Romano, "Charity and Community in Early Renaissance Venice," *Journal of Urban History* 11 (1984), p. 66. Guzzetti, *Venezianische Vermächtnisse,* pp. 19–20.

98. Guzzetti, *Venezianische Vermächtnisse,* p. 57.

99. Cohn, *The Cult of Remembrance,* p. 198; Chabot, "Risorse e diritti patrimoniali," pp. 60–65.

100. In the first quarter of the fourteenth century they made 6.3 percent.

101. Statuta veneta, Liber 4: 31. Fernanda Sorelli, "Gli ordini mendicanti," in *Storia di Venezia,* vol. 2 (Roma: 1995), pp. 915–918. Antonio Rigon, "Influssi francescani nei testamenti padovani del Due e Trecento," *Le Venezie francescane,* n.s. 2 (1985), pp. 106–107.

102. Guzzetti, *Venezianische Vermächtnisse,* p. 123.

103. Guzzetti, *Venezianische Vermächtnisse,* pp. 124, 165.

104. SAG, reeks 330, reg. 14, f. 170 (= II) verso, 1st act, 01/31/1409. Nine years later the testatrix substituted brother Augustiin van der Steene for the deceased priest, Janne Seys.

105. Silver objects were common as bequests to the executors.

106. Guzzetti, *Venezianische Vermächtnisse,* p. 186.

107. SAG, reeks 330, reg. 12, f. 57 verso, 3rd act, 01/14/1401.

108. Coutume Gand, rubrica XXVII, 7.

109. Coutume Gand, rubrica XXVI, 21.

110. Reeks 330, reg. 12, f. 76 verso, 5th act, 03/29/1401.

111. SAG, reeks 330, reg. 14, f. 237 recto–verso, 1st act, 01/20/1410.

112. SAG, reeks 330, reg. 12, f. 15 recto, 3rd act, 10/02/1400.

113. SAG, reeks 330, reg. 9, f. 305 recto, 2nd act, 05/14/1393.

114. SAG, reeks 330, reg. 12, f. 21 verso, 6th act, 10/19/1400. For full assistance the formula was: *ate, dranke, cleederen, coussin ende steen*, meaning food, drink, clothes, and accommodation.

115. Archivo notarile, testamenti, notary Ariano Passamonte, protocol, act 90, 01/12/1393. Franceschina was the deceased daughter of a brother of the testatrix, Beria, widow of Nicoletto Rizo.

116. For servants in Venice see Dennis Romano, *Housecraft and Statecraft. Domestic Service in Renaissance Venice, 1400–1600* (Baltimore: Johns Hopkins University Press, 1996). For Ghent see Marc Boone, "La domesticité d'une grande famille gantoise d'après le livre de comptes de Simon Borluut," in *Les niveaux de vie au Moyen Age*, ed. J.-P. Sosson, S. Thonon, and T. van Hemerlyck (Louvain-la-neuve: Academia-Bruylant, 1999), pp. 77–90. For Florence see Christiane Klapisch-Zuber, "Célibat et service féminin dans la Florence du XVe siècle," *Annales de démographie historique* 1981, pp. 289–302; English version "Female Celibacy and Service in Florence in the Fifteenth Century," in *Women, Family and Ritual in Renaissance Italy* (Chicago: University of Chicago Press, 1985), pp. 165–77.

117. Guzzetti, *Venezianische Vermächtnisse*, pp. 171–79.

118. See note 93.

119. Archivio notarile, Testamenti, notary Giorgio de Gibellino, ced. 35, 05/16/1377.

120. "Table of the Holy Ghost" was a denomination for parochial institutions providing for the poor.

121. Jacques Chiffoleau, "Sur l'usage obsessionel de la messe pour les morts à la fin du Moyen-Age," in *Faire croire. Modalités de la diffusion et de la réception des messages religieux du XIIe au XIVe siècle*, Collection de l'École française de Rome 51 (Roma: École française de Rome, 1981), pp. 235–56.

122. Probably because that was the age of Christ when he died.

123. Kateline Hottenspoers, SAG, reeks 330, reg. 14, f. 7 verso, 1st act, 11/16/1407. Lisbette sGauyen (sGaeyen), SAG, reeks 330, reg. 14, f. 17 verso, 1st act, 12/05/1407.

124. For an instance of a long list of properties the income of which was designated for Masses, see the testament of Lisbette van de Moure ende van der Coudeberg (note 107).

125. Walter Simons, "The Beguine Movement in the Southern Low Countries: a Reassessment," *Bulletin van het Belgisch historisch Instituut te Rom* 59 (1989); Walter Simons, "Een zeker bestaan: de Zuidnederelandse begijnen en de Frauenfrage, 13de–18de eeuw," *Tijdschrift voor Sociale Geschiedenis* 17 (1991), pp. 125–46; Walter Simons, "Begjinen en begarden in het middeleeuwse Dowaai," *De Franse Nederlanden*, 17 (1992); Walter Simons, *Cities of Ladies. Beguine Communities in the Medieval Low Countries, 1200–1565* (Philadelphia: University of Pennsylvania Press, 2001).

126. Mario Fois, "I religiosi: decadenza e fermenti innovatori," in *Chiesa di Venezia tra medioevo e età moderna*. A cura di Gianni Vian (Venezia: Edizioni Studium Cattolico Veneziano, 1989), pp. 156–60. Antonio Rigon,

"I problemi religiosi," in *Storia di Venezia*, vol. 3: *La formazione dello stato patrizio*. A cura di G. Arnaldi, G. Cracco, and A. Tenenti (Roma: Istituto dell'Enciclopedia italiana e Fondazione Giorgio Cini, 1997), pp. 933–56.

127. Fernanda Sorelli, *La santità imitabile. La "Leggenda di Maria da Venezia" di Tommaso da Siena*. Miscellanea di studi e memorie 23 (Venezia: Deputazione di storia patria per le Venezie, 1984), pp. 110–117; Fernanda Sorelli, "Per la storia religiosa di Venezia nella prima metà del Quattrocento: inizi e sviluppi del terz'ordine domenicano," in *Viridarium floridum. Studi di storia veneta offerti dagli allievi a P. Sambin*. A cura di M.C. Billanovich et al. Umanesimo e medioevo 54 (Padova: Antenore, 1984), pp. 89–114.

128. From the first quarter of the fourteenth century onward women came to be excluded from the prestigious *scuole grandi*. Richard Mackenney, "Devotional Confraternities in Renaissance Venice," in *Voluntary religion*, ed. W.J. Shields and D. Wood (London: Blackwell, 1986), pp. 85–96, and Linda Guzzetti and Antje Ziemann, "Women in Fourteenth-Century Venetian Scuole," *Renaissance Quarterly* 55 (2002), pp. 1151–95.

129. See note 110.

130. SAG, reeks 330, reg. 12, f. 7 recto, 4th act, 10/15/1400.

131. Archivio notarile, testamenti, notary Luca Novello, 08/21/1382.

132. Archivio notarile, testamenti, notary Antonio Nigro, 07/20/1378.

133. Danneel, *Weduwen en wezen*, pp. 376–77.

134. Hughes, p. 277.

135. Danneel, *Weduwen en wezen*, p. 377.

136. Danneel, *Weduwen en wezen*, p. 340; Guzzetti, *Venezianische Vermächtnisse*, p. 91; Sorelli, *Donne a Venezia*, p. 8.

137. For a different view on this issue see Dennis Romano, "Gender and Urban Geography of Renaissance Venice," *Journal of Social History* 23 (1989), pp. 2, 339–53.

138. For London see Marian K. Dale, "The London Silkwomen of the Fifteenth Century," *Economic History Review*, 1st ser., 4 (1933), pp. 324–35; reprinted in *Sisters and Workers in the Middle Ages* (Chicago: University of Chicago Press, 1989), pp. 26–38; C.M. Barron and A.F. Sutton, eds., *Medieval London Widows* (London: Hambledon Press, 1994); Kay E. Lacey, "Women and Work in Fourteenth and Fifteenth Century London," in *Women and Work in Preindustrial England*, ed. Lindsey Charles and Lorna Duffin (London: Croom Helm, 1985), pp. 24–82; Barbara A. Hanawalt, "The Widow's Mite: Provisions for Medieval London Widows," in *Upon My Husband's Death: Widows in the Literature and History of Medieval Europe*, ed. Louise Mirrer (Ann Arbor: University of Michigan Press, 1992), pp. 21–45. For Cologne: see Margret Wensky, *Die Stellung der Frau in der stadtkölnischen Wirtschaft im Spätmittelalter* (Köln: Böhlau, 1980); Martha C. Howell, *Women, Production and Patriarchy in Late Medieval Cities* (Chicago: University of Chicago Press, 1986), pp. 124–58.

CHAPTER 5

NEITHER EQUALITY NOR RADICAL
OPPRESSION: THE ELASTICITY OF
WOMEN'S ROLES IN THE LATE MEDIEVAL
LOW COUNTRIES

Eric Bousmar

Introduction: Toward a New Paradigm

In this essay I propose a new interpretation of gender relations in the southern Low Countries (Flanders, Brabant, and neighboring principalities) during the Burgundian period (late fourteenth to sixteenth centuries), in order to resolve contradictions and apparent paradoxes arising from literature on (and primary sources from) the Low Countries. How can we reconcile very clear signs of gender inequality and patriarchal oppression on the one hand, with a relatively favorable position of women in the field of private law (inheritance, property rights, commercial capacity) as well as with hints of affection and trust, on the other hand? How can we reconcile measures of female exclusion from guild activities and public offices with evidence of female successes in economic and political businesses?

By formulating a new paradigm this interpretation diminishes the antagonism between the egalitarian trend mainly postulated by legal historians, and the patriarchal inequality mainly observed by social historians. Female subjugation (which is not to be denied) was tempered by a "taking-over" principle that enabled women to assert themselves and to exercise power in political and economical matters, although not on equal footing with men. This model should not only be seen as a tool for historians but also as a tentative description of late medieval mental representations.

Moreover, this model does not limit its scope to the "private" sphere—as traditionally embedded in marriage and maternity—but explains how women had access to the public sphere and how continuity was experienced between the two spheres by contemporaries, men and women alike.[1]

Household and maternity were definitely regarded as the domain of women, but they were not confined to it (despite all moralistic writing and preaching on the housewife). As substitutes for a dead father or a dead/absent husband, women were entitled to a wide range of opportunities, leading some of them to become preeminent entrepreneurs or political figures. This elasticity of female possibilities, on the ground of their familial and lifecycle position as well as of their sexual morality, constitutes an extension of M.C. Howell's model of gender and patriarchy.[2] It makes clear that, however great and impressive the accomplishments of individual women might have been in the late medieval Low Countries, those women were by no means "exceptional": they had the opportunity to go through a door *potentially* open to *all* women. Moreover, they did so *not as equals* with men, but rather as substitutes. This exemplifies the limits of this particular gender pattern (and perhaps of all European and American gender patterns before the second feminist wave in the twentieth century).

An Egalitarian Trend?

Analysis of Low Countries customary law (*consuetudines*) by legal historians such as the authoritative John Gilissen focused on the opposition between so-called egalitarian and inegalitarian trends, and they concluded that the egalitarian trend predominated. Can this view stand up to the critic?[3]

It is clear indeed that a number of customary rules implied equal rights for men and women. In most of the legal systems the surviving spouse had a right of usufruct. Urban customs enabled daughters as well as sons to inherit movable goods, including houses. The parental authority over children was almost equally shared; in some customs the widow could take over paternal authority, elsewhere she gained at least considerable legal guardianship. Sometimes the mother could even share the parental authority with the father (contrary to the Northern Italian situation). We can thus authoritatively speak of equality or quasi-equality between husband and wife, boys and girls, with regard to *those* rules.[4] These rules are typical for the Low Countries, especially but not exclusively of urban laws. Such practices must have had an obvious impact on gender and family relations.

Nevertheless, inequality remained *the* rule. Not only were there many particular rules that implied a clear advantage to men (such as many inheritance principles privileging men or the mostly tacit prohibition against women taking on public responsibilities other than those associated with feudal tenure), but there were also encompassing fundamental principles that established a male-dominated society. Marital authority is the most striking. "The husband is lord and master in his house, during matrimony" (*Den man es heere ende meester van sijnen huyse, 't huwelijk gedurende*) says, for instance, a draft of the general custom of the county of Flanders in the beginning of the sixteenth century.[5] This principle implied the legal incapacity of the wife (with two exceptions important enough to mention in a comparative context: she could defend herself on her own in penal matters before a court as well as make her will). Her husband was supposed to administer her goods as well as his own and the common properties. This shows how relative the equality of inheritance concerning urban movable goods was: a woman could well inherit but could not manage such properties if and as long as she was married. The husband managed even the incomes that his wife could get as a *coopwijf* or public merchant.[6]

Despite legal latitudes offered to her, in the customary law or in learned law (both Roman and canon) a woman was supposed to be ultimately obedient. Indeed, the unmarried woman (unless legally and formally emancipated by her father) was subordinated to the father's authority and, as we have seen, the married wife to her husband's. Only the widow had greater legal autonomy. Its implications were, however, ambivalent. As demonstrated by Marianne Danneel, depending upon her socioeconomic situation, a widow's independence could work to her disadvantage (for example, pauperization and burden of children) as well as to her advantage (power and assertiveness). Moreover, this autonomy could be very provisional (second and third marriages were not rare and entailed renewed marital subordination).[7]

If we consider a number of rules from the perspective of the evolution of private law, it is indeed legitimate to speak of gender equality regarding a particular rule, but only as far as *that* very rule is concerned. There can be no doubt about general gender inequality in Low Countries customary law. An egalitarian model of gender relations thus cannot satisfy the historian, even concerning the great delta of northern Europe. From an anthropological and social perspective the opposition between egalitarian and inegalitarian trends is a false problem despite its longevity.[8] The explanation of the Low Countries gender-relations pattern thus has to be found elsewhere; I will now turn to this task.

Constructing a Model

In this enterprise I opted for an empirical historical anthropology. Such an approach seems to be the best fitted to integrate aspects of past life that are usually studied separately, as argued by Peter Burke.[9] This is particularly appropriate for the present stage of inquiry. In addition to legal history ground-breaking contributions often come from social historians[10] who deal with various issues like marriage, family, women's work, social mobility, and so on, which relate to the gender question without addressing it as such. Relying on their work, I propose a more coherent and comprehensive model of gender construction in the Burgundian Netherlands through a study of the perception of the body, marriage, sexuality, and female assertiveness. My research includes first-hand analysis of a large variety of fifteenth-century primary sources (narratives and other forms of literature such as novels and poetry, diplomatic sources, iconography, judicial accounts, and even some artifacts), representing both the urban world (in which the particularities of a "Flemish" gender pattern are especially developed) and the court of the dukes of Burgundy who ruled most of the Low Countries at that time.

The present model is of course not definitive but aims to bring together various research traditions and to offer a common analytical tool. The main theses are as follows. Gender relations were characterized by an intense feeling of corporeity, a differential sex life, and a female *subjugation* tempered by a "taking over" principle, which allowed women to take on many kinds of responsibilities *as substitutes* in the absence of a man, as when the father or the husband was dead or temporarily absent, *or as auxiliaries* of father or husband. This principle introduced *elasticity* into the definition of gender roles (perhaps causing some psychological insecurity to men) that enabled lucky women to fulfill most "typical" male occupations, excepting knighthood and public offices such as bailliff, mayor, alderman or chancellor. Such a pronounced elasticity is certainly the most striking feature of the gender pattern experienced in the late medieval Low Countries.

But this elasticity also needs to be understood in the larger context of the functions of marriage and the bipolar organization of sexual life. Despite the circumstances of its formation, its often underestimated political function, and the husband's uncontested authority, the marital link was also characterized by affection and collaboration. This explains, as we shall see later, how subordination could coexist along with the "taking over" principle throughout the lives of married couples. We also need to emphasize that sexuality, although seen as positive in itself, was reserved for decent women only in wedlock, whereas men had a much larger set of possibilities, including the procreation of bastard children (the famous "double standard"). Women were clearly divided into two groups on the basis of their morality and sexual behavior. First, there were the honest and honorable women—being chaste or at least faithful to their husbands—among whom daughters and widows could exercise an uncontested power on the grounds of the aforementioned "taking over" principle. Second, there were the so-called dishonest women, who were not really marginalized but rather confined to a certain social function—that of whore.

Such a bipartition did not apply to men. This is of course one of the key limits that society imposed on women. Even courtly love and the service of the ladies—those two cornerstones of courtly culture—emphasized female subjugation and passivity rather than an "elevation" of the lady.

Body and Gender

Before the era of the Reformation and the beginning of the "Prozeß der Zivilisation" first described by Norbert Elias, lay people had a positive and "holistic" experience of body and sexuality, despite any official Church policy of encouraging asceticism (*"contemptus mundi"*). This explains major cultural phenomena in the Low Countries such as going to the stews, often quite innocent nudity, evidences of eroticism and scatology in fine arts and literature, which, for the most part, should not be seen as a release from an oppressive morality. On the contrary, it was supported in the elite circles by the ideology of Nature (as constructed two centuries earlier by Jean de Meung and others).[11]

The medieval perception of the human body is usually characterized in ecclesiastical and learned conceptions by a strong dichotomy between flesh and soul. Inspired by the philosophy of late antiquity, patristic and monastic traditions developed a contemptuous discourse about the earthly world, especially in matters of body and sexuality. This corpus of doctrine is known as *"contemptus mundi."* Asceticism and sexual renunciation were regarded as the only way to salvation, and all obstacles on this path were systematically despised. Although since the twelfth and thirteenth centuries clerics had more understanding of Nature on a pure cognitive level, they still viewed flesh and sexuality in a very negative way on the moral level. The misogynistic male Latin culture was rooted in this vision.

Medieval and early Renaissance lay attitudes toward the body were quite different. The work of historians of mentalities shows how only very slowly from the sixteenth and seventeenth centuries onward did the strong dichotomy between soul and flesh, spirit and body, begin to dominate lay culture. Growing self-control and mastery of all bodily aspects of life such as table manners, decent ways of blowing one's nose, spitting, defecating, passing wind and urinating, or of seduction and sexual matters, are at the heart of the long trend that the famous sociologist Norbert Elias coined as the "Prozeß der Zivilisation."[12]

As I have argued elsewhere, linguistic evidence in the late Middle Ages might show how the body was still regarded as an essential—and not accessory—part of the person.[13] As in modern English, phrases like anybody or somebody refer not to a mere somatic reality but to the whole person. Similar survivals exist in modern French and Dutch. But in

Middle French and Middle Dutch, such uses were much more lively and not frozen locutions: not mere survivals but actual expressions of thought and feeling.

The average medieval lay perception of the person would have been more holistic than dichotomous, and would have approached the modern phenomenological concept of "corporeity" ("to be a body" rather than "to have a body").[14] As a result, body and sexuality would not have had any negative value judgment. We can find hints of such an attitude in various manifestations, to which we shall now turn, discussing briefly public stews, nudity, costume, and obscenity.

Medieval public stews were very often linked with prostitution, as we can deduce from the presence not only of vats but also of beds in some inventories as well as from the explicit link made in many judiciary sources. Nevertheless, we cannot pretend *a priori* that every stew was a locus of prostitution. The municipal legislation of Mons, a medium-scale city in the county of Hainaut, for example, very cautiously established a number of honest stews, where men and women were to be present alternatively and never on the same day, which were distinguished from the dishonest stews.[15] Besides, the elites had their own private stews, be it in ducal palaces or in noble and rich burgher houses, sometimes even with beds. There was indeed a proper medieval bathing culture. If we are to believe some literary texts (for example, stories of adulterous love), well-being and relaxation in the stews were likely to be coupled with sex and good eating but not necessarily with prostitution as such. This would indicate that physical well-being was not undervalued by the lay culture, and that the holistic body perception could include specific rituals like bathing in the stews.

Nudity is our second point in this discussion. To be nude was and still is an ambiguous situation. "To be nude in one's shirt" in front of other people was a humiliation, frequently used as a dishonorable penalty imposed on criminals and rebels. On the other hand, artists depicted female and male nudity, sometimes in contexts that clearly cannot support the idea that such representations were intended as stigmatization. Instead, they are more likely to be connected with a positive body experience than with sexual repression. Some manuscript miniatures even depicted genitals, both male and female, accurately and without shame.[16]

Third, this situation is mirrored by garment and costume, most of all within the elite. Cutting and fulling resulted in prominent bellies and décolletés for the ladies and damsels, in wide shoulders and accentuated genitals for (younger) men (and this even in religious painting like Memling's martyrdom of Saint Sebastian). This resulted in gender polarity at court and in the upper class. As an effect, gestures too were gendered: the man was free to move whereas the lady needs an arm to hold her dress against the hip or her belly when walking, an attitude widely attested by miniatures.

Fourth, there is the obscenity question. As elsewhere in the medieval West, many sexual and scatological elements may be observed in urban and court culture. Outstanding examples are the famous *Cent nouvelles nouvelles* at the court of Burgundy, building on the tradition of the *fabliaux* and of the Italian short story, the snowpops festival held in Brussels in 1511, or the poems written by Jehan Molinet.[17] Are these trivial elements a form of compensation for a growing sexual repression, as argued by Herman Pleij? Or are they an expression of a world still untouched by such a repressive movement, as Robert Muchembled believes? Although this is a matter still open to discussion, my own arguments point in the second direction. There was no compensation needed because there was still no large-scale effective repression. Sexual and scatological triviality would have for the most part to be seen as an expression of a holistic state of mind (supported by the ideology of Nature in the case of the elites), both for men and women. Indeed, even noble ladies possessed saucy texts. For example, the countess of Saint-Pol owned the famous *Evangiles des Quenouilles*, which are full of racy comments supposedly made by old women about their husbands or younger men,[18] and the widow Christine de Pizan memorialized the pleasure of her wedding night in a poem. Of course, a distinction has to be drawn between a positive experience of body and sexuality and freedom in one's sex life. For the honest women sex was only available with one's husband but could be gratifying. A man was able to choose a wider choice of partners without shame.

Marriage and Gender

Since in the eyes of the Church marriage was the only place for legitimate sexual activity for both males and females (but essentially for females as far as lay society is concerned), which functions did this social and religious institution fulfill? Was there expectation of mutual affection and pleasure, or was it a family business?[19]

The decision to wed was made by the family head (thus in most cases a man) and by the larger family (the so-called *amis charnels* in Middle French and *vrienden en magen* in Middle Dutch). The groom and bride could, however, discreetly influence the negotiations. The degree of choice is still debatable. Myriam Carlier suggests that in most cases, couples decided their marriage partner whereas financial negotiations for the marriage contract were left to the fathers and extended family.[20] Choice was less operative at the top of the social hierarchy—nobility and urban elites—where material and political interests were greater.

Marriage was not only an economic matter but also a way of enhancing one's status and standing. This explains the cases of abduction and forced marriages observed in the Low Countries.[21] But there is more. Marriage was also intrinsically a political alliance, a source of solidarity between two groups, be it in higher politics or in networks in the middle and lower classes. Primary sources make clear that political and military help was expected from kin. It was considered treasonous for kin to choose the enemy's side. It was also treasonous to contract a matrimonial link with the enemy. The link established between two groups by marriage worked as a political link. This political alliance was sealed through the copulation of two bodies, a private event that had public consequences.

Public implications of marriage and conjugal coitus were no obstacles to spousal affection. Couples could meet before the wedding and even in some cases choose their partners. Efficient collaboration in the shop or the workshop, or—in the case of the nobility—in the management of a manor or a princely state was impossible without a minimum of good understanding and spousal friendship. Evidence exists for the urban middle-class of artisans and shopkeepers as well as for the duchesses of Burgundy, who held an important position in the administration of what was one of the preeminent states of the time.[22] The extent to which this good understanding could be valued is evident in the supple practices adopted by officials toward matrimonial litigation. In the diocese of Cambrai, which covered a large part of the Low Countries, marriage annulments could be achieved on the basis of mutual incompatibility, itself a broad interpretation of canon law prescriptions.[23]

(Dis-)honest Women and Men

I already explained that I do not believe sex was seen by most lay people, male and female alike, as negative or immoral. However, gender clearly determined who could practice sexuality more freely. From this perspective "honest" women formed a group from which men took their wives and in which daughters and widows were allowed to exercise serious economic and political responsibilities when acting as substitutes of a dead or absent father or husband. Public fame largely determined membership. So it could be written in ducal patent letters that Marguerite de Carvin from Lille "governed herself honestly and kept herself well as an honorable daughter and maiden should do, and is thus commended in manners and honest conversation" (*se gouvernoit honnestement et se maintient comme fille et damoiselle de bien et d'onneur doit faire, et est tellement recommandée en meurs et conversation honneste*), a compliment based on testimonies by her neighbors.[24] It is striking how many slanders and insults against the sexual honesty of women were repressed by urban courts: to attack the slanderer was perhaps the only way for the insulted woman to preserve her reputation and to guarantee her membership in the group of honest women.

Otherwise she could easily switch to the other category, that of defamed women and girls: harlots and whores. I agree with Guy Dupont that prostitutes in the Low Countries were integrated into urban society, contrary to the classical historiographical view of the prostitute as marginal and excluded.[25] They had a role and a task to perform, though they did not enjoy the same status as honest women. It is thus important to stress how the female population was divided in two groups with different expectations and possibilities, based on how public fame evaluated their reputation in matters of sexual conduct.

As for men, such a distinction was of no significance, according to the so-called double standard. At the end of the Middle Ages bastard children were almost a sign of status for men, and visiting prostitutes was not defaming. In the lay system of values, sexual iniquities committed by men were incest, homosexuality, bestiality, and intercourse with the Devil.[26]

The Elasticity of Gender Roles

Thus the question arises as to the extent of women's liberty in such an obviously sexist and androcentric society. Although the reproductive sphere was indeed specific to women, male ideology could never entirely confine them to it. As elsewhere in Europe at that time, household and child-rearing were considered proper to women. For example, birth and its surrounding rituals were exclusively feminine. In 1456, as reported in the bailliff accounts, a man called H. vanden Damme was fined 15 pounds by the local baillif in Malines for spying—or at least listening to—his maid during the delivery.[27] This was supposed to be an exclusive female event. As demonstrated by A. Delva, pregnant women were, at least in the cities, accompanied and supported by qualified midwives. Birth iconography shows only women around the bed: some of them prepare a bath for the newborn baby and a meal for the mother. Consequently, only women were prosecuted for crimes of abortion and infanticide.[28]

A certain learned discourse, especially by clerics, tended to confine women to the household. Herman Pleij and other literary historians have illustrated this point. Dirc Potter, a poet at the court of Holland, described the ideal housewife as follows: "Thou, good wife, look for thy house, don't go wild, don't make any confusion." The negative image of the bad housewife corresponded to this imperative statement. So the *Reynaerts historie* (late fourteenth century) describes maids who prefer to dance all night and sleep long and softly in the morning.[29] Didactic literature, be it in the new humanistic trend or in the older scholastic tradition, also clearly attribute the role of housewife to married women.[30]

But were women therefore confined to the private sphere and excluded from all processes of production and decision? Were they exiled from the public to the private space? To answer these questions, it is necessary to distinguish between rural and urban contexts. In the country it seems that a more radical pattern existed, men caring for the fields, women for the cattle, the fowl, and the garden. But through that household-extended activity, country women had the opportunity to go far away from home to sell their products (eggs, butter, fruits, and vegetables) at an urban market. In such a travel- and sell-activity, they were surely supposed to be assertive.[31]

In the cities, the elasticity of gender patterns was greater but so were the risks of pauperization and prostitution. Contrary to the image of a rigid role and gendered space, urban women took part in economic life,[32] be it inside the household economy as auxiliaries and subordinate partners to their husbands, or outside, as unskilled wage-earners, for example, in the textile industry, or as servants (both situations that could be regarded as a mere natural extension of housewifery).[33] So their position was either marginal or subordinate. They seldom come up in the sources, but at times their competence and economic power can be observed, as in the case of the Ghent widows studied by M. Danneel. Some women might also achieve a career as a "public merchant" (*coopwijf* or *femme marchande publique*), a status more or less comparable to that of *femme sole* in England; nonetheless, even she was ultimately subordinate to the husband, who was legally responsible for the administration of his wife's incomes, and who was supposed to accept tacitly her economic activities.[34]

As a substitute for father or husband, noble women and urban middle and upper class women could show economic and political assertiveness and be accepted by society. A typical example is the duchess of Burgundy, Isabel of Portugal, who had important functions during the reign of her husband Philip the Good. She not only managed the ducal finances but also often exerted power by marital delegation.[35] One can find parallels in wives of other dukes[36] and in kinswomen of the prince governing the Netherlands on his behalf in the sixteenth century, such as Margaret of Austria and Mary of Hungary, or later the royal bastard Margaret of Parma.[37]

The unquestioned presence of women in the public space is also demonstrated by the phenomenon of female spies and messengers in wartime. The idea was surely that women (as much as priests and friars) could easily go "through the lines" and wander under the pretext of usual occupations such as going to the market to sell butter and eggs. Burgundian ducal accounts show that they could be prostitutes as well as honest women like wives of lower urban officers. But some of them could nevertheless have been suspected if their stories failed to convince, such as a woman at the end of the fifteenth century who pretended to be on pilgrimage and was arrested in the Brabantine city of Nivelles.[38]

Even though the housewife was the ideal of theoretical and didactic literature, and maternity, child-rearing and household daily management were considered proper to women, it was still not unusual nor socially unacceptable to see women active in the public space. They functioned there in activities that might have been seen as ultimately derived from housewifery, or as auxiliaries or substitutes to men (but significantly never in their own right as men's equals). In such instances, they could even exert authority and power, demonstrating assertiveness and expertise.

Courtly Subjugation: The Chivalric Gender Pattern

Let us finally pay special attention to gender patterns at court and in the nobility. What I call the chivalric gender pattern was rooted in ordinary Low Countries patterns and was far from any glamorous idealization of the Lady.[39] The theme of service to ladies was one of the core elements of chivalric and courtly culture. It was staged in important ceremonies and rituals (such as tournaments and jousts) that contributed to the cohesion and self-consciousness of the aristocratic elites. It was one of the traditional duties imposed by clerics upon the ideal knight.

But service to ladies was also a generalization of the textual courtly love relationship found in literature from the twelfth century on. Courtly love was an idea familiar to aristocratic circles in the Burgundian Netherlands. At and around the ducal court new romances were composed and old romances and epics were changed from verse to prose. Both old and new could be found in the luxurious manuscripts of the ducal library and in those of high aristocratic status, such as the lord of Gruuthuse, the lord of Wavrin, and the Croy family. In these texts heroic knights acted for the love of a maid whom they rescued and frequently married. This pattern typically staged male activity and female passivity.

In the classical view courtly love was adulterous and involved a lady of higher rank and a knight of lower status: she imposed heroic deeds upon him and gave herself only progressively to him, according to some critics, in a platonic way. Rüdiger Schnell has shown, however, that no consistent and established doctrine existed. There was only a courtly discourse about true and good love. Literary texts show not only a variety of opinions but also a variety of love phases. A romance could describe a whole relationship, or a poem may have concentrated on one moment of hope or despair, uncertainty or trust in the reciprocity of the feelings.[40] Such a love was, however, only a literary (and fictive) phenomenon, even if some chronicles gave the appearance of courtly love to the relationship between their characters: courtship, seduction, and flirting matched the external form of courtly love.

Forms of service to ladies and theatrical representations of courtly love took place at the Burgundian court, which shows how highly the chivalric gender pattern was regarded by the top of society. What can explain this high ideological value in European late medieval aristocratic circles and particularly at the Burgundian court? It had a double function: on the one hand the organization of a mixed court society obligated by politeness, on the other hand the prevention of potential gender transgression by women. The first function—politeness between genders—was particularly important in a society that extolled beauty, emphasized sexual characters through clothing, and viewed the female presence at court as essential. Prevention of transgression in its turn can be explained by the fact that in those circles a woman could achieve the highest possible form of power through the exercise of feudal authority as subsitute for kin, husband, or child. Men could thus, by opposing female passivity to male activity (consciously or not), stress subjugation in the place of "taking over" (and of potential assertiveness), and ease their fears of female power.

Conclusion

Neither equality, radical oppression nor patriarchy characterized gender patterns in the late medieval Low Countries. Undeniable female subjugation was *tempered by* a "taking over" principle that enabled women under favorable circumstances to assert themselves and to exercise power and authority in the public space, as *auxiliaries* or full *substitutes* to a father or husband. By this means women were not confined to a private sphere and a prominent *elasticity* pervaded gender roles. But the actual "takeover" as a substitute was limited to the group of honest women; moreover, the structural opportunities offered to these women in the absence of the father or husband could mean assertiveness and power for some women or oppression and decadence for others, depending upon their concrete socioeconomic situation and personal aptitudes. The model is supple and can account for the variety of observed life situations.

Although I focused here on lay men and women, I think that such a model can be applied to the condition of religious and semireligious women as well. When accepted by the male ecclesiastical hierarchy and by the lay society their assertiveness could be justified in the same way. Holy women, mystics, and visionaries were acting in the eyes of their contemporaries as substitutes, that is as representatives of a higher being (a saint, an angel, or God).[41]

In this study it was necessary to limit some aspects of gender such as the importance of matrilinear filiation in family strategies or the differential use of violence by men and women.[42] Moreover, there is still a lot of research to be done in the field of legal as well as social and cultural history (studies are needed on sources from legal practice, like those by R. Jacob, M. Howell, and M. Danneel on Douai and Ghent). New archival findings may confirm or complicate the model elaborated here. For example, evidence for women at work should be analyzed very carefully, considering whether such women acted as auxiliaries, substitutes, *coopwijf*, in high or low status activities, inside or outside a guild. The comparative question also needs to be raised, especially regarding Italian gender patterns.[43] Is this model valid for all northwestern Europe in contrast to the near absence of elastic roles in Italy and the Mediterranean? Should we perhaps try to measure "differential elasticities"? If present, how should we explain them? And how did these patterns evolve in later times?

In the north, since approximatively the seventeenth century, the model altered progressively under the influence of the "Prozeß der Zivilisation," so that in nineteenth-century bourgeois culture the holistic perception of the body had disappeared along with most of the effects of the "taking over" principle (cf. the impact of the French "Code civil" on the Continent). The double standard ruled sexual life more than ever. Late medieval and Renaissance housewife ideology finally had its revenge on social praxis. New major changes in gender relations could only appear with the rise of feminism, which affirmed the principle of *equality*.

Notes

An earlier version of this chapter appeared as E. Bousmar, "Een historisch-anthropologische kijk op gender in de Bourgondische Nederlanden (15de eeuw)," *Verslagen van het RUG-Centrum voor Genderstudies—1999—nr. 8*, ed. N. De Bleeckere, M. Demoor, and K. Heene (Ghent: Academia Press, 1999), pp. 35–53. It offers a synthesis of my doctoral dissertation, to be published by Brepols Publishers as *Des compagnons inégaux. Le vécu des relations hommes / femmes dans les Pays-Bas bourguignons (ca. 1440–ca. 1510): mentalités et comportements*.

1. The interpretation is therefore completely different and hopefully more accurate than M. Greilsammer's model, which focused only on marriage and maternity. See M. Greilsammer, *L'envers du tableau. Mariage et maternité en Flandre médiévale* (Paris: A. Colin, 1990) and E. Bousmar, "Mariage et maternité en Flandre et Brabant (1250–1600). A propos d'un livre de Myriam Greilsammer," *Revue d'histoire ecclésiastique* 88 (1993), pp. 805–15.

2. Howell makes clear that female high-status labor activities in the Low Countries and the Rhineland derive from the patterns of household economy. Martha C. Howell, *Women, Production, and Patriarchy in Late Medieval Cities* (Chicago: Chicago University Press, 1986). See also *The Marriage Exchange.*

Property, Social Place and Gender in Cities of the Low Countries, 1300–1550 (Chicago: Chicago University Press, 1998).

3. References for factual material and historical analysis discussed in this section can be found in J. Gilissen, "Le statut de la femme dans l'ancien droit belge," *Recueils de la Société Jean Bodin pour l'histoire comparative des institutions,* vol. 12: *La femme* (Brussels, 1962), pp. 255–321; see also the *summa* by Philippe Godding, *Le droit privé dans les Pays-Bas méridionaux du 12e au 18e siècle* (Brussels: Académie royale de Belgique, 1991) and the study of familial structures by Robert Jacob, *Les époux, le seigneur et la cité. Coutume et pratiques matrimoniales des bourgeois et paysans de France du Nord au moyen âge.* Publication des Facultés universitaires Saint-Louis, vol. 50 (Brussels: P.F.U.S.L., 1990), whose "geographical northern France" in fact concerns Low Countries cities.

4. See the use of the phrase "egalitarian" by M. Danneel, "Gender and the Life Course in the Late Medieval Flemish Towns," "in *Secretorum Scriptorum". Liber alumnorum Walter Prevenier,* ed. W. Blockmans, M. Boone, and Th. de Hemptinne (Louvain/Apeldoorn: Garant, 1999), pp. 227, 230–31. The legal situation was quite different in northern Italian cities. A good summary can be found in C.E. Meek, "Women, Dowries and the Family in Late Medieval Italian cities," in *The Fragility of Her Sex? Medieval Irish Women in Their European Context,* ed. C.E. Meek and M.K. Simms (Dublin: Four Court Press, 1996), pp. 136–52.

5. Quoted by Gilissen, "Le statut de la femme," p. 289, n. 3.

6. *Coopwijf:* a tacit status by which a limited legal capacity was attributed to some married woman in order to practice an autonomous commercial activity (only partially comparable to that of *femme sole* in England, whose autonomy was greater). See Gilissen, "Le statut de la femme," pp. 295–298; Godding, *Le droit privé,* p. 80; and M. Danneel, *Weduwen en wezen in het laat-middeleeuwse Gent,* Studies in Urban Social, Economic and Political History of the Medieval and Early Modern Low Countries, vol. 3 (Apeldoorn/Louvain: Garant, 1995).

7. M. Danneel, *Weduwen en wezen.* On the high rate of female remarriages, which seems typical for the Low Countries especially in contrast with Italy, see M.C. Howell, "The Social Logic of the Marital Household in Cities of the Late Medieval Low Countries," in *The Household in Late Medieval Cities, Italy and Northwestern Europe Compared. Proceedings of the International Conference Ghent, 21st–22nd January 2000,* ed. M. Carlier and T. Soens, Studies in Urban Social, Economic and Political History of the Medieval and Early Modern Low Countries, vol. 12 (Louvain-Apeldoorn: Garant, 2001), pp. 194–96.

8. It was the basis of much historical research and is still recently at the core of Myriam Greilsammer's work, in which, building on an insight of J. Gilissen, she tried to explain the urban egalitarian trend by the needs of economic growth. See Greilsammer, *L'envers du tableau.*

9. P. Burke, "Overture: The New History, Its Past and Its Future," in *New Perspectives on Historical Writing,* ed. P. Burke (Cambridge: Cambridge University Press, 1991), pp. 1–23.

10. It is impossible here not to mention the Ghent school of Walter Prevenier and his former students (among others, Marc Boone, Thérèse de Hemptinne, Peter Stabel, Marianne Danneel, and Myriam Carlier). A recent and fundamental synthesis, *Le prince et le peuple. Images de la société du temps des ducs de Bourgogne, 1384–1530*, ed. Walter Prevenier (Antwerp: Fonds Mercator, 1998), includes many insights and data on gender, sexuality, household, and social networks. See also Myriam Carlier, *Kinderen van de minne? Bastaarden in het 15de eeuwse Vlaanderen* (Brussels: Koninklijke Vlaamse Academie van België, 2001).

11. This section is discussed at length, with full references, in E. Bousmar, "Het weerbarstige lichaam. Profane cultuur en het officiële ascetisme van de Kerk in de Bourgondische Nederlanden," in *Het lichaam m/v*, ed. Kaat Wils, Alfred Cauchies reeks, vol. 3 (Leuven: Leuven University Press, 2001), pp. 40–54 and 274–75.

12. Norbert Elias, *Über den Prozess der Zivilisation. Sociogenetische und psychogenetische Untersuchungen*, 2nd edition (Bern/Munich: Franke, 1969) and R. Muchembled, *L'invention de l'homme moderne: culture et sensibilités en France du XVe au XVIIIe siècle*, 2nd edition (Paris: Fayard, 1994).

13. E. Bousmar, "L'importance du corps dans les mentalités, à l'aube du processus de 'civilisation des mœurs' (2e moitié du XVe siècle). Eléments d'enquête," *LIIe congrès de la Fédération des Cercles d'archéologie et d'histoire de Belgique / Cinquième congrès de l'Association des Cercles francophones d'histoire et d'archéologie de Belgique. Herbeumont, 22–25 août 1996. Actes* (Namur: Division du Patrimoine du Ministère de la Région wallonne, 1996–2000), vol. I, pp. 127–28 [summary] and vol. II, pp. 351–60 [full text].

14. I refer here (among others) to the thought of the famous French philosopher Maurice Merleau-Ponty.

15. L. Devillers, ed., *Bans de police de la ville de Mons du XIIIe au XVe siècle* (Mons: Publications de la Société des Bibliophiles belges siégeant à Mons, 1897), and E. Bousmar, "Whores, Beggars and Laborers: Regulation Purpose and the Penal Discourse of a Medium-Scale City (Mons, 13th– early 16th c.)," paper read at the Third European Social Science History Conference (Amsterdam, April 12–15, 2000, session on "Politics of Expulsion in Medieval Cities"), to be published.

16. Bousmar, *Des compagnons inégaux*, section 3.4.2 and also "Iconographie et genre. Le cas des Pays-Bas bourguignons (XVe siècle): quelques pistes et résultats de recherche," *Women's Studies. Etudes féministes en Belgique 1997–2000* (Brussels: Sophia-Réseau de coordination des études féministes, 2002), pp. 127–36.

17. F.P. Sweetser, ed., *Les Cent nouvelles nouvelles* (Geneva: Droz, 1966); H. Pleij, *De sneeuwpoppen van 1511: literatuur en stadscultuur tussen middeleeuwen en moderne tijd* (Amsterdam/Leuven: Meulenhoff, 1988); Paul Verhuyck, "Jean Molinet et les étapes de la vieillesse: 'du bas mestier les plus grans coups sont oultre,'" in *Les niveaux de vie au moyen âge: mesures, perceptions et représentations*, ed. J.-P. Sosson, Cl. Thiry, S. Thonon, and T. Van Hemelryck (Louvain-la-Neuve: Academia-Bruylant, 1999), pp. 421–50.

18. Madeleine Jeay, ed., *Les Evangiles des Quenouilles* (Paris/Montréal: Presses de l'Université de Montréal, 1985).

19. E. Bousmar, "Des alliances liées à la procréation: les fonctions du mariage dans les Pays-Bas bourguignons," *Mediaevistik*. *Internationale Zeitschrift für interdisziplinäre Mittelalterforschung* 7 (1994), pp. 11–69, and *Des compagnons inégaux*, chapter 4.

20. M. Carlier, "Solidariteit of sociale contrôle? De rol van vrienden en magen en buren in een middeleeuwse stad," in *Hart en marge in de laat-middeleeuwse stedelijke maatschappij: handelingen van het colloquium te Gent (22–23 augustus 1996)*, ed. M. Carlier, A. Greve, W. Prevenier, and P. Stabel, Studies in Urban Social, Economic and Political History of the Medieval and Modern Low Countries, vol. 7 (Apeldoorn/Leuven: Garant, 1997), p. 80. See also Bousmar, "Les fonctions du mariage," and M. Danneel, *Weduwen en wezen*.

21. See Myriam Greilsammer, "Rapts de séduction et rapts violents en Flandre et en Brabant à la fin du moyen âge," *Tijdschrift voor Rechtsgeschiedenis/Revue d'histoire du droit* 56 (1988), pp. 49–84; W. Prevenier, "La stratégie et le discours politique des ducs de Bourgogne concernant les rapts et les enlèvements de femmes parmi les élites des Pays-Bas au XVe siècle," in *Das Frauenzimmer: die Frau bei Hofe in Spätmittelalter und Früher Neuzeit. 6. Symposium der Residenzen-Kommission der Akademie der Wissenschaften in Göttingen*, ed. J. Hirschbiegel and W. Paravicini, Residenzenforschung, vol. 11 (Stuttgart: Thorbecke Verlag, 2000), pp. 429–37, as well as the earlier case-studies by this author on the same issue.

22. Monique Sommé, *Isabelle de Portugal, duchesse de Bourgogne: une femme de pouvoir au XVe siècle* (Villeneuve-d'Ascq: Presses universitaires du Septentrion, 1998); Christine Wheightman, *Margaret of York, Duchess of Burgundy, 1446–1503* (Gloucester, New York: St. Martin's Press, 1989); Bousmar, *Des compagnons inégaux*, section 6.4.

23. Monique Vleeschouwers-van Melkebeek, "Aspects du lien matrimonial dans le Liber sentenciarum de Bruxelles (1448–1459)," *Tijdschrift voor Rechtsgeschiedenis/Revue d'histoire du droit* 53 (1985), pp. 67–74; and also "Classical Canon Law on Marriage. The Making and Breaking of Households," in *The Household in Late Medieval Cities, Italy and Northwestern Europe Compared. Proceedings of the international conference Ghent, 21st–22nd January 2000*, ed. M. Carlier and T. Soens, Studies in Urban Social, Economic and Political History of the Medieval and Early Modern Low Countries, vol. 12 (Leuven-Apeldoorn: Garant, 2001), p. 21.

24. Carlier, "Solidariteit," p. 77, n. 17.

25. Guy Dupont, *Maagdenverleidsters, hoeren en speculanten: prostitutie in Brugge tijdens de Bourgondische periode (1385–1515)*, Vlaamse historische studies, vol. 10 (Bruges: Genootschap voor Geschiedenis, 1996); and also "'Des filles de legiere vie': de draaglijke lichtheid van het bestaan als prostituee in het laat-middeleeuwse Brugge," in *Hart en marge*, pp. 93–103. I am currently investigating the foundation of late fifteenth-century repentent houses (Magdalens) in Low Countries cities (Lille, Mons, Valenciennes, and Tournai) and the influence of Dowager Duchess Margaret of York (the sister of Edward IV and widow of duke of Burgundy, Charles the Bold) in this process.

26. M. Boone, "State Power and Illicit Sexuality: The Persecution of Sodomy in Late Medieval Bruges," *Journal of Medieval History* 22 (1996), pp. 135–53, and Bousmar, *Des compagnons inégaux*, chapter 5.

27. *de Hennen vanden Damme, de ce qu'il estoit derrière une montée pour escouter après sa baiselette, qui estoit en grant travail d'enfant, lequel n'appartenoit poynt à oyr à hommes, dont ledit escoutète en a receu par composition 15 livres.* Quoted by L.-Th. Maes, "Les délits de mœurs dans le droit pénal coutumier de Malines," *Revue du Nord* 30 (1948), pp. 11–12. Literally a "composition" is not a fine but a sum paid to avoid a trial.

28. Ann Delva, *Vrouwengeneeskunde in Vlaanderen tijdens de late middeleeuwen*, Vlaamse historische studies, vol. 2 (Bruges: Genootschap voor Geschiedenis, 1983); Greilsammer, *L'envers du tableau*.

29. *Ghi, goede wive, verwaert u huus / loopt niet in 't wilde, maect gheen confuus;* maids *die liever dansen in den nacht / en 's morgens slapen lanck en zacht,* Herman Pleij, *De sneeuwpoppen van 1511. Literatuur en stadscultuur tussen middeleeuwen en moderne tijd* (Amsterdam/Leuven: Meulenhoff, 1988), p. 260.

30. Pleij, *De sneeuwpoppen*, pp. 278–79. Differential gender patterns in devotion follow the same spatial partition and might explain why male devotional diptychs of male sitters appear on panels (a semipublic issue) and that of female worshippers in books of hours (a more private way of representation). See Andrea G. Pearson, "Personal Worship, Gender, and the Devotional Portrait Diptych," *The Sixteenth Century Journal* 31 (2000), pp. 99–122.

31. There is a fine study based on the city of Binche in the county of Hainaut, by Claire Billen: "Le marché urbain: un espace de liberté pour les femmes rurales?" in *Les femmes et la ville en Belgique: histoire et sociologie,* ed. J.-P. Nandrin and E. Gubin, Publication des Facultés universitaries Saint-Louis Collection Travaux et Recherches, vol. 28 (Brussels: P.F.U.S.L., 1993), pp. 41–56.

32. See especially Peter Stabel, "Women at the Market. Gender and Retail in the Towns of Late Medieval Flanders," in *Secretorum Scriptorum. Liber alumnorum Walter Prevenier,* ed. W. Blockmans, M. Boone, and Th. de Hemptinne (Leuven/Apeldoorn: Garant, 1999), pp. 259–76.

33 On household collaboration, see Howell, "The Social Logic." On servants, see M. Danneel, "Quelques aspects du service domestique féminin à Gand, d'après les registres et les manuels échevinaux des Parchons (2ème moitié du XVe siècle)," in *Sociale structuren en topografie van armoede en rijkdom in de 14de en 15de eeuw: methodologische aspecten en resultaten van recent onderzoek. Handelingen van het colloquium gehouden te Gent op 24 mei 1985,* ed. W. Prevenier, R. Van Uytven, and E. Van Cauwenberghe, Studia Historica Gandensia, vol. 267 (Ghent: Universiteit Gent, 1986), pp. 51–72.

34. See Godding, *Le droit privé,* and Danneel, *Weduwen en wezen.*

35. See Monique Sommé, *Isabelle de Portugal.*

36. See W. Prevenier and W. Blockmans, *De Bourgondiërs: de Nederlanden op weg naar eenheid 1384–1530* (Amsterdam: Meulenhoff, 1997), pp. 51, 54 ff., 64, 72, 113, 116. As a dowager, Margaret of York played a similar role in the Burgundian-Habsburg Netherlands, by counseling Mary and Maximilian,

and later on their son Archduke Philipp the Handsome. See Ch. Weightman, *Margaret of York*. On earlier princesses, see Th. de Hemptinne, "Les épouses des croisés et pélerins flamands aux XIe et XIIe siècles. L'exemple des comtesses de Flandre Clémence et Sibylle," in *Autour de la première croisade. Actes du colloque de la Society for the Study of the Crusades and the Latin East (Clermont-Ferrand, 22–25 juin 1995)*, ed. M. Ballard, Byzantina Sorboniensia, vol. 14 (Paris: Presses de l/Université Paris-Sorbonne, 1996), pp. 83–95; and also her "Deux princesses au pouvoir: les règnes de Jeanne et Marguerite de Constantinople," *Septentrion* 25 (1996), pp. 73–75; in M. Margue, ed., *Ermesinde et l'affranchissement de la ville de Luxembourg. Etudes sur la femme, le pouvoir et la ville au XIIIe siècle*, Publications du CLUDEM, vol. 7 (Luxembourg: CLUDEM, 1994).

37. Laetitia Gorter-van Roijen, "De regentessen van Karel V in de Nederlanden. Beeld en werkelijkheid," *Tijdschrift voor Geschiedenis* 110 (1997), pp. 169–97; Barbara Welzel, "Die Macht der Witwen. Zum Selbstverständnis niederländischer Statthalterinnen," in *Das Frauenzimmer: die Frau bei Hofe in Spätmittelalter und Früher Neuzeit. 6. Symposium der Residenzen-Kommission der Akademie der Wissenschaften in Göttingen*, ed. J. Hirschbiegel and W. Paravicini, Residenzenforschung, vol. 11 (Stuttgart: Thorbecke Verlag, 2000), pp. 287–309. See also Laura Gelfand's chapter in this volume, "Regency, Power and Dynastic Visual Memory: Margaret of Austria as Patron and Propagandist."

38. Rosalba Vandewiele, "Les champs relationnels à la fin du moyen âge et à l'aube des temps modernes: le regard de l'arrière-pays," in *Les champs relationnels en Europe du Nord et du Nord-Ouest des origines à la fin du Premier Empire*, ed. S. Curveiller (Calais, 1994), pp. 157–69; Bousmar, *Des compagnons inégaux*, section 6.3.1.); Anne Godfroid follows both in her "Les femmes dans les guerres d'Ancien Régime," in *Femmes et guerre 16e–20e s. Dossier*, ed. A. Godfroid and K. Celis, Archives générales du Royaume et Archives de l'État dans les Provinces, Service éducatif, Dossiers Première série, vol. 18 (Brussels: AGR, 1997), pp. 14–15.

39. Eric Bousmar, "La place des hommes et des femmes dans les fêtes de cour bourguignonnes (Philippe le Bon-Charles le Hardi)," in *A la cour de Bourgogne. Le duc, son entourage, son train*, ed. J.-M. Cauchies, Burgundica, vol. 1 (Turnhout: Brepols, 1998), pp. 11–31 [with an addendum, first published in *Fêtes et cérémonies aux XIVe–XVIe siècles. Rencontres de Lausanne (23 au 26 septembre 1993)*, ed. J.-M. Cauchies, Publications du Centre européen d'Etudes bourguignonnes XIVe–XVIe siècles, vol. 34 (Neuchâtel: C.E.E.B., 1994), pp. 123–43]; idem, *Des compagnons inégaux*, chapter 7; Bousmar and M. Sommé, "Femmes et espaces féminins à la cour de Bourgogne au temps d'Isabelle de Portugal (1430–1457)," in *Das Frauenzimmer: die Frau bei Hofe in Spätmittelalter und Früher Neuzeit. 6. Symposium der Residenzen-Kommission der Akademie der Wissenschaften in Göttingen*, ed. J. Hirschbiegel and W. Paravicini, Residenzenforschung, vol. 11 (Stuttgart: Thorbecke, 2000), pp. 47–78. For a good introduction to the chivalric and courtly culture, including some datas from the Low Countries, see W. Paravicini, *Die ritterlich-höfische Kultur des Mittelalters*, Enzyklopedie deutscher Geschichte, vol. 32 (Munich: Oldenbourg, 1994).

40. R. Schnell, "Die 'höfische' Liebe als 'höfische' Diskurs über die Liebe," in *Curialitas. Studien zur Grundfragen der höfisch-ritterlichen Kultur*, ed.

J. Fleckenstein, Veröffentlichungen des Max-Planck-Instituts für Geschichte, vol. 100 (Göttingen: Vandenhoeck und Ruprecht, 1990), pp. 231–301.

41. And this can be said as well of Joan of Arc (at least by the other side, that of the French Armagnacs and partisans of the Dauphin, enemies of the Burgundians), and Colette de Corbie, the Franciscan reformer and visionary supported by the Burgundian court, or Liedewij van Schiedam, the maid who suffered a long and ecstatic agony, and of so many mystics in earlier centuries (who could adopt a passive and receptive pose to justify— even in their own eyes—their assertive discourse), and even of economically active beguines. For Jeanne, among many studies, see Jan van Herwaarden, ed., *Joan of Arc, Reality and Myth* (Hilversum: Verloren, 1994) and Jelle Koopmans "Jeanne d'Arc auteur de sa propre légende," in *Jeanne d'Arc entre les nations*, ed. A.J. Hoenselaars and Jelle Koopmans (Amsterdam: Rodopi, 1998), pp. 5–15; for Colette: Martine Thiry-Stassin, "Les 'Nourritures terrestres' dans la vie de sainte Colette de Corbie," in *'A l'heure encore de mon escrire': Aspects de la littérature de Bourgogne sous Philippe le Bon et Charles le Téméraire*, ed. Claude Thiry (Louvain-la-Neuve: Les lettres romanes, 1997), pp. 207–18, and Elizabeth Lopez, "Sainte Colette et la maison de Bourgogne," in *Le Banquet du Faisan, 1454: l'Occident face au défi de l'Empire ottoman*, ed. M.-Th. Caron and D. Clauzel (Arras: Artois Université Presse, 1997), pp. 289–301; for Liedewij: Ludo Jongen and Cees Schotel, eds., *Het leven van Liedewij, de maagd van Schiedam. De middelnederlandse tekst naar de bewaarde bronnen uitgegeven, vertaald en van commentaar voorzien* (Hilversum: Verloren, 1994); more generally: Michel Lauwers, "Paroles de femmes, sainteté féminine. L'Eglise du XIIIe siècle face aux béguines," in *La critique historique à l'épreuve. Liber discipulorum Jacques Paquet*, ed. J.-M. Cauchies and G. Braive, Publications des Facultés universitaires Saint-Louis Collection Travaux et Recherches, vol. 17 (Brussels: P.F.U.S.L., 1989), pp. 99–115, and J. Dor, L. Johnson, and J. Wogan-Browne, eds., *New Trends in Feminine Spirituality: The Holy Women of Liège and Their Impact* (Turnhout: Brepols, 1999); as well as the many contributions in this volume on religious women. On a sixteenth-century transitional Brabantine figure mixing late medieval and early modern features, see Ruth Timmermans, "Een laat-middeleeuwse mystieke vrouw met moderne ideën. Religiositeit, lichaam en taal in verbeelden en handelen van Maria van Hout († 1547)," in *Het lichaam (m/v)*, ed. Kaat Wils, Alfred Cauchies reeks, vol. 3 (Leuven: Leuven University Press, 2001), pp. 71–86 and 277–79.

42. On the first, see Bousmar, *Des compagnons inégaux*, section 4.2.

43. A recent step in this direction is the international colloquium organised at Ghent by Myriam Carlier in January 2000: Myriam Carlier and Tim Soens, eds., *The Household in Late Medieval Cities, Italy and Northwestern Europe Compared. Proceedings of the international conference Ghent, 21st–22nd January 2000*, Studies in Urban Social, Economic and Political History of the Medieval and Early Modern Low Countries, vol. 12 (Leuven-Apeldoorn: Garant, 2001).

PART TWO

ART AND PERFORMANCE

CHAPTER 6

VISIONARIES IN THE PUBLIC EYE:
BEGUINE LITERATURE AS PERFORMANCE

Mary A. Suydam

In the last twenty years two exciting developments in scholarship—one textual and one performative—have changed the way many medievalists approach texts and authors. First, textual studies scholars like Brian Stock have persuasively argued that medieval readers and writers had a different relationship with their texts than do modern readers.[1] Second, scholars in the field of sermon studies have focused on the relationships between written texts and their oral performance.[2] So far, application of both textual and sermon studies perspectives has been limited to the "textual communities" of educated, Latin-reading clerical males—the people who produced written texts and performed them as sermons.[3]

Another and quite different "textual community" in the southern Low Countries consisted of the *mulieres sanctae* ("holy women"), or, as they were coming to be known, beguines, a few of whom were ecstatic visionaries.[4] These women did not have access to, or authority over, the wide array of Latin texts available to clerics. Although many could read and perhaps write only their native vernacular language, a few (such as Hadewijch of Antwerp) possessed some knowledge of Latin and knew important traditional texts. Nevertheless, despite their lack of Latinate authority, some of these women fired the imagination, lay and clerical, of their contemporaries and achieved notoriety within their culture. This notoriety was based upon their reputation for extraordinary sanctity, as well as upon their fame as healers of the living and the dead (in terms of release or mitigation of time in purgatory). Their healing powers were demonstrated by an astonishing array of ecstatic manifestations.

A few of these women documented their activities themselves; admiring clerics preserved the memory of others.[5] In this essay I argue that the written texts—both self- and other-authored—of the ecstatic experiences of thirteenth-century "holy women" like Ida of Nivelles, Ida of Leuven, Lutgard of Aywières, and Hadewijch of Antwerp should be regarded as performative rather than as purely literary.[6] A performance perspective, which focuses upon the public aspects of events described in texts, is a more useful tool for understanding the interdependence between these women and their audiences.[7] These beguines expressed an array of astonishing public behaviors, including trance-induced dancing, mystical songs, and divine healing. Such ecstatic manifestations should be regarded as public performances rather than privately received "visions" because they took place in front of audiences and affected these audiences. Moreover, a performance perspective helps explain why such activities were textually recorded at all.

As explained in the introduction, daily life in the southern Low Countries had an oral and public character. For women as well as for men noteworthy events were expected to take place in front of other people, and written documentation was a secondary feature.[8] The beguine movement reflected these oral and public features. These semireligious women either lived in rented apartments or in beguinages, generally centrally located within towns. Jocelyn Wogan-Browne and Marie-Élisabeth Henneau describe some beguinages as "towns within towns" and note that they "tend to be laid out. . .as separate buildings linked by streets, a fact which creates a more varied and open sense of communal, indeed of civic, life than even the largest of earlier female abbeys."[9] Moreover, their emphasis upon emulation of Christ through dedication to a life of poverty and service to others meant that beguines served the public as teachers, nurses, and caretakers of the poor.[10] Thus, rather than individuals rapt in private ecstasy, beguine visionaries were full participants in their communal life of prayer, work, and service.

Women who began religious lives as beguines but eventually joined Cistercian or Dominican convents brought these spiritual interests with them.[11] This is apparent in the *Vitae* of Low Countries "holy women"— devout women such as Marie d'Oignies, Ida of Leuven, and Beatrijs of Nazareth, all of whom eventually professed monastic vows, yet continued to live communally and to care for others.[12] They were not solitary recluses who spent most of their lives passively absorbed in the presence of the Divine. Examining the records of spectacular visions and other spiritual phenomena of these holy women, it is striking that most of them occurred in communal spaces, most often during Mass. Consequently, there were almost always audiences who witnessed and perhaps participated in these events. Where there is audience, there is performance. In this chapter I argue first that visionary manifestations should be regarded as a type of performance. Second, I hypothesize that the textual communities of producers and readers who told stories of these women reflect performative concerns. That is, they argue for a performative model of holiness and, especially in the writings produced by beguines themselves, are intended to foster performances in others.

Theories of Performance: Drama and Ritual

When reconfigured to take medieval culture into account, the performance theories of Manfred Pfister and Richard Schechner and the concepts of ritual advanced by Schechner and Victor Turner have particular usefulness for reconceptualizing Low Countries ecstatic experiences and their subsequent retellings as "sacred performances." Pfister's *The Theory and Analysis of Drama* (1977) specifies how drama differs from literature. A literary text is generally written by one author and read by one individual at a time; in contrast, theatrical performances are characterized by "a collectivity of production and reception."[13] "Collectivity of production" means that no one person is solely responsible for a theatrical production. A "collectivity of reception" indicates that a group of people (an audience) engages with the work rather than a single reader. Stories written about beguine holy women demonstrate both characteristics. Consider an example from the *Vita* of Lutgard of Aywières, at this time a Benedictine nun:

> Lutgard had been keeping up her night vigils, on and on, and one night the nuns were to see, up above her, for a sizable portion of the night, the glittering of a light brighter than the sun. . .This light was transfused into, not merely to herself alone, but also into those who beheld it. They experienced it in the terms of Our Lady's promise, as "an augmenting of the Grace of the spiritual life."[14]

For now, let us take this story at face value. At first glance it seems to be a typical example from the stock of stories about holy women. Lutgard, seemingly lost in contemplation, glowed with a visible light. However, the story as actually presented is far more complex. Lutgard was not alone in her cell, but was "keeping the vigils" in company with other nuns. Lutgard's intense and public performance of these prayers resulted in a transformation of herself and of others, as the nuns also received "an augmenting of the Grace." Finally, the story was related and translated by either Lutgard or nuns who knew her, then told through the mediation of a Dominican monk, Thomas de Cantimpré, and further mediated by generations of copyists. Behind the facade of narrative and narrator stands a dynamic and ongoing collectivity of production and reception.

Lutgard not only *had* an ecstatic experience (was a passive recipient); she also *did* something for others within a communal space. Further, her *performance* had transformational qualities—it was efficacious for her and her audience. Action and transformation are exactly the characteristics emphasized in the ritual and theatrical performance theories of Richard Schechner.[15] He defines performance as a "quality of action"; that is, the performer *does* something. Moreover, the performer does something in the presence of and for an audience.[16] According to Schechner, performances can be viewed from two perspectives. The first is that of a continuum ranging from performances in everyday life (for example, gestures of greeting, the "performance" of an academic professional at a conference) to those of religious rituals and ceremonies (for example, the rite of baptism). The second perspective is that of a web of differing types of performances within a culture, all of which interact with and animate each other.[17] For example, within the formal ritual of the Mass are recognized social gestures of greeting and eating. Conversely, modern Veteran's Day parades often reflect their origins in civic religious processions—the parade of civic leaders, the placing of wreaths on monuments, the participation of important local clubs and civic groups. Schechner notes that all performances involve some degree of ritualization in their use of conventions that an audience can recognize.[18]

"Performance" is thus a much broader term than the popular limitation to theatrical performances. By viewing performances and rituals as a web, we can see that many performances have ritual aspects. This broader conception of performance means that scholars need to delineate types of performances and the relationships between them. However, in the case of religious performances distinctions are fraught with difficulties. For example, Schechner distinguishes the category of contemporary performances—even those with religious themes—from that of ritual by specifying that rituals such as the Mass are "efficacious," meaning that they cause something to happen or bring something into being. Rituals are also public and participatory.[19] Modern theatrical performances, however, such as the play *Agnes of God*, involve some sense of separation from "real life" and their primary purpose is entertainment. Like ritual, they take place in delineated spaces and they often occur "outside time." However, unlike ritual, they involve play or pretence, and the audiences are witnesses rather than active participants. So, for Schechner, the Mass is a ritual rather than a performance. Its purpose is not to entertain an audience, but to bring about a transformation in that audience. Further, the audience participates in the ritual and is not a passive witness.

Schechner's work is quite helpful in specifying exactly what we mean by the term "performance." On the other hand, his distinctions between religious and theatrical performances apply to modern Western cultures. In the medieval southern Low Countries, the genre we consider "theater" was still in its infancy and had not acquired the rigid separation from religious ritual that is more typical in post-sixteenth-century European cultures.[20] It is quite clear that performances such as Lutgard's transformative vigil were understood by the cleric chronicling them to have ritual qualities of efficaciousness. Thus, Schechner's separation of theatrical and ritual performances is not useful for studying the culture of the medieval southern Low Countries.

Precisely because medieval ecstatic performances had ritual qualities, the theories of ritual advanced by Victor Turner are germane. Turner stated: "By 'ritual' I mean prescribed formal behavior for occasions not given over to technological routine, having reference to beliefs in mystical beings or powers."[21] Such formal behavior, in the sense of actions sanctioned and practiced by authorized members of a society, could encompass many kinds of performances. Turner was particularly interested in the type of ritual in which an individual's status is changed. During such rituals, called "rites of passage," individuals frequently spend transitional periods of time in which they are not part of either the previous social state nor a different, transformed, social state. Turner used Arnold van Gennep's (1873–1957) term "liminality" to describe states that are "not this/not that" or "betwixt and between."[22] During the liminal states brought about by some kinds of rituals, there is the potential for creativity. Although the goal is reintegration into communal norms, the reflexivity and sense of being "outside the bounds" occasioned by liminal states may in fact subvert those norms. Thus, Turner transformed the definition of ritual from that of conservative guarantor of the status quo (now confined to the concept of "ceremony") to one with the possibility of dynamic social change. Eventually Turner located liminality in more diffuse situations (called "liminoid") than those of formalized rituals, especially in industrialized cultures, in which people of different social statuses could take part: civic parades and games, pilgrimages, the arts, and even subversive literature.[23]

Turner's focus upon ritual as formalized behavior makes it difficult to incorporate the seemingly spontaneous and informal nature of beguine ecstatic performances.[24] Because beguine religious performances were never part of the formalized rituals of the Church, they might fall into the category of "liminoid" events. In fact, Caroline Bynum has questioned the usefulness of the concept of liminality for medieval holy women, noting that women were never part of the communal norm but always occupied liminal space within medieval cultures.[25] That is, they could not reintegrate into the community if they were never considered part of it. However, since Turner viewed social process as dynamic and ongoing, one might suspect that these liminoid women performed "outside the bounds" in a bid to move to the center of their culture.

Yet, as essays in this volume document, women in the southern Low Countries were not liminal to their culture in many arenas: legal, social, economic, and religious. It is true that women were seldom the subjects of the formal (official) rituals of the Church—at the altar they did not bring about transformations or create liminal spaces in which transformations could occur. However, medieval holy women in the southern Low Countries were admired by clerics and sought out by all kinds of audiences. That is, they occupied a respected and understood space within their culture. Furthermore, many of their own transformations (such as Lutgard's described earlier) occurred within the sacred spaces—but outside the altar—of the Church.[26]

The difficulty seems to be with our own perception that ecstatic performances occupy a liminal space between theater and ritual. While everyone would accept that the Mass is both a performance *and* a formal ritual,[27] visionary and other ecstatic "acts" are generally regarded as spontaneous, unstructured demonstrations of exceptional individual piety rather than as either performances or rituals with transformational (efficacious) qualities.

Schechner's and Turner's profound insights about the dynamic nature of performance and ritual are useful theories for understanding beguine ecstatic performances in the medieval southern Low Countries. On the other hand, their categorizations are based upon the contemporary cultures they analyzed. In the Middle Ages no clear-cut categories called "theater" and "ritual" existed. Because a closer examination of the records of beguine ecstatic acts reveals both transformative (in the sense of efficaciousness) and performative (in the sense of actions done in the presence of and for others) ritual components I propose that the term "sacred performance" can incorporate and extend the insights of both Schechner and Turner.[28]

Like ritual, beguine holy women's ecstatic acts were efficacious. Their actions "brought something into being" that was not solely for their individual benefit nor for entertaining others. In the example cited earlier, Lutgard's intense efforts at prayer resulted in her "gaining possession of heaven," so powerfully that her ecstatic experience also transformed the nuns in her community.[29] In fact, Low Countries holy women routinely performed transformative acts during these ecstatic moments, exorcising demons, relieving purgatorial suffering, and intervening on behalf of individuals or communities.[30] Ecstatic performances allowed women the opportunity to become agents of transformation in a way not possible within the institutional structures and formal rituals of the Church. Consequently, these ecstatic manifestations were transformative ("efficacious") for the holy woman, too, in that each experience confirmed and augmented her spiritual status, not only for herself, but for others. Unlike the office of priesthood, there was no ordination or other ritual that granted women like Lutgard or Ida permanent sacral functions. Their status as "holy women" was a contingent category that depended upon continued public performances (and their reenactment via texts) that could demonstrate their authority to all.[31]

In this sense Low Countries women's identity as "holy" was produced *through* repeated performances rather than being expressed *by* performances.[32] There is not a quality called "holiness" manifested at particular times. Instead, "holiness" *as perceived by themselves and others* was generated and guaranteed by continued successful performances of holiness. This contingent aspect of female sacrality is masked by the narrative accounts, which, persuaded by the sum of performances, retroactively regarded such women as possessing an identity or essence of holiness that was expressed through a lifetime of visible sacred performances.[33] The narrative accounts also mask the continuous renegotiation of "holiness" within the web of cultures—local, clerical, transregional—that shaped the ongoing understanding of beguine women's performances.[34]

For every visionary "taken up in the spirit" there was a listening and participating audience. Later audiences of readers and writers also inserted their own understandings of these events in order to record them and/or read/interpret them for others. Thus, I believe that we need to approach texts by and about beguine holy women from a focal point of negotiated performance rather than from a reader's perspective, that is, rather than as a private communication from one author to an unseen audience of silent, individual readers.[35] Furthermore, thinking of religious women as performers restores both the contingent nature of their identity and their agency in successfully converting a series of conditional performances into a fixed identity of "holiness," itself a contested term. That is, there was no universal, one-size-fits-all model of sanctity, but many cultural models struggling for acceptance.[36]

This performance perspective explains why beguine performances eventually had to be written down, either by themselves or others. Texts provided a mechanism for construction, negotiation, and, most of all, ongoing engagement with the many models of sanctity, long after the original performances had ceased. The ongoing collectivity of production and reception of the "absent presence" of the original performers demonstrates serious engagement with, and sometimes struggle over, conceptions of a saintly life. Paradoxically, as the saintly model became universalized in the early modern period, engagement with saintly performances faded and records of "holy women" became mere personal expressions of individual piety. Let us see how sacred performances and models of sanctity reemerge from two kinds of texts: texts about "holy women" (hagiography) and texts by them.

Sacred Performances: Stories About Holy Women

When one thinks of performance one thinks of dramatic action, of the kinesthetics of bodies moving in space. Indeed, the presence of nonlinguistic signs is a distinguishing feature of dramatic texts.[37] When the Cistercian nun Ida of Nivelles was gripped with a six-week fever in order to free a dead man from purgatory, this was not an individual private encounter between a soul and God, but an intensely embodied experience that involved everyone in her community. Others had to take care of Ida while she was incapacitated; her body sweat mingled with the other odors in the convent, and her actions called forth the prayers of others.[38] Her actions were clearly understood to be not an ordinary illness, but a "wrestling" with the supernatural. We cannot recover this lived experience, but we can heighten our own spatial and kinesthetic awareness to re-envision the texts about such events as pointing to a performance-oriented model of holiness rather than distantly authored personal recollections.

A notable feature of many of these stories is the close attention to physical details that seem superfluous to modern readers accustomed to a model of tranquil and disembodied spirituality. For example, when Ida enters into ecstasy, the author takes pains to point out that "her entrails were so jarring under that grief that she could not refrain from copious vomiting of blood."[39] At the time of her first eucharistic ecstasy, her hagiographer lovingly details Jesus's physical appearance, the color and curliness of his hair, and the make and color of his garments. Not content with this description, another author adds several more lines describing how Jesus repeatedly circled the rectory and returned to stand in front of her.[40]

Focusing on, rather than ignoring, these aspects of beguine devotional literature restores the rhetoric of public speech and space practiced by most medieval writers and readers but de-emphasized by silent, private, modern readers. Manfred Pfister has called attention to the fact that literature is "time-distant" while dramatic texts are "here-and-now."[41] This "time-distant" approach to literature was not practiced by medieval authors or readers. It is now recognized that medieval writers did not expect a silent reader to engage privately and quietly with their work.[42] Instead, they could expect their work to be written, copied, read, and received communally. In short, they wrote for a public audience who would hear their stories as a performance and who would be actively engaged with the texts. Thus, their devotional works are full of lively stories that could be reinterpreted, added to, and even enacted with rhetorical flourish.

The many details are thus "scripts for action" and should be regarded as foreground rather than background. Consider the following example from Thomas de Cantimpré's *Vita* of Lutgard, describing Lutgard's intervention on behalf of Jacques de Vitry, a man unaware of his spiritual peril:

> Blessed Lutgard was spiritually alert to the bonding of his heart and the guile of the devil, and she betook herself to implore the Lord for him with abundant

tears. Achieving no progress by such praying, she accused the Lord of being cruel in this matter. He replied, "The man you are praying for is resisting the thrust of your prayers.". . .Blessed Lutgard went on and dealt quite impatiently with the Lord. With loud cries she shouted at him: "What is it you are doing, Lord, supposedly so benign and so just? Either you separate me from yourself, or you go ahead and free the man I am asking for, even if he is not willing!" Wondrous thing! With no delay between the request and the deed, he was freed there and then, and turned to bless his liberator, and also her who was handmaid to him. With eyes thus opened after his liberation, he perceived the peril he had not been able to see before.[43]

One can certainly imagine this story being enthusiastically read and reenacted before monastic audiences. But who is the source of the story, Lutgard or Thomas? Thomas is ostensibly the "author," but there is more of a "collectivity of production" than we are used to in modern literature. Thomas himself relates that all of the stories in his *Vita* originated either with Lutgard herself or a beguine or nun who knew her well.[44] Jody Enders has described the "rhetorical mode" pervasive in many aspects of educated clerical life: the use of dramatic gesture, voice, and staging to convince courts or to argue debate points in the *quodlibet*, or I would add, to preach before audiences.[45] Certainly the clerical writers of beguine *Vitae* (such as Thomas de Cantimpré and Jacques de Vitry) came from similarly educated backgrounds.[46] As popular preachers in their own right they were quite familiar with rhetorical devices in their own performances before audiences. It is reasonable to assume that Thomas shaped the narrative of Lutgard in rhetorical ways that would suit its retelling before clerical and/or popular audiences. In fact Jacques's success as a popular preacher stemmed from his skill in the use of *exempla* (entertaining stories that prove a moral point).[47]

Yet Jacques described the beguine Marie d'Oignies as a "living exemplum."[48] That is, Marie and other holy women did not tell moral stories; they themselves were the moral story. Jacques also admitted that he was initially unsuccessful as a preacher until Marie took him aside and helped him shorten his sermons.[49] Schechner's concept of the web of performance is particularly helpful here. Rather than searching for the source of a performance, we should focus on the interaction of the "rhetoric of performance" available in all levels of Low Countries culture—scholastic, clerical, legal, economic, and "popular." It is quite possible that Lutgard herself, or other companions, shaped the story about Jacques's spiritual restoration with such interesting use of space, dialogue, and kinesthetics. The description of Lutgard's vocal speech and dialogue, her tears and loud supplications, are nonlinguistic signs that provide "scripts for action" and point away from a unitary conception of authorship.

Moreover, a performance perspective recognizes the physical presence of Jacques, signaled by his turning to Lutgard. This brief notation indicates that in this story Lutgard was depicted as vocally praying in a communal space rather than silently communing "alone with the Lord." She was also portrayed as a performer willing to abandon communion with God rather than fail at spiritual restoration. Restoring this "rhetoric of public space," as medieval readers would have done, enables Lutgard's actions among and for others to emerge.

Jacques's presence and role in this story is also tantalizing. As bishop Jacques was both Lutgard's and Thomas's spiritual superior. Yet in the story Lutgard clearly saves Jacques from some spiritual peril. If not she, then Thomas structured the story in this way. As presented in this account, Lutgard is a dynamic spiritual leader whose sanctity is recognized by both local and extra-regional clerics. Jacques, the bishop, is most resistant, but his protestations are of no avail. In fact Lutgard is working on his behalf!

Yet we must always be aware that the story in its current form has been mediated by a series of later performers: Thomas himself, as well as later generations of monks who copied his works. Although Lutgard told many of these stories to Thomas, she spoke only a Dutch dialect. But our copies of Thomas's *Vita* of Lutgard exist now in three manuscripts, two in Latin and one in Old French.[50] Each manuscript tells a somewhat different version of this story. A literary interpretation seeks to discover the "authentic" text, from which all other texts derive, whereas a performance model of textuality regards each text as a performance in its own right. Each audience—the foreign cleric (Jacques), the local monk (Thomas), and the groups of beguines and nuns—understood and shaped this "script for performance" differently.

Sacred Performances: Beguine Narratives

A second type of Low Countries devotional writings was composed by holy women themselves: records of ecstatic experiences, usually referred to as visionary *literature*. Elsewhere I have described how such texts were intended to evoke a transformative power in the listener/reader.[51] Religious medieval ecstatic texts were written documents intended to guide ongoing oral and social performances. They are not static records of one long-ago private visitation. Moreover, even such directly authored texts have been mediated for audiences by generations of copyists. The same monastic scriptoria that transcribed and copied *Vitae about* holy women also transcribed and copied books *by* them. Consequently, it is not necessarily the case that records by holy women describe their own experiences more clearly than do works written about them.[52]

A performance model of textuality is less concerned with authorial intent than with recognizing such texts as ongoing sources for transformation. John Dagenais has described this process as the "ethics of reading."[53] Jean Alter suggests a model of theatrical "reading" that views texts as "a set of fixed notations for past and future performances."[54] According to Alter, a fully staged text necessarily involves more than one reading.[55] This "staged text" model allows for the ongoing mediation of performers and audiences in beguine ecstatic textuality.

Victor Turner's concept of ritual as "social drama" also provides insight into the nature of ecstatic textual performances. Turner observed that societies continually wrestle with tension, ambiguities, and conflicts. Such conflicts generate change in dynamic ways, a process Turner called "social dramas." Turner identified five stages of social drama: breech, crisis, redress, reintegration, *or* schism. By focusing upon social change as drama, he defined the dramatic impulse as the ground of social life. Among the Ndembu people Turner studied, he discovered that "a multiplicity of conflict situations is correlated with a high frequency of ritual performance."[56] Turner began to associate rituals with social dramas. In fact, rituals may serve as a redressive phase in social dramas.[57]

Turner also argued that social dramas are sites for negotiation of conflicts between groups and individuals. In this manner, "social dramas" can be agents of social change and of transformation in societies. In times of social change, marginalized individuals may press for inclusion and legitimacy. Ordinary norms may be questioned. Redress of grievances may be sought.[58]

To envision beguine and religious ecstatic literature as a "set of fixed notations of past and future performances" means enlarging one's awareness of such texts' theatrical (or rhetorical) use of space, as demonstrated in examples from the *Vita* of Lutgard. It also means a consideration of the "social drama" of complex negotiation enacted within and by the text. Consider this example from the *Visionenen* of Hadewijch, a beguine from the region of Brabant:

> I was taken up in the spirit for a short while at Matins on Assumption Day and I was shown the three highest heavens which one names after the three highest angels: the Thrones, the Cherubim, and the Seraphim. And then came to me the eagle from the four living creatures, that sweet St. John the Evangelist, and he said: "Come and see the things I saw as a man, all of which you have seen transparent and complete, and that which I saw as a representation you have understood, and you know what they are."[59]

According to Hadewijch, this vision occurred on Assumption Day. On this occasion of the assumption of Mary into heaven, Hadewijch also was "taken up" in the spirit. Moreover, she was "taken up" to the very highest

heavens, among the Thrones, Cherubim, and Seraphim.[60] Within the public
setting of a parish church, the eagle as Saint John (the symbol of the mystic) invited Hadewijch to see "all the things I saw as a man," but which
Hadewijch saw more fully than he. Attention to the performance aspects of
the text emphasizes its public setting with a presumed public audience,
affirming Hadewijch's importance within her community. At this point
Hadewijch addressed God directly:

> And I fell on my face with great woe, and that woe cried aloud: "Ah! Ah!
> Holy Friend and True Power, why do you let those who are ours wander in
> alien ways, and why do you not flow through them in our oneness? I have
> my whole will with you and love and hate with you, as you."

Hadewijch's text switches from external to internal dialogue, while
emphasizing the continuation of vocal speech. At first she questions God
about the fate of "those who are ours," a probable reference to the
beguines' dedication to the religious quest for identity with *minne*, or God as
an aspect of divine love. The next line then "undoes" this question by
declaring her union of will with God's will. At this point her speech takes a
curious turn and reveals the unusual social drama being performed within it:

> For I am now no Lucifer, since you have again given me certainty, as those
> who are now Lucifer do, and wish that good and grace be granted to them
> who do not have it, neither in living nor in works, nor in service, and they
> wish to end labor and enjoy grace, and they set themselves up on high
> because you give them a little of your goodness, and so they wish to have it
> as a right. And they fall from your heavenly honor; this you have made known
> to me.

Hadewijch declares that she is not *now* as Lucifer, implying that in a
previous time, she was. She defines Lucifer's quality as wishing to have as
a right what may only be given through God's grace. Such ones fall from
heaven, where Hadewijch is at present. There has been a breech, but
reintegration has already occurred. The text continues:

> And hereupon I erred before the living and the dead, those whom I desired
> to free from purgatory and hell as my right. But of this you are blessed; with-
> out anger you gave me four from among the living and the dead who then
> belonged to hell. Your goodness tolerated my ignorance and my thoughtless
> desires, [as of] your boundless charity which you gave yourself to men. In
> this I fell and became Lucifer because I did not know this, although I did no
> evil [according to] you. This was the one thing in which I fell under [the
> control of?] men, so that I remained incomprehensible to them, and they
> were cruel to me. Through love I wanted to snatch the living and the dead

from the abyss of despair and wrongdoing, and I caused their pain to be lessened, and sent those dead in hell to purgatory, and brought those living in
hell to the heavenly way [of life]. Your goodness forgave me and showed me
that for this I had fallen under those people.

At this point the cause of Hadewijch's earlier "fall" or "breech" becomes
apparent. She freed four souls from hell. Reading Hadewijch's text from a
performance perspective makes one aware that she *did* something—she
performed some action that caused these souls to be transformed. Moreover, this action was public, because others knew of it and she suffered for
her actions. Curiously, the speech claims that she only "fell" among "men,"
not from God, who forgave her for this (theologically) unforgivable act.
Thus, this aspect of Hadewijch's speech both explains her previous action
and claims divine forgiveness for it. Moreover, Hadewijch does not say that
the action she performed was ineffective—quite the reverse. The dead souls
were permanently transformed. Although the speech acknowledges wrongdoing, it also claims victory. Further, the text both acknowledges the status
quo of the Church's theological position, and claims a successful breech and
reassertion of that status quo. In fact:

> Then you took my self into your self, and gave me to know how you are, and
> that you hate and love in one being, so that I understood that I must hate and
> love with you, and be in everything being. Hereby this I know, [and] so
> I desire of you that you make those who are ours complete with us. . .
>
> And he [God] took me out of the spirit in that highest satisfaction of
> wonder beyond reason, and there I enjoyed him as I will eternally. That hour
> was short and when I came to myself he brought me again into the spirit
> and said to me thus: "As you now enjoy, so shall you eternally enjoy."

Not only does Hadewijch not "fall" from heaven as a result of her
action, she is "taken up" to the very highest heaven and enjoys God "as she
will eternally" in a public dimension, a church on a holy festival day. Thus
she is vindicated before the world.

Hadewijch's speech, which performs sorrow and enacts triumph simul-
taneously, is incomprehensible without a consideration of three factors: the
performance dimension of the experience itself, the transcription through
which the speech has been mediated to successive audiences, and the tension and resolution of the social drama within the text.

First, awareness of the performance aspects of Hadewijch's dialogues
enables one to grasp the nature of her true victory. Through public action
she accomplished the forbidden act of the translation of souls from hell to
(eventual) heaven, and for this she was publicly excoriated before being
publicly vindicated. The vision is cast in terms of a dialogue because it was

performed for an audience—the ones who wronged Hadewijch and the ones who understand her status as a true holy woman. This audience is necessary to witness and to affirm her current, triumphant, status. The vision is not a record of a private encounter with the divine. Through the performance of this vision, Hadewijch's identity as holy woman is re-produced, erasing (but not completely!) the previous performance that cast suspicion upon her status.

Second, the audience who transcribed the record of this performance were clerics. Certainly they knew that Hadewijch's actions were not permissible. It is impossible to know to what extent Hadewijch was the author of the words we now have. Regardless, a performance standpoint is more concerned with the reception of her vision. The simultaneous acceptance of wrongdoing combined with Hadewijch's exultant transformation allows clerical misgivings to dissolve before the powerful vision of mystical union. Acceptance of Hadewijch's words as the words of a "holy woman" refocuses this social drama upon transformation (reintegration), while the wrong actions (breech) fade into the background. Yet the tension has not been wholly erased. Hadewijch's actions remain unforgivable and yet forgiven.

The continuing presence of tension within this social drama allows it to be reenacted in what John Dagenais has called the "ethics of reading." By personally engaging with Hadewijch's drama of error and triumph, absorbing the nonlinguistic signs of "falling" and "assumption," readers can absorb the beguine emphasis upon divine union into their own "ethical system" in a more direct manner than is possible when one merely reads the words of Hadewijch's encounter, long ago.[61] Multiple productions and receptions of ecstatic texts insure ongoing mediation of performers and audiences in beguine and other ecstatic textuality.

This fully staged text is neither purely oral/performative nor literary. Jacques Derrida has argued that there are no neat dichotomies between spoken and written words; one cannot be said to come before or to be superior to the other.[62] In the foregoing example, the performance of the Assumption Day liturgy dedicated to Mary, a cultural and theological understanding of the status of the living and the dead, the afterlife, and of divine grace, and an understanding of the beguine concepts of divine union are all "intertextualities" of the ecstatic text. Thus, the process of producing and receiving the text interweaves textual, dramatic, ritual, and performative elements.[63]

Conclusion

In conclusion, foregrounding the presence of performance and ritual aspects of texts by and about beguines and other Low Countries religious women enables a richer understanding of the meaning of their ecstatic acts. Within their culture holy women were not isolated individuals who were passive recipients of God's grace. They were doers, performers who accomplished religiously important actions within and for their communities. As Joanna Ziegler will document in chapter 8, at least one of them carefully practiced her performance skills.[64] Moreover, their actions were models ("scripts for action") for future ethical performances. Collectively enacted, collectively produced, collectively received, Low Countries ecstatic "scripts for action" demonstrate that the ecstatic acts of holy women, too, were an important aspect of the complex urban landscape of the southern Low Countries. Further restoration of the "social dramas" within beguine textuality highlights the contested nature of medieval holiness and the tension and interactive webs between local and Latinate clerical models. Finally, acknowledgment of multiple audiences and performances brings these female ecstatic performers back into the limelight of public activity from which they have too long been assumed to have been absent.

Notes

1. For example, Paul Saenger notes that for most of the Middle Ages, texts were read aloud. Further, "literacy" implied the ability to read, whereas the ability to write was a highly technical skill possessed only by a few. Additionally, many manuscripts had elaborate decorations, imparting a strong visual quality to the written word. See Paul Saenger, "Silent Reading: Its Impact on Late Medieval Script and Society," *Viator* (Spring 1982), pp. 368–444; Brian Stock, *The Implications of Literacy: Written Language and Models of Interpretation in the Eleventh and Twelfth Centuries* (Princeton, N.J.: Princeton University Press, 1983); *Listening for the Text: On the Uses of the Past* (Baltimore: Johns Hopkins University Press, 1990); and Laura Kendrick, *Animating the Letter: The Figurative Embodiment of Writing from Late Antiquity to the Renaissance* (Columbus: Ohio State University Press, 1999).

2. Pope Urban II's sermon, which led to the First Crusade, illustrates the differences between a written sermon and its actual performance. Notes for Urban's sermon, preached in different parts of France, differ widely. Again, Bernard of Clairvaux wrote literary versions of sermons that were constructed according to the sermon genre but were not actually performed before an audience. His performed sermons were not written down but can be reconstructed from monastic notes. See Jean LeClerq's Introduction to *Bernard of Clairvaux: Selected Works*, trans. G.R. Evans (New York: Paulist Press, 1987), pp. 28–29. For an introduction to models of holiness in sermon studies, see *Models of Holiness in Medieval Sermons, Textes et Études du Moyen Âge*, ed. Beverly Mayne Kienzle, Edith Wilks Dolnikowski, Rosemary Drage Hale, Darleen Pryds, and Anne T. Thayers (Louvain-La-Neuve: Fédération Internationale des Instituts d'Études Médiévales, 1996), pp. vii–xx.

3. Recent scholarship has begun to focus on the audiences' reception of these sermons. A good example is Jacqueline Hamesse, Beverly M. Kienzle, Debra L. Stoudt, and Anne T. Thayer, eds., *Medieval Sermons and Society: Cloister, City, University* (Louvain-La-Neuve, Fédération Internationale des Instituts d'Études Médiévales, 1998).

4. Walter Simons points out that already by 1177 lay men and women in the diocese of Liège formed "textual communities" of readers who read translated versions of Latin scriptures. See Simons, *Cities of Ladies: Beguine Communities in the Medieval Low Countries, 1200–1565* (Philadelphia: University of Pennsylvania Press, 2001), p. 30. In this chapter I am interested in the production of texts rather than their consumption.

5. In the last twenty years the scholarship on beguines and other "holy women" has greatly increased as their writings have been translated and edited (such as the many editions of medieval women's writings published by Paulist Press). Understandably, the first focus of scholars has been upon these newly available writings. Notable examples of scholarship from this literary perspective include Barbara Newman, *From Virile Woman to WomanChrist: Studies in Medieval Religion and Literature* (Philadelphia: University of Pennsylvania Press, 1995), and *Sister of Wisdom: St. Hildegard's Theology of the Feminine* (Berkeley: University of California Press, 1987); Elizabeth Petroff, *Medieval Women's Visionary Literature* (New York: Oxford University Press, 1992) and *Body and Soul: Essays on Medieval Women and Mysticism* (New York: Oxford University Press, 1994); Paul Szarmach, *An Introduction to the Medieval Mystics of Europe* (Albany: State University of New York Press, 1993). Two new publications that begin to explore other aspects of female mystical writings are Juliette Dor, Lesley Johnson, and Jocelyn Wogan-Browne, eds., *New Trends in Feminine Spirituality: The Holy Women of Liège and Their Impact* (Turnhout: Brepols Publishing, 1999), and Mary Suydam and Joanna Ziegler, eds., *Performance and Transformation: New Approaches to Late Medieval Spirituality* (New York: St. Martins Press, 1999).

6. My research for this chapter is based upon the *vitae* of Ida of Nivelles, Lutgard of Aywières, Ida of Leuven, and the self-recorded visions of Hadewijch of Antwerp. The *vita* of Ida of Nivelles was possibly written by the Cistercian Goswin of Bossut, that of Lutgard by the Dominican Thomas de Cantimprè, and the *vita* of Ida of Leuven was anonymously compiled. All three *vitae* exist in very different and interpolated manuscripts. Editions of texts and explanations of the authors and redactions are found in Martinus Cawley, trans., *Lives of Ida of Nivelles, Lutgard, and Alice the Leper* (Lafayette: Guadalupe Translations, 1987); and *Ida of Louvain* (Lafayette: Guadalupe Translations, 1990). The collection of Hadewijch's visions exist in five different manuscripts. A very good modern Dutch edition based on MS. A with facing medieval Flemish is Imme Dros, trans., *Hadewijch: Visioenen* (Amsterdam: Uitgeverij Prometheus/Bert Bakker, 1996). A medieval Dutch edition based on MS. C was published by Jozef van Mierlo, *Hadewijch: Visioenen* (Leuven: De Vlaamsche Boekenhalle, 1924–25).

7. Recent scholarship on visionary literature in general has largely overcome stylistic criticism by arguing that women writers did not intend to create

systematic narratives. However, the literary perspective has a much more problematic feature: it necessarily emphasizes a model of unitary authorship. For example, Amy Hollywood states: "to compare the type of piety offered in the hagiographies with Mechtild, Porete, or Eckhart's theological formulations. . .ignores central differences in perspectives. . .We must look at women's. . .own formulations of their theological and mystical teachings. . .despite the recognition that women's writings themselves internalize and are mediated through male-dominated culture" (*The Soul as Virgin Wife: Mechtild of Magdeburg, Marguerite Porete, and Meister Eckhart* (Notre Dame: University of Notre Dame Press, 1995)), p. 6. Such a model of authorship obscures the layered nature of medieval textual productions by ignoring the scribes (sometimes across several generations) who composed, transcribed, copied, and read these women's works aloud. Although authors like Brian Stock have persuasively critiqued modern assumptions of authorship and readership, such assumptions are still quite prevalent in writings about medieval women.

8. Several scholars have argued that in the southern Low Countries there was a marked emphasis upon oral and public validation of all kinds of legal and social actions. See, for example, Ellen Kittell, "Women, Audience and Public Acts in Medieval Flanders," *Journal of Women's History* 10, no. 3 (Autumn 1998), pp. 74–96. See also Linda Guzzetti's essay, chapter 4, in this volume.

9. Jocelyn Wogan-Browne and Marie-Élisabeth Henneau, "Liège, the Medieval 'Woman Question,' and the Question of Medieval Women," in Juliette Dor, Lesley Johnson, and Jocelyn Wogan-Browne, eds., *New Trends in Feminine Spirituality*, pp. 14–15. For a discussion of the oral nature of Low Countries daily life, see our introduction to this volume.

10. For a short introduction to the phenomena of beguines in the southern Low Countries, see our introduction to this volume.

11. The *Vitae* of holy women like Lutgard of Aywières and Ida of Nivelles stress their continued care for others. These women traveled to other religious houses to help troubled members, and others traveled to their convents to seek their aid. See Martinus Cawley, trans., *Lives of Ida of Nivelles, Lutgard, and Alice the Leper.*

12. For a discussion of the beguinages of Oignies and Nivelles, see McDonnell, *The Beguines and Beghards in Medieval Culture*, pp. 59–70, and Walter Simons, *Cities of Ladies*. Ida of Leuven and Beatrijs of Nazareth both became Cistercian nuns.

13. Manfred Pfister, *The Theory and Analysis of Drama* (Cambridge: Cambridge University Press, 1988), p. 11. It is important to emphasize that my essay is *not* arguing for an origin of theater in the actions of beguine and religious holy women, though that may be an intriguing area for further research. Rather, I emphasize the performance aspects of beguine "literature" and seek to demonstrate the consequences for our understanding of Flemish holy women's multiple roles within medieval Flemish culture.

14. *Lutgarde ergo crebrius continuante vigilias, accidit una nocte, ut super eam a monialibus super solis splendorem per magnum spatium noctis, iubar luminis videretur.*

Quod utique lumen transfusum interius non solum in ipsam, sed et in illas quae viderunt illud, spiritualis vitae gratiam augmentavit (Martinus Cawley, trans., *Lives of Ida of Nivelle, Lutgard and Alice the Leper*, Lutgard I: 12).

15. Richard Schechner, *Essays in Performance Theory* (Routledge: New York, 1988); Victor Turner, "Social Dramas and Stories About Them," in *On Narrative*, ed. W.J.T. Mitchell (University of Chicago Press: Chicago, 1981), pp. 137–64.

16. Schechner, *Essays in Performance Theory*, p. 30.

17. Schechner, *Essays in Performance Theory*, pp. xii–xv.

18. For example, in the southern Low Countries the appearances of witnesses before aldermanic courts had both ritual and performance aspects. Witnesses did something in a public hearing. Their actions and words had recognized social conventions that others could recognize. Ellen Kittell, "Women, Audience and Public Acts in Medieval Flanders," pp. 76–78.

19. For a similar perspective on the public nature of liturgy, see Cheslyn Jones, Geoffrey Wainwright, and Edwin Yarnold, S.J., *The Study of Liturgy* (New York: Oxford University Press, 1978), p. 13: "Liturgy is celebrated *with* others and the relationships between the members of the worshipping community are of the highest importance. *Private* acts of *public* worship are a contradiction in terms."

20. Although there were popular forms of pure entertainment, one of the striking features of late medieval drama (as well as that of the medieval sermon, which was often a form of monologue) is its interactive character. Most plays were religious and were intended to move the spectator toward genuine penitence and transformation. Still debated is the question whether medieval religious drama was a new creation, or whether "Christian drama reemerged from ritual as theater did in its most ancient Greek beginnings" (Gail McMurray Gibson, *The Theater of Devotion: East Anglian Drama and Society in the Late Middle Ages* (Chicago: University of Chicago Press, 1989)). See also Karl Young, *The Drama of the Medieval Church*, 2 vols. (Oxford: Clarendon Press, 1933).

21. Victor Turner, *The Forest of Symbols: Aspects of Ndembu Ritual* (Ithaca: Cornell University Press, 1967), p. 19.

22. Turner, *Forest of Symbols*, pp. 95–97.

23. Victor Turner, *From Ritual to Theater* (New York: Performing Arts Journal Publications, 1982), pp. 24–37. For Turner, the difference between agricultural and industrial cultures lay in the close connection between work and play in the former and their separation in the latter.

24. Ronald Grimes makes this point about Turner's formal definition in "Victor Turner's Definition, Theory, and Sense of Ritual," in *Victor Turner and the Construction of Cultural Criticism*, ed. Kathleen Ashley (Bloomington: Indiana University Press, 1990), pp. 141–46. It is true that Turner's later work does allow for more inclusive conceptions of ritual, but his more formalized definition continues to be widely used, even though, as Grimes notes, "Turner's theory differs radically from his definition." Grimes also notes that Turner's sense of dramatism and performance animates his understanding of ritual, but that Turner does not always specify exactly what constitutes dramatic or performative elements.

25. Caroline Bynum, "Women's Stories, Women's Symbols: A Critique of Victor Turner's Theory of Liminality," in *Fragmentation and Redemption: Essays on Gender and the Human Body in Medieval Religion* (New York: Zone Books, 1991), pp. 27–51.

26. This does not mean that such women did not have critics and detractors. Yet, although some women were persecuted or vilified, it is not surprising to us that women like Lutgard and Ida were quite at home within their culture.

27. Many writers have remarked upon the dramatic and performative qualities of the Mass. See, for example, Karl Young, *The Drama of the Medieval Church* (Oxford: Clarendon Press, 1933); O.B. Hardison, *Christian Rite and Christian Drama in the Middle Ages: Essays in the Origin and Early History of Modern Drama* (Baltimore: Johns Hopkins Press, 1965).

28. Further, following research by Kittell and others, I hypothesize that medieval women in the southern Low Countries were not liminal within their culture.

29. *coelum secundum promissum domini possidebat* (Lutgard, I: 11). Thomas Driver has argued that ritual can effect powerful changes in the lives of individuals: "Rational political methods alone cannot bring about transformation of society. . .because they cannot fuse the visionary with the actual. . .Nor can ideas alone do this, for in order to bear fruit ideas require flesh-and-blood performance" ("Transformation: The Magic of Ritual," in *Readings in Ritual Studies*, ed. Ronald Grimes (New Jersey: Prentice Hall, 1996), p. 181).

30. For exorcism of demons, see Lutgard, II: 34–35, 38. For restoration of the dead to life, see Ida of Leuven, I: 18, 40–41, 28–29. For purgatorial revelations, see Ida of Nivelles, 24, 29, 40–41; Lutgard, 29, 31, 37, 53, 66–67, 70; Alice, 33, 37, 43, 47. For discovery of secret sins subsequently confessed to the holy woman, see Ida of Nivelles, 34, 36, 38, 43, 44; Lutgard II: 47, 48, 50, 78, 54; Ida of Leuven, 53, 54. On Ida of Leuven's miraculous ability to tell the moment of elevation of the Host at distant Masses, see II.6.9, 40; on her enabling a priest's Eucharistic devotion, see II.19.15, 44 (Cawley, *Lives*). On Tiedala of Nivelle's enabling another priest's devotion, see McDonnell, *Beguines and Beghards*, pp. 328–29.

31. Since the fourth-century victory over the Donatists, a priest's status is not contingent upon personal qualities of holiness. Holy women had no such security.

32. Judith Butler's insights in contemporary gender theory are relevant to the perception of certain beguine women as holy: she states that identity is produced through performances and thus always contingent, rather than identity being prior and essential and thus expressed through performances. See Butler, "Imitation and Gender Insubordination," in *The Second Wave: A Reader in Feminist Theory*, ed. Linda Nicholson (New York: Routledge, 1997), pp. 300–15.

33. According to Butler and other feminist theorists who de-emphasize fixed subjectivity, we naturally try to deny the contingency of our performances and to establish a unitary self, free from the contingencies of performance.

See also Chris Weedon, *Feminist Practice and Poststructuralist Theory* (Cambridge: Blackwell Press, 1994), pp. 74–106.

34. See Ulrike Wiethaus's essay, chapter 7, in this volume.

35. Of course, there is a great difference between these two literary genres.

36. See Beverly Mayne Kienzle et al., eds., *Models of Holiness*,, especially E.L. Saak, "*Quilibet Christianus*: Saints in Society in the Sermons of Jordan of Quedlinburg, OESA," pp. 317–38, who identifies three models of holiness: exemplary, revolutionary, and transformational.

37. Pfister, *Theory and Analysis of Drama*, p. 10. See also Schechner, *Essays in Performance Theory*, p. 103: "Drama does not depend upon written text, but upon carefully scripted actions."

38. The story is recounted in Cawley, trans., *Lives, Ida*, pp. 17–18.

39. *quod concussione viscerum suorum et dolore non modico se a vomitu multi sanguinis continere non posset* (ibid., p. 26). Almost identical wording is used of one of Marie d'Oignies's ecstasies; see Margot King, trans., *Two Lives of Marie D'Oignies* (Toronto, Peregrina Publishing, 1998), p. 109.

40. Cawley, trans., *Lives, Ida*, p. 54.

41. Pfister, *Theory and Analysis of Drama*, p. 15.

42. For example, see Brian Stock, *Listening for the Text: On the Uses of the Past* (Baltimore: Johns Hopkins Press, 1990); John Dagenais, *The Ethics of Reading in Manuscript Culture: Glossing the Libro de Buen Amor* (Princeton: Princeton University Press, 1994); Mary Suydam and Joanna Ziegler, eds., *Performance and Transformation: New Approaches to Late Medieval Spirituality*. In regards to beguine devotional practices see Mary Suydam, "Writing Beguines: Ecstatic Performances," *Magistra* (Summer 1996), pp. 137–69.

43. *Hujus igitur consolationi intentus assidue, praedicationis officium segniter omittebat. Pia ergo Lutgardis, vinculum cordis ejus et dolos diaboli in spiritu sentiens aggressa est in multis lacrymis pro eo dominum deprecari. Cumque nihil proficeret in orando, et Dominum super hoc argueret ut crudelem, respondit dominus orationisbus inquit, tuis in contrarium homo nititur pro quo petis. . .Pia Lutgardis impatientius agens Domino, magnis vocibus inclamavit: Quid est, ait, quod agis, benignissime ac justissime Domine? Aut separa me a te, aut hominem pro quo peto, Libera, etiam non volentem. Mira res! Nulla mora inter rogatum et factum penitus intervenit sed prorsus et protinus liberatus, liberatori sud et ejus famulae benedixit, sensitque apertis oculis post liberationem periculum quod ante, humano amore caecatus, vedere non poterat* (Cawley, trans., *Lives*; Lutgard, II: 4, 28).

44. Ibid., Lutgard, I: 2.

45. Jody Enders, *Rhetoric and the Origins of Medieval Drama* (Ithaca: Cornell University Press, 1992).

46. Both Thomas and Jacques were Dominican preachers and had university educations. See McDonnell, *Beguines and Beghards*, pp. 20–27.

47. Two recent articles exploring Jacques de Vitry's sermons are Carolyn Muessig, "Audience and Sources in Jacques de Vitry's 'Sermones Feriales et Communes,'" and Cynthia Ho, "*Corpus Delicti*: The Edifying Dead in the *Exempla* of Jacques de Vitry," in *Medieval Sermons and Society*, ed. Jacqueline Hamesse et al., pp. 183–202, 203–218.

48. Margot King, trans., *Two Lives of Marie D'Oignies*, p. 39.
49. Ibid., pp. 121–22. In fact, the episode narrated above actually concerns Jacques de Vitry who, according to the story, was spiritually healed by Lutgard: *Nec grande post haec tempus excessit cum idem ven. Jacobus ad episcopatum acconensem in transmarinis partibus est electus* (Cawley trans., *Lives*; Lutgard II: 4, 28).
50. See note 6. See also Mary Suydam, "Sacred Performances: Beguine Textuality," in *Performance and Transformation*, ed. Mary Suydam and Joanna Ziegler, pp. 177–80.
51. Mary Suydam, "Writing Beguines," pp. 137–69; "Sacred Performances: Beguine Textuality," pp. 169–210.
52. Generally scholars tend to view works by women as more "authentically authored" than books about them. For example, see Amy Hollywood, *The Soul as Virgin Wife*.
53. John Dagenais, *The Ethics of Reading in a Manuscript Culture*.
54. Suydam, "Writing Beguines." See Jean Alter, *A Sociosemiotic Theory of Theatre* (Philadelphia: University of Pennsylvania Press, 1990).
55. Alter, *A Sociosemiotic Theory of Theatre*, p. 165: "Each reading, or re-reading, brings more precision to various imaginary stage features, adding or changing them, playing with the repertory of nonverbal signs."
56. Victor Turner, *The Ritual Process: Structure and Anti-Structure* (Ithaca: Cornell University Press, 1977), p. 10.
57. "I consider the term 'ritual' to be more fittingly applied to forms of ritual behavior associated with social transitions, while the term 'ceremony' has a closer bearing on religious behavior associated with social states. . .Ritual is transformative, ceremony confirmatory" (Victor Turner, *The Forest of Symbols*, p. 5).
58. Victor Turner, *Dramas, Fields, and Metaphors* (Ithaca: Cornell University Press, 1974). For critiques of Turner's ideas, see David Raybin, "Aesthetics, Romance and Turner," and Thomas Pavel, "Narratives of Ritual and Desire," in *Victor Turner and the Construction of Cultural Criticism*, ed. Kathleen Ashley, pp. 21–41 and 64–69. Turner's insight that social dramas are inherent within ritual has altered scholarly perspectives of ritual from those of conservative, rigid structures to ones emphasizing transformation and change.
59. Hadewijch, *Visioenen*, pp. 68–72. My translation throughout.
60. Hadewijch uses the concept of layered heavens advanced by Isidore of Seville and Gregory the Great in the *Moralia*. For a description of the medieval depictions of different levels of heaven, see Gustav Davidson, *A Dictionary of Angels* (New York: Free Press, 1967), p. 336.
61. John Dagenais, *Ethics of Reading*, 28.
62. Jacques Derrida's trenchant critique of Claude Levi-Strauss's romantic privileging of speech over writing is particularly pertinent here. The point is not that present speech/performance is superior to absent writing/literature. As Derrida notes: "By radically separating language from writing, by placing the latter below and outside, believing that it is possible to do so. . .one thinks in fact to restore the status of authentic language . . ." According to

Derrida, all acts of differentiation are "writing" already (*Of Grammatology*, trans. by Gayatri Chakravorty Spivak (Baltimore: Johns Hopkins University Press, 1976), p. 120).

63. "This means that 'oral performance' and 'written composition' cannot really be separated. 'Performance' may refer to *both* the vision-enacted-in-the-here-and-now *and* to the performance (dictation) of a written work. Likewise, composition can refer to the written work as a product, as well as to the act (performance) of constructing and interpreting an enacted performance" (Suydam, "Writing Beguines," p. 168).

64. The likely possibility that other beguines did so will be a fruitful avenue for further research.

CHAPTER 7

THE DEATH SONG OF MARIE D'OIGNIES: MYSTICAL SOUND AND HAGIOGRAPHICAL POLITICS IN MEDIEVAL LORRAINE

Ulrike Wiethaus

Introduction: The Sound of Mysticism

Sound is possibly the least studied aspect of medieval Christian mysticism today, neglected in favor of textual and visual data. Medieval sound-scapes, whether liturgical or extra-liturgical, were, however, an integral part of medieval religious life, both in terms of spiritual experiences and theory.[1] Apart from the sacraments, liturgical sound provided a sensual medium that connected the sacred and the earthly with intense immediacy. Doxological in nature, it symbolized harmony between the Divine and the cosmos; sound generally was understood to supply the fiber out of which all of cosmic reality was fashioned.[2] It is this ontological understanding of the liturgy, combined with a sense of great aesthetic pleasure, that we find most frequently expressed in mystical experiences of sacred music.

The celebration of Mass, like sound itself offering a temporal opening between sacred and earthly realms, frequently determined the overall *Gestalt* of mystical acoustic experiences. To quote Saint Gregory the Great's (ca. 540–604) formulation of the cosmological map of such experiences,

> Who among the faithful could doubt that at the very moment of the immola-
> tion, the heavens open at the priest's voice? In this mystery of Jesus Christ the
> choir of angels are present; the lowest beings are associated with the highest, the
> earthly join the heavenly, and the visible and invisible become a single reality.[3]

Since both clergy and laity participated in this multisensory event, audience participation sometimes could be intensely responsive, especially so among mystics.[4]

Variations of acoustic miracles were documented surprisingly often in the subculture of the new mendicant orders.[5] Echoing Saint Gregory the Great's musicological understanding of Mass, the prolific Dominican Thomas de Cantimpré (ca. 1200–70), for example, reported the following sonic miracle by an unnamed holy woman from Oignies. According to Thomas, the holy woman

> knew without any hesitation the time of the coming of Christ on the altar through the ministry of the priest, however secretly it came about. Each time it happened, the cooing of a dove echoed in her throat with such a sound that no mortal could imitate it. . . .she uttered cries of such sweetness that there was no doubt that she was being called to the supper of the Lamb in which, with invisible power, the almighty Father joins heavenly to earthly, the lowest to the highest.[6]

The story highlights the focus of this essay—the connection between women's desire to participate actively in the liturgy, the narrative ambiguities of sonic mysticism as a religiously significant event, and the complex communal context of the beguines'"new" mysticism. As a social activity, neither music nor mystical performance can be separated from their communal, geographic, and social context. Medieval women's home, a realm where female musical traditions could flourish, was not a site for the textual production of songs and the recording of melodies. This resulted in the loss of what we may assume to have been a rich tradition of instrumental and vocal music focused on women's work and their life cycle.[7] Religious views on the seductive dangers of the female voice have confounded our already dismally meager knowledge of women's musical traditions. Saint Jerome (ca. 347–419), for example, explicitly forbade women to be trained as musicians.[8] Dante illustrated this fearful view of women's musical powers in his depiction of the foul-smelling but seductive siren in *The Divine Comedy*.[9] Marie d'Oignies's first biographer, Jacques de Vitry (1170–1240), reminded his readers of the misogynist stereotype early on in Marie's *vita*:

> May wretched and foolish women take heed and lament, they who light the fire of lust with their lascivious songs and make embers burn with their breath and thus alienated from the song of the angels, perish in their vanity. Their laughter is turned to tears, their joy into eternal sorrow, their song into wailing.[10]

Women's restricted access to musical technologies and public performances determined in some way the social meaning of all liturgical events.[11]

The prohibition for women to speak in Church extended to music. The one exception to this rule has been the convent. Indeed, "within convents, liturgical singing became the most common activity of the nuns: they sang the Divine Office and Mass, played instruments, acted as choral directors, and demonstrated the technical and philosophical expertise necessary for composition."[12] Saint Gregory of Nyssa's (ca. 331/40–ca. 395) *Life of St. Macrina* is among the earliest sources about musical activities in female monasteries. It movingly describes nuns lamenting Saint Macrina's death.[13] In terms of liturgical chanting, nuns were generally on a somewhat more equal footing with monks until the spectacular yet controversial rise of polyphony and musical quantification in university settings during the thirteenth century.[14] Cloistered religious women, however, have always only represented a small percentage of the female population. Thus, centuries of prohibition against laywomen's liturgical participation led scholars to the conclusion: "in Christianity, we clearly do not have. . .a gynaecocentric liturgical culture."[15]

Given this background, acoustic mysticism at times functioned to reclaim women's right to speak in Church, albeit in highly original ways.[16] My preliminary study of gender differences in the production of sonic mystical phenomena suggests that medieval religious women generally tended to produce more polysemic, kinetic, and unusual sound-related performances, including musically induced group ecstasies, melodies produced without the use of vocal chords, levitations, and innovative musico-theological imagery. Men, on the other hand, seem to have generated mystical phenomena linked to their theological and musicological training such as miraculous composing and theorizing or melodic auditions during their celebration of Mass.[17]

As related by her biographers, the beguine Marie d'Oignies's manifestations of sonic mysticism fit the general pattern of the "new" or "modern" female spirituality that began in the late twelfth century in the southern Low Countries.[18] The new forms of mysticism channeled women's effort to overcome the prohibition of being more than passive participants in the liturgy; they validated their religious claims psychosomatically in manifestations such as extreme fasting and eucharistic ecstasies. Nonetheless, all these mystical phenomena, precisely because of their extraordinary character, still underscored women's exclusion from liturgical participation.

Despite ecclesiastical prohibitions and reservations, however, the beguines' new liturgically oriented devotional practices, including acoustic mysticism, helped to articulate their religious insights, to legitimate their ambiguous religious status, even to prove their usefulness to the Church. The writings by the first generations of beguines in the Low Countries, France, and Germany thus contain numerous references to music and mysticism. The authors Hadewijch of Brabant (active first half of thirteenth century), the German Mechthild of

Magdeburg (ca. 1212–82), and the French Marguerite de Porete (d. 1314) used musical knowledge both thematically and structurally.[19] Following the conventions of courtly love lyrics, which were generally performed with musical accompaniment, musical tropes often functioned as a literary coding of mystical experiences. For example, Hadewijch compared the *unio mystica* to a melody; she declared, "the pride of Love counsels me to hold / So firmly to her that I may encompass / Union above comprehension: / The melody surpasses every song!"[20] Because of its rhymed nature and structural borrowings from courtly love poetry, it is possible that at least some of Hadewijch's and Mechthild's poetry was performed as songs or accompanied by instruments when read to an audience. In contrast to the extraordinarily skilled beguine authors, illiterate or semi-literate beguines such as Marie d'Oignies produced more distinctly psycho-physiological sonic phenomena, such as singing for extensive periods of time, uttering unusual sounds, or manifesting miraculous physical responses to their surrounding soundscapes. The following analysis will highlight some of the problems generated by the necessity to translate female sonic mysticism into communicable religious knowledge.

Biography as Destiny: The Influence of Marie's Biographers Jacques de Vitry and Thomas de Cantimpré

Born into a wealthy merchant family in Nivelles and married at a young age, Marie d'Oignies and her husband chose to serve a leper's colony in nearby Williamsbroux. Marie gained renown as a charismatic healer and eventually moved to a cell in a newly established community of Augustinian canons that also housed women.[21] Thanks to a confluence of historical events and personal interests, Marie's local cult at Oignies eventually gained the attention and approval of influential clergy, and Marie became known as a paragon of beguine spirituality. However, the stereotype of Marie's preeminence as a beguine owes perhaps more to the antagonistic agendas of her two renowned biographers, the Frenchman Jacques de Vitry, and the Brabantine Thomas de Cantimpré, than to her own spiritual aspirations or the complex reality of female religious life in the region.[22] Read closely, the biographical data reveal—perhaps unwittingly so—a disturbing underside of the devotion one might expect to find in hagiographical accounts. For example, as Marie lay dying, her first biographer Jacques de Vitry noted that she was

> untroubled by any sound which she knew pertained to God or to His Church. For instance, it did not bother her when we were sitting beside her in the church and were singing in a loud voice almost directly in her ears. She was equally undisturbed when a large group of masons were hammering right next to her during the erection of an altar, which we had arranged to be built and which was to be consecrated by the Bishop of Toulouse.[23]

The sonic scene beside the new altar captures the extent of Marie's relevance for the community at Oignies as Jacques understood it: validating religious men's activities, but not guiding them.[24] Her wish to die with devotion in a sacred space appears to have been less important than the more profane deadline of masons' finishing the altar in time for its consecration by the bishop from Languedoc. Were it not for its supernatural insensitivity, Marie's sick but reportedly unperturbed body would have been rendered invisible by the canons' effort to create a presence of the Sacred through liturgical chanting (which she was forbidden to join) or their noisy architectural expansion of the church at Oignies.[25]

Jacques's vignette also captures another aspect of the new mysticism that Marie came to represent, this time geographical: the nexus of local and transregional presssures in the formation of ecclesiastical standards of beguine orthodoxy. As we shall see, Jacques, who became a preacher for the crusades to Southern France and Palestine after Marie's death, had a vested interest in strengthening the links between the north and south of European Christendom. Indeed, the composition of Marie's *vita* cannot be fully understood without awareness of this charged north–south axis. In a similar vein, Thomas de Cantimpré's appeal for local patronage after Jacques's election as bishop cardinal in Italy shaped the focus of his biographical *Supplement* to Jacques's *vita*. Even the most local of Marie's biographical sources, the succinct *History of the Church of Oignies*, made an effort to create some sort of synchronicity between local and Middle Eastern events.

Jacques de Vitry knew Marie personally for the last years of her life, a phase during which Marie's regional reputation was well-established; Thomas noted that Jacques was already Marie's fifth confessor.[26] Born in Reims and educated in Paris, Jacques's religious allegiances were formed by an international career in a Church whose administrative structure spanned most of Europe; during the era of the crusades, the Church attempted to strengthen her reach even beyond the Continent. In his *Supplement* to Jacques's *vita* of Marie, Thomas stressed his predecessor's status as a foreigner and reported Marie to have urged Jacques to "abandon France and remain. . .at Oignies."[27] Rather surprisingly for a Dominican, Thomas also criticized Jacques's "excessive" academic learning at the university in Paris and noted elsewhere that Jacques was reprimanded for his biography's inappropriate "elegant style."[28] Apart from currying favors for the little-known Augustinian house at Oignies, Thomas's insistence on Jacques's outsider status possibly disguises discomfort with the (discursive) appropriation of local religious practices for personal career politics; perhaps they also imply a criticism of Jacques's past French loyalties at a time when the French royal crown made claims on Flanders.[29]

I suggest that Marie's sonic mysticism, and in particular her so-called Death Song, was molded into a narrative structure that preserved traces of key junctures and concerns not just of Marie's activities, but also of her biographers' careers; like the layers of an archeological site, Marie's hagiographies absorbed strands of intertwined lives and encounters that altered the course of the biographers' existence as much as the memory of Marie's holiness. Although sonic miracles could occur at the death scene of any saintly woman, the key to accessing underlying biographical currents is the fact that only Marie's Death Song became explicitly associated with issues of Christian orthodoxy and preaching. Jacques de Vitry phrased the Death Song performance as follows. As Marie lay dying, "she. . .began to sing in a high and clear voice and for three days and three nights did not stop praising God and giving thanks: she rhythmically wove in sweet harmony the most sweet song about God, the holy angels, the blessed Virgin, other saints, her friends and the Holy Scriptures."[30] During this sung exegesis, Marie is said to have expounded the tenets of Christian faith in astonishing depth and innovation. Immediately after the completion of her song, however, she died, unable to continue her musical preaching; equally surprising, those present during her performance could neither remember nor understand much of what she sang.

The Death Song performance reiterates themes that Jacques applied to other parts of his hagiographical text as well. In contrast to the other two biographical sources, Jacques minimized references to Marie's specialized role as a gifted holy woman in her local community, but maximized universal themes of orthodoxy and obedient devotion to the Church. Instead of her ministry to the sick and socially marginalized, Jacques stressed Marie's extraordinary acts of penance. Standardized and reduced to a more human dimension, these acts could be more easily reproduced or held up as a model for communities anywhere than could Marie's exceptional endurance and healing gifts. Local personal fame and universally applicable virtuous behavior created contradictory assessments of Marie's accomplishments in all three biographical sources. It will be the task of this essay to tease out their points of contact, their connections, and implications.

Biography as Flattery: Pleasing a Traveling Troubadour

The local scene of Marie's slow dying, her miniscule and emaciated presence beside the unfinished altar and the chanting canons, are brought into deeper relief by the presence of a well-traveled Church official, Bishop Fulk (Fulquet) of Toulouse (ca. 1155–1231). Nobody, including his fellow poets Dante (1265–1321) and Petrarch (1304–74), would forget that Fulk began his career as a Genovese merchant and troubadour in Marseilles.[31] Fulk's presence in Oignies seems to offer the most suitable key to unlock the multiple meanings of Marie's Death Song. Given Fulk's fame as troubadour, the many references to sound and mystical phenomena in Marie's biography, and especially her dogmatically focused Death Song were most likely formulated as Jacques's homage to the former minstrel. After all, Marie's *vita* is dedicated to Fulk and supposedly written upon his request.[32]

Jacques's reverence for Fulk was not without its own problems, however. Having joined the Cistercian order in about 1202, Fulk rose to the position of bishop of Toulouse by 1205. The wealthy bishopric, also a center of Albigensians, a subgroup of the heretical Cathars, enabled Fulk to command a substantial militia force of his own. Unwaveringly loyal to Rome, Fulk proved himself to be one of the shrewdest supporters of Simon de Montfort the Elder's (ca. 1153–1218) military campaigns against Albigensians and their alleged supporters.[33] Unlike Jacques, sympathizers with Languedoc had little sympathy to spare for the troubadour turned bishop. The anonymous author of the second part of the Occitan *La Chanson de la croisade albigoise* wrote disparagingly about the effects of Fulk's musical talents.

> And I tell you that the bishop, who is so violent that in all that he does, he is a traitor to God and to ourselves, has gained by means of lying songs and beguiling phrases which kill the very soul of any who sing them, by means of those verbal quips he polishes and sharpens, by means too of our own gifts through which he first became an entertainer, and through his evil teaching, this bishop has gained such power, such riches, that no one dares breathe a word to challenge his lies. Yet when he was an abbot and a cowled monk [in the Cistercian abbey of Thoronet in the Provence], the light was so darkened in his abbey that there was no goodness or peace until he was removed.[34]

The mission of Fulk's journeys to the Low Countries and beyond was to gather troops and financial assistance in the siege of towns and castles loyal to Count Raymond VI.[35] The as yet unknown Jacques took up Fulk's cause through the means available to him, that is, preaching and writing. Composing his supplement to Marie's *vita* roughly fifteen years later, Thomas remembered the results of the former minstrel's visit as less than glamorous. Not only religious idealists from that region of "great holiness" joined the fight against Languedoc. Thomas described at length how some "stupid and irreverent people" on their way to Southern France threatened to kill a fellow neighbor from Nivelles, Marie's birthplace, for the simple reason that he criticized their uncouth manners.[36]

Framed by its musical interludes, Marie's programmatic *vita* outlines Jacques's pastoral views of orthodox lay spirituality in conformity with

Fulk's anti-heretical agenda. Its key ingredients are obedience to the Church, self-effacement, humility, excessive sensitivity to the demands of confession, and the power of the Eucharist. The tendentiousness of such ideal holiness becomes more pronounced when contrasted to the biography of a contemporaneous Cistercian nun from the Low Countries, the Jewish convert Rachel, or as known by her Christian name, Catherine of Louvain. According to her sympathetic biographers, Thomas de Cantimpré and Caesarius of Heisterbach, Rachel was intellectually precocious and so motivated to study Christianity that she amazed and exhausted her priestly instructor and his female assistant Martha, possibly another beguine. Referring to her religious instruction, it was noted,

> the explanation of these matters. . .was so complete that at the age of six and a half she comprehended [everything] by means of such great understanding of the spirit, so that rarely did the priest repeat any explanation. . .What evidence of wonder! Rachel could never be satisfied, nor did she tire of hearing the word of God.[37]

Eager for conversion, little Rachel is shown to have demonstrated initiative, courage, eloquence, and serenity. These are all virtues that the adult Marie as well displayed in her choice to serve lepers, to foretell the future and distant events, and to heal the sick and to raise the dead, yet such demonstrations of courage and independent action become neglected in Jacques's effort to stress Marie's subordination to clerical authority.

Jacques's support of Fulk's missions no doubt advanced his own fledgling career in the Church. Marie died in 1213; in the same year, Jacques began preaching the Albigensian crusade. As Jacques's rise from relative obscurity to prominence suggests, the cosmopolitan Fulk provided Marie's biographer with an entry to a world beyond the newly founded Church at Oignies, impoverished as it was and pitifully endowed with nothing but "a rent of three hens."[38] It is thus not surprising that Jacques painted Fulk's encounter with Marie with dramatic strokes. Fulk "received so much consolation from looking at her that for an entire day no material taste of food he ate could dispel that taste of honey from his mouth"; Marie "greatly lightened her servant's bitterness which he was suffering on account of his exile."[39]

Biography as Geography: From Lorraine to Palestine and Back

Whether Marie understood herself as a far-reaching beacon of orthodoxy or as a local healer, the Albigensian crusade was not the only international religious crisis, however, that shaped the biographers' approach to Marie's very local sanctity. Somewhat strenuously perhaps, the anonymous author of the *History of the Church of Oignies* linked the founding of his small community to Saladin's (1138–93) immensely important victory over Christian armies in Palestine. It is hard to see much of a causal connection between Augustinians clearing a patch of land in Lorraine and the sultan of Egypt and Syria's brilliant military accomplishments in Palestine; however, the missing compositional link is not Marie's, but Jacques de Vitry's presence at Oignies. As in the *vita*, a desire for patronage, this time Jacques's very own, shaped the *History*'s framing of local religiosity. Anonymous begins his pithy oeuvre with a summary statement of anti-Islamic sentiment and a tendentious image of Saladin, then adds a critique of the laxity of Christians in the Holy City, and finally, in a seeming *non sequitur*, he evokes Jacques's early studies in Paris, undertaken before he moved to Oignies.

> It was the time when God permitted the Kingdom of Jerusalem, with all the Christians living there, to be subdued and slaughtered with cruelty and hostility by the impious Saracen king, Saladin, a cruel tyrant. This their countless sins required. It was the year 1187 AD. . . . Our most reverend father and lord, Jacques de Vitry, the confessor of Louis, the king of France, was studying sacred theology in Paris.[40]

Rhetorically at least, Jerusalem had to be evoked, because by the time of the *History's* composition, Jacques had advanced from the status of an obscure biographer to the position of cardinal bishop of Tusculum. Between his humble beginnings in Oignies and his illustrious final appointment in Italy, Jacques had been assigned the bishopric of Acre. In 1214, one year after Marie's death and his preaching tour against the Albigensians, we find him busy raising money and manpower to fight Muslims in Palestine. The bishopric of Acre, a rich and vibrant port city that served as a launching pad for crusading efforts, became his in 1216. The anonymous historiographer from Oignies couched Jacques's impressive career trajectory in reverent terms, praising the cardinal bishop because long ago, he had "disdained worldly riches and preferred the company of poverty" when he had moved to Oignies after his studies in Paris.[41]

While in Palestine, Jacques indeed did not forget his humble beginnings at the new community. We learn from Anonymous that "later, when he advanced to a worthier lot, he endowed our church [at Oignies] with linen vestments, the relics of the saints, and other church ornaments, books, and many privileges of the apostolic see."[42] Thomas de Cantimpré expanded the transfer of these gifts into high drama in his own hagiographical version, complete with Marie's prophesies, a devastating fire, a miraculous sea crossing, and a dancing prior.[43]

Even though Jacques and Fulk connected the community of Oignies to an international nexus of historical forces, local religious culture was never merely a passive and stable "feminine" background to a trend-setting "masculine" international cast of players. Communally experienced crises such as famine and war demanded thoughtful religious responses; personal ties within communities evoked nuanced story telling that recorded the local ebb and flow of tensions and affections.[44] And finally, neighbors and relatives who actually joined crusades and pilgrimages were remembered through prayers by loved ones and their whereabouts abroad were tracked in holy women's visions.

"If you look carefully. . .": Biography and Local Community

If the Albigensians in Languedoc fell short of Marie's exemplary conduct so did some local people in the Lorraine as well, at least according to Jacques. As a friendly and collegial nod to Fulk, but certainly as a provocation to those who were critical of the beguines' ecstatic extravagance, Jacques intended Marie's biography "to strengthen the faith of the weak, instruct the unlearned, incite the sluggish, stir up the devout to imitation, and confute the rebellious and the unfaithful."[45] Did the Frenchman Jacques raise a few local eyebrows when he invoked beguine spirituality as a bulwark of orthodox sanctity? After all, in contrast to members of the clerical caste, the majority of religious women tended to live and work in the region of their birth; they and their families were thus well-known locally.[46] Thomas de Cantimpré expressly pointed to his local roots as a validation for the truth of his account of Marie's miracles: "I have seen and known many religious men and women in Lorraine where there is a great abundance of holiness. As a man brought up in that region, I have accepted their visions and secret visitations."[47]

Indeed, conflict and misgivings shaped some of the local interpretations of the early beguines, especially because not all beguines were as wealthy as Marie nor gifted with the desirable healing powers ascribed to her. In his prologue, Jacques defended at length the more unusual aspects of their lives against what might possibly have been rather levelheaded critics. When these local skeptics observed some of the beguines' frequent and unusually intense trances and ecstasies, they judged "them to be either insane or idiots, and they consider prophecies and the revelations of the saints (sic) to be fantasies or illusions of sleep."[48] Marie's spiritual gifts of healing, her ability to predict the future, and especially her care for the dead served the community well and soothed the impact of collectively endured crises and difficult personal transitions by endowing liminal life experiences with larger religious meaning, most poignantly so in matters of illness, injuries, travel, and death. In terms of communal benefits of beguine spirituality, ecstasies and trances on the other hand were mere byproducts of perhaps rarer, but more practical supernatural skills. As highly individual union experiences with the Divine, altered states of consciousness were socially useless and even constituted a burden to the community. The ecstatics needed care, shelter, and food, yet were unable to acquire these essential provisions for themselves. For some of them, excessive fasting and wearing nothing but rags might have developed into a pious virtue by existential necessity.

Marie's biographers, especially Thomas, noted her socially beneficial gifts. In yet another evocation of death- and illness-related themes, he described her ability to track spirits in purgatory, heaven, and hell, and her healing powers, which technically consisted of a combination of prayer and the laying-on of hands. In a typical story of successful healing, Marie's special gifts became the last resort after all else had failed. To cite just one example, Thomas tells us that "a certain boy who lived in Oignies was dangerously ill and was continually bleeding from the ear. Although no medical art could effect a cure, he was perfectly restored to health by the medicine of her prayers and by the laying on of hands."[49]

Marie as a mystic thus is extraordinary in her healing gifts, but, as a beguine, ordinary in her attentiveness toward the ill, dying, and the dead. Beguines specialized in these female works by offering necessary spiritual services. Many of them simply stayed with the dying as a form of medieval hospice care, or visited the dead during wakes and at their graves. All that these services, whether mystical in exceptional cases or soberly pastoral among ordinary beguines, had in common were that they responded to existential situations of personally experienced liminality; they were rendered at a point when medical care had proven useless or superfluous. Beguines found their pastoral niche through mediating between the known and unknown, between death and life, between present and future.

Of Marie's three biographical sources, it is Oignies's anonymous historiographer who found the local element of Marie's career as a healer and prophetess the least unobjectionable, especially as it lived on in her relics. And not surprisingly so: like Jacques de Vitry's material gifts of valuable ornaments and other treasures, Marie's miracle-working relics formed part of Oignies's cultural capital. In the anonymous historiographer's words,

> In those days there flourished at Oignies that most precious pearl of Christ, Marie d'Oignies. Those who enjoyed her patronage have transmitted to posterity the story of her life, which was endowed with the virtue of many miracles. In God's name she cured the sick, cleansed lepers, and drove out demons from possessed bodies and, what is more, raised the dead. Her very clothing is in our reverent possession still. When women in labor are wrapped in it, they are freed from the danger of death and rejoice in a happy birth.[50]

Her powers were seen as especially efficacious for women in labor, a sign that Marie's married status was recognized as a plus for the lay community rather than a female blemish as male clerics since Saint Jerome would have it. As in the case of other beguines, Marie's pastoral efforts and the efficacy of her relics continued traditionally female work in a spiritual vein.[51]

Final Moments: Death, Song, and a Hagiographical Battle of Postmortem Interpretation

Community-oriented pastoral care seems to have been a central aspect of the beguines' self-chosen religious role. In contrast, issues of orthodoxy, support and validation of the priesthood, and submission to ecclesiastical authority became the focus of women's mystical life during the beguines' "discovery" by clerics. The movement's subsequent clerical reinterpretation was tailored to fit more abstract and thus universally applicable models of standardized female religiosity. This process of discursive redefinition and a certain disempowerment is not only documented in several *vitae*, but also reflected upon in the less numerous beguine-authored spiritual writings. The period of a "textualization" and thus new categorization of beguine spirituality implied that their status in the Church had to be renegotiated as well. The literate beguines dealt self-consciously with both ends of the religious spectrum; Mechthild of Magdeburg, for example, reported her frequent visits to the sick and dying, but she also engaged in heated debates about theological matters, including the conflict-ridden intra-ecclesiastical status of women like her.[52] Both Hadewijch and Marguerite Porete were respected as teachers by their respective communities, but persecuted by outsiders; Marguerite was eventually burned at the stake.

Of course, aspects of both spiritual dimensions also left their mark in the male-authored written sources of beguine lives. Presented in a peculiar descriptive mix of beguine autonomy and subordination, they still cause contradictory assessments today.[53] Since they did not belong fully to either secular women's realm nor to religious men's sacred spaces, beguines could more easily move between the two social worlds, and in the process infuse both with new meaning altogether. Marie's dying body challenged the profane nature of the stone masons' work in the church of Oignies with its clearly intrusive presence. Like the dying Marie, beguines and holy women of the new orders as well boldly interrupted male liturgical authority through sonic mystical performances.[54]

Marie's cult flourished at the margins of Latinate literate culture, but remained anchored within the boundaries of the sacred space, the region, and the community where she had lived. As Thomas and the anonymous author of the history of the church of Oignies testified, Marie's locally known body continued to heal through her clothing and her relics. Although Jacques noted her strong connection to her community, especially to women, he dramatically reinterpreted references to the power of her relics.[55] If we add to this omission of her wonder-working relics the fact that he described Marie's self-inflicted bodily immolations at great length, a narrative focus not pursued by the other two authors, we may suspect an intentional effort to undermine the supernatural powers of Marie's body. Instead of her acts of healing, for which she became locally renowned, Jacques concentrated on Marie's orthodoxy that, in imitation of her relics' efficacy, would extend even beyond the grave:

> After her death, she did not desert those whom she had loved in her life and returned to many and she frequently spoke to holy women of proven conduct. She taught her friends what they should do and warned them of dangers and removed from their hearts all doubt by certain and secret signs.[56]

Read against the evidence of her cult as provided by the anonymous historiographer, Jacques's embellishment of Marie's death, including her Death Song, thus appears even more as idiosyncratic invention. As noted above, the Death Song constitutes a mode of communication that, according to Jacques's symbolic accounting, lasted for three days and three nights. Not surprisingly, Jacques stressed supernatural intervention rather than personal stamina when describing Marie's musical feat.

> She thus began to sing in a high and clear voice. . .for three days and three nights. . .she rhythmically wove in sweet harmony the sweetest song. . .she rejoiced with a continuous cry. . . .Once when she had cried aloud for a whole day,. . .her throat became so hoarse that by the following evening she could barely speak. . . .The next morning our percussionist began to play her lyre even louder and more piercingly than usual, for that night an angel. . . had taken away all her hoarseness and put into her breast an unction of wondrous sweetness. Her windpipe was opened and her voice renewed and for almost the entire day she did not cease from praising God and men heard a voice of great exaltation and harmonious modulation, although the doors were shut and everything blocked up.[57]

Two factors are significant here. One, that in so far as religious music was understood to connect heaven and earth, Marie's sonic miracle at the time of death manifested somatically the Gregorian claim that religious music dissolved boundaries between life and death, earthly life and heavenly existence.[58] Marie's dying is thus transformed into a dynamic process of transition; the miracle functions to minimize the trauma of loss of life by prefiguring the completion of dying—the happy reception of sinless souls in heaven's choirs.

But Jacques de Vitry extended Marie's miracle even further. Following his anti-heretical program, he reported, as noted earlier, that Marie had sung an entire *summa* during those three days and nights. His claims are somewhat precarious even on the surface of the textual evidence; he had to admit that the two eyewitnesses, Marie's maidservant and the prior, could neither understand nor remember the things she sang about.[59] But never mind. In Jacques's words,

> At first she began her antiphon in a very high tone and then in an even higher one. She sang about the Holy Trinity, about the Trinity in unity and the unity in Trinity. She sang these praises for a very long time and inserted marvelous and, as it were, ineffable things into her song. She expounded the Holy Scriptures in a new and marvelous way and subtly explained many things from the Gospels, the Psalms and the Old and New Testaments, which she had never heard interpreted. She uttered many things about the Trinity and from there she descended to the humanity of Christ, the blessed Virgin, the holy angels, the apostles and the other saints who followed them.[60]

Ironically, even Jacques himself could barely catch the meaning of her words:

> She began to sing I know not what in a low voice for a very long time, for at that time she could not raise her voice. When I approached closer, I could understand only this little bit of her song: "How beautiful you are Lord, our King."[61]

Compared to manifestations of sonic mysticism among other dying religious women, even other beguines, Marie's theological singing is no doubt unique; Jacques's own description of another, more typical beguine's death scene highlights the point. He recounts how at the side of the dead beguine, Marie caught a glimpse of the Virgin Mary and a "multitude of heavenly maidens" chanting divine praises while hovering over the female corpse. Nothing of declamatory theological significance occurs.[62] Since no mention is made of Marie's theological expertise at any other point of this *vita* or in the other sources on her life, it seems that in her dying moments only, can Jacques de Vitry's Marie take on a masculine role, and thus resolve the liturgical and theological paradox of female submission vis-à-vis beguine innovation, crystallized in the scene of a dying female singing and teaching.

In contrast, Thomas de Cantimpré invoked Jacques's telling of Marie's Death Song as more consistent with her social role as mystical healer. In the *Supplement*, the dead Marie demonstrates her authority and independence by exercising literally tight control over her relics, especially the bones and skin related to speech and voice. The *Supplement*'s story seems to stage Jacques's Death Song motif with a great sense of irony, perhaps intentionally so in light of Thomas's criticism of Jacques's overly zealous theological studies earlier in the text. The death scene's chapter title in the *Supplement* seems rich with *double entendre* and allusion: "How she predicted that after her death, her mouth would close tight. How after her death, she would not allow the teeth of her mouth to be removed unless prayers had been offered beforehand."[63] Not song, but silence. Not obedience, but the grisly resistance of a very real corpse. Not theological abstraction, but concrete physical exertion. Thomas described the incident of Marie's willfully silent corpse as follows, a scene that, it should be noted, is delicately and with good reason omitted in the *History of Oignies*.

> The prior of Oignies [who had been present during her death song performance] with some friends and fellow thieves transferred the body of the dead woman to a hidden place. He laid the head down on his knee and grasped the chin with his right hand while he pushed down hard on the forehead. However, in accord with the words of the prediction she made while she was alive, he was unable to open her teeth or even her lips. Then he tried a knife and other iron tools to no avail; so, frustrated, he arranged to put the body back on the bier.[64]

As a nod to his illustrious visitor from Southern France, Jacques appears to have transformed a female death scene into a rhetorical device, underscoring that the holy women of the region were orthodox; unlike Albigensian heretics, they would only pronounce theological statements at the time of their death, and even then remained tactfully unintelligible to their audiences. Thomas, critical perhaps of Jacques's omission of Marie's miraculous gifts as healer and the potency and authority of her relics, replaced the image of a mumbled death song with a grim corpse with tightly locked jaws.

Conclusion

It is thanks to the Latinate interpretations of their lives that the holy women's "great abundance of holiness" could evolve from local relevance to transregional significance; naturally, it had to change its meaning in the process. Sifting through the layers of Marie's biographical sources, we find other, more hidden dimensions of her sonic mysticism in the vernacular roots of her Death Song. Jacques made a point to note that Marie's Death Song was not delivered in Latin, but in French, the common language of southern Brabant and Lorraine. Whether Jacques's rendering of the story of Marie's dying is true or not, the Death Song's vernacular character hints at a spiritual matrix of meaning that linked religious women, death, mysticism, and music in unexpected, but not atypical ways. The fact that women both before and after Marie produced sonic miracles at the limits of life offer us clues about an extraordinary liturgical tradition that is indeed gynecocentric. For example, on her deathbed, Saint Elisabeth of Thuringia (1207–31), one of the patron saints of the beguines, staged miraculous songs without moving her lips. About 200 years after Saint Elisabeth's death performance, Saint Catherine of Bologna (1413–63), an accomplished and highly educated convent musician and also already recognized as a saint during her lifetime, had a near-death vision of a lute player, who revealed to her that she would not yet die. Saint Umiliana (1219–46), well-known for her care for the ill and poor, is said to have emitted miraculous sounds from her body while suffering from stomach cramps. Her pain disappeared for as long as the music lasted.[65] The Dominican Heinrich Seuse (ca. 1295–1366), to cite yet another example, left us a story about a holy woman's visionary dream, during which she saw him being lovingly embraced by a group of angelic children singing the praise of God. The devout children were revealed to be deceased nuns who once were in Seuse's pastoral care.[66] In the Cistercian tradition, Saint Bernard of Clairvaux's *vita* includes a story of a female harpist called to his bedside in order to heal him while he suffered from a headache.[67] On the local level, like common beguines' care for the sick, and no matter its ideological readings, Marie's dying became transformed into a dynamic process of spiritual transition, minimizing the trauma of loss of life by prefiguring the happy reception of souls in the choirs of heaven.

And so we return full circle to the ideological layers placed upon the liminal event by Marie's biographers and their illustrious visitor. Fulk of Toulouse, troubadour and infamous defender of Christian orthodoxy, might have taken note of both authors' symbolic linkage of death, song, and theological utterance. After all, according to the contemporaneous *Chanson de la Croisade contre les Albigeois*, he was held responsible for the deaths of scores of people from Languedoc. Although warmly welcomed in a region that the South of France knew best through its militias and mercenaries, Fulk's journeys only brought suffering and destruction to his own local community. Likening the defender of orthodoxy to the Antichrist, the Occitan Anonymous remembered in the *Chanson* that

> once he [Fulk] was elected bishop of Toulouse, a fire has raged throughout the land that no water anywhere can quench. For he has destroyed the souls and bodies of more than five hundred people, great and small. In his deeds, his words and his whole conduct, I promise you he is more like Antichrist than a messenger from Rome.[68]

Like Marie's Death Song, the *Chanson de la Croisade*, too, is a song about death. And although performed in different regions, both songs were framed by the presence of the same key player, and the same key issue, religion's power to determine the meaning of life and death.

Notes

An earlier version of this paper was presented at the 35th International Congress of Medieval Studies, Kalamazoo, 2000. I wish to thank in particular Margot H. King, Mary Suydam, and Ellen Kittell, but also the panelists of my session and my audience for their insightful comments, support, and feedback.

1. See Ernst Benz, *Die Vision. Erfahrungsformen und Bilderwelt* (Stuttgart: Ernst Klett Verlag, 1969), section VI: 2 ("Die himmlische Musik") and section VII: 2 ("Vision und Liturgie"); on possible neurological predispositions for musically induced ecstatic states, see Robert Jourdain, *Music, the Brain, and Ecstasy* (New York: William Morrow and Company, Inc., 1997).

2. During Mass, but also during extraliturgical states of trance and ecstasy, frequently at the moment of death, the music of angels could be made audible to the devout. Taking her clue from Isaiah's vision of the throne of God surrounded by singing seraphim, the Early Church believed that angels would perpetually sing praises in honor of the Divine. This notion developed into the view that during liturgy, angelic choirs would merge their voices with human song in praise of the resurrected Christ. See Reinhold Hammerstein, *Die Musik der Engel: Untersuchungen zur Musikanschauung des Mittelalters* (Bern and München, 1962); Cyprian Vagaggini, *Theological Dimensions of the Liturgy* (Collegeville, Minnesota: The Liturgical Press, 1976).

3. St. Gregory the Great, *Dialogues* 4, 58. Quoted in Vagaggini, *Theological Dimensions*, p. 352.

4. See C. Clifford Flanigan, Kathleen Ashley, and Pamela Sheingorn, "Liturgy as Social Performance: Expanding the Definitions," in *The Liturgy of the Medieval Church*, ed. Thomas J. Heffernan and E. Ann Matter (Kalamazoo, Michigan: Medieval Institute Publications, 2001), pp. 695–715.

5. Wiethaus, "Music and Visions in the Works of Blessed Heinrich Seuse (ca. 1295–1366)," unpublished paper presented at the conference on "Music, Mantra, and Medicine" at Elon College, 1998.

6. . . .*ut ubicumque in ambitu monasterii esset, horam adventus Christi in altario per ministerium sacerdotis, quantumcumque secreto fieret, sine ulla/m? haesitatione cognosceret; voceque facta in gutture ejus turturea, tanto modulamine resonaret, ut nullus mortalium eam sono imitari valeret. Horum testis ego sum, qui celebrans in loco, turturiam illam vocem audivi; vidique in eam aliud valde mirabile. . .plausus tantae ducledinis emittebat, ut dubitari non posset vocari eam ad coenam nuptiarum agni, in qua pater omnipotens, caelestia terrenis, ima summis virtute invisibili conjungebat.* Thomas de Cantimpré, *Vita Mariae Oignaciensis, Supplementum*, ed. Arnold Rayssius in *AASS*, June vol. 5 (June 23) (Paris, 1867), chapter 18, pp. 572–81 (hereafter abbreviated as *Supplement*). Translated into English in *Two Lives of Marie d'Oignies: The Life by Jacques de Vitry. Supplement to the Life by Thomas de Cantimpré, and The Anonymous History of the Church of Oignies*, trans. Margot H. King and Hugh Feiss (Toronto: Peregrina Publishing Co., 1998), pp. 242–43.

7. See the discussion of our contemporary loss of knowledge about secular women's spiritual practices in Peter Biller, "The Common Woman in the

Western Church in the Thirteenth and Early Fourteenth Century," in *Women in the Church,* ed. W.J. Sheils and Diana Wood (Oxford: Basil Blackwell for The Ecclesiastical History Society, 1990), pp. 127–59. For an example of secular women's subversive use of sound performances, see Kathy Lavezzo, "Sobs and Sighs Between Women. The Homoerotics of Compassion in *The Book of Margery Kempe,*" in *Premodern Sexualities,* ed. Louise Fradenburg and Carla Freccero (New York: Routledge, 1996), pp. 175–99. On music and women's spirituality cross-culturally, see overview and annotated bibliography by Jennifer Rycenga and Karen Pechilis Prentiss, "Music," in *Encyclopedia of Women and World Religion,* vol. 2 (New York: Macmillan Reference USA, 1999), pp. 687–93.

8. Discussed in context in Sophie Drinker, *Music and Women. The Story of Women in Their Relation to Music* (New York: The Feminist Press at The City University of New York, reprint 1995), p. 160 ff. See also J. Michele Edwards, "Women in Music to ca. 1450," in *Women and Music: A History,* ed. Karin Pendle (Bloomington and Indianapolis: Indiana University Press, 1991).

9. In *Purgatorio* XIX, 7–36, Dante used two strategies to mark the Siren's female song as vile and her powers as less threatening. Not only is her body described as malformed, but she cannot sing and be beautiful until he looks at her. ". . .there came to me in a dream a woman, stammering, with eyes asquint and crooked on her feet, with maimed hands, and of sallow hue. I gazed upon her: and even as the sun revives cold limbs benumbed by night, so my look made ready her tongue, and then in but little time set her full straight, and colored her pallid face even as love requires. When she had her speech thus unloosed, she began to sing so that it would have been hard for me to turn my attention from her" (. . .*mi venne in sogno una femmina balba, / ne li occhi guercia, e sovra in pie distorta,' con le man monche, e di colore scialba. / Io la mirava; e come 'l sol conforta / le fredde membra che la notte aggrava, / cosi lo sguardo mio le facea scrota/ la lingua, e poscia tuta la drivazza / in poco d'ora, e lo smarrito volto, / com' amor vuol, cosi le colorava. / Poi ch'ell' avea 'l parlar cosi disciolto, cominciava a cantar si, che con pena / da lei avrei mio intento rivolto*). Quoted in *The Divine Comedy. Purgatorio. Italian Text and Translation,* trans. Charles S. Singleton (Princeton: Princeton University Press, 1975), pp. 200–201. See also note 60.

10. *Attendant haec, et lugeant miserabiles et fatuae mulieres, quae lasciviae suae cantilenes ignem libidinis accendunt, et anhelitu suo prunes ardere faciunt, et idcirco a cantu Angelorum alienae in vanitate sua pereunt; quarum risus in luctum, gaudium in dolorem aeternum, cantus convertetur in ululatum.* Jacques de Vitry, *Vita De B. Maria Oigniacensi in Namurcensi Belgii Diocesi,* ed. Daniel Papebroeck in *AASS,* June vol. 5 (June 23) (Paris, 1867), chapter 34, pp. 542–72 (hereafter abbreviated as *Vita*). In addition to this *Vita,* the other biography of Marie d'Oignies is Thomas de Cantimpré, *Supplement* (see note 6). Both biographies and the anonymous history of Oignies (hereafter *History*) are translated into English in Margot H. King and Hugh Feiss, *Two Lives of Marie d'Oignies.* All quotations refer to these editions.

11. See Sophie Drinker's classic and still relevant study, *Music and Women*, chapter 12; Kimberly Marshall, "Symbols, Performers, and Sponsors: Female Musical Creators in the Late Middle Ages," in *Rediscovering the Muses. Women's Musical Traditions*, ed. Kimberly Marshall (Boston: Northeastern University Press, 1993), pp. 140–69; Anne Bagnall Yardley, " 'Ful weel she soong the service dyvyne': The Cloistered Musician in the Middle Ages," in *Women Making Music. The Western Art Tradition, 1150–1950*, ed. Jane Bowers and Judith Tick (Urbana and Chicago: University of Illinois Press, 1986), pp. 15–39. For individual medieval cloistered women who proved to be the exception to the rule, see the work of Therese Schroeder-Sheker on the Cistercian Mechthild of Hackeborn (1241–98), "The Use of Plucked-Stringed Instruments in Medieval Christian Mysticism," *Mystics Quarterly* XV (3) 1989, pp. 133–40; on Saint Gertrude the Great (1256–1302/03), another Cistercian, see Vagaggini, *Theological Dimensions*, chapter 22; on the earlier Benedictine Hildegard of Bingen (1098–1179), see *Saint Hildegard of Bingen. Symphonia*, trans. Barbara Newman (Ithaca and London: Cornell University Press, third edition, 1995).

12. Rycenga and Pechilis Prentiss, "Music," p. 688.

13. Discussed in Drinker, *Music and Women*, p. 188 ff.

14. On the rise of polyphony at Paris, where Jacques de Vitry studied, see Craig Wright, *Music and Ceremony at Notre Dame of Paris: 500–1500* (Cambridge: Cambridge University Press, 1989), parts V and VI.

15. Teresa Berger, "Women as Alien Bodies in the Body of Christ? The Place of Women in Worship," in *Liturgy and the Body*, pp. 112–21, quotation p. 113. Berger cites two main reasons for women's exclusion from liturgical participation: the prohibition to enter the priesthood and menstrual taboos. For medieval antecedents in the early Christian Church, see Berger, *Women's Ways of Worship. Gender Analysis and Liturgical History* (Collegeville, Minnesota: The Liturgical Press, 1999), chapters 1–2. On Hildegard of Bingen's liturgical compositions, see Margot Fassler, "Composer and Dramatist: 'Melodious Singing and the Freshness of Remorse," in *Voice of the Living Light. Hildegard of Bingen and Her World*, ed. Barbara Newman (Berkeley and Los Angeles: University of California Press, 1998), pp. 149–76. However, nuns were allowed to perform public liturgies during special processions, at least during the fourteenth century. See Jo Ann Kay McNamara, *Sisters in Arms. Catholic Nuns Through Two Millennia* (Cambridge and London: Harvard University Press, 1996), p. 328.

16. Carolyn Muessig suggests this possibility in her essay on Marie's Death Song, "Prophecy and Song: Teaching and Preaching by Medieval Women," in *Women Preachers and Prophets through Two Millennia of Christianity*, ed. Beverly Mayne Kienzle and Pamela Walker (Berkeley: University of California Press, 1998), pp. 146–59, but see Michel Lauwers's argument in his study, " 'Noli Me Tangere': Marie Madeleine, Marie d'Oignies et les Penitentes du XIIIe Siecle," *Mélanges de l'École française de Rome* 104 (1992), pp. 209–68. Given Jacques de Vitry's authorial agenda, it is very difficult to establish precisely what Marie d'Oignies knew and to what extent she was

capable to teach theological matters generally and especially while close to death and in the grip of a debilitating illness. A more clear-cut case can be made for Hildegard of Bingen's subversive use of the liturgy as a means to authoritative teaching; see Bruce Wood Holsinger, "The Flesh of the Voice: Embodiment and the Homoerotics of Devotion in the Music of Hildegard of Bingen (1098–1179)," *Signs* 19, 1 (1993), pp. 92–126; on the issue of prohibiting beguines to preach, see Michel Lauwers' interesting perspective in " 'Noli Me Tangere,' " p. 243 ff.

17. Ulrike Wiethaus, "Healing Sounds: Gender, Music, and Visions in Medieval Mystical Texts," unpublished paper presented at the 34th International Congress on Medieval Studies, Kalamazoo, 1999.

18. See Bernard McGinn, *The Flowering of Mysticism. Men and Women in the New Mysticism, 1200–1350* (New York: Crossroad, 1998), chapter 4, "*Mulieres Religiosae*: Experiments in Female Mysticism."

19. In her path-breaking survey of references to music in German literature, Kerstin Bertels discusses in particular Mechthild of Magdeburg (1212–ca. 1282/92) and Heinrich Seuse; other mystics considered include writings by the Dominicans Margaretha Ebner (ca. 1291–1351) and Elsbeth Stagel (d. 1360). See Bertels, *Musik in deutschen Texten des Mittelalters*, Europäische Hochschulschriften, Reihe 1: *Deutsche Sprache und Literatur* (Frankfurt am Main: Peter Lang, 1997); Vaggagini extensively analyzes Gertrud the Great's works in *Theological Dimensions*, chapter 22.

20. *Fierheit raedt mi dat ic hanghe / So vaste in minnen dat ic bevanghe / Een wesen boven alle sinne / Die toen verhoghet alle sinne*, Hadewijch, *Poems in Stanzas*, 31:5, in Marieke J.E.H.T. van Baest, ed. and trans., *Poetry of Hadewijch* (Leuven: Peeters, 1998), p. 218. I have used the more poetic translation by Columba Hart, *Hadewijch. The Complete Works* (New York: Paulist Press, 1980), p. 217.

21. The issue of whether Marie lived as anchoress or in some kind of beguine community is not resolved. See Margot King, *Two Lives*, p. 174, n. 60 for a summary of the debate. On medieval women saints as healers, see Elizabeth Jensen Bauer, "Medieval Women and the Care of the Sick: Some Evidence from Hagiography," *Magistra. A Journal of Women's Spirituality in History* 5, 1 (1999), pp. 79–97. On beguines from the Low Countries and their work in *leprosaria*, see Michel Lauwers, " 'Noli Me Tangere,' " p. 216 ff.

22. For better or worse, contemporary scholars are more cautious in their evaluation of these two authors than previous generations. For example, Wilhelm Preger, in his *Geschichte der deutschen Mystik im Mittelalter* (Leipzig: Dörffling und Franke, 1874), chastised Jacques for showing little inner disposition for the female lives he described with too much eloquence; to Preger, Jacques was only interested in the external power of the Church; he was a vain sycophant. Marie interested him only insofar as her piety could be exploited to defend an embattled *ecclesia* (pp. 44–45). Thomas does not fare much better. In Preger's stern assessment, Thomas, although more idealistic than Jacques, demonstrated weak powers of judgment; his head in the clouds, he had little understanding of human nature and the ways of the

world; naïvely, he believed everything pious nuns told him (ibid., pp. 46–47). The biographies of Marie d'Oignies are detailed in notes 6 and 10.

23. . . .*cum iuxta eam et quasi ad aures eius in ecclesia alta voce cantaremus, cum campanas diu et fortiter pulsaremus, cum etiam quoddam altare ut consecraretur ab episcopo Tolosano, cum multis caementariis percutientibus cum malleis iuxta eum erigeremus; numquam aliquo tumultu gravari poterat, quem ad Deum vel ad eius ecclesiam pertinere sciebat; Vita,* chapter 105.

24. Margot H. King has noted de Vitry's careful circumscription of Marie's authority vis-à-vis the canons. See *Two Lives,* p. 182. See also Lauwers's nuanced discussion in " 'Noli Me Tangere,' " p. 237 ff. Rita Lejeune argues for the closeness of beguine to Cathar spirituality, and points out that Cathars were documented for the Liège area since the eleventh century; furthermore, prince bishop of Liège, Hugues de Pierrepont (d. 1229), in contrast to Fulk and Jacques, practiced tolerance toward Cathars, which might also have prompted Jacques to demonstrate the beguines' obedience to their priests and confessors. See Rita Lejeune, "L'Évéque de Toulouse Folquet de Marseille et la Principaute de Liège," in *Melanges Felix Rousseau. Études sur l"histoire du pays mosan au moyen âge* (Brussels: La renaissance du Livre, 1958), p. 446 ff. On examining similarities and differences between Marie's spirituality and Catharism, see the monograph by Iris Geyer, *Maria von Oignies. Eine hochmittelalterliche Mystikerin zwischen Ketzerei und Rechtgläubigkeit,* Europäische Hochschulschriften vol. 454 (Frankfurt/Main: Peter Lang, 1992) and Patricia Deery Kurtz's study, "Mary of Oignies, Christine the Marvelous, and Medieval Heresy, *Mystics Quarterly* 14, 4 (1988), pp. 186–97. Muessig summarizes Jacques's misogynistic position in "Prophecy and Song," 146 ff., and in Muessig, *The Faces of Women in the Sermons of Jacques de Vitry* (Toronto: Peregrina Publishing, 1999), pp. 108–114.

25. On the association of saintliness with the inability to feel physical pain, see the helpful study by Esther Cohen, "The Animated Pain of the Body," *American Historical Review* 105, 1 (February 2000), pp. 36–68.

26. *Supplement,* chapter 20.

27. *Cuius peregrinationem famula dei devote valde suscipiens, exegit ab eo precum instantia, ut cum fratribus de Oignies derelicta Gallia permaneret; Vita,* chapter 2.

28. "his theological studies in which he was immoderately interested,". . .*relictis theologicis studiis, quibus fervebat immodice. . .; Supplement,* ibid.; the "elegant style" is discussed by Thomas in his *Vita S. Lutgardis virginis* in *AASS,* June vol. 3 (June 16), vol. 1, p. 5. See also Margot H. King, *Two Lives,* p. 161, n. 10, and Preger, *Geschichte der deutschen mystik,* pp. 44–45, for commentaries on Jacques's style. Rita Lejeune argues that Jacques's florid style was intentionally devised as a homage to the skilled poet Fulk; see "L'Évéque de Toulouse," pp. 433–48.

29. See David Nicholas, *Medieval Flanders* (London and New York: Longman Group UK Limited, 1992), p. 150 ff.

30. *Incepit enim alta voce et clara cantare, nec cessavit spatio trium dierum et noctium Deum laudare, gratias agree, dulcissimam cantilenam de eo, de sanctis angelis, de*

beata virgine, de sanctis aliis, de amicis suis, de divines scriptures; Vita, chapter 98.
Marie reportedly had the help of a seraph as she sang (ibid.). In her list of
the perfect, Hadewijch reports, "a beguine called Helsewent, who lived near
Vilvoorde, is [number] twenty-seven. She died singing." Quoted in
Sr. Helen Rolfson, trans., "These Are the Perfect, Clad As Love. Hadewijch
Saw Each of Them With His/Her Seraphim," *Vox Benedictina* 5, 2, 3 (1988),
p. 207. The Dutch *Lijst der Volmaakten* is edited and reprinted in
H.W.J. Vekeman, *Het Visioenenboek van Hadewijch* (Nijmegen-Bruges:
Dekker & van de Vegt-Orion, 1980), pp. 192–207.

31. Unlike the *Chanson de la croisade contre les Albigois* (see later, note 41), both
poets have kind words for their fellow colleague. Dante (1265–1321)
remembered Fulk in *Canto IX* of the *Paradiso,* letting him introduce himself as "Folco the people called me to whom my name was known, and this
heaven is imprinted by me, as I was by it. . . .Here we contemplate the art
which so much love adorns, and we discern the good by reason of which
the world below again becomes the world above" (*Folco mi disse quella gente
a cui / fu noto il nome mio; e questo cielo / di me s'imprenta, com' io fe' di lui;. . .
Qui si rimira ne l'arte ch'addorna/ cotanto affetto, e discernesi 'l bene / per che 'l
mondo di su quell di giu torna*) in Dante Alighieri, *The Divine Comedy,*
pp. 100–101. Petrarch (1304–74) mentioned Fulk as "Folquet whose name
is the pride of Marseilles, and who deprived Genoa of that honor when he
exchanged his lyre and songs for a kinder and more devout vocation" (*Folco,
que' ch'a Marsiglia il nome ha dato / Ed a Genova tolto, ed all'estremo / Cangio
per miglior patria abito e stato*), *Triumph* I, part IV, lines 38–57. Quoted in
Robert Briffault, *The Troubadours* (Bloomington: Indiana University Press,
1965), p. 190. On Fulk's visits to the Low Countries and their effects, see
Rita Lejeune, "L'Évêque de Toulouse."

32. Prologue, *Vita,* chapter 9.

33. See, *inter alia,* Jonathan Sumption, *The Albigensian Crusade* (London and
Boston: Faber & Faber, 1978), p. 112 ff. On the Cathars, see M.D. Lambert,
Medieval Heresy. Popular Movements from Bogomil to Hus (London: Edward
Arnold Publishers, 1977), pp. 108–151.

34. William of Tudela and Anonymous, *La chanson de la croisade albigeoise,* edition bilingue, ed. Henri Gougaud (Paris: Berg International, 1984), Laisse
145; trans. Janet Shirley, *The Song of the Cathar Wars. A History of the Albigensian
Crusade* (Hants, England: Scholar Press, 1996), p. 75.

35. Lejeune suggests that Fulk went north three times in search for assistance: in
1211 or 1212, in 1213, and in 1217 (L'Évêque de Toulouse," pp. 434, 440).

36. *Supplement,* chapter 4; see also Lejeune, "L'Évêque de Toulouse," p. 444 ff.

37. The story is edited, translated, and introduced by Michael Goodich,
"Caesarius of Heisterbach (ca. 1225) and Thomas of Cantimpré (ca. 1263)
on Catherine of Louvain," in *Other Middle Ages. Witnesses at the Margins of
Medieval Society,* ed. Michael Goodich (Philadelphia: University of Pennsylvania
Press, 1998), pp. 26–32. For its context and aspects of Jewish–Christian
relations at the time, see Aviad Kleinberg, "A Thirteenth-Century Struggle
Over Custody: The Case of Catherine of Parc-aux-Dames," *Bulletin of*

Medieval Canon Law 20 (1990), pp. 51–67. The fifteenth-century text cited by Goodich, which combines both Thomas's and Caesarius's versions, is printed in *AASS*, May 4 I, 532–34; for Caesarius of Heisterbach, see *Dialogue de miraculis*, ed. Joseph Strange, 2 vols. (Cologne: J. Heberel, 1851), 2.25, pp. 95–98. Interestingly, Hadewijch also tells of another adolescent Jewish convert, Sara, who, like Rachel, is praised for her education: "She [Sara] understood all tongues and was familiar with every science. . .she was a perfect mother of God." Quoted in "These Are the Perfect," p. 206.

38. *History*, chapter 4. The *vita* is intended as a preaching manual for Fulk and others. *Licet autem tu dices valde tibi et aliis multis esse commodum, si contra haereticos provinciae tuae, ea quae Deus in sanctis modernis in diebus nostris operatur, in publicum posses praedicare; ego tamen non acquievi, earum quae adhuc vivunt, virtutes et opera scripto commendare, quia nullo modo sustinerent*; Prologue to *Vita*, chapter 9.

39. *Unde cum vir quidam magnus, licet in oculis suis parvus die quadam loqueretur ei, . . .ex visu eius tantam recepit consolationem, ex verbo autem eius tantam dulcedinem, quod per totum diem illum nullus materialis cibi sapor ex ore eius expellere potuit, quem susceperat mellitum saporem. . . .Ex quo tamen factum, ut pius animarum consolatory servi sui, pro se exulantis maxime relevaret amaritudinem; Vita*, chapter 41.

40. *History*, Introduction.

41. *History*, chapter 7.

42. Ibid.

43. *Supplement*, chapter 13 ff.

44. For a description of local crises such as famine and warfare, see Galbert of Bruges, *The Murder of Charles the Good, Count of Flanders*, ed. and trans. James Bruce Ross (New York: Harper Torchbooks, 1967).

45. Thomas J. Heffernan pointed out that hagiographies were intended to create and support social cohesion, and that "the author of sacred biography is the community, and consequently the experience presented by the narrative voice is collective"; see Heffernan, *Sacred Biography. Saints and Their Biographers in the Middle Ages* (Oxford and New York: Oxford University Press, 1988), p. 19. The case of the early beguines in the Low Countries might be more complex, however, since some *vitae* explicitly address interpretative tensions between the clerical authors and the local community. Local resistance to the beguines in France, especially in regard to their public roles, is analyzed by Renate Blumenfeld-Kosinski, "Satirical Views of the Beguines in Northern French Literature," in *New Trends in Feminine Spirituality: The Holy Women of Liège and Their Impact*, ed. Juliette Dor, Lesley Johnson, and Jocelyn Wogan-Browne (Brepols: Liège, 1999), pp. 237–51; a summary of critical views of the beguines has been compiled by Ernest W. McDonnell, *The Beguines and Beghards in Medieval Culture, with Special Emphasis on the Belgian Scene* (New York: Octagon Books, 1969), especially pp. 439–56.

46. However, this circle could extend beyond regional boundaries. Hadewijch noted in her list of the perfect that female friends would visit her both in spirit and in body from far away; she knew a recluse "who dwells far away

on craggy rocks," and people in Thuringia, England, Jerusalem, Paris, Bohemia, and "on the other side of the Rhine"; as an example of multiple forms of long-distance communication and unusual communicators, Hadewijch wrote, "a virgin from Cologne, called Verlana. . .also used to come often to me in spirit and also to send me spirits, angels, seraphim, saints, and people" ("These Are The Perfect," pp. 207–209).

47. *Multos enim in Lotharingiae partibus, ubi maxima sanctitatis copia est, religosos religosasque vidi atque cognovi, quorum etiam visions atque visitationes secretas accepi, utpote homo illis in partibus educatus; Supplement,* chapter 11.

48. . . .*quaecumque vero non intelligent, derident et despiciunt. . . .Ipsi vero spiritum quantum in se est extinguunt, et prophetias spernunt: quia spirituales quosque, quasi insanos vel idiotas despiciunt, et prophetias sive sanctorum revelationes tamquam phantasmata vel somniorum illusiones reputant; Prologue, Vita,* chapter 10.

49. *Quidam puer juxta Oignies periculosa aegritudine laborabat: nam per eius auriculam continue a capite eius sanguis defluebat: cumque nulla arte medicinali curare posset, medicina orationum ejus et appositione manus sanitati perfectae restitutus est; Vita,* chapter 55.

50. *History,* chapter 6.

51. The courtly author Christine de Pizan (1364–1430) gave us a glimpse of women's public functions as caretakers, thus highlighting the continuum between the community work of holy women and laywomen. In the quotation that follows, Christine especially stressed the asexual (and thus slander-free) nature of such public work by emphasizing the older age of female caregivers.

> . . .If you watch carefully, for every young woman you will see twenty or thirty old women dressed simply and honestly as they pray in these holy places. And if women possess such piety, they also possess charity, for who is it who visits and comforts the sick, helps the poor, takes care of the hospitals, and buries the dead? It seems to me that these are all women's works and that these same works are the supreme footprints, which God commands us to follow.

> Christine de Pizan, *The Book of the City of Ladies,* trans. Earl Jeffrey Richards (New York: Persea Books, 1982), I.10.I, p. 26.

52. See Marianne Heimbach's study, *"Der Ungelehrte Mund" als Autorität: Mystische Erfahrung als Quelle kirchlich-prophetischer Rede im Werk Mechthilds von Magdeburg* (Stuttgart/Bad Cannstatt: Frommann-Holzboog, 1989).

53. See most recently, Annette Esser, "Marie d'Oignies: Female Visions of Strength" in *Women Christian Mystics Speak to Our Times,* ed. David B. Perrrin (Franklin, Wisconsin: Sheed & Ward, 2001), pp. 71–89.

54. Christina Mirabilis challenged liturgical taboos, for example, by musically redefining both spatial and gendered sacrality. Violating the prescription that women should not sing in public, Christina brilliantly staged memorable sonic events both in the Church and outside of it. If we can trust her biographer, Thomas de Cantimpré, she carefully chose liminal time and space to mark her acoustic transgressions as exceptions to the rule. Her performances were eventually recognized as sacred, and their liminality thus safely brought within the

boundaries of orthodoxy. Thomas described her innovative liturgical mimesis as follows: "While she was in that place [close to the German border], Christina went to the vigils of Matins every night after everyone had left the church and the doors were locked. Then, walking on the church pavement, she would utter such sweet songs that they seemed to be the songs of angels and not of human origin. The song was so marvelous to hear that it surpassed the music of all instruments and the voices of all mortals." Perhaps even more shocking were Christina's public musical performances in her own village, St. Trond. Frequently, her singing took place on fence palings, a cleverly chosen stage that poignantly symbolized her trespassing. In Thomas's account, a different reason, however, is given; nonetheless, even his interpretation underscores the sacredness of her liturgical activity: "Many times she would stand erect on fence palings and in that position would chant all the Psalms for it was very painful indeed for her to touch the ground while she was praying" *Vita*, chapter 39. On the frequently used topos of "sweetness" in descriptions of supernatural music, see Bartels, *Musik in deutschen Texten*, p. 66 ff., pp. 74, 76. Many of Hadewijch's visions as well occurred at or after Matins (see *Hadewijch. The Complete Works*, note 34).

55. Jacques's selectivity becomes clear when we juxtapose the *Historia*'s description of the healing function of Marie's clothing (see note 52) with Jacques's stereotypical denouncements of female clothing in chapter 37, and Marie's fabric relics as mere moral symbol. "What do you have to say to this, you extravagant and ostentatious women. . .you who manifest degenerate bestiality while you array yourselves as though you were temples?. . .In contrast, the clothes of this holy woman have been kept as relics because they smell sweetly. They are precious garments because no matter how thin they were, she was never conquered by cold. They have been sanctified because of the cold and, precisely because of this sanctification, they have been kept carefully after her death by the devout and are honored with a pious love." *Quid ad haec dicitis superfluae mulieres et pomposae?. . .quae vos degeneres et bestiales ostenditis, circumornatae ut similitude templi. . . .vestimenta sanctae mulieris hujus habentur pro reliquiis et redolent. Hae sunt vestes pretiosae, nullo frigore, quantumcumque tenues essent, superatae; et ideo propter frigus sanctificatae, propter sanctificationem vero post obitum ejus a devotis diligenter conservantur et affectu pietatis honorantur; Vita*, chapter 37.

56. *Post mortem etiam quos dilexerat in vita, non deseruit; sed ad aliquos rediens, sanctas etiamet probatae vitae mulieres frequenter alloquens, amicos suos docuit in agendas, et praemunivit in periculis, certis et secretis signis, omnem a cordibus eorum dubitationem removens; Vita*, chapter 109. Hadewijch as well communicated with entities in the spirit world; see note 37 and also Frank Willaert, "Hadewijch und ihr Kreis in den 'Visionen,' " in *Abendländische Mystik im Mittelalter. Symposium Kloster Engelberg 1984*, ed. Kurt Ruh (Stuttgart: J.B. Metzlersche Verlagsbuchhandlung, 1986), pp. 368–88.

57. *Incepit enim alta voce et clara cantare, nec cessavit spatio trium dierum et noctium Deum laudare, gratias agere, dulcissimam cantilenam de Deo. . .rithmice dulci modulatione contexere. . .continuo clamore jubilans. . .Cum autem tota die usque ad*

noctem clamasset, raucae factae sunt fauces ejus, ita quod in principio noctis vix aliquam vocem poterat edere. . .Facto autem mane tympanistria nostra altius et clarius solito incepit citharizare: angelus enim. . .illa nocte abstulerat omnem rauctitatem a gutture, immittens pectori ejus mirae suavitatis unctionem: et sic reparatis arteries et renovata voce; per totam fere diem non cessavit a Dei laude. Vocem exultationis et consonantiam modulationis tantum hominess audeibant; clauses enim ostiis et omnium exclusis; Vita, chapters 98 and 99. In chapter 98, Jacques emphasized that Maria did not compose her songs, thus diminishing her agency and independence, and noted again that if the community outside of Saint Nicholas would have heard her, they might have thought of her as a fool (*fatuus*); this is possibly the reason why she was kept behind locked doors while singing.

58. See among others Francois Marty, "From Senses to Sense," in *Liturgy and the Body*, special edition of *Concilium* 3 (1995), ed. Louis-Marie Chauvet and Francois Kabasele Lumbala, pp. 22–29. The biblical paradigm is David's healing of Saul (1 Sam. 16.14–23; 18.10; 19.9); in Marie's circle, the summoning of a female harpist to heal Bernard of Clairvaux's headache must have been a well-known story. See Arno Paffrath, *Bernhard von Clairvaux. Leben und Wirken—dargestellt in den Bilderzyklen von Altenberg bis Zwettl* (Köln: Dumont Verlag, 1984), p. 30 ff.

59. *Prior noster et ancilla mulieris secum in ecclesia remanserant, et ii multa de arcanis caelestibus, quae illa dicebat, intelligere non poterant; quaedam autem intellexerunt; sed pauca, pro dolor! Retinere potuerunt; Vita,* chapter 99.

60. *Primo autem summo et supreme tono Antiphonam suam inchoavit a sancta scilicet Trinitate, Trinitatem in Unitate, et Unitatem in Trinitate diutissime laudans, et mirabilia quasi ineffabilia cantilenae suae interferens. Quaedam etiam de divinis Scripturis, novo et mirabili modo exponens; de Evangelio, de Psalmis, de novo et de veteri Testamento quae numquam audierat, multa et subtiliter edifferens. A Trinitate vero ad Christi descendit humanitatem, dehinc ad beatam Virginem, ab hinc de sanctis Angelis et de Apostolis, et de aliis sequentibus Sanctis multa pronuntians; Vita,* chapter 99.

61. *Diutissime. . .coepit nescio quid submissa voce cantare, non enim jam vocem poterat exaltare. Cum autem magis appropinquastem, non nisi modicum de cantilena ejus potui intellegere, hoc scilicet: Quam pulcher es Rex noster Domine; Vita,* chapter 107.

62. See *Vita*, chapter 52.

63. *Miracula post mortem, potissimum in spiritu blasphemiae depulso. Qualiter dentes ex ore suo, post ejus obitum, sicut praedixerat, nisi oratione praemissa, vix auferri permisit. Supplementum, "Capitula," Caput III.* See also Patrick J. Geary, "Coercion of Saints in Medieval Religious Practice," in *Living with the Dead in the Middle Ages* (Ithaca and London: Cornell University Press, 1994), pp. 116–25.

64. *Tunc prior de Oignies cum aliquibus secretioribus amicis, defunctae corpus ad locum secretum transferens; caput illius super genus supinatum deposuit, sicque mento ejus dextera apprehenso, sinistra vero frontem deorsum cum virtute retorsit; sed nec sic dentes vel faltem labia, secumdum verbum quod vivens praedixerat, aperire praevaluit. Tunc cultellum et ferramenta alia adhibens cum nil proficeret, jamque frustrat spe corpus in feretro relocare disponeret; Vita,* chapter 3.

65. These incidents are collected in Joseph von Görres, *Die christliche Mystik*, 5 vols. (1836; repr. Graz: Akademische Druck-u. Verlagsanstalt, 1960). Georges Duby notes, "it seems clear that there existed a privileged relationship between women and the deceased" ("Women and the Dead" in *Women of the Twelfth Century*, vol. 2, ed. Georges Duby, trans. Jean Birrell (Chicago: The University of Chicago Press, 1997), p. 14).

66. See Heinrich Seuse (1295–1366), *The Life of a Servant*, in *Henry Suso. The Exemplar, With Two German Sermons*, trans. and ed. Frank Tobin (New York: Paulist Press, 1989), chapter 5. The German text can be found in Karl Bihlmeyer, *Heinrich Seuse. Deutsche Schriften* (Stuttgart: Kohlhammer, 1907).

67. See also note 11. The adolescent Bernard refused to listen to the harpist, however, possibly because she was female. Harps, kitharas, and lyres were and still are regarded as the musical instruments most conducive to healing. See Paffrath, *Bernhard von Clairvaux*, pp. 423–24.

68. *Chanson de la croisade albigeois*, Laisse 145.

CHAPTER 8

ON THE ARTISTIC NATURE OF ELISABETH OF SPALBEEK'S ECSTASY: THE SOUTHERN LOW COUNTRIES DO MATTER

Joanna E. Ziegler

Elisabeth as Mystical Performer in Medieval Historical and Modern Theoretical Terms

Around 1270 Philip, abbot of Clairvaux and Cistercian monk, left Spalbeek, near Liège in what would later become Belgium, where for the previous six months he had experienced what he would later describe as a "virgin. . .herself entirely a miracle." Upon returning to his monastery in France, the abbot set down his recollections of the events that he had witnessed and which he had found so astonishing in that small farming village. That document, which has become familiar through the centuries as the *Life of Elisabeth of Spalbeek*, is extraordinary, no less for its content than for the sense of both conviction and frustration that infuses the narration.[1] In this remarkable text the cleric finds himself only partly adequate to the task, repeatedly declaring that he would not believe, had he not seen things with his own eyes; and what he saw appears to challenge him as a writer: "Let it suffice for the present to have written these things about the description of the Hours, although many other things about contingent issues have been passed over, either because of a failure of memory or on account of the difficulty of the material from which my feeble pen recoils."[2]

The subject of this wonder and confusion was the extraordinary young Flemish-speaking holy woman, Elisabeth of Spalbeek, whose growing notoriety had captured the abbot's attention. More than 700 years later our lives met when I, too, became intrigued with the mystery and meaning of Elisabeth's life in the context of my own academic, aesthetic, and spiritual journey. Ultimately, this encounter led me to a profoundly affecting and challenging conclusion, which until now neither scholars of mysticism nor medieval art historians have considered: *ecstatic mysticism of the sort Elisabeth practiced and Philip witnessed is fundamentally artistic in nature and requires us to engage it on predominantly visual and artistic terms.* Moreover, my approach brings forward the more affirmative and resourceful characteristics of female mysticism as opposed to the current predominant emphasis on mysticism as both the function and expression of neurosis and pain. A further logical question is what role her homeland, the southern Low Countries, with its rich artistic culture, played in this form of mystical expression.

Abbot Philip had heard about Elisabeth while making his annual rounds, including a visit to the nuns at Herkenrode, near Elisabeth's home. The stories of her activities (including displaying the stigmata) were so unlikely to him that he visited her and spent approximately six months observing her behavior. It must have been an inspiring, if baffling, time for the abbot, because in setting forth his observations he took great care to describe Elisabeth's activities faithfully and in elaborate detail, and to position them, at the same time, as legitimate reflections of Church teachings.[3] He found this no easy task.

To help the process he interviewed local people, which suggests that Elisabeth's reputation was well-established in the region. Other monks came to witness as well; whether they did so at Philip's behest we shall never know. Her authenticity as a visionary was tested by the court of Philippe III of France;[4] and her relationship to other renowned spiritual women in the Flemish-speaking areas was examined; scholars have surmised that she may even have known Hadewijch.[5] Her performances each Friday were witnessed, again and again, and meticulously recorded upon Abbot Philip's return to Clairvaux—even though he found aspects of the performances profoundly puzzling. Clearly, her activities took on the nature of staged events, performed for audiences on a regular basis, the small chapel attached to her living quarters providing the environment and venue of a theater. The abbot's text, therefore, is a description of a performance—a record of what Elisabeth's audiences watched.

Elisabeth was not the only holy woman to become prominent in her time. The end of the thirteenth century in the southern Low Countries was favorable to women who practiced a sort of intensely physical and heightened spirituality that in our own time we have come to associate with women mystics[6] and ecstatics. The culture was fertile, promoting and sustaining a feminine spirituality that resulted in one of the most stimulating versions of mysticism in the history of Christianity. In the southern Low Countries many of these women, like Elisabeth, were beguines and lived with female family members, although the majority of beguines in the southern Low Countries lived in groups and were housed in beguinages.[7]

Let me be clear that in this essay I am referring to a group of exceptional women, who, as I have argued elsewhere, often were viewed as potentially disruptive to the community.[8] Religious and secular leaders of the beguine movement in the southern Low Countries often strove to keep the women, especially the "enclosed" beguines, from engaging in heightened spirituality—with its portent of uncontrollability. The relationship between the promotion of saintly women (through writing and preaching) like Elisabeth and the normative religious life of ordinary beguines still remains somewhat ambiguous.[9]

Nonetheless, there certainly was a proliferation of saintly biographies, sermons, and other writings in the thirteenth and early fourteenth centuries, composed by male clerics with time and inclination enough to observe these extraordinary women closely and record their lives. Thus flowered a variant on the genre of literature called hagiography,[10] writings about the lives of holy women, or *vitae*, to which Abbot Philip's report more or less belongs—more or less, because the *Life of Elisabeth of Spalbeek* differs from most beguine *vitae*. Walter Simons in his 1994 article, "Reading a Saint's Body," observed this difference and proposed that Abbot Philip's work is not a record of Elisabeth's life nor of her miracles, as is usually the case. This variance—the distinctiveness of Elisabeth's *vita*—is crucial to an understanding and interpretation of the *vita*.

Abbot Philip eschewed the conventional categories and devices that clerics employed to describe and promote feminine spirituality in the period. He did not write, for instance, about any acts of mercy she may have performed, such as caring for the sick or tending lepers. Such acts were centrally featured in promoting the *vita apostolica* of "holy women" (*mulieres religiosae*).[11] Nor do we learn about Elisabeth's family background or economic standing, so that another of the defining characteristics of women's *vitae* contemporary with Elisabeth's—the notion of voluntary poverty—is again totally missing from the text. Lastly, Abbot Philip was not her confessor; he did not spend a lifetime in intimate conversation, guiding and observing her spirituality. His time with her was brief.

Rather, Elisabeth's *vita* is predominantly a notation of her remarkable ecstatic movements in which, to the abbot's astonishment, she vigorously propelled her body in all sorts of patterns and contortions through the space of her chapel, often incorporating a small wooden crucifixion diptych as a devotional object. These movements culminated in the performance of the Passion, in which Elisabeth assumed the roles of Christ, John, and Mary, the entire event building in a crescendo to the climatic revelation on her own body of the blood and marks of the stigmatic five wounds of Christ.[12]

Certain aspects of these ecstatic activities were common to the great women's spiritual culture of the time. Many *vitae* depict remarkable occurrences of ecstasy and rapture in their female subjects.[13] Dyan Elliott has suggested, "[b]y the end of the fourteenth century, an entire genre devoted to spiritual discernment had developed which adduced general principles for deciphering the source of mystical inspiration." In Elliot's words again, the hagiographers "dwelt lovingly on these bodily manifestations as *ipso facto* proofs of sanctity."[14] Thus, Elisabeth's *vita* certainly should be viewed as part of this vigorous current of writing about the physical nature of women's mystical experience that arose in the thirteenth century.[15]

For all of its period emphases, though, Abbot Philip's text is still atypical. For example, pain and suffering, essential features of the genre, are downplayed in Elisabeth's *vita*. There is also an absence of reference to any excessive austerity on Elisabeth's part—which so frequently accompanies women's rapture and ecstasy and which in the decades after Elisabeth's death, would become suspect, even to the point of censure.

Also, Philip, in his account, seems to advance his own curiosity and questions about the activities, rather than use the text, as was common, to vindicate those occurrences as a sign of blessedness. It is as though Elisabeth's movements, in and of themselves, are as interesting to him as their symbolic and theological meanings. Moreover, he calls attention to the public nature of Elisabeth's mysticism—that people gathered to watch, including the abbot himself. He does not shy away, therefore, from her significance as spectacle. In fact, if anything, he seems carried away by her performance as something to be reckoned with in its own right rather than as merely an end, as merely (in Elliott's words) an "effective shorthand for denoting sanctity."[16]

My present purpose is to explore Elisabeth's *vita* in order to begin the process of marking out the unique characteristics of spiritual practices in the southern Low Countries—for males as well as females, authors, devotees, and audiences. Elisabeth's *vita* is part of the body of mystical literature surrounding a number of exceptional holy women who came to prominence in northern Europe in the thirteenth century. Because Abbot Philip's documentation of Elisabeth's mystical practices differs so markedly from other accounts, I will focus on those distinctions, paying special attention to the *artistic* nature of her practice, and exploring a number of the methodological issues at stake in treating that practice as "art." The latter part of this study will link the external form of Elisabeth's spirituality to theater, opening, I hope, a new perspective into the incredibly prolific, creative, and influential trends in mysticism from the southern Low Countries.[17]

Elisabeth's Appeal: Some Personal Considerations

I first learned about Elisabeth in the late 1980s while I was researching a book on the late medieval origins of the Pietà theme in the southern Low

Countries.[18] In studying the Chapel, Abbot Philip's *Life of Elisabeth* soon became the principal document. Historical analysis of that *Life* has enabled scholars to understand the religious context of Elisabeth's gestures and ecstasy, as well as those of other beguine examples, as part of a language of contemporary monastic and clerical ideology.[19] As an art historian, however, I was taken with different questions regarding Elisabeth, questions centering on the purely and manifestly visual aspects of her mystical practices.

How does Elisabeth's *vita* differ from the others, and why? What was it about her activities that was so challenging to the abbot, who as a Cistercian had ready access to the formula of women's *vitae*? Indeed it would have been perfectly acceptable (and probably expected) for Philip to adopt the compositional devices and narrative recipes of contemporary hagiography.[20] At the time Philip took to writing his report, the Cistercians and Dominicans were well on the way toward establishing a standard form for writing about women visionaries and ecstatics in the Low Countries.[21] In 1216, Jacques de Vitry had written the *vita* of Marie D'Oignies, considered by most scholars to be a prototype of the genre.[22]

Why, then, did Philip depart from the literary conventions of his contemporaries? What is this "difficulty of matter" to which Philip referred? Might it not prove instructive and valuable, I wondered, to follow his lead, and try to understand what he found discomfiting and agitating (even exhausting) about Elisabeth's practices—indeed about her nature—and which other hagiographers of the time found either absent in their subjects, or too unsettling or downright irregular to record?[23] It is this very departure of Philip from hagiographical conventions that provides the clue, I believe, to what distinguishes the spiritual life of the exceptional practitioners in the southern Low Countries.

Especially intriguing—indeed challenging—from a visual point of view are Elisabeth's motions that in his text Philip frequently is at pains to describe. Philip often wonders what to make of Elisabeth, apparently having no ready category in which to fit some of her activities, repeatedly saying of certain actions that they are performed, ". . .with a manner that may neither be heard nor told"[24] or "in a manner that I may not tell."[25] Moreover, his comments underscore the theatrical nature of Elisabeth's activities—the great physical demands of the activities, the presence of onlookers, the use of props and costumes, and the repetition of the performance with precision each time.

Some examples from the abbot's description of the physical nature of Elisabeth's actions follow:

. . .Thus grabbing herself by the hairs on both the right and left side of the head, she rouses herself and drives herself bending from this side and then from other in an inaudible and inexplicable manner with blows of her hands[26]. . .she strikes her own breast for a long time in a strong and very swift manner, so that as can be comprehended by certain of our more perspicacious attendants through counting more than calculating, sometimes she strikes her breast a hundred times with the double and continuous blows from both her hands[27]. . .and when she, as has been said, is leaning to the earth on one foot, from one side of her upper torso she bends her whole body toward the earth: and standing in this position for a long time the girl stands bent over to the other side of her upper torso as if she were vigorously swinging as a pendulum, (and in a manner) even beyond the strength of a man, sustains her hanging body on the one wounded foot[28]. . .sometimes while violently ripping from the front of her brow her hair that had recently been cut sufficiently short, she strikes the ground with her head in an amazing fashion without moving her feet.[29]

Philip describes at length Elisabeth's use of what apparently was a prop, a painting of the crucifixion on a folding panel. The relationship between her performance and the two-dimensional object is worth quoting at length:

Immediately a certain diptych icon which has an exquisitely depicted image of the crucified Lord is offered to her; holding the icon open with its parts unfolded in both her hands, she contemplates her most sweet Lord with the greatest devotion. And frequently she recalls these words, frequently repeating: "Here, soerte, Here" that is, "Lord, Sweet, Lord." With her purest lips, whence diffused grace radiates clearly she often sweetly kissed the feet of the Lord's image. . .and from considering the image she even slips off into contemplation of the truth while holding the image with the same grip as she held it before the rapture. Whenever her lips touch the foot of the crucifix and so thus her neck and head meet as for a kiss, they are elevated for a little while from the ground. In between these kisses, she produces from the intimate depths of her heart lavish, profound, joyful, and passionate expressions of longing along with a certain serene excitement of her breast and throat as well as of the sweet-sounding whispers from her lips. Afterwards she fixes her gaze upon the same image with a completely focused concentration and. . .without ever letting her attention waver, sets her gaze upon the image. The same panel is held so strongly by the girl's fingers that, when the tablet itself is seized by another or it is shaken or moved as if by someone trying to rip it out of her hands, never does she let go of it with her fingers, but her own body moves in accord with the movements of the tablet.[30]

At the conclusion of this part of the performance Philip says, "After she has been caught up in ecstasy, in as much as she has come back to herself, she rises and exits her bed swiftly, and she moves through her room with a marvelous and composed gait, as if she trusts in an angelic hand by which she is being led."[31] He even describes special clothing, or costume: "But in truth, after she had arisen, so always has she donned a tunic of wool against her flesh as an undergarment and then put on above that a white linen garment that hangs down just a little above the ground with its hems falling below her ankles and measuring the virgin's full height."[32] Finally, this performance, he tells the reader, is repeated and, moreover, repeated with precision: "However, she repeats these movements that I have just described above both frequently and in exacting detail."[33]

Philip's cryptic and often frustrated attempts to describe—indeed to *re-present* in words—Elisabeth's physical movements pose an equally vexing intellectual and scholarly conundrum: if physicality and somatic spirituality were so central to medieval women's religious experience—and we know from the *vita* that the body in motion is unquestionably what perplexed and fascinated Philip—then, is written description of the sort that scholars customarily provide the only, or even the optimum, means of approaching that physicality?[34] We must be fully aware that unlike most accounts of women's spiritual experiences, Philip's does not attempt to transcribe or interpret Elisabeth's *writing*, as is often the case, but rather her *movements*. This is, in fact, about her body—not her words. In Elisabeth's practice, the flesh necessarily has become the word.

The text, as Philip presents it, redolent with both promise and frustration, begs an alternative form of illumination to help retrieve and fathom its subject—and hence to help locate more accurately the status of both the text and its subject in the history of late medieval religion in the southern Low Countries. For me, that alternative became dance, along with visual analysis grounded in the discipline and practices of art history.

It became evident to me that whatever Elisabeth had been doing, it was experienced *and rationalized* in her time as something *seen*. Philip, convinced that Elisabeth's actions brought the message of Christ's passion and redemption to even the most unlettered among her audience, clearly makes the point that Elisabeth's message was embodied—and abundantly accessible—in her physical actions:

> . . .Even in the male sex, that is to say in the person of blessed Francis, this very phenomenon has previously revealed itself: so as each sex, not only from the witness of the Scriptures, but also from the living exemplars of the human condition, might find in the cross of Christ that which each person might honor, venerate, revere, imitate, love, and nothing of an excuse that a person, however uneducated or simple, whom the birth of the chaste Virgin redeemed, could offer as a pretext, so that one might say: "I am not able to learn about by reading or understand such profound mysteries, because I do not know how to read." Or since the book has been closed, since an ordinary person, just as much as the literate person, might have the ability to learn from reading a living image of our own salvation and an animated

history of redemption not in the parchments or in the documents, but in the limbs and body of our young girl we recall here, of course here I mean, of an unmistakably alive and lively Veronica.[35]

To *visualize* these aspects of the text—to picture Elisabeth, to see in formal terms the art and drama of her moving performance, which Philip so lovingly and carefully describes as an "alive and lively" image—in a state as close to the one that inspired his writings, this became the goal, my fascination and preoccupation.

For reasons that I will develop later, traditional methods of literary and historical analysis could not help. Perhaps because I am professionally trained in visual analysis and the performing arts, and also perhaps because certain details were pointing me in that direction, I turned to the processes I know best—art, dance, and theater—to help me picture what had taken place on those Fridays at the Spalbeek Chapel nearly eight centuries ago. Ultimately, I was convinced of the need to introduce another perspective, differing from the accepted ones, in order to enable Elisabeth—her beauty and power, and the transcendent radiance of her performance—to step forward into the light.

In 1992 with assistance from my institution, the College of the Holy Cross, I arranged for dancer and choreographer Paula Hunter to choreograph and perform portions of the *Life of Elisabeth of Spalbeek*. We videotaped her interpretation, through dance, of key sections of Abbot Philip's text. This project dramatically affirmed the course of my work on Elisabeth, strengthening and enhancing my relationship to her, the Chapel, and to mysticism. Naturally, of course, it unsettled all my notions of how—and whether—traditional forms of analysis can reveal the once-living artistic experience buried within the mystical texts. Whatever else, Elisabeth was, in my opinion, first and foremost an artist, the unique manifestation of her mysticism an art form, and Philip's description a true example of *ekphrasis*, a written description of a work of art, or "the verbal representation of visual representation."[36]

With this affirmation at hand and with a long-standing conviction that the later medieval Low Countries constitute a world of form and materiality[37]—of artistically and materially rendered representation—I would now like to set this thesis in motion: *the southern Low Countries do matter.* This region is consummately visual and artistic in the construction and expression of the myriad identities that comprise its culture—political, social, and spiritual.

Elisabeth was the quintessential performer—actor, dancer, and seer, all at once—and her mystical activities comprised a theatrical event, or, should we wish to categorize the matter in contemporary terms, it was "performance art."[38] We must, however, proceed cautiously with the reference to performance art, lest the current feminist interpretation of the term be construed as our only meaning of performance.[39] That interpretation—applying such contemporary and as yet unresolved concepts, as "embodied subjectivity" and "body art"—would fix Elisabeth's practices in a language and order that is wholly modernist rather than medieval. Needless to say, this topic deserves further treatment in another study dedicated solely to body art models and historical approaches to the body. For the present, it is probably sufficient to say that the politicized nature of body art is entirely alien to Elisabeth and her audience, both historically and philosophically.

In his confusion and struggle with defining Elisabeth's activities, Philip did not, of course, use the word "art" because the concept of performance as art was not available to him in the way it is to us. But his rhetorical flourishes, his puzzlement, descriptions, and, above all, his enduring and specific recall as a spectator, all underscore his conviction that he had beheld a series of exceptional events, which did not happen just once but repeatedly, in the same dramatic manner and with the same profound effect upon the spectator. This, I contend, is not just enactment of ritual,[40] but *theater*—the transformation of the actor into character, the use of a stage and props, the presence of spectators, the repeatability of the "script," the use of the body moving through time and space as in dance and choreography, and, most mystifying of all in the creative arts, the transformation of practice into a dependably transcendent aesthetic spectacle.[41]

It is not at all surprising that a woman who became one of the most renowned holy women in all the Low Countries had displayed her spirituality in the form of elaborate public spectacle. As cultural historian Peter Arnade has argued, by the fifteenth century the Burgundian court was visible, communicating itself in highly elaborate forms of public ritual. These rituals were rich in visible ceremony and public symbol, so much so, as Arnade claims, "[c]rafting state power in the Burgundian Netherlands involved a world of representation. . ."[42] Burgundian state ritual is not the only manifestation of the prolific and brilliant visual modes of expression in that region. After all, the southern Low Countries comprised a unique artistic environment, one that was recognized in its time, as well as in ours, as immensely rich, productive, and original—competitive, indeed on a par with, Florence *by the fifteenth century*. Such complex and confident statements of representation and public symbol as we see manifested in the fifteenth-century political and artistic realms did not suddenly spring forth from vacant ground. The fifteenth century was, I am convinced, the maturing of a visual culture that had been developing steadily for at least two centuries. And religion, no less than politics, participated and contributed to that development. It, too, was marked by the distinct cultural nature of the Low Countries, which since the late medieval period, as Johan Huizinga contended long ago, sought to display its beliefs in terms of public symbols.[43]

Yet our approach to these exceptional late medieval women—Elisabeth's contemporaries—has traditionally been through word- and discourse-oriented disciplines, by scholars of literature, history, religious history, theology, and feminism, with a concentration on theological and sociological issues and questions. The evidence for the spirituality of these women is viewed largely as textual and/or verbal; it is viewed as a discourse about words rather than forms. My approach—placing Elisabeth in the category of artist—puts forward and examines different issues because it operates within a different framework from previous approaches. For example, it allows us to circumvent customary questions of whether the activities of mystics are "real" or "genuine." In the art of dramatic theater those questions are quite beside the point. We can think about what it means to be part of something sacred without being limited to or bound by the religious sphere alone. We can, as scholars, engage concepts that the academy has customarily reserved for poetry and mythology—passion, love, and transcendence—as aesthetic aspects of mystical activities. Lastly, it helps to situate Elisabeth's history within a context of Low Country history that is consistent, as I remarked earlier, with past and current interpretations: that of a religion marked by intensely visual public ritual and theater.

My first goal, then, is to have Elisabeth's mysticism regarded and understood as a moving, kinesthetic form of visual art—an art of depiction rather than fixed form or material, the product of a living being whom we call "artist"—and included in the history of medieval art, along with the static visual arts of painting, sculpture, and architecture.[44] Just as important to identifying Elisabeth of Spalbeek as an artist is establishing the means—defining the criteria—by which we get there. The process of discerning the nature and the character of this art is what interests me—the questions we ask, and the direction in which they point us. Yet, in genuinely working through the issues and questions that arise around the correlation between art and mysticism, our understanding of *both* will be considerably enriched.

This brings us to my second and ultimate goal: that future work will take Elisabeth's history as a starting point for drawing new comparisons, first between Elisabeth and her contemporaries in the Flemish-speaking areas, and then between the great holy women of the Flemish-speaking areas and those of other parts of northern Europe.

Elisabeth's Mystical Visions: Stage and Staging

Elisabeth, for various reasons—most importantly her mystic performance—has simply never been taken up as an appropriate subject of inquiry by art historians.[45] One might reasonably ask why this approach had not been considered heretofore. One obvious reason is that Elisabeth is not, of course, an exhibitable object—even though it is clear that Abbot Philip regarded the persona and the performance as all but indistinguishable.[46] For the discipline of art history, *objects matter*. Art history was shaped as an academic discipline in the late nineteenth century, when rigid taxonomy and classification of objects and styles prevailed.[47] In other words, the history of art arose in a materialist framework, wherein objects were uniformly the subject of studies grounded in taxonomic methods, based on chronology and material. Moreover, not only did objects matter, but the history of art was motivated by a quest for objects that embodied "aesthetic quality" and "greatness," exclusively the products of "male genius."[48]

By definition, then, Elisabeth, her surroundings, and her devotional props were invisible to the discipline. Even the chapel at Spalbeek would be considered ordinary and humble from the perspective of the canon of architectural history. No towering Gothic cathedral, lacking vaults and buttresses, it is a small, austere, and simple stone shell, apparently cobbled together over time. It grew by accretion over the centuries, apparently in three phases, the last one occurring in the seventeenth century.[49] It lacks "unity of style," until recently the pedigree of buildings worthy of study, and, of course, it is in Belgium, a country that non-Belgian art historians have celebrated for its Early Renaissance painting but denigrated for the sameness of its high medieval architecture.[50] Even the country's grand churches, from Saint Rombout in Mechelen to Saint Gummaris in Lier, for example, have generated scant interest among students of the field. No wonder, then, that the chapel at Spalbeek has existed in somnolent anonymity all these centuries.

A fresco program on the walls of the interior eastern hemicycle, dated as early as 1350 and as late as 1500, suffers a similar anonymity.[51] There are representations of a Trinity, Saint Cornelius, Saint Hubert, a knight (probably Saint Quirinus of Neuss), a Pietà (with John the Evangelist and the *arma Christi*), Saint Gertrude of Nivelles, Saint Bernard, and Saint Gudule of Brussels.[52] The wall paintings are not of very high quality, if considered against well-known contemporary examples in Italy. From a traditional standpoint of connoisseurship the figures are poorly drawn, perspective is lacking, and the overall workmanship is mediocre. Although the iconography is rich, the references to Saint Hubert and the Four Marshals and to Saint Gertrude—a popular patron saint of Low Country beguines—are deeply embedded in local cult traditions, rather than reflecting universal themes. What is more, as far as we know, the props and objects of Elisabeth's mysticism—for example, the diptych mentioned by Philip[53]—no longer exist and can only be described by comparison with such similar devotional objects as have been preserved elsewhere.

Apparently, the inviolability of the inert *material* object[54] remains too ingrained in the training of art historians to be transgressed. This rigidity has lessened in some notable areas over time; such nonclassical works as posters, photography, installation art, and performance art, for example, are now treated as worthy of study by art historians along with the familiar and canonical works of art. Unfortunately, this trend has not yet embraced the art of performance in the Middle Ages. I contend that if we in the discipline now accept true performance and body art as worthy of study, we *must*, in retrospect, accept as well similar art of past ages in that study.[55]

Nor have most scholars of mysticism pursued the dramatic or aesthetic nature of mystical activities, for the obvious reason of the separation of the study of art from that of the study of religious texts.[56] There are some exceptions. Most notably, in 1995 Mary Giles published an outstanding essay entitled "Holy Theatre/Ecstatic Theatre,"[57] in which she drew a number of promising comparisons between the so-called "Holy Theatre" of playwrights and stage directors Peter Brook and Jerzy Growtowski—along with their predecessors Antonin Artaud and Jacques Copeau—and the "Ecstatic Theatre" of the sixteenth-century Spanish mystic, Sor María Juana. Although the period Giles studies, the sixteenth century, follows Elisabeth's era, Giles's essay alerts us to the parallels—dramatic, theatrical, spectatorial, and so on—between contemporary drama and what I term premodern ecstasy.[58]

Despite the encouraging introduction of new theoretical insights, such as Giles's, the study of mysticism remains firmly in the grip of entrenched views and values that have impeded a more inclusive understanding of the inherent visual and theatrical aspects of mysticism such as those exemplified by Elisabeth. For example, mystical texts themselves—rather than the specific and unique practices and phenomena they describe—remain the primary interest of inquiry, and a literary interest, at that. Most scholars of mysticism are trained in English departments, a few in History, even fewer, interestingly enough, in Religion. Generally speaking, these scholars continue to treat mystical texts—writings either by or about the mystics—as though they are static, occupying a fixed place in time. Mary Suydam's recent work, however, an example of the more inclusive approach, crosses many boundaries and urges us to free the text from its limiting identification as literature, which emphasizes a singular, one-on-one experience between reader and text. Suydam views the interpretation of mystical texts as metamorphosing over time, and, most importantly, regards the texts themselves as sites for dramatic interaction.[59] She proposes that the marginalia on the original texts, which were added over time—even across centuries—constitute a sort of conversation happening among readers from different generations and different epochs. These texts often were read aloud and thus were dramatic renditions involving audiences in convents, beguinages, and perhaps in abbeys, as well.

Another reason why performances, such as Elisabeth's, have heretofore not been viewed as art is that the means and the end are often confused in our current view. The mystics' pain and suffering are seen as the sole content and singular meaning of their spiritual acts. The profound beauty, power, and exultation of women's love of Christ, the art of the moving body, and the genuine creative dramatic appeal of the theater of mysticism are all obscured by this emphasis on neurosis and pain—a feminine subjectivity that appears to relish these more disquieting, one might even say revolting, physical aspects. This perspective makes it virtually impossible to see the real accomplishments of these women as among our highest and most glorious aesthetic aspirations—as impossible as it would be for us to find truth, beauty, and inspiration in the freakish events displayed in supermarket tabloids.

Finally, scholarship overlooks the fact that all of this happened because Elisabeth loved God—a love that inspired extraordinary expressions, moments of "dancing,"[60] acting, and transformation that she shared with her onlookers. This is not unlike other great visual works of art inspired by faith. The love of Christ, manifested in *outward form*, is what really mattered to Elisabeth, as well as to Abbot Philip.[61] No matter what our interpretation, that is the simple, incontestable fact of Elisabeth's accomplishments, the surest thing that scholars today have to work with and the imperative rationale for visual analysis.

Theater and mysticism have been linked before, most notably by theater people. We recall that Growtowski and Brook labeled their work "Holy Theatre" and made frequent reference to spirituality, mysticism, and ecstasy—that is to say, the "religion" of theater. In the nineteenth century, the Italian actress Eleanora Duse, arguably the greatest of her day, was considered by many admirers and biographers to manifest the "mystics" philosophy,[62] and Duse herself believed her art was inspired by the deep mystical workings of her nature. The American theater and film *enfant terrible*, Orson Welles, also thought he possessed something akin to sacred, mystical powers: "I'm a medium, not an orator. Like certain oriental and Christian mystics, I think the 'self' is a kind of enemy."[63]

The central element in the comparison of mysticism and theater, I think, lies in the nature of practice and performance, and in how they interact and take life from each other. Artistry occurs when technique, gained by daily practice, is so encoded in the mind and body that pure freedom from technique, at the moment of performance, can be achieved. There is little that is truly spontaneous or unprepared—not to be confused with improvisational—about performance and creativity.

The mysticism of Elisabeth clearly displays this relationship between repetitive practice and performance. This, importantly, is what Paula Hunter's choreography revealed. There are movements, described by Abbot

Philip, that almost certainly must have been practiced to be accomplished and, most significantly, to be repeated dependably. How, for example, *does* one stand "on one leg with the head bowed to the ground" without having practiced this movement? The element of practice enabled Elisabeth to perform motions that literally astounded and bewildered her spectators—and to perform them repeatedly. She embodied the paradox of artistic creativity: that true creativity is *freedom from* the very rigor and practice that prepares and sustains the art.

The writings of Philip attest to the fact that this apparent contradiction was as enigmatic in his time as it is today. Our acknowledgment and acceptance of that paradox is important, however, as it helps us understand the genuinely artistic content of Elisabeth's mysticism—it is what brings us to *an encounter* with what is, in the terminology of specialists, ineffable and noetic about Elisabeth's mysticism.

Uniting mysticism and art allows us to penetrate Elisabeth's "subjectivity," which had an outward form, a material form, in her Friday performances—partly in the choreography, partly in her dramatic reshaping of the Passion story. Visual analysis can help us understand—indeed it can reveal—the aesthetic nature of that form. But we must remember that the form is not "empty"; rather, it dramatically brings to life and communicates her beliefs and feelings to a group, to an audience. Form—Elisabeth's performance—is the communicated (and communicable) dimension of mystical activity. Translated into familiar formal terminology, it is spatial, dynamic, and three-dimensional. With this language, we come nearer to a historical understanding that within the performative domain, individuals, like Elisabeth, shaped and expressed religious concepts.[64]

By viewing the outward manifestation of her mysticism as art, we learn that formalization and practice—the foundation of art making—constitute the foundation of mystical ecstasy, as well. This revises our general conception of ecstasy, bringing it more in line with creative practices than with hysteria or madness. If Elisabeth shares with the performing arts the interdependent interaction of technique (practice) and performance (the event), we need only reaffirm the relationship between performance and the visual arts, and their legitimate place in art history.

Elisabeth had an image of Christ that she communicated to her audiences. To this end, though, the images had to be conceived, formed, displayed, and transmitted. Undeniably visual, they were expressed as form: in theater, dance, and performance. In her ability to express and to form her love of God—and to give form to her love of God—she was an artist, whose full, powerful, and transcendent range of image making—her iconography, to be sure—can now, more than seven centuries after her remarkable life, begin to be tapped.

With Elisabeth's visual expression—the representational form—in place, I hope scholars will be moved to put other texts to similar sorts of analyses. Especially for those tilling the mystical vineyards of the Flemish-speaking areas, comparative study, focusing on the formal and visual characteristics, will yield, I suspect, a fuller picture of the southern Low Countries at the end of the Middle Ages. There, in that small but amazingly creative corner of Europe, a spiritual practice (for clerics as well as practitioners) flourished. It was founded on exceptionally sophisticated visual and artistic principles— indeed infinitely complex and imaginative principles, in which language and imagination grew together—that bespeak a young and vigorous culture that was the southern Low Countries.

Notes

This article is revised and expanded from the original version, which appeared in the *Jaarboek Koninklijk Museum voor Schone Kunsten Antwerpen 2000/Antwerp Royal Museum 2000*, pp. 265–79. I introduce a new perspective on the material here, however, by directing the issues toward women in the medieval southern Low Countries, with footnotes and bibliography amended and expanded accordingly. I wish to thank Marcia Brennan (Rice University) for her always-sensitive criticism and encouragement—and friendship. Her intellectual presence, in the form of any number of suggestions, flows throughout this text. Joe Vecchione has edited this work, motivating me to write both more clearly and more passionately, by helping me keep sight of the commitments that drive my thinking. I hope he is not disappointed with the results. This is dedicated to Sophie.

1. The translation here is based on the Latin text *Vita Elizabeth sanctimonialis in Erkenrode, Ordinis Cisterciensis, Leodiensis dioecesis*, that is drawn from the text of codex Bruxellensis (Ms. B) with emendations from the codex 135 Academiae Leodiensis (Ms. L) as an appendix to Codex #2864–71 found in the *Catalogus codicum hagiographicorum bibliothecae Regiae Bruxellensis*, I (Brussels, 1886), 362–78; and K. Horstmann, "Prosalegenden: Die Legenden des Ms. Douce 114," *Anglia* VIII (1885), pp. 102–195, in particular pp. 107–118 (cited hereafter as Horstmann, "Prosalegenden"). Father Vodoklys, S.J. is currently preparing a new translation of the Latin *vita*. All translations are from the Latin text and have been generously provided by Father Vodoklys and are cited hereafter as *Vita Elisabeth*/Vodoklys. For examination of the textual tradition, see Patricia Deery Kurtz, "Mary of Oignies, Christine the Marvelous, and Medieval Heresy," *Mystics Quarterly* 14 (1988), pp. 186–96 and Amandus Bussels, "Was Elisabeth van Spalbeek Cisterciënserin in Herkenrode?" *Cîteaux in de Nederlanden* II (1951), pp. 43–54, especially 43, note 1. For recent interpretations, see Susan Rodgers and Joanna Ziegler, "Elisabeth of Spalbeek's Trance Dance of Faith: A Performance Theory Interpretation from Anthropological and Art Historical Perspectives," in *Performance and Transformation: New Approaches to Late Medieval Spirituality*, ed. Mary A. Suydam and Joanna E. Ziegler (New York: Saint Martin's Press, 1999), pp. 299–347; Elliott Visconsi,

" 'She Represents the Person of Our Lord':The Performance of Mysticism in the *Vita* of Elisabeth of Spalbeek and the *Book of Margery Kempe*," *Comitatus* 28 (1997), pp. 76–89; Walter Simons, "Reading a Saint's Body: Rapture and Bodily Movement in the Vitae of Thirteenth-Century Beguines," in *Framing Medieval Bodies*, ed. Sarah Kay and Miri Rubin (Manchester: Manchester University Press, 1994), pp. 10–23; and Walter Simons and Joanna Ziegler, "Phenomenal Religion in the Thirteenth Century and Its Image: Elisabeth of Spalbeek and the Passion Cult," *Studies in Church History* 27 (1990), pp. 117–26. This essay is part of my long-term project to integrate Elisabeth into a broader conception of creativity, dance, and ecstasy—one in which the medieval example will become paradigmatic.

2. *Vita Elizabeth*/Vodoklys, Latin, section 18; and Horstmann, p. 114.

3. Simons, "Reading a Saint's Body," pp. 11–13.

4. Elisabeth held some fame as a visionary; perhaps she knew Hadewijch. This is reviewed by G. Hendrix, "Hadewijch benaderd vanuit de tekst over de 22e volmaakte," *Leuvense Bijdragen* 67 (1978), pp. 129–45. She was called in as a sort of clairvoyant in a bizarre case at the court of Philippe III of France, after the sudden death of the dauphin. See J. de Gaulle, "Documents historiques," *Bulletin de la Société de l'Histoire de France* I (1884), pp. 87–100; Richard Kay, "Martin IV and the Fugitive Bishop of Bayeux," *Speculum* 40 (1965), pp. 460–83, which Simons warns may not be "always accurate"; and Remco Sleiderin, "Een straf van God: Elisabeth van Spalbeek en de dood van de franse kroonprins," *Madoc* 11/1 (April 1997), pp. 42–53.

5. See previous note.

6. Of course the word "mystics" may not actually be accurate. I use it throughout this essay, however, for ease and to give a general sense of a sort of spiritual practice that is associated with the many exceptional holy women written about in the *vitae*, whom scholars customarily call mystics.

7. The literature on the subject of the beguines is abundant. For a review of pertinent sources, see Mary Suydam, "Beguine Textuality: Sacred Performance," in *Performance and Transformation*: (1999), pp. 169–210; and Walter Simons, "Les Béguines au moyen âge," in *Béguines et Béguinages*, ed. Marianne Trooskens (Brussels: Archives générales du Royaume, 1994), pp. 7–25 [also in Dutch as "Begijnen in de middeleeuwen," in *Begijnen en begijnhoven*, ed. Marianne Trooskens (Brussels: Archives générales du Royaume, 1994), pp. 7–25] and his *Cities of Ladies: Beguine Communities in the Medieval Low Countries, 1200–1565* (Philadelphia: University of Pennsylvania Press, 2001). Unfortunately this work came to press just after I wrote this chapter. For the Belgian beguinages, see Pascal Majérus, *"C'est femmes qu'on dit béguines. . ."* *Guide des béguinages de Belgique. Bibliographie et sources d'archives*, 2 vols. (Brussels: Archives générales du Royaume, 1997).

8. I made the point some time ago that the great named holy women stood apart from their "ordinary" beguine counterparts in "Reality as Imitation. The Dynamics of Imagery among the Beguines," in *Maps of Flesh and Light: New Perspectives on the Religious Experience of Medieval Women*, ed. Ulrike Wiethaus (New York: Syracuse University Press, 1996), pp. 112–126.

This argument has recently been taken up by Penny Galloway, "Neither Miraculous Nor Astonishing: The Devotional Practice of Beguine Communities in French Flanders," *New Trends in Feminine Spirituality: The Holy Women of Liège and Their Impact*, ed. Juliette Dor, Lesley Johnson, and Jocelyn Wogan-Browne (Brussels, Belgium: Brepols, 1999), pp.107–128.

9. Galloway, "Neither Miraculous nor Astonishing"; see note 8.

10. For a provocative review of the (presumed nineteenth-century) distinction between hagiography and historiography, see Felice Lifshitz, "Beyond Positivism and Genre: 'Hagiographical' texts as Historical Narrative," *Viator* 25 (1994), pp. 95–113; and for an excellent series of essays investigating the colloboration between educated male cleric and often less educated female holy woman, see Catherine M. Mooney, ed., *Gendered Voices: Medieval Saints and Their Interpreters* (Philadelphia: University of Pennsylvania Press, 1999).

11. The literature on the promotion of *mulieres religiosae* is vast. On the point of the creation of a paradigm relationship between apostolic poverty and the male cleric, see Carolyn Muessig, *The Faces of Women in the Sermons of Jacques de Vitry* (Toronto: Peregrina Publishing Company, 1999). On the misogynistic stereotypes of beguines, see Renate Blumenfeld-Kosinski, "Satirical Views of the Beguines in Northern French Literature," in *New Trends in Feminine Spirituality*, ed. Dor et al., pp. 237–49.

12. In his *De Scandalis Ecclesiae*, the Franciscan Gilbert of Tournai practically accused Elisabeth of fraud and called for an investigation of her stigmata. See Simons and Ziegler, "Phenomenal Religion," pp. 122–23, where we suggested that Philip's report was responding to the Franciscan attempt to monopolize the urban beguines.

13. See the superb essay on the relationship of gender to mystical pain and suffering by Dyan Elliott, "The Physiology of Rapture and Female Spirituality," in *Medieval Theology and the Natural Body*, ed. Peter Biller and A.J. Minnis, York Studies in Medieval Theology I (York, England: York Medieval Press, 1997), pp. 141–74. A number of new approaches in the last decade have also emerged in gender studies and feminist writing on the relationship between the mystic and the hysteric. See, for example, Amy M. Hollywood, "Beauvoir, Irigaray, and Mystical," *Hypatia* 9/4 (Fall 1994), pp. 158–84; and Ulrike Wiethaus, *Ecstatic Tranformation: Transpersonal Psychology in the Work of Mechtild of Magdeburg* (New York: Syracuse University Press, 1996).

14. Elliott, "The Physiology of Rapture," p. 152.

15. For example, Elliot claims, "Physical proofs, often cruel ones, were freely practiced on a given saint's immobile body. . .Such tests need not arise from any particular doubts but were often engineered to exploit the spectacle value inherent in the enrapt female form" (p. 162).

16. Elliott, "The Physiology of Rapture," p. 162.

17. The scholarship on the relationship between "embodiment" and mysticism is large, and increasingly fragmented. One would read Caroline Bynum's major works, naturally. Feminist approaches would include, among others, Karma Lochrie, *Margery Kempe and Translations of the Flesh* (Philadelphia: University of Pennsylvania Press, 1991); Linda Lomperis and Sarah Stanbury,

eds, *Feminist Approaches to the Body in Medieval Literature* (Philadelphia: University of Pennsylvania Press, 1993); and Laurie Finke, *Feminist Theory, Women's Writing* (Ithaca and London: Cornell University Press, 1992). An exciting volume of solid documentary research in Peter Biller and A.J. Minnis, eds., *Medieval Theology and the Natural Body* (York, England: York Medieval Press, 1997).

18. Ziegler, *Sculpture of Compassion: The Pietà and the Beguines in the Southern Low Countries, c.1300–c.1600* (Brussels, Belgium: Institut historique belges de Rome, 1992).

19. Simons, "Reading a Saint's Body," pp. 10–23.

20. Simons, "Reading a Saint's Body," pp. 10–23, especially pp. 13–16.

21. Ibid., p. 13, and note 34. Scholars of our own time have made a subfield in medieval studies devoted to the genre of feminine *vitae*. Bynum's work, especially that which issued from *Holy Feast and Holy Fast: The Religious Significance of Food to Medieval Women* (Berkeley, CA: University of California Press, 1987), produced these *vitae* as a group that can be analyzed collectively. It would be interesting to know more of the historiography of the creation of this field of study.

22. For a comprehensive compilation of the sources, see the entry on Jacques de Vitry by Walter Simons, "Jacques de Vitry (ca. 1160/70–May 1, 1240), in *Dictionary of Literary Biography*, vol. 208, ed. Deborah Sinnriech-Levi and Ian S. Laurie (Detroit: A Bruccoli Clark Layman Book, 1999), pp. 157–62.

23. The *vitae*, as Bynum work has taught us, offer many bizarre and odd anecdotes but they are of a different order, they are "unbelievable" to our culture, whereas Elisabeth's doings, as I argue below, are perfectly "believable." It may be that in the future we will want to explore other *vitae* by using the method I propose below, as a way of finally confronting the issue of "believability," something scholars have ignored, surprisingly.

24. Horstmann, "Prosalegenden," p. 109.

25. Horstmann, "Prosalegenden," p. 112.

26. *Vita Elizabeth*/Vodoklys, Latin, section 4; Horstmann, "Prosalegenden," p. 108.

27. *Vita Elizabeth*/Vodoklys, Latin, section 10; Horstmann, "Prosalegenden," p. 112.

28. *Vita Elizabeth*/Vodoklys, Latin, section 10; Horstmann, "Prosalegenden," p. 113.

29. *Vita Elizabeth*/Vodoklys, Latin, section 4; Horstmann, "Prosalegenden," p. 109.

30. *Vita Elizabeth*/Vodoklys, Latin, section 7; Horstmann, "Prosalegenden," p. 110.

31. *Vita Elizabeth*/Vodoklys, Latin, section 3; Horstmann, "Prosalegenden," p. 108.

32. *Vita Elizabeth*/Vodoklys, Latin, section 4; Horstmann, "Prosalegenden," p. 108.

33. *Vita Elizabeth*/Vodoklys, Latin, section 4; Horstmann, "Prosalegenden," p. 109.

34. Cf. note 17. For immense theoretical sophistication on the medieval body, but without posing the issue of textuality as the venue, see Sarah Kay and Miri Rubin, eds., *Framing Medieval Bodies* (Manchester and New York: Manchester University Press, 1994). There is some revisionist thinking taking place recently around "the body" and women's spirituality, pointing toward the emphasis as resulting from the male clerical writers of women's words and experiences, which focus on the "external" in order promote women's sanctity. See the eight essays in Mooney, ed., *Gendered Voices* (1999).

Some scholars prefer to focus on themes of pain and suffering, rather than simply generalizing around "physicality." See E. Ross, " 'She Wept and Cried Right Loud for Sorrow and for Pain': Suffering, the Spiritual Journey, and Women's Experience in Late Medieval Mysticism," in *Maps of Flesh and Light*, ed. Ulrike Wiethaus, pp. 45–59; D.F. Tinsely, "The Spirituality of Suffering in the Revelations of Elspeth von Oye," *Mystics Quarterly* 21 (1995), pp. 121–47; and A. Hollywood, "Spirituality Transformed: Marguerite Porete, Meister Eckhart and the Problem of Women's Spirituality," in *Meister Eckhart and Beguine Mystics, Hadewijch of Brabant, Mechthild of Magdeburg, and Marguerite Porete* (New York: Continuum, 1994), pp. 87–113.

35. *Vita Elizabeth*/Vodoklys, Latin, section 16.

36. James A.W. Heffernan, *Museum of Words: The Poetics of Ekphrasis from Homer to Ashbery* (Chicago and London: University of Chicago Press, 1993), especially the Introduction. I am developing ways to argue for the ekphrastic character of Elisabeth's life. Perhaps the hagiographic genre may be seen more appropriately in light of ekphrasis (" 'speaking out' or 'telling in full' " Heffernan, *Museum of Words*, p. 6), for language that "strives to keep power under control" Heffernan, *Museum of Words*, p. 7.

37. On the later medieval Low Countries and women's "fluency" (especially the beguines) in the language of materiality, as I call it, see my *Sculpture of Compassion* (1992), esp. chapter 5, "Materiality and Tactility: Social Facts and Experiential Essences of the Beguines," pp. 95–110.

38. For a serious discussion of medieval mysticism and performance art, see Anne-Marie Lombardi, "Women's Philosophical Voice, Expression, and Inquiry: Explorations in Medieval Mysticism, Performance Art and Ecological Feminism," M.A. thesis, the University of Montana, 1994, especially the chapter on "Feminist Art, Aesthetic, and Discourse: The Performance of Karen Finley"; and Nanda Hopenwasser, "A Performance Artist and Her Performance Text: Margery Kempe on Tour," in *Performance and Transformation*, pp. 97–132.

39. The feminist interpretation of performance art I refer to is exemplified by Amelia Jones, *Body Art/Performing the Subject* (Minneapolis: University of Minnesota Press, 1998) and the review in *Art History* 22/1 (March, 1999) by Marsha Meskimmon, pp. 142–48. For an overview of examples of contemporary feminist performance art itself, see the videotape "Reclaiming the Body: Feminist Art in America" (Michael Blackwood Productions).

40. Performance and ritual have long been linked in an exciting area of study. For a review, see Mary Suydam, "Background: An Introduction to Performance Studies," in *Performance and Transformation* (1999), pp. 1–26, especially 1–10. Now, did Elisabeth's contemporaries think of her as an "artist?" This is an important question, one that is, however, beyond the scope of this essay. To what extent people in 1300 were aware of a concept of art per se is extremely difficult to gauge, despite our understanding of the predominance of skill and craft in the period.

41. Maurice Bloch develops a complex relationship among formalized language and communication, authority, and religion in his article, "Symbols,

Song, Dance and Features of Articulation: Is Religion an Extreme Form of Traditional Authority?" *Archives europeénes de sociologie* 15 (1974), pp. 55–81.

42. Peter Arnade, *Realms of Ritual: Burdundian Ceremony and Civic Life in Late Medieval Ghent* (Ithaca and London: Cornell University Press, 1996), p. 34.

43. Arnade's work bears significantly on our ability to take up the Huizinga problem in a new historical and anthropological approach.

44. See Joanna E. Ziegler, "Skipping Like Camels, or Why Medieval Studies Neglects the Dance," *Medieval Feminist Forum*, no. 32 (Fall 2001), pp. 24–31.

45. For all the work on performance art by contemporary feminists, including art historians and art critics, only the literature people have explored the medieval mystics from the point of view of performance art.

46. Even Jeffrey Hamburger's most recent revisionist interpretation of medieval "art" and women tries to reformulate the importance of women as artists by looking at the medium of drawings. See Jeffrey Hamburger, *Nuns as Artists: The Visual Culture of a Medieval Convent* (Berkeley and Los Angeles: University of California Press, 1997).

47. There are copious texts treating the historiography of art history. Most helpful to the present discussion are Kathryn Brush, *The Shaping of Art History: Wilhelm Voege, Adolph Goldschmidt, and the Study of Medieval Art* (Cambridge: The Cambridge University Press, 1996) and Thalia Gouma-Peterson and Patricia Mathews, "The Feminist Critique of Art History," *The Art Bulletin* 69/3 (September 1987), pp. 326–57.

48. For an example (unfortunately not in medieval studies) of this more positive feminist framework, see Marcia Brennan, "Krasner and Pollock: Touching and Transcending the Margins of Abstract Expressionism," *Abstrakter Expressionismus: Konstruktionen Asthetischer Erfahrung*, ed. Roger M Buergel and Vera Kocket (Dresden and Amsterdam: Verlag der Kunst, 2000). The "canon" of art history, as reconsidered by feminists, is problematized as inclusively male and exclusively female. For example, see Nanette Salomon, "The Art Historical Canon: Sins of Omission (1991)," in *The Art of Art History; A Critical Anthology*, ed. Donald Preziosi (1990; Oxford and New York: Oxford, 1998), pp. 344–55. However, the canon as comprising the "grand" media has not yet, to my knowledge, been questioned by feminists or, accordingly, augmented. Yet, as I am arguing here, women artists may indeed have been recognized long ago, if the definition of art is extended to include other media than the traditional ones.

49. H. Jaminé, "Église de Spalbeek," *Bulletin de la société scientifique et littéraire du Limbourg* 16 (1884), pp. lxii–lxvi; and *Bouwen door de eeuwen heen: Inventaris van het cultuurbezit in België. Architectuur, 6n I, Provincie Limburg. Arrondissement Hasselt* (Ghent, 1981), pp. 421–23.

50. Even the grand Gothic architecture of the Low Countries has not been deemed "worthy" of study by North American art historians, as "Gothic" is still considered, even if problematically so in some people's views, a French accomplishment. See Joanna E. Ziegler, "Gothic Architecture in the Duchy of Brabant," Ph.D. diss., Brown University, 1984 and Kathryn Brush, *The Shaping of Art History* (1996).

51. *Bouwen door de eeuwen heen*, p. 423. The dating is problematic, for there is really no evidence other than visual. The fresco is not in good condition and it is difficult to see the drawing style clearly. Also, Limburg was hardly a main center for artistic practice, thus posing the usual difficulty of how to gauge the chronology and style.

52. Some preliminary reattribution was suggested in W. Simons and J. Ziegler, "Phenomenal Religion," pp. 117–26.

53. See above, p. 186, for Philip's narration of Elisabeth and the diptych.

54. Arguably, the "inviolability" of the object arose with the Italian Renaissance. Michelangelo certainly set that issue in the foreground of his conception of "art," especially opposing that characteristic to northern devotional sculpture. On this, see Joanna E. Ziegler, "Michelangelo and the Medieval Pietà: The Sculpture of Devotion or the Art of Sculpture?" *Gesta* 34/1 (1995), pp. 28–36. This may be an additional example of the privileging of certain aspects of art that resulted from the dominance of the Italian model, a "story" that is brilliantly evoked in Stephen Melville, "The Temptation of New Perspectives," in *The Art of Art History*, pp. 401–412.

55. See the review of Suydam and Ziegler, eds., *Performance and Transformation* (1999) by Amy Hollywood in *Hypatia* 16/2 (Spring, 2001), pp. 106–107, in which she wonders about the nature of Elisabeth's performance itself. Marcia Brennan has also suggested that further clarification is warranted regarding the relationship between performance as an interpretive model and "body art," as described here. I think this is certainly an issue for art historians—including myself—to take up, especially if we should see fit to bring historical performance into the canon of Western art.

56. Although far beyond our boundaries, the following study, very interestingly, seeks to propose that "artistic creation" is an "essential part" of Shamanism, largely due to the "long and arduous preparation." See Andreas Lommel, *Shamanism: The Beginnings of Art*, trans. Michael Bullock (New York and Toronto: McGraw-Hill, 1967), with series of reviews compiled in "Shamanism: The Beginnings of Art," *Current Anthropology* 11 (February, 1970), pp. 39–48. Importantly, the reviews are written by anthropologists, not art historians or art critics, although the latter are the ones who would benefit most from Lommel's enlightening understanding of artistic practice, as a process of the formation and transmission of images—despite his emphasis on sickness and weakness of the shaman.

57. Mary E. Giles, "Holy Theatre/Ecstatic Theatre," in *Vox Mystica: Essays on Medieval Mysticism in Honor of Professor Valerie M. Lagorio*, ed. Anne Clark Bartlett (Cambridge and Rochester, USA: D.S. Brewer, 1995), pp. 117–28. It is with deep regret that I did not cite this wonderful essay—so close in spirit to my own pursuits—in my "Introduction" to *Performance and Transformation* (1999), pp. xiii–xxi.

58. More recently, in the anthology of essays *Performance and Transformation*, eleven scholars examine the public and theatrical nature of mystical activities, including those of Elisabeth of Spalbeek.

59. Mary Suydam, "Writing Beguines: Ecstatic Performances," *Magistra* 2 (1996), pp. 137–69; and idem, "Beguine Textuality," in *Performance and Transformation*, pp. 169–210.

60. Dancing was prohibited in churches and in religious ceremonies and thus the presence of dance in mystical events needs to be more thoroughly researched than it has to date. Simons points out, importantly in this context, that "the endless repetition of these decrees [prohibiting dancing] must prove that such dances were not unusual, however, and some texts appear to single out women as the prime suspects" ("Reading a Saint's Body," p. 13). Along with my article, "Skipping Like Camels" (as in note 44) see Pierre Riché, "Danses profanes et religieuses dans le haut Moyen Age," *Histoires sociale, sensibilités collectives et mentalités. Mélanges Robert Mandrou* (Paris, 1985), pp. 159–67; Jeannine Horowitz, "Les danses cléricales dans les églises au Moyen Age," *Le Moyen Age* 95 (1989), pp. 279–92; Jean-Claude Schmitt, *La Raison des gestes dans l'Occident médiévale* (Paris: 1990), pp. 90–91.

61. For the challenge to the widely held view that mysticism is "characterized by intense, ineffable, subjective experiences" only and may be rather involved in public expressions of social and political justice, see Grace M. Jantzen, "Feminists, Philosophers, and Mystics," *Hypatia* 9/4 (1994), pp. 186–206; idem, *Power, Gender, and Christian Mysticism* (Cambridge: Cambridge University Press, 1995). While I agree with Jantzen's powerful problematization of the naming of the mystic (in her phrase, "who gets to be a mystic"), I continue to see room for exploring individual manifestations of religious understanding, such as Elisabeth's. While it may be wise to avoid the public/private dichotomy, the notion of a "self" may be operative nonetheless in precisely the terms I'm laying out here: as a communicated, expressed form.

62. This is especially clearly treated in Eva Le Galliene, *The Mystic in the Theatre: Eleonora Duse* (New York: Farrar, Straus & Giroux, 1966). See also Jean Stubbs, *Eleanora Duse* (New York: Stein and Day, 1970); and Giovanni Pontiero, *Duse on Tour: Guido Noccioli's Diaries, 1906–07* (Manchester: Manchester University Press, 1982).

63. Simon Callow, *Orson Welles: The Road to Xanadu* (New York and London: 1995), p. xi.

64. See Jantzen as in note 61.

CHAPTER 9

REGENCY, POWER, AND DYNASTIC VISUAL MEMORY: MARGARET OF AUSTRIA AS PATRON AND PROPAGANDIST

Laura D. Gelfand

When the widowed Margaret of Austria (1480–1530) made her triumphal entry into the Netherlands, where she was to act as regent from 1507 to 1530, she was welcomed as their "princesse naturelle," and she capitalized on this perception through her patronage[1] (figure 9.1). Margaret was the last ruler of the Netherlands who could claim, on her mother's side, descent from the Valois, a family whose political status had peaked, yet who were still seen as the "natural" rulers of the Burgundian Netherlands, an area that stretched from Holland and Belgium to areas of modern day France including Burgundy and Alsace-Lorraine (figure 9.2). On her paternal side, Margaret of Austria's Habsburg lineage put her in a tenuous position as governor over a potentially unruly Netherlandish people. Margaret's patronage of devotional portrait diptychs and the display of her collection in Mechelen reflects this hereditary tension and frames the political situation in which she served as regent. Specifically, she commissioned a number of paintings with strong Valois associations that were intended to capitalize on the popularity of her maternal family. Margaret's mobilization of art to shore up hereditary and political claims demonstrates both the significant role patronage and display played in Margaret's propagandistic strategies and her clear understanding of the politics of iconography and style.

9.1   Bernard van Orley, *Portrait of Margaret of Austria*, Brussels, Musée des Beaux-Arts. Girandon/Art Resource, NY.

The Valois and Devotional Portrait Diptychs

Over the first half of the fifteenth century the Burgundian dukes of the house of Valois regularly commissioned devotional portrait diptychs, hinged panels with the Virgin and Child on one panel adjoining a portrait of the original owner in prayer.[2] Devotional portrait diptychs were used primarily for private devotion and passed down through family lines, although some of them were placed above their original owner's tombs following their deaths. The proximity of the owner in prayer to the Virgin and Child make these images particularly conducive to establishing the affective closeness fervently desired by late medieval patrons. Additionally, devotional portrait diptychs almost certainly originated within the pages of books of

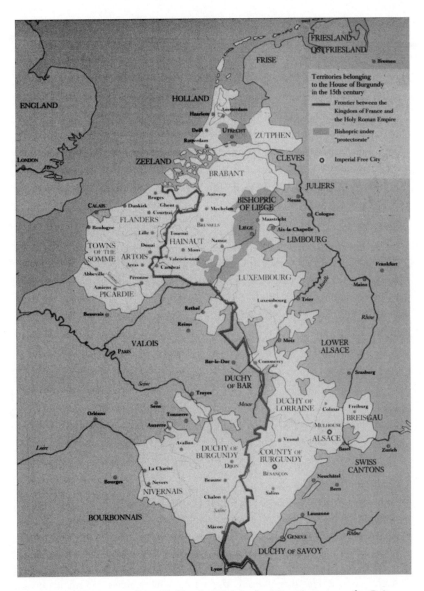

9.2 Map of territories controlled by the Valois in the fifteenth century, after Poiret.

hours where the portraits of owners were placed next to prayers that pleaded for the Virgin's intercession with Christ for aid in achieving salvation.[3] The desire for salvation with which owner portraits were originally associated remained when they were painted on panels rather than illuminated in texts. These paintings were to achieve great popularity during the fifteenth century, but few examples originated outside of the Burgundian Netherlands where they were painted between 1400 and 1530.[4] This geographically circumscribed production was probably due to the diptych's role as a Valois dynastic signifier.[5]

The first devotional portrait diptychs usually show the figures in three-quarter or full-length, as they appeared in the books of hours in which they originated, but as diptychs grew increasingly popular, painters began to depict the owner and the Virgin in the half-length style first popularized by Rogier van der Weyden.[6] In this way the artist increased the perceived intimacy between the sitter and the Mother and Child, emphasizing the connection between the three participants, and creating a more satisfying devotional paradigm for the image's owners. Soon after this format was created for the Valois dukes, diptychs began to be commissioned by members of the court, many of whom were ducal favorites.[7] Even after the popularity of devotional diptychs had extended to more bourgeois members of society, the paintings continued to be produced primarily in territories ruled by the Valois.[8] The limited popularity of devotional portrait diptychs in areas outside the Burgundian Netherlands indicates that the portrait diptych form was clearly associated with the Valois dukes in the lands they controlled.

The first devotional portrait diptychs created for the Valois Burgundian dukes were quite large and they were located in the Chartreuse de Champmol, the Valois family mausoleum founded by Philip the Bold and Margaret of Flanders in 1383.[9] These diptychs were hung on the walls of the church and acted as a portrait gallery illustrating the royal lineage of the dukes. The particular significance of the Virgin and Child to the Burgundian dukes remains unknown. However, the desire by this newly powerful branch of nobles to create an image or a sign with which they would be associated is in keeping with the practice of other contemporary rulers. The diptychs found at Champmol would have complimented the ducal tomb sculptures while furthering the desire of its founders to create a monument that would rival St. Denis, the burial site of the French kings in Paris. Only a single painting survives that may once have been part of this series, the *Virgin and Child* (Berlin, Dahlem Museum), attributed to Jean Malouel and dated about 1400 (figure 9.3).[10] This large work was painted with tempera on a cloth support. The Virgin holds the Child who reaches toward a now-missing donor portrait that would have hung to the viewer's left. Millard Meiss and Colin Eisler believed that a portrait of Philip the Bold or his son John the Fearless may have hung beside this image, thus forming the first known Valois devotional portrait diptych.[11] The authors suggested that the portrait of John the Fearless, now known only through an eighteenth-century copy, was the pendant to the Berlin *Virgin and Child*, an argument

9.3   Malouel, *Virgin and Child*, Staatliche Museen zu Berlin-Preissischer Kulturbesitz Gemäldegalerie. Photo: Jorg P. Anders.

supported by visual evidence.[12] This portrait of John the Fearless may have been the one taken by the German Carthusian, Dom Étienne, when he visited Champmol in 1791.[13] Diptychs that featured portraits of the Valois dukes served an important role at Champmol, encoding dreams of dynastic power that would continue to resonate for Margaret and others long after the death of Charles the Bold.

Hapsburg Rule and the Burgundian Netherlands

The fifteenth-century Burgundian Netherlands surrounded France on its northern and eastern borders and relations between the French kings and the Valois dukes of Burgundy were historically troublesome. The initial gift of Burgundy to Philip the Bold by his father, King Jean le Bon, was extended to Flanders through Philip's marriage to Margaret of Flanders. The Valois controlled this far-flung duchy beginning in the late fourteenth century despite repeated threats from the French and they expanded their territories through marriage and war. Although the peripatetic Valois court moved continuously, for the majority of the fifteenth century their most important courts were in Bruges and Dijon, cities located at the northern and southern extremes of Valois lands. A century of Valois control caused the dukes to be seen by the linguistically and socially varied populace over whom they ruled as their natural governors.

A crisis over inheritance and control of the Burgundian Netherlands began during the years preceding and following the death of Margaret's mother, Mary of Burgundy. When Charles the Bold died without leaving a male heir in 1477, the French king, Louis XI, moved onto Burgundian lands including the duchy of Burgundy. Louis claimed the lands for the French Crown by promoting a spurious reading of the initial gift of the lands to Philip the Bold.[14] French Salic laws dictated that without a male heir to assume possession, the properties in the Hainaut, Namur, Picardy, and Artois were to revert to France.[15] It is important to note that the legality of Louis's claims was controversial and involved his self-interested "interpretation" of the initial gift that Jean le Bon had made to his son Philip the Bold in 1363. Louis XI claimed that the duchy of Burgundy was a royal appanage of the French Crown and that it had temporarily been placed with a branch of the royal family for maintenance. The king argued that these lands were subject to French laws and should rightfully revert to the Crown in the absence of a male heir. Supporters of Mary's claims saw the duchy of Burgundy as a fief rather than an appanage and believed that the lands had been inherited by Jean le Bon because he was the closest relative to the preceding duke, Philip of Rouvres, rather than because he was king. According to the Burgundian interpretation, male succession was not necessary as it had not been specified in the original gift of Burgundy to Philip the Bold. Additionally, although French laws forbid women from succession, territories outside of France had no such stipulations. The French king's desire to reclaim these lands resulted in the need by descendants of the Valois to establish their identity as the rightful rulers of a Burgundian territory that existed independent of French royal rule.

Battles over the regency of the Netherlands began in 1482, immediately after the death of Mary of Burgundy, whom the vast majority of the Flemish had supported over the French, and were fought continuously for more than a decade.[16] Maximilian I, Mary's husband, was a Hapsburg and therefore seen by the Flemish as a foreign prince, one with whom they felt they had little in common and whose taxation policies served to alienate them. His control of the Netherlands remained tenuous both before and during Margaret's regency. Maximilian's troubles were already evident in the contract signed by Flemish towns granting him permission to marry Mary of Burgundy in which he was specifically forbidden to act as regent in the event of Mary's death.[17] After Mary's untimely death many towns preferred French governance to the German alternative and Ghent, one of the three most powerful Flemish towns, was particularly strident in its protestations of Maximilian's regency, supporting France's claims over those of the archduke.[18] Additionally, and humiliatingly, Bruges rebelled against Maximilian's taxes to fund his war with the French and actually held him captive from February to May of 1488.[19] Maximilian's war effort and his struggles with the Flemish cities in revolt combined to create a period of severe inflation, further aggravating the situation.[20] Commynes, the French chronicler, even used Maximilian's pretensions to govern Flanders as an example of the virtues of Salic laws, which forbade female inheritance, arguing that French laws would have prevented the succession of this foreign prince.[21] Maximilian's appointment of his daughter, Margaret of Austria, to the position of regent of the Netherlands in 1507 was a wise choice: Margaret was a Valois descendant on her mother's side and thus a more acceptable governor to the Netherlandish people. Additionally, she was a highly skilled administrator who was able to move into the position of regent easily and operate with greater popular approval than Maximilian ever could.

Margaret of Austria and Devotional Portrait Diptychs

During Margaret of Austria's regency, from 1507 to 1530, the devotional portrait diptych began to experience something of a renaissance. After Margaret's death, however, the production of these paintings slowed and had stopped altogether by 1560. Thus, her commissions and those by members of her court represent both a resurgence and the final flourishing of a format that had been waning in popularity after over a century of enthusiastic production. Significantly, Margaret is one of only two women known to have commissioned portrait diptychs, commissioning at least four of them.[22] Recently, Andrea Pearson has examined Margaret's diptych commissions in light of Margaret's role as regent and her wish to display her piety. Pearson links Margaret's diptych commissions to trends in female piety through an examination of their format and scale, seeing them as both smaller and more closely centered on Christ than diptychs patronized by male owners.[23] The diptych format offers owners the opportunity to interact with the Virgin and Child when they open and close the hinged panels as well as allowing them privileged access to the holy figures as they are depicted in close proximity to the Virgin and Child. This is, in and of itself, a remarkable type of representation, one that each devotional diptych owner tailored to his or her own spiritual needs. The devotional possibilities inherent in the form were surely important to Margaret, but I would emphasize that her diptych commissions also testify to her perception that this particular format, which had previously been the purview of Burgundian men, was available for appropriation thanks to her remarkable status as regent. Further, Margaret's commissions also indicate that she believed the diptych format conveyed a message of dynastic and thus, political significance.[24]

Examination of Margaret's other artistic commissions and the display of her portrait collection reveal patterns of patronage that she used to support her political agenda. Margaret's artistic patronage has been criticized by some scholars as *retardataire*, but more careful analysis suggests that the archaizing forms and styles found in her commissions were deliberate efforts to draw attention to her Valois pedigree and to link her regency to the Valois Golden Age of the previous century.[25] Because she was a woman the types of objects and the iconography available for appropriation and propagandistic display was limited. Unlike her Valois ancestor, Philip the Good, Margaret could not emphasize her military prowess through the creation of an order of knights like the Order of the Golden Fleece, founded as part of his marriage ceremony in 1430.[26] Nonetheless, she used patronage strategically to encourage popular support for her precariously positioned regency. Artistic policy and visual language played an important role in her struggle to control the rebellious Netherlands. Recognition of her Valois lineage is found both in her patronage of the arts and in her political maneuvering for the restoration of Burgundy and the other southern territories lost to the French.[27] The artistic and intellectual milieu established by Margaret in her palace at Mechelen was famous throughout Europe. As regent she played an important role in European politics while raising her nephew, the future Holy Roman Emperor, Charles V, and his four sisters.[28] At Mechelen she employed numerous court artists, and was an extremely active patron of both art and architecture as well as works of music and literature; in fact, Margaret was arguably one of the first great woman bibliophiles.[29] Examination of the collections housed here together with her commissions reveals her astute exploitation of Valois dynastic signs in her strategies for patronage and display.

A previously unidentified connection between early Valois diptychs and the collection of Margaret of Austria is found through studying the provenance and copies of Jan van Eyck's *Virgin in a Church*, dated to the first half of the 1430s.[30] The postcard sized *Virgin in a Church* (figure 9.4), is the pendant panel to a wing that would have shown the original owner in prayer. The patron of this diptych may have been Philip the Good, the great-grandfather of Margaret of Austria, and it was inherited by Margaret

9.4   Jan van Eyck, *Virgin in a Church*, Staatliche Museen zu Berlin-Preissischer Kulturbesitz Gemäldegalerie. Photo: Jorg P. Anders.

together with the rest of Philip's collection, entering her own collection in Mechelen where it was copied several times.[31] A painting mentioned in the July 17, 1516 inventory of Margaret's collection matches the description of Jan van Eyck's *Virgin in a Church* Diptych: *Ung autre tableaul de Nostre-Dame, de duc Philippe, qui est venu de Maillardet, couvert de satin brouché gris, et ayant fermaulx d'argent doré et bordé de velours vert. Fait de la main de Johannes.*[32]

"Johannes," when it appears in the inventories of Margaret of Austria, usually indicates that the artist is Jan van Eyck.[33] "Duc Philippe" is Philip the Good and the inclusion of a painting of the Virgin together with a gilded silver closure strongly suggests that the work was a diptych that closed with hinges and clasps. Further, it may be possible to reconstruct the original appearance of Jan van Eyck's diptych by examining copies of the *Virgin in a Church* that include an owner panel and were made while the painting was in Margaret's collection. The presence of a devotional portrait diptych by a famous artist featuring an important member of the Valois dynasty in Margaret's own collection may help explain her predilection for commissioning diptychs. The work may also have underscored the dynastic charge the format conveyed to Margaret herself and to knowledgeable visitors to her court.

At least two copies of Jan's diptych were made by the Master of 1499, who presumably had access to the painting at Margaret's court in Mechelen.[34] The *Diptych of Christiaan de Hondt* (figure 9.5(a) and (b)),[35] shows the original owner in a domestic interior adjoining a close copy of the *Virgin in a Church* and this diptych may indeed be a copy of Jan van Eyck's original diptych with a different owner portrait included.[36] Christiaan de Hondt, abbot of the Abbey of the Dunes, near Bruges, from 1496 to 1509, is shown in a private chamber with a devotional diptych hung within the drapes of the bed behind him. A book of hours is placed on the *prie-dieu* before the abbot and he kneels on a cushion. The dog beside him may refer to the donor's surname but it may also have been the personal pet of the abbot.[37] This chamber resembles an early to mid-century interior rather than contemporary furnishings from the beginning of the sixteenth century, and it is reminiscent of the domestic interiors painted by Jan van Eyck and Robert Campin.[38]

Consideration of a second diptych by the Master of 1499 provides further evidence for the presence of Jan's *Virgin in a Church* diptych in the collection of Margaret of Austria and for the reconstruction of its original appearance. The owner panel in the *Diptych of Margaret of Austria* (figure 9.6) shares a common source with the *Abbot De Hondt* owner panel although its pendant is not a copy of the *Virgin in a Church*.[39] In the Ghent painting, Margaret's portrait is placed within an almost identical chamber. Differences between the two panels result primarily from the deeper placement of Margaret within the room, the tiny scale of the Ghent work, and the greater simplicity of the wooden ceiling in Margaret's chamber. It is highly unlikely that this is a depiction of the actual living space of either owner, rather, both panels probably share a common source. Surprisingly, the significance of the repetition of the domestic setting in the Ghent and the Antwerp diptychs has not been previously discussed. However, the copies of this owner panel for two different patrons in works by an artist who had access to Jan's original diptych may suggest that the Ghent and Antwerp diptychs include copies of Jan van Eyck's *Virgin in a Church* Diptych owner panel.

It is also possible to identify the Ghent *Diptych of Margaret of Austria* in the 1516 inventory of Margaret of Austria's collection: *Ung demy tableaul ou est Madame painete en une chambre faict de telle main que celluy de Maillardet.*[40] The size of the painting described in the inventory would certainly match the diminutive Ghent diptych.[41] The singling out of the *chambre* in which Margaret is depicted, the one that is so similar to that in the *Diptych of Christiaan de Hondt,* may indicate that this was a particularly important feature of the work.[42] If the Ghent owner panel is indeed a copy after the Eyckian original, the sitter's domestic interior setting may well have served as a distinguishing element.

Jan Gossaert, one of Margaret's court painters, copied the Madonna panel from Jan van Eyck's *Virgin in a Church* for the left wing of the *Diptych of Antonio Siciliano* (Rome, Galeria Doria-Pamphili).[43] This diptych is dated about 1513 and was probably made while both the owner and Gossaert were in Mechelen where they could have seen van Eyck's painting in Margaret's collection. The Siciliano diptych shows the owner kneeling with his patron saint in a landscape that may reflect a request by its Italian patron for an example of this well-known specialty of Northern painters. Antonio Siciliano and Gossaert both had access to Margaret's collection in Mechelen where they could have seen Jan's *Virgin in a Church* diptych. Both were in Mechelen at the same time and Gossaert, as a court artist, certainly had access to the palace and its collections while Siciliano, as an important visitor, may well have been invited to Margaret's court.

Additionally, copies survive of a half-length devotional diptych by Bernard van Orley, another court painter in Mechelen, that depicts the regent in half-length at prayer by a tapestry-draped table seated across from the Virgin and Child (figure 9.7).[44] In its half-length format and depiction of an intimate relationship between the owner and the Christ Child this work recalls the devotional portrait diptychs of Rogier van der Weyden created during the second half of the fifteenth century. Like these earlier diptychs, the painting acts as a stimulus for prayer by the owner during her lifetime and encourages prayer for her after her death. Christ addresses Margaret directly while pulling away from his mother to move forcefully toward her. The imperative call, *Veni*, is placed beneath His outstretched hand and Margaret looks up from her devotional text with her positive response, *Placet*, inscribed above her. The fact that multiple copies of this diptych exist indicates that it may have been a gift from Margaret to individuals of particular importance. Its significance as a Valois signifier may have made it suitable for those upon whom Margaret particularly wished to impress this dynastic message.

Members of Margaret's court in Mechelen also commissioned their own diptychs; the most well-known extant example is Jan Gossaert's *Diptych of*

9.5(a) Master of 1499, *Diptych of Christiaan de Hondt*, Antwerp, Koninklijk Museum voor Schone Kunsten. Photo: Museum.

9.5(b)   *Diptych of Christiaan de Hondt.*

9.6 Master of 1499, *Diptych of Margaret of Austria*, Ghent, Museum voor Schone Kunsten. Photo: Museum.

9.7 Bernard van Orley, *Diptych with the Virgin and Child and Margaret of Austria*; current location unknown.

9.8   Jan Gossart, *Diptych of Jean Carondelet*, Louvre, Paris. Réunion des Musées Nationaux/Art Resource, NY.

Jean Carondelet in the Louvre (figure 9.8).[45] This diptych may have been commissioned by Carondelet before he undertook a potentially dangerous diplomatic mission.[46] The inclusion of a skull on the reverse of the owner's panel would have enabled the diptych to function as a tomb marker in the event of his death and in this way it is similar to several earlier diptychs that were also intended to serve a funerary function.[47] Margaret is also known to have commissioned diptychs for members of her court, such as the diptych by Jan Vermeyen for Cardinal Erard de la Marck, her close political advisor.[48]

Commissioning devotional portrait diptychs enabled Margaret to link herself and her court with the golden age of the Valois, her maternal ancestors. Her diptychs may have been part of a strategic campaign intended to capitalize on the Flemish preference for Valois over Hapsburg governors. But how might Margaret have displayed her diptychs and other portraits? Fortunately, we know a great deal about the exhibition of Margaret's collection in Mechelen thanks to the survival of two inventories. As heir to Philip the Good's manuscripts, paintings, tapestries, and decorative objects, Margaret could claim one of the most impressive art collections in Europe and she actively added to it with numerous commissions of her own.[49] Dagmar Eichberger's invaluable examination of Margaret's collection has revealed that it was unusually rich in portraits, many of which had been inherited from the Valois ducal collections. Margaret carefully planned the exhibition of her portrait collection in order to emphasize specific dynastic links and deemphasize others. Inventories of her palace in Mechelen, taken in 1516 and in 1523/24, convey the large scale of the collection as well as how it was displayed. It has been suggested that Margaret was with her court recorder while the inventories were taken and it may be her interpretation of the identities of the figures in the paintings as well as her attributions that are recorded in the inventories. The regent seems to have been actively involved in the display of her collection and she carefully controlled the placement of objects within the palace. Thus these inventories provide evidence for Margaret's programmatic arrangement of her extensive portrait collection.

By 1524, Margaret owned a total of eighty portraits not including six devotional diptychs and triptychs that included her own portrait and portraits of her family.[50] Eichberger has found that the organization of the portraits exhibited in the public rooms of Margaret's palace highlighted the importance of the Burgundian-Hapsburg families and their allies.[51] Thirty portraits were hung in the Première Chambre, the most public room in the palace, and twenty-nine of these depicted famous members of the European courts, nearly all of whom were related to Margaret by blood or by marriage. Most prominent in this room were portraits of the Valois Burgundian dukes. Distinctly less prominent were images of the Hapsburgs. Only one portrait of Margaret's father, Maximilian, was included and rather than emphasizing his status as Holy Roman Emperor, it followed an iconographic prototype established by the Burgundian dukes, showing Maximilian dressed in the robe and collar of the Golden Fleece.[52] Thus even the sole portrait of Maximilian shown in the regent's public rooms was designed to stress his links to the Netherlands. The portrait may have been intended to counter the widespread perception by the Flemish that Maximilian was a foreign prince with no real right to govern their lands.

Conclusion

The events that followed Margaret of Austria's death provide further evidence that Margaret's devotional portrait diptychs were the result of politically inspired patronage. Mary of Hungary, Margaret's niece and the woman who succeeded her as regent of the Netherlands, was not a Valois and she moved her court from Mechelen, the court center established by Charles the Bold, to Brussels where she commissioned work that more appropriately reflected her own lineage.[53] This work was typically created in the Renaissance style derived from Italy and embraced by the Hapsburg rulers beginning with Maximilian I and reaching its climax with Charles V and Philip II. The Burgundian-Valois line effectively came to an end with Margaret of Austria, and those who followed her conveyed their genealogies and political aspirations using the Renaissance style.

Margaret was in a weak position as a female regent over a region that had emphatically displayed its resentment of Hapsburg rule and was suffering from economic setbacks following the disastrous monetary policies of her father. Among other strategies, she asserted the appropriateness of her governance of the Netherlands through thoughtful, symbolic display and politically inspired commissions. Artistic policy and visual language played an important role in Margaret's governance and in her push for the restoration of southern territories to create a second Burgundian golden age. The devotional portrait diptychs created for Margaret and the display of artwork at her court in Mechelen may be seen as part of a carefully orchestrated campaign using the visual arts to draw upon the Valois associations incorporated within these works of art. Margaret exploited the artistic means by which she could convey dynastic lineage, and in so doing broke the gendered boundaries that had prevented women from having their portraits included in devotional portrait diptychs.

Notes

1. There are numerous studies of Margaret's life; a good, accessible biography of Margaret is by Charity Willard, "Margaret of Austria: Regent of Netherlands," in *Women Writers of the Renaissance and Reformation*, ed. Katharina Wilson, (Athens: University of Georgia Press, 1987), pp. 350–62. Other works consulted for information on Margaret's life and regency include E.E. Tremayne, *The First Governess of the Netherlands: Margaret of Austria* (London: Methuen, 1908); M. Bruchet, *Marguerite d'Autriche: Duchesse de Savoie* (Lille: Imprimerie L. Danel, 1927); G. de Boom, *Marguerite d'Autriche-Savoie et la Pré-Renaissance* (Paris and Brussels: E. Duchatel, 1935); J. de Iongh, *Margaret of Austria, Regent of the Netherlands* (New York: Norton, 1953); and P. Guérin, *Marguerite d'Autriche-Bourgogne, Archduchesse de Brou* (Lyon: Bellier, 1992). Any discussion of Margaret of Austria or her collection would be incomplete if it failed to mention the important work of Dagmar Eichberger. Of her numerous articles, "Margaret of Austria's Portrait Collection: Female Patronage and Dynastic Ambitions and Artistic Quality," *Renaissance Studies* 10/2 (1996), pp. 259–79, is among those most relevant to the present study.

2. For further discussion of the development and functions of devotional portrait diptychs see Laura D. Gelfand, "Fifteenth-Century Netherlandish Devotional Portrait Diptychs: Origins and Function," Ph.D. diss., Case Western Reserve University, 1994.

3. Ibid., see chapter 2, 12–37.

4. Fouquet's *Melun Diptych*, dated about 1450, is one of only a few French devotional portrait diptychs. Other than an anomalous single devotional panel by Bernard Strigel, which makes up half of the *Diptych of Hans Funk*

(Alte Pinakothek, Munich), the devotional diptych is virtually unknown in Germany. Not a single Italian or Spanish example survives and there are no Eastern European examples. The *Wilton Diptych* in the National Gallery in London offers an important early example of the form that is not associated with the Valois. The most recent text on this much-published diptych is D. Gordon, L. Monnas, and C. Elam, eds., *The Regal Image of Richard II and the Wilton Diptych* (London: Harvey Miller, 1997).

5. Gelfand, "Fifteenth-Century Netherlandish Devotional Portrait Diptychs," pp. 38–54.

6. S. Ringbom, *Icon to Narrative; The Rise of the Dramatic Close-up in Fifteenth-Century Devotional Painting*, 2nd ed. (Doornspijk, Netherlands: Davaco, 1984; originally pub. Abo Akademie: 1965) is an important source for information about the significance of these changes.

7. Rogier van der Weyden painted several diptychs including the *Diptych of Jean Gros*, the *Diptych of Philippe of Croy*, and the *Diptych of Laurent Froiment*. For illustrations of all of Rogier's diptychs see Dirc De Vos, *Rogier van der Weyden; The Complete Works* (Antwerp: Mercatorfonds, 1999).

8. Hans Memling's well-known painting the *Diptych of Martin van Nieuwenhove*, Friedlander, vol. 6, plates 52 and 53 (Bruges, Memlingmuseum) and the *Diptych with the Mystic Marriage of St. Catherine and the Donor Jan du Celier*, Friedlander, vol. 6, plate 54 (Paris, Louvre).

9. C. Monget, *La Chartreuse de Dijon, d'après les documents des archives de Bourgogne* (Montreuil-sur-Mer: Notre-Dame des Près, 1898) is still the single best source for documentation about Champmol.

10. Reproduced in color in C. Eisler, *Masterworks in Berlin; A City's Paintings Reunited* (Boston: Little Brown and Co., 1996), p. 95.

11. M. Meiss and C. Eisler, "A New French Primitive," *Burlington Magazine* 102 (1960), p. 238.

12. The work measured "4 pieds 6 pouces de large sur 5 pieds 6 pouces de haut." It is difficult to translate exactly how large this would have been, although it suggests a fairly large work. P. De Winter, "The Patronage of Philippe le Hardi, Duke of Burgundy (1364–1404)," Ph.D diss., New York University, 1976, pp. 826–27.

13. De Winter, "Philippe le Hardi," pp. 826–27.

14. See P. Viollet, "Comment les femmes on été exclues en France de la succession à la couronne," *Memoires de l'Académie des Inscriptions et Belles-Lettres*, 34, 2nd part (Paris, 1893), pp. 5–58. Salic laws were a relatively new development, instituted after the death of Louis X, and coming into definitive acceptance only during the reign of Charles VII. The document in which Jean le Bon initially gave Burgundy to Philip the Bold is reprinted in A. de Ridder, *Les droits de Charles-Quint au duché de Bourgogne* (Louvain and Paris: Typographe de C. Peeters, 1890), pp. 152–58.

15. Y. Cazaux, *Marie de Bourgogne* (Paris: A. Michel, 1967), pp. 191–92. See also R. Wellens, "Les États Generaux des Pays-Bas des origines à la fin du règne

de Philippe le Beau, (1464–1506)," *Anciens pays et assemblées d'États* 64 (1974), pp. 155–56.

16. For a thorough analysis of the rights that Mary of Burgundy had over various parts of the duchy of Burgundy see W.P. Blockmans, ed., "Marie de Bourgogne, 1477," *Anciens pays et assemblées d'états*, 80 (Huele, Belgium: U.G.A., 1985).

17. This is reprinted in W. P. Blockmans, *Handelingen van de Leden en van de Staten van Vlaanderen; regeringen van Maria van Bourgondie en Filips de Schone (5 January 1477–26 September, 1506)* (Brussels: Palais der Academies, 1973), vol. 1, no. 18 B, C: 37. The text is published in an edited form by J. Dumont, *Corps universel diplomatique du droit des gens* (Amsterdam-La Haye: P. Brunel, 1726–31), vol. 3: 10. A French copy that was signed by Mary of Burgundy was published by O. Delepierre, *Chronique des faits et gestes admirables de Maximilien I durant son mariage avec Marie de Bourgogne* (Brussels: n.a., 1839), pp. 446–49.

18. See W.P. Blockmans, "Autocratie ou polyarchie? La lutte pour le pouvoir politique en Flandre de 1482 a 1492, d'après des documents inédits," *Bullétin de la Commission Royale d'Histoire* 140 (1974), pp. 258–368. Maximilian's problems were particularly severe with the city of Ghent but Bruges was subject to periodic rebellions as well.

19. For a detailed description of the conflict between Maximilian and the city of Bruges see R. Wellens, "La révolte brugeoise de 1488," *Handelingen van Genootschap voor Geschiedenis "Societé d'Emulation te Brugge"* 102 (1965), pp. 5–52.

20. P. Spufford, *Monetary Problems and Policies in the Burgundian Netherlands, 1433–1496* (Leiden: Brill, 1970). The author clearly elucidates the financial impetus behind the wars and revolts waged following the death of Mary of Burgundy.

21. P. de Commynes, *The Memoirs of Philippe de Commyes*, 2 vols, ed. Samuel Kinser and trans. Isabelle Cazeaux (Columbia, SC: University of South Carolina Press, 1973), p. 382.

22. The only other extant diptych that includes a female donor is the Louvre *Diptych of Margaret of York* (1446–1503). The owner was Margaret of Austria's step-grandmother with whom she lived in Mechelen from 1493 to 1497 and 1499 to 1501.

23. A. Pearson, "Margaret of Austria's Devotional Portrait Diptychs," *Woman's Art Journal* 22/2 (Fall 2001/Winter 2002), pp. 19–25. I thank the author for sharing this material with me before its publication.

24. Further discussion of Margaret of Austria's artistic policies and use of style is found in my article, "The Iconography of Style: Margaret of Austria and the Church of St. Nicolas of Tolentino at Brou," in *Widowhood and Early Modern Visual Culture*, ed. Alison Levy (Aldershot, England: Ashgate Press, 2003), pp. 145–159.

25. For criticism of Margaret's patronage see J. Riviére, "Réévaluation du mécénat de Philippe le Beau et Marguerite d'Autriche en matière de

ceinture," *Publication du Centre Européen d'Études Bourguignonnes (XIV–XVIe siècles)* 25 (1985), pp. 103–118. A discussion of her use of style in architecture is found in E. van den Bosseche, "Margareta van Oosterrijk: Prinses van de Renaissance?" *Handelingen van de Koninklijk Kring voor Oudheidkunde, Letteren en Kunst van Mechelen* 76 (1972), pp. 61–86.

26. Wim Blockmans and Walter Prevenier, *The Promised Lands: The Low Countries Under Burgundian Rule, 1369–1530*, trans. E. Fackelman (Philadelphia: University of Pennsylvania Press, 1999), pp. 74–75.

27. Philip the Good's use of artwork as propaganda is discussed in J.C. Smith, "The Artistic Patronage of Philip the Good, Duke of Burgundy (1419–1467)," Ph.D. diss., Columbia University (1979), pp. 7–38. The ways in which Margaret of Austria and her father, Maximilian, connected themselves with this Valois past through the collection and commissioning of chronicles aggrandizing their dynastic legacy is intelligently addressed in G. Small, *George Chastelain and the Shaping of Valois Burgundy: Political and Historical Culture at Court in the Fifteenth Century* (Rochester, NY: The Boydell Press, 1997), p. 217.

28. For more on Margaret's court in Mechelen see G. van Doorslaer, "Coup d'oeil sur la Ville de Malines durant la Régence de Marguerite d'Autriche," *Bulletin du Cercle Archéologique, Littéraire et Artistique de Malines* 17 (1907), pp. 5–28; Musée de Brou, *Van Orley et les Artistes de la Cour de Marguerite d'Autriche* (Brou: Musée de Brou, 1981); and G. Doutrepont, *Jean Lemaire de Belges et la Renaissance* (Brussels: M. Hayez, 1974). For an extremely informative treatment of the upbringing of Charles V, see T. Juste, "Charles-Quint et Marguerite d'Autriche. Étude sur la minorité, l'emancipation et l'avenement de Charles-Quint à l'Empire," *L'Académie Royal des Sciences, des Lettres et des Beaux-Arts de Belgique* 7 (1859), pp. 1–175.

29. Margaret's activities as a writer of poetry compliment her remarkable patronage of literary, visual, and musical arts. Her political agenda was furthered by her commissions in all these areas as has been discussed by Catherine M. Müller, "Marguerite d'Autriche (1480–1530): Poétesse et mécène, in *Reines et princesses au Moyen Âge*" (Montpellier: Université Paul-Valéry/Cahiers du C.R.I.S.M.A., 2001), pp. 763–76. For her literary patronage see F. Thibaut, *Marguerite d'Autriche et Jean Lemaire de Belges, ou de la littérature et des arts au Pays-Bas sous Marguerite d'Autriche* (Paris: E. Leroux, 1888; reprinted Geneva: Slatkine Reprints, 1970).

30. Some of the most relevant treatments of the work including discussions of possible dates for its completion are found in: E. Panofsky, *Early Netherlandish Painting* (Cambridge: Cambridge University Press, 1953), pp. 144–48; S.J. Herzog, "Zur Kirchenmadonna van Eycks," *Jahrbuch der Berliner Museen* 6 (1956), pp. 2–16; C. Purtle, *The Marian Paintings of Jan van Eyck* (Princeton: Princeton University Press, 1982), pp. 144–56.

31. Another copy of Jan's painting, now lost, was formerly in the possession of F. Cacault, the representative of France in Naples, Florence, and Rome. This copy and its dimensions are published in J. Weale and M. Brockwell, *The van Eycks and Their Art* (London: John Lane, 1912), p. 169.

32. The inventory is reproduced in full in M. Le Glay, *Corréspondance de l'Empereur Maximilien Ier et de Marguerite d'Autriche* (Paris: J. Renouard, 1839), pp. 480–82. Thanks to Erik Inglis for bringing this particular entry to my attention.

33. J. Duverger, "De Werken van 'Johannes' in de Verzamelingen van Margareta van Oosterijk," *Oud Holland* 45 (1928), pp. 210–20. The inventory lists another painting by "Johannes" now identified as the *Arnolfini Wedding Portrait* (London, National Gallery); *Ung grant tableau qu'on appelle Hernoulle-Fin avec sa femme dedens une chambre, qui fut donné a Madame par don Diego, les armes duquel sont en la couverte dudit tableaul. Fait du painctre Johannes.* Le Glay, *Corréspondance*, p. 79.

34. For paintings by the Master of 1499 and the likelihood that he was actually Gerard Hoorenbout, see P. Eeckhout, "Les trois diptychs du Maître de 1499," *Bullétin Musées Royaux des Beaux-Arts de Belgique* 1–3 (1985–88), pp. 49–62. An attribution to Hoorenbout, a miniaturist who worked for Margaret from at least 1515 to 1521, would certainly be possible given the familiarity the painter displays with objects in the collection of Margaret of Austria.

35. P. Vandenbroek, *Catalogus schilderkunst 14e en 15e eeux, Koninklijk Museum voor Schone Kunsten* (Antwerp: Koninklijk Museum voor Schone Kunsten, 1985), pp. 125–30.

36. The reverse of the owner panel of the Antwerp diptych shows Robert de Clercq, abbot of the Abbey of the Dunes from 1519 to 1557, in prayer facing an image of the Salvator Mundi that was painted by the Master of 1499 at the same time as the reverse of the painting. De Clercq's portrait seems to have been added about 1519 and Eeckhout believes that this was also painted by the Master of 1499 and provides an indication of the evolution of his style. Eeckhout, "Les Trois diptychs," p. 50 and fig. 2.

37. Margaret is shown in the Ghent diptych with her own dog, Bouté; however there is no evidence for her ownership of a monkey. It is, unfortunately, not possible to ascertain whether or not the dog included in the De Hondt diptych was the property of the abbot.

38. Herzog suggested that this interior is reminiscent of those from the early fifteenth century and cited examples of similar interiors including Jan van Eyck's *Arnolfini Wedding Portrait* (London, National Gallery of Art) and the Eyckian miniature of the *Birth of St. John* in the Turin-Milan Hours (Turin, Museo Civico, fol. 93v.), as well as Campin's *Werl Altarpiece* and the *Merode Altarpiece* (New York: The Cloisters). Herzog, "Zur Kirchenmadonna van Eycks," pp. 14–15.

39. Musée de Brou, *Van Orley et les Artistes*, pp. 54–55, states that the Virgin panel is by another painter altogether while Eeckhout, "Les Trois Diptychs," p. 58, believes it, like the portrait of De Clercq, is another example of the later style of the Master of 1499. The painting has suffered from a good deal of past restoration. Additionally, the Virgin and Child panel may refer back to an earlier painting. However I have not been able to identify a specific model.

40. Le Glay, *Corréspondance*, p. 482. The term "Maillardet," found in both entries, is mysterious. The name doesn't appear in any of the correspondence

between Margaret and Maximilian and is not mentioned in any of the other inventory lists. In correspondence with Dagmar Eichberger, she indicated that the identification of this person has eluded her as well. The fact that the name appears in both the entries cited, however, might indicate a link between the two objects and support the identification I have proposed for the paintings in the inventory.

41. The panels are each 30.5 × 14.6 cm., see Vandenbroek, *Catalogus schilderkunst*, pp. 125–30.

42. Eichberger proposes that the Ghent diptych entered Margaret's collection after the inventory of 1524 and is mentioned there as *Receu puis cest inventoire fait ung double tableau; et l'ung est N(re) Dame habille de blue, tenant don enffant droit, et en aultre Madame a genoux, adorant ledit enffant*, published in Michelant, "Inventaire des vaisselles, joyaux, tapisseries, peintures, manuscrits, etc. de Marguerite d'Autriche, regente et gouvernante des Pays-Bas, dressé en son palais de Malines, le 9 Juillet 1523," *Académie Royale de Sciences des Lettres et de Beaux-Arts de Belgique, Bulletin* 3 ser. 12.2 (1870), p. 87. However, De Boom, *Marguerite d'Autriche*, p. 142, argued that this inventory entry refers to one of the half-length van Orley diptychs. If one assumes that the Ghent Diptych would have entered Margaret's collection immediately upon its completion (sometime in the first decade of the sixteenth century) it is possible that this entry refers to an unknown, later, full-length diptych.

43. This work is described and reproduced in S.H. Herzog, "Jan Gossaert called Mabuse (ca. 1478–1532): A Study of His Chronology with a Catalogue of His Works" (Ph.D. diss, Bryn Mawr College, 1974), cat. no. 8: 226.

44. See M.J. Friedlander, *Early Netherlandish Painting*, trans. H. Pauwels and S. Herzog, (Leiden: A.W. Sijtoff: 1972), vol. 8, p. 109 and plate 115. There are three copies of van Orley's half-length diptych with Margaret of Austria.

45. Friedlander, *Early Netherlandish Painting*, vol. 8, plates 10 and 11.

46. Herzog, "Jan Gossaert called Mabuse," p. 8. For information on Jean Carondelet see L. Gachard, "Jean Carondelet," *Biographie Nationale de Belgique*, vol. 3 (1866), p. 349. For more on his patronage and that of his brother see M. le Suchet, "Étude biographique sur Jean et Ferry Carondelet (1469 a 1544)," *Mémoires de l'Academie de Besançon* (1901), pp. 1–39.

47. A marvelous grinning skull is found on the verso of a *Portrait of a Man* that made up half of a diptych by the Master of 1480, (North Carolina, Mint Museum of Art) and the *Diptych of Josse van der Burch* (Cambridge, MA: Busch-Reisinger Museum) includes the donor's coat of arms and a funerary inscription. See Gelfand, "Fifteenth-Century Netherlandish Devotional Portrait Diptychs," pp. 139–53.

48. Eichberger, *Devotional Objects in Book Format*, p. 296 and n. 53. This diptych was commissioned from Margaret's court painter in 1528. There may have been two copies of this diptych, as is detailed by Eichberger. She also mentions the presence of a third diptych with a portrait of Erard de la Marck and indicates this had already been divided by the time of the 1523/24 inventory (Michelant, "Inventaire des vaisselles," p. 86). Eichberger notes that this is the

only diptych in Margaret's collection to include a portrait of anyone other than a family member.

49. Albrecht Dürer toured the collection with Margaret in 1521 and his somewhat acerbic commentary is found in his journals. J.-A. Goris and G. Marlier, *Albrecht Dürer: Diary of His Journey to the Netherlands, 1520–1521* (Greenwich, CT: New York Graphic Society, 1971), pp. 95–98.

50. D. Eichberger and L. Beaven, "Family Members and Political Allies: The Portrait Collection of Margaret of Austria," *Art Bulletin* 74 (1995), p. 226. If all the devotional images are included together with the secular portraits, Margaret's collection actually numbers closer to 100 portraits. In order to put this into perspective, Philip of Cleves, a contemporary noble collector, had only thirty-three portraits.

51. Eichberger and Beaven, "Family Members and Political Allies," p. 230.

52. Maximilian was shown wearing the collar of the Golden Fleece in accordance with Burgundian practice for formal portraiture (Michelant, p. 68), *Item, ung aultre tableau de la portraiture de l'empereur Maximilian, pere de Madame, que Dieu pardoint, habille d'une robbe drapt d'or, fouree de martre, a ung bonnet noir sur son chief, portent le colier de la Toison d'Or, tenant un rolet en ca main dextre.*

53. Boogert, Bob van den, "Hapsburgs imperialisme en de verspreiding van renaissancevormen in de Nederlanden: de vensters van Michiel Coxie in de Sint-Goedele te Brussel," *Oud Holland* 106, no. 2 (1992), p. 75.

INDEX

Page numbers in italics refers to illustrations.

Melitta Breznik

Mutter.

Chronik eines Abschieds

Luchterhand

Melitta Breznik
Mutter.

»Es ist später als Du denkst«

Inschrift auf einem Marmorstein
in Laas, Südtirol

Als ich auf die Welt kam, so erzählte Mutter, war ich ein hässliches, untergewichtiges Etwas, umhüllt von einem bittersüßen Geruch, der von einer käsigen, schuppigen Schicht auf meinem Körper herrührte. Zwei Wochen hatte ich mir nach dem errechneten Geburtstermin Zeit gelassen, sodass die Ärzte schon gemeint hatten, ich würde kaum lebend zur Welt kommen. »Mit einundvierzig wollte ich kein Kind mehr, aber als ich Dich in meinen Armen hielt, war alles gut.«

I

17. Oktober. Seit gestern bin ich hier bei Mutter. Ihre Stimme am Telefon klang verändert, der dunkle Ton fehlte, die Melodie der Sätze war ungewohnt eintönig, karg. Sie habe starke Bauchschmerzen, immer wieder erbrochen. Der Arzt habe gemeint, sie solle auf Blähendes und Fettes verzichten, aber das tat sie ohnehin. Kein Lauch, kein Kohl, Mutter hatte den Speiseplan der Familie an ihre Bedürfnisse angepasst, nur manchmal gab es in meiner Kindheit Käferbohnensalat mit Kürbiskernöl für Vater, mit kleingehackten Zwiebeln und Knoblauch, wie es in der Gegend üblich war. Mutter war Ende der Vierzigerjahre aus Frankfurt am Main in diese steirische Kleinstadt gekommen und hatte gelernt zu kochen, wie es die Männer hier von ihren Frauen erwarteten.

Seit Mutter Ende achtzig war, wurden die Wege zum Einkaufen beschwerlicher. Eines Tages zeigte sie mir Unterlagen über eine ihrem Alter angepasste kleine Wohnung. Dann war alles schnell gegangen. Mutter entwickelte unerwarteten Eifer, und wir pilgerten von einem Einrichtungshaus zum anderen, um das neue Mobiliar auszusuchen, das sie sich von ihrem Ersparten und etwas Geld von mir anschaffte. Sie wollte fast nichts mitnehmen, es sollte ein Neuanfang sein, für diesen letzten Abschnitt in ihrem Leben, der mit einem Umtrunk für die ehemaligen Nachbarn der Burggasse in ihrer neuen Bleibe begann.

Seit zwei Jahren lebt sie hier mit sieben älteren Frauen in dem zweistöckigen Wohnhaus nicht weit vom Stadtzentrum. Der Gesellschaftsraum im Parterre bietet genügend Platz, um gemeinsam Kaffee zu trinken oder Karten zu spielen, vormittags kümmert sich eine Sozialhelferin der Gemeinde darum, wenn etwas zu organisieren ist, ein Besuch des Hausarztes oder der Krankenpflege. Es gibt keine Männer hier, aus der Generation der Kriegsteilnehmer sind die meisten verstorben oder im Altersheim. Mutter hat sich gut eingelebt, der Alltag mit begehbarer Dusche, kleiner Kochzeile und Terrasse gestaltet sich komfortabler als in ihrer alten Wohnung, in der sie nach der Trennung von Vater die letzten fünfundzwanzig Jahre verbracht hat. Sie liebt es, in der warmen Jahreszeit ihren Mittagsschlaf im Liegestuhl vor ihrem Wohnzimmer im Freien zu halten und den Wind in den Haaren zu spüren. In einem kleinen Beet zieht sie Petersilie, Thymian und Pfefferminz, lässt Kletterrosen am Windschutz emporwachsen, die sie mit Hingabe pflegt, meist gemeinsam mit Frau Gabriel, die ihr seit einigen Jahren einmal in der Woche schwere Haushaltsarbeiten abnimmt.

Zunächst zögerte ich hierherzukommen, denn Mutter litt, seit ich mich zurückerinnern kann, an Unpässlichkeiten, die immer wieder verschwanden, so schnell wie sie gekommen waren, und ich hoffte, es würde auch diesmal so sein. Ich hatte meinem Bruder, der in einer benachbarten Kleinstadt lebt, telefonisch die Lage geschildert, er wusste bereits Bescheid, und ich bat ihn, am selben Tag bei Mutter vorbeizuschauen und mir über ihren aktuellen Zustand zu berichten, da ich nicht wisse, ob meine Anreise nötig sei. Die nächsten Wochen in Basel hatte ich bereits verplant, ich führte Gespräche mit Chefärzten von psychiatrischen Kliniken, in denen ich mir meine nächste Arbeitsstelle vorstellen konnte. Zudem hatte ich ein Jahr Auszeit genommen, um an einem Buch zu arbeiten. Für die Recherchen dazu war ich zunächst nach Griechenland gereist, ins Gebiet der Felsen von Meteora, wo mein Vater einige Monate als Wehrmachtssoldat stationiert gewesen war. Eine Reise hatte mich auch nach Südengland geführt, nach Romsey, eine kleine Stadt nahe Southampton. Dort war er zwei Jahre lang als Kriegsgefangener interniert gewesen. Viel Zeit verbrachte ich in Archiven in Wien, London und Freiburg im Breisgau, um Unterlagen über Einheiten zu studieren, denen mein Vater im Laufe des Kriegs zugeteilt worden war. Ich war auf der Suche nach der Katastrophe, deren Schatten ihn als Vater hatten versagen lassen. Er hatte sich im Laufe der Jahre, als Quartalstrinker, nach und nach vom Leben zurückgezogen. Zum Abschluss meiner Recherchen war ich nach Frankfurt gefahren, genauer gesagt nach Bergen-Enkheim und Fechenheim, Vororte, in denen Mutter aufgewachsen war und wo sie während des Krieges Vater kennengelernt hatte. Zuletzt hatten Mutter und ich vor ein paar Jahren dort Station gemacht, wir waren unterwegs zu vier psychiatrischen Kliniken in Hessen, auf der Suche nach Dokumenten über ihre Mutter, die dort interniert gewesen und unter unklaren Umständen zu Beginn der Vierzigerjahre verstorben war.

Von Frankfurt aus telefonierte ich mehrmals täglich mit Mutter, in der Hoffnung, sie würde sich erholen. Doch als sie mir sagte, sie könne das Bett kaum mehr verlassen, machte ich mich ohne weiteres Zögern auf den Weg hierher. Bei meiner Ankunft war ich überrascht, Mutter fröhlich zu sehen. Als ich sie, noch an der Türe, nach dem ersten Kuss auf ihre weiche Wange, die vertraut roch, vorsichtig umarmte, noch unsicher, wie fest ich sie berühren durfte, fühlte sie sich federleicht an. Fast war ich versucht, sie, die einen Kopf kleiner war als ich, hochzuheben wie ein Kind. Die Berührung löste in mir ein Gefühl von Geborgenheit aus, doch diese Nähe stellte sich meist nur in kurzen Momenten ein, als Auftakt meines Besuches und dann beim Abschied. Dazwischen war jeder körperliche Kontakt mit einem alten Tabu belegt. Nur nicht zu nahe, nicht zu lange die Hand halten, übers Haar streichen, nur nicht.

2

Mutter trägt ein gelbes Hauskleid. Es ist ein einfach ge-
schnittenes Stück, das sie vor ein paar Jahren selbst genäht hat. Das Gelb passt zu ihren Haaren, die sich in
dünnen Wellen weich um ihr Gesicht legen. Es ist später Vormittag, und wir sitzen auf der sonnenerwärmten
Terrasse ihrer Wohnung, ein lauer Oktobertag hat sich
über die Stadt gebreitet, mild und unerwartet. Mutter
wirkt zerbrechlich und hat Mühe, Haltung zu bewahren
und so zu tun, als fühle sie sich besser als in den Tagen
davor. Meinen Vorschlag, den Hausarzt zu konsultieren,
verwirft sie mit einer ablehnenden Geste, ein weiteres
Insistieren würde nichts fruchten. Also erzähle ich von
meiner Reise und beginne mit den Vorbereitungen für
das Mittagessen, lege den Inhalt der Einkaufstasche auf
dem Klapptisch aus, während sie zurückgelehnt im Ses-
sel sitzt und die Sonne das Weiß ihrer Haare zum Leuchten bringt. Ich kenne Mutter nicht anders als mit dieser
Frisur, und in mir tauchen Bilder aus meiner Kindheit
auf, von der Friseurgehilfin, die über die mit Locken-
wicklern bestückten Köpfe hinweg Tageskonversation
führte. Das Geschnatter der Frauen schien sich gegenseitig aufzuladen, jede gab Geschichten über diesen und

jene zum Besten. Die Rede war meist vom Werk, diesem zwischen dunkel bewaldeten Bergen schnaubenden Ungeheuer, das über die Jahre immer wieder einen der Ehemänner, Väter oder Verlobten bei der Arbeit am Hochofen oder am Stahlhammer verschlungen hatte. Ich war neun Jahre alt und wünschte mir, Mutter würde sich für eine Färbung entscheiden, dunkelblond, was mir die Frage meiner Mitschüler ersparen würde, warum ich bei meinen Großeltern wohnte. Mutter sagte oft, das rasche Ergrauen habe kurz nach meiner Geburt begonnen, buchstäblich über Nacht.

Mutter und ich schneiden Gemüse, das ich an einem Marktstand in der Altstadt gekauft habe. Suppenhuhn vom Bauern aus der Gegend soll es geben, gewürzt mit Lorbeer, Majoran und Petersilie, so, wie sie es für mich gekocht hatte, wenn ich fiebrig von der Schule nach Hause kam und mich sofort ins Bett legte. Gelegentlich gab es auch sonst Hühnerbrühe, die Bouillon wurde am Sonntag mit Griesnockerl vor dem Schnitzel serviert. Die Sonne wärmt mir den Rücken, während wir einträchtig schälen, zerkleinern und die bunten Stücke in einer Glasschüssel sammeln. Ich beobachte, wie Mutter die Karotten in Scheiben schneidet, alle anderen mir bekannten Köchinnen verarbeiten sie zu länglichen Stiften. Die Suppe wird aussehen wie in meiner Kindheit, Erbsen und Möhren, kleine grüne Kugeln und orange Medaillons, die mit den golden glänzenden Fettaugen und der frisch geschnittenen Petersilie an der Oberfläche im Teller ein appetitliches Bild abgeben. Im Stillen wünsche ich mir, sie solle durch meine Fürsorge rasch genesen. Wenn ich in der Gegend wohnen würde, könnten wir öfter miteinander kochen, dann wäre es selbstverständlich, einträchtig Strudelteig zuzubereiten, der so schmeckt, wie er immer geschmeckt hat. Als Jugendliche hat mich die Angst davor, eine Hausfrau zu werden wie meine Mutter, die mittags mit dem Essen auf ihren Mann und die Kinder wartet, davon abgehalten, mit ihr am Herd zu stehen. Erst als ich über dreißig war und als Ärztin in der Schweiz arbeitete, wollte ich wissen, wie sie die Marillenknödel zubereitete, fragte nach dem Rezept für den Topfenstrudel, den Kaiserschmarren, die Rindsrouladen. Vielleicht hätte Mutter mein Leben aufgefressen, wenn ich in ihrer Nähe geblieben wäre. Ich behalte den Gedanken für mich.

Das Huhn kocht in einem großen Topf langsam vor sich hin, Mutter hat sich aufs Sofa im Wohnzimmer gelegt, ich sitze allein auf der Terrasse, es weht ein warmer Herbstwind, und für einen kurzen Moment ist es wie früher, als ich noch klein war. Gleich würde Vater nach seiner Arbeitsschicht im Werk müde zur Tür hereinkommen und, nachdem er die Hände und das Gesicht gewaschen hätte, mit der Zeitung in der Hand in der Küche Platz nehmen, bis die Gemüse-, Gulasch- oder die Griesnockerlsuppe angerichtet war. Dann würden wir zu Tisch gerufen werden.

Während wir langsam die heiße Suppe löffeln und Mutter mir von ihren Nachbarinnen im Haus erzählt, stelle ich mir vor, es würde so sein wie bei meinen früheren Besuchen. Mutter hatte sich in meiner Gesellschaft meist schnell erholt. Möglicherweise ist es die Erschöpfung nach der Magenverstimmung, die sie in diese düstere Herbststimmung abgleiten lässt, unter der sie in den letzten Jahren zunehmend leidet. Nach einem halben Teller Suppe klagt sie über Bauchschmerzen und kurz darauf erbricht sie alles. Sie schleppt sich vom Badezimmer ins Bett und schläft erschöpft ein. Ich wasche in der kleinen Küche leise das Geschirr und beschließe, am nächsten Morgen mit Mutter ins Krankenhaus zu fahren. Mutters Zustand ist ernster, als wir beide es wahrhaben wollen. Verzagt setze ich mich an den Esstisch gegenüber der offenen Tür zum Schlafzimmer, sehe Mutter auf ihrem Bett liegen, zugedeckt mit einer rostbraunen Wolldecke, die sie bis zu den Schultern hochgezogen hat, beobachte von weitem ihr Gesicht, dessen Züge sich langsam glätten, und beginne in mein Tagebuch zu notieren.

Draußen vor den hohen Fenstern zur Terrasse zieht sich das Licht langsam aus der Landschaft zurück. Die Welt beschränkt sich auf das schwach von der Stehlampe erleuchtete Wohnzimmer mit dem goldgelben Sofa, die darauf drapierten Kissen, den Esstisch mit vier Stühlen aus hellem Holz, die Anrichte, auf der Gegenstände für Mutters täglichen Gebrauch bereitliegen. Fein säuberlich nebeneinander finden sich dort das Blutdruckmessgerät, die ovale Pillendose, ein Pack Taschentücher, ein kleiner Stapel ungleich quadratisch zurechtgeschnittener Zettel für die Einkaufsnotizen, darauf ein Kugelschreiber mit der Aufschrift einer Bank. Zuhinterst steht ein Wochenkalender, den Mutter von ihrer Nichte geschenkt bekommen hat, er zeigt »Frauen von Tahiti am Strand« von Gauguin, ein buntes Bild, friedvoll. Eines der beiden dunkelhäutigen Mädchen sitzt nachdenklich im Sand und sieht am Betrachter vorbei, sie trägt ein blassrosa Kleid, die zweite junge Frau kauert mit in sich gekehrtem Blick daneben. Im Hintergrund ein satter hellgrüner Streifen, der sich gegen die anbrandenden sanften blauschwarzen Wellen des Wassers abhebt.

3

Mitternacht, die Deckenleuchten in allen Zimmern sind eingeschaltet. Vielleicht ist Mutter ins Bad gegangen. Zunächst lausche ich, stehe auf, sehe durch die offene Schlafzimmertüre, sie liegt ruhig im Bett, schläft tief. Ich gehe ganz nah zu ihr hin, um ihre Atemzüge zu hören, so wie ich es früher getan habe, als Kind, denn ich hatte oft Angst um sie, um ihr Herz, das eines Tages versagen würde. Manchmal kam der Hausarzt, wenn Mutter bleich auf dem Küchensofa lag, schwer Luft holte und eine Hand an ihren Brustkorb hielt, als müsste sie in ihrem Leben innehalten. Nachdem der Arzt ihr eine Spritze gegeben hatte, saß ich still in einer Ecke, bis sie eingeschlafen war. Vater hatte im Wohnzimmer den Fernseher lautlos geschaltet und ließ sich nicht blicken. Tags darauf war der Spuk vorbei und Mutter arbeitete wieder im Garten, an der Nähmaschine, oder war in der Küche mit dem Einkochen von Marillenmarmelade beschäftigt.

Am Morgen erzähle ich Mutter von der hell erleuchteten Wohnung und sie schüttelt den Kopf, sagt, sie sei nicht aufgestanden, um auf die Toilette zu gehen. Nach einer Weile meint sie, das Licht von letzter Nacht sei ein Gruß ihrer Mutter aus dem Reich der Toten. Auch wenn ich es nicht wahrhaben will, vielleicht ist die Zeit gekommen, Abschied zu nehmen. In den letzten Jahren, wenn ich sie nach einem Besuch an der Haustüre umarmt hatte und zum offenen Autofenster hinauswinkte, dachte ich oft, ich würde sie zum letzten Mal sehen. Ich rang um Fassung, bis die kleine Gestalt, die mir im Schein der Eingangslaterne nachwinkte, in der Kurve der Siedlungsstraße aus dem Sichtfeld verschwunden war. Erst dann ließ ich meinen Tränen freien Lauf und versuchte mich auf der Fahrt nach Graz zum Verladezug, der mich durch die Nacht ans andere Ende von Österreich tragen würde, langsam zu beruhigen. Bei einem ihrer häufiger werdenden Krankenhausaufenthalte im vergangenen Sommer hatte sie mich bis zur Eingangstüre begleitet, und ich sagte ihr, dass ich aller Wahrscheinlichkeit nach nicht rechtzeitig bei ihr sein könnte, wenn sie sterben würde. Mutter meinte, mit einem verlegenen Lächeln um den von Falten gezeichneten Mund, »diesen Gang muss ich wohl alleine hinter mich bringen«. Immer bedrängte mich das Gefühl, dass es noch irgendetwas gab, das ich ihr sagen sollte, etwas, das nicht verloren gehen durfte zwischen uns. Als sie in der hohen verglasten Empfangshalle stand, in ihrem dunkelblauen japanischen Morgenmantel, mit den notdürftig frisierten Haaren, den blauen Augen, denen noch immer ein Glanz innewohnte, sprang mich ihr Alter an. Ich hatte diese Tatsache in den Jahren davor immer wieder verdrängt.

Mutter hatte vor dem Zubettgehen einer Untersuchung im Krankenhaus zugestimmt. Mit einem leisen Stöhnen holt sie ihre Schuhe aus der untersten Lade des Vorzimmerschrankes, wobei sie sich nicht helfen lässt. Ich trinke noch ein Glas lauwarmes Wasser im Stehen, frühstücken mag ich nicht, ich habe keinen Appetit. Während der zehnminütigen Fahrt schweigen wir, und als ich Mutter vor dem Haupteingang aussteigen lasse, geht sie langsam, auf ihren Rollator gestützt, in ihrer dickköpfigen Selbstständigkeit, die sie nicht auf mich warten lässt, die schräge Rampe hinauf. Nachdem ich eilig das Auto geparkt habe, hole ich sie ein, in der Hand die kleine Reisetasche, die sie für solche Fälle mit dem Notwendigsten gepackt im Kleiderschrank bereithält. Wir sind bei der gläsernen Schiebetüre angelangt, bleiben kurz stehen, und als ich zu ihr hinübersehe, erwidert sie meinen besorgten Blick.

Das Warten im Vorraum zu den Untersuchungszimmern erträgt sie mit Geduld, wir wechseln nur ab und zu einen Satz, das Schweigen von vorhin ist einer Erwartung gewichen. Unsere Aufmerksamkeit richtet sich auf die grauen Türen, hinter denen sich das medizinische Personal zu schaffen macht, bald wird Mutters Name gerufen. Neben uns sitzen zwei ältere Frauen, die sich unablässig mit lauten Stimmen über ihre Gebrechen unterhalten. Ihr Gerede irritiert mich, und so betrachte ich die weiß getünchten Wände, die großflächigen Fenster, mit Sicht auf einen Innenhof, der mit einem für diese Jahreszeit ungewöhnlich grünen Rasen bewachsen ist.

Kaum jemand außer dem Gärtner wird ihn je betreten, ein Unort zwischen den Gebäuden. Das Krankenhaus ist mir vertraut, ich habe hier einen Teil meiner Turnuszeit absolviert, doch kann ich jetzt nicht das tun, was ich sonst als Arzt tun würde, Patienten untersuchen, behandeln, ihnen zuhören und am Abend nach Dienstschluss nach Hause gehen. Jetzt sitze ich hier im Warteraum als Tochter meiner kranken Mutter.

Die junge Ärztin, die uns begrüßt, bemüht sich, Mutter beim Ausziehen zu helfen, versucht so sanft wie möglich an ihrem Bauch zu tasten, um herauszufinden, wo es wehtut. Die Kunst des Handanlegens nach alter Manier, dieses inzwischen fast nebensächlich gewordene Ritual, dem von jungen Ärzten kaum mehr hohe Aussagekraft beigemessen wird, wie lange wird es sie noch geben? Mich wird später einmal niemand mehr so berühren, wie Mutter jetzt berührt wird. Man wird mich am Eingang zum Spital in einen Diagnosetunnel schieben, an dessen Ende mir die Ergebnisse der Untersuchung von einer Computerstimme mitgeteilt werden.

Mutter verzieht immer wieder den Mund, lässt aber, ohne sich zu beklagen, alles über sich ergehen, erträgt stoisch den Druck des Ultraschallkopfes, den die Ärztin an Mutters Bauchwand presst. Die junge Frau dreht den Bildschirm unter fortlaufenden Erklärungen in meine Richtung, damit ich die ineinanderfließenden grauweißen Flächen, welche die unterschiedlichen Organe darstellen, besser sehen kann. Gleich zu Beginn habe ich ihr gesagt, ich sei Kollegin, hätte hier im Krankenhaus einen Teil meiner Ausbildung absolviert, arbeite jedoch seit Jahren in der Psychiatrie. Ihre Art, mit Mutter und mir umzugehen, wirkt natürlich, sie ist durch meine Anwesenheit nicht eingeschüchtert und erklärt uns, sie könne wegen der aufgeblähten Darmschlingen nicht feststellen, was der Grund für die Beschwerden sei. Ein MRI würde weiterhelfen, und wenn wir Glück hätten, gäbe es am Vormittag noch einen Untersuchungstermin.

Während sich Mutter langsam anzieht, hole ich einen Rollstuhl am Informationsschalter in der Eingangshalle und schiebe sie mit einem dankenden Gruß für die Ärztin zurück in den Wartebereich. Nach einer halben Stunde, während der wir still nebeneinander sitzen und lustlos und unkonzentriert in den dort ausliegenden bunten Magazinen blättern, krächzt hell eine Frauenstimme aus dem Lautsprecher Mutters Namen. Sie solle zum Röntgentrakt kommen. Nachdem das MRI durchgeführt ist, werden wir mehr über die Ursache ihrer wochenlangen Übelkeit wissen, die ich inzwischen nicht mehr auf eine Infektion zurückführe. Mutter ahnt vermutlich dasselbe, aber wir sprechen es nicht aus. Vor zwanzig Jahren hatte sie bereits eine Operation wegen Unterleibskrebs hinter sich gebracht, später war sie an Brustkrebs erkrankt und musste sich nach dessen Entfernung einer Bestrahlung unterziehen. Sie hatte alles ohne Murren akzeptiert, die bleierne Müdigkeit, die sie überwältigt hatte, bezeichnete sie als »Schlafkrankheit«, die es ihr endlich erlaube, ungestraft im Bett zu bleiben. Sie hatte sich »durch-gekämpft«, wie sie einmal sagte, und nie den Anschein erweckt, als hätte sie Angst vor dem Tod.

Mutter ist in den Untersuchungsraum verschwunden. Im Fenster gegenüber der Wartekoje, in der ich Platz genommen habe, spiegeln sich die Umrisse meines Körpers, mein Gesicht kann ich nicht erkennen, es ist überlagert von den Umrissen der auf dem Parkplatz in der Morgensonne schimmernden Autos. Ich sehe einige Menschen, die hierhergekommen sind, um eine Untersuchung zu machen, deren Ergebnis vielleicht ihr Leben verändern wird, eine junge Frau mit einem schreienden Kind, das sie auf dem Arm trägt, ein alter Mann, der auf Krücken gestützt ein Bein schleppend nachzieht.

In meine Beobachtungen versunken, reagiere ich zunächst nicht, als mich ein Arzt anspricht, den ich aus dem Studium kenne und den ich hier nicht erwartet hätte. Wir hatten gemeinsam für die Anatomieprüfung gelernt und mit anderen Studenten, die zu unserer Seziergruppe gehörten, an den Wochenenden Ausflüge aufs Land unternommen, um dem alles durchdringenden Gestank nach Formalin zu entkommen. Auf seine Frage, warum ich hier sei, erzähle ich von Mutter. Er gibt mir seine Telefonnummer, ich verspreche, mich bei ihm zu melden. In einer anderen Situation hätte ich mich darauf gefreut, Erinnerungen über Bekannte aus der gemeinsamen Zeit auszutauschen, doch ich mag nicht reden, habe mir am Morgen einen Harnisch übergestreift, um gewappnet zu sein. Die junge Ärztin gibt mir nach einer Weile Bescheid, ich könne Mutter in den zweiten

Stock begleiten, sie würde auf alle Fälle stationär aufgenommen, ich solle im Sekretariat der Röntgenabteilung fragen, ob ich mit dem zuständigen Kollegen über den Befund sprechen könne.

Während Mutter im Sechsbettzimmer auf der Station erschöpft von den Anstrengungen des Morgens vor sich hin döst, sitze ich im Untergeschoss des Krankenhauses in einem dunklen Raum neben dem zuständigen Oberarzt. Er zeigt mir die Schichtaufnahmen, erklärt, die gesamte Bauchhöhle sei zugewachsen, was in absehbarer Zeit jegliche Nahrungsaufnahme verhindern würde, der Speisebrei könne kaum noch vom Magen in den Darm passieren. Aller Wahrscheinlichkeit nach handle es sich um Bauchspeicheldrüsenkrebs in fortgeschrittenem Stadium, die Metastasen hätten bereits eine beträchtliche Größe erreicht. Ich betrachte den Schirm, während er in einer schwungvollen Bewegung, die von einem schnalzenden Ton der zuschnappenden Haltevorrichtung begleitet wird, die Magnetresonanzschichtbilder auf einer milchig weiß hinterleuchteten Glasfläche platziert. Er erklärt mir in kollegialem Ton, was da an grauen Flecken im Bauchraum einer alten Frau zu sehen ist. Normalerweise sitzt er hier alleine in diesem konturlosen Zimmer, dessen Wände in der Tiefe der Dunkelheit verschwinden, und diktiert Befunde, die dann von den Kollegen an der Bettenfront den Opfern mitzuteilen sind. Verwüstung, Zersetzung, das sind die Worte, die sich mir aufdrängen, während er in seinen Erklärungen innehält, die Hand, mit der er an den unscharfen Konturen der Krebsgeschwülste entlangfährt, sinken lässt. Als sich unsere Blicke begegnen, murmelt er, da könne man wohl nichts mehr machen. Mit einem leisen »Danke« stehe ich von meinem Platz auf, nehme die Hand des Kollegen, die er mir mit einem verlegenen Lächeln entgegenstreckt, halte inne, als er seine Linke an meinem Oberarm legt und mit einem Räuspern sagt, es tue ihm leid.

Der Weg vom Untergeschoss hinauf zur Station erscheint mir lang, ich setze mich nach dem ersten Treppenabsatz auf einen der Warteplätze im Zwischengeschoss, den Blick durch eine Glasfront auf den Hügel gegenüber gerichtet, an dem sich mehrere Zeilen mit Einfamilienhäusern hinaufziehen bis knapp unter den Waldrand. Dort in einer der obersten Straßen habe ich früher oft bei meiner Schulfreundin übernachtet, bin mit einem kleinen Rucksack, gefüllt mit Nachthemd, Schulheften und Gemüse, das mir Mutter aus unserem Schrebergarten mitgegeben hatte, vor der Eingangstüre gestanden und habe gewartet, bis meine Freundin mir öffnete. Bei ihr zu Hause konnte ich ein Wochenende lang in ein anderes Leben eintauchen. Ihre Mutter kam ursprünglich aus London, und es gab Curry mit Chutney zu Mittag und um fünf Uhr schwarzen Tee mit Milch. Ich fühlte mich aufgehoben in der Familie meiner Freundin, doch gleichzeitig dachte ich an meine Mutter, wusste, dass Vater bei Vollmond abends betrunken nach Hause kommen würde.

Während ich aus dem Fenster sehe, befinde ich mich

in einem zeitleeren Raum, den ich nach Belieben dehnen kann, fühle meinen Körper nicht. Auch wenn ich weiter in der Kindheit verweile, einer Zeit, als Mutters Tod noch fern lag, wird mein Zögern ihr Leben nicht verlängern. Als ich bei ihr im Zimmer ankomme, sieht sie mich fragend an, und ich bitte sie, mir auf den Gang hinaus zu folgen. Sie nimmt meine Hand, wir gehen zu einer Sitzecke, nehmen Platz. »Es ist Krebs«, ich blicke Mutter in die Augen, versuche zu schildern, was ich auf den Bildern gesehen habe, berichte vom Chaos in ihrem Bauch, den Ablegern, die sich überall eingenistet haben und schuld an ihren Beschwerden sind. Mutter senkt ihren Blick. »Ich hatte bereits so etwas erwartet. Was meinst Du, gibt es noch Chancen?« Ich verneine. Alle Behandlungen würden nur das Leiden verlängern, doch wir sollten die Befundbesprechung abwarten.

Am Nachmittag sitzen wir im Büro des Chefarztes, er meint, er könne nicht vorhersagen, wie lange Mutter noch zu leben habe, die Zeitspanne reiche von ein paar Wochen bis zu einigen Monaten. Nach einem Moment des Schweigens sagt Mutter, sie würde das Schicksal annehmen, das ihr bevorstehe. Sie erhebt sich als Erste von ihrem Stuhl, und als sie das Büro bereits verlassen hat, hält der Chefarzt mich diskret an der Schulter fest, sagt freundlich, wir sollten uns melden, wenn wir Hilfe und Rat benötigten. Ich nicke ihm dankend zu, doch im Stillen denke ich, dass wir immer allein zurechtgekommen sind, ich habe in meiner Familie nichts anderes gelernt. Draußen auf dem Flur, nachdem ich die Türe hinter uns geschlossen habe, sagt Mutter unvermittelt mit fester Stimme »Komm wir gehen heim sterben«. Wir verabschieden uns bei den Schwestern und Ärzten, die geschäftig ihrer Arbeit nachgehen, einige grüßen knapp, alles ist gesagt, jedes weitere Wort zu viel. Man fühlt als Betroffener Scham, wenn man den Ablauf der Routine des Heilens mit den Belangen des Todes stört. Wir fahren nach Hause, Mutters »zu Hause«. Das Fenster im Schlafzimmer steht offen, ich habe am Morgen vergessen, es zu schließen. In der Wohnung ist es eiskalt und still.

4

Nach der Rückkehr aus dem Krankenhaus sagte Mutter, sie wolle einschlafen und nicht mehr aufwachen, ich solle ihr doch eine Spritze verabreichen. Sie bat mich darum, meine ärztlichen Kenntnisse dafür zu verwenden, ihr einen leichten Tod zu ermöglichen. Ich war überrascht und entsetzt, doch ich erinnerte mich an einen früheren Satz von ihr, den ich damals ihrem trockenen Humor zugeschrieben hatte. »Wenn es so weit ist, hilfst Du mir, damit ich von hier verschwinden kann und nichts mehr mitbekomme.« Als ich ihr sagte, ich würde ihr den »Erlösungstod«, wie sie es nannte, verweigern, reagierte sie unwirsch. An den darauffolgenden Abenden, nachdem sich Mutter für ihre Bitte entschuldigt hatte und die Spannung zwischen uns sich langsam legte, haben wir lange Gespräche geführt und versucht uns vorzustellen, wie sich die nächsten Wochen oder Monate entwickeln würden. Ich beschrieb ihr, was aus medizinischer Sicht zu erwarten sei, wenn sie keine Nahrung mehr zu sich nehmen könne und aufhören würde zu trinken. Schließlich sagte Mutter, sie wolle die Zeit des Abschieds miterleben, wie auch immer sie sich gestalten würde.

Seit heute ist ihre Stimmung leichter, und sie verfolgt meine Vorbereitungen zu ihrem einundneunzigsten Geburtstag mit Neugier. 24. Oktober, das Telefon klingelt, Gratulationen, Blumensendungen. Mutter erzählt ihren Freunden, dass dies ihr letzter Geburtstag ist, und die Pausen lassen ahnen, wie ihre Gesprächspartner um Fassung ringen, nicht glauben können, was sie hören. Sie versprechen, in den nächsten Tagen vorbeizukommen, und Mutter sagt, sie sollen kommen, ja doch. Zunächst dachte ich, ich könnte für zwei Tage nach Basel fahren, um meine Stellenverhandlungen weiterzuführen und um ein paar warme Kleidungsstücke zu holen. Doch ich werde hierbleiben, Mutter braucht jemanden, der ihr Gesellschaft leistet, eine Kleinigkeit kocht und ihr beim Aufstehen hilft, wenn der Schwindel sie plagt. Selbst wenn die Frauen der Hauskrankenpflege zwei Mal am Tag vorbeikämen, mein Bruder abends nach der Arbeit den Einkauf erledigen würde, ließe es mir keine Ruhe, Mutter über Stunden hinweg alleine zu wissen. Ihr Dahindösen, ihren Schlaf werde ich unaufdringlich mit den Geräuschen der notwendigen Verrichtungen in Küche und Wohnzimmer begleiten, werde mich mit ihr an früher erinnern, wenn wir gemeinsam alte Fotos betrachten, werde ihr etwas vorlesen, mit ihr Karten spielen, werde versuchen, ihr so gut ich kann die Angst vor dem Tod zu nehmen. Ein feiner akustischer Teppich aus Geschirrgeklapper, Rascheln von Zeitungsseiten, dem Rauschen des Wasserstrahls auf dem Boden des stählernen Abwaschbeckens, dem hellen Quietschen der Kühlschranktür, dem kurzen Knipsen des Lichtschalters soll den Tod noch eine Weile davon abhalten, ans Fenster zu klopfen. Es soll sein wie damals, als ich in meiner Kindheit mit Bauchschmerzen auf dem Sofa lag und Mutter den weiten Raum, der sich hinter meinen Augenlidern auftat, mit der Musik ihres vorsichtigen Tuns in der Küche füllte.

Die ganze Familie ist zu Mutters Geburtstag gekommen, und ich habe Champagner und belegte Brötchen beim Wirt in der Altstadt bestellt. Sie scheint sich zu freuen, liegt auf dem Sofa, nimmt an den Gesprächen teil, sieht uns beim Essen zu. Sie will, dass wir essen, auch wenn sie nichts zu sich nehmen kann, sie nippt an ihrem Glas, nimmt einen winzigen Schluck. Es herrscht eine friedliche Stimmung, nicht traurig, eher aufgeräumt, vertrauter als bei früheren Familientreffen. Mutter ist mittendrin, mit warmen Wangen, die röter leuchten als sonst. Die Haut in ihrem Gesicht riecht nach der Creme aus der blauen Dose, die sie seit ihrer Jugend verwendet und deren Duft ich mit meiner Kindheit verbinde. Erinnerungen an die Umkleidekabine des Stadtbades werden wach, Mutter hat einen Fuß auf den kniehohen Holzlattenrost gestellt und verteilt die weiße Masse auf den Unterschenkeln. Sommerferien, wir haben gemeinsam unsere morgendlichen Bahnen im Freibad gezogen. »Mama, weißt Du noch, wie wir um die Wette geschwommen sind?« Ich halte ihre kalten Hände, sitze neben ihr auf dem Sofa und lege meinen Kopf an ihre Schulter, beobachte meinen Bruder, wie er versucht, ein

Foto von uns zu machen, wie unabsichtlich, und ich denke, dass ich das Bild später nicht mehr ansehen werde, weil es unerträglich sein wird. Mein Bruder ist bemüht, fröhlich zu wirken, seine beiden Söhne sind zu Beginn etwas schüchtern, doch mit der Zeit reden alle durcheinander, erzählen heitere Begebenheiten. Es ist, als hätten alle ein stilles Übereinkommen getroffen. Die Urenkelin spielt mittendrin auf dem Teppich, in der nahen Kirche läuten die Glocken den Abend ein, ich stehe auf und schließe das Fenster, weil man das eigene Wort nicht versteht.

Als ich im August bei Mutter zu Besuch war, habe ich zum ersten Mal mitbekommen, wie sie zu Mittag beim Geläut halblaut das »Vaterunser« betete. Es überraschte mich, weil in unserer Familie nie laut gebetet worden war. Mit sieben Jahren ging ich in die Vorbereitung für die Erstkommunion, und damals gab es niemanden in der Familie, der mich begleitete oder der mit mir die Sprüche und Gebete eingeübt hätte. Ich schämte mich ein wenig, weil ich von den Sonntagsmessen, dem Duft von Weihrauch und dem hellen Klingeln der Ministrantenglocken fasziniert war. Es war etwas Besonderes, oben im Chor neben der Orgel zu stehen und mit den anderen Schülern unserer Klasse »Großer Gott wir loben Dich« zu singen. Wir waren nicht religiös zu Hause, Vater glaubte an nichts mehr, wie er beteuerte, »wenn Gott wirklich Gott gewesen wäre, dann hätte er so manches nicht zugelassen«. Worauf er damit anspielte, konnte ich damals nicht sagen, doch später vermutete ich, er meinte seine Erlebnisse im Zweiten Weltkrieg. Mutter war vor einiger Zeit wieder in die evangelische Kirche eingetreten, ein lang gehegtes Bedürfnis, wie sie sagte, das mich, als sie mir davon erzählte, zutiefst erstaunte. Sie war protestantisch erzogen worden, es existierte in unserem Familienalbum ein Bild von ihr zur Konfirmation, auf dem sie, gekleidet in ein dunkles Kostüm mit weißem Spitzenkragen vor einer Atelierkulisse, die eine weite Landschaft zeigt, eine Hand auf eine Stuhllehne legt und ein wenig kokett in die Kamera blickt. Soweit ich mich erinnern kann, gab es von meiner Firmung kein einziges Bild. Der Termin war für meine Eltern eher eine gesellschaftliche Pflichterfüllung, und als ich meinen Bruder vor Tagen danach fragte, erinnerte er sich nicht daran, mein Pate gewesen zu sein. Gelegentlich kam es vor, dass wir auf einer Familienwanderung eine malerische Dorfkirche betraten, an deren Eingang Vater, kaum für uns andere wahrnehmbar, seine Finger ins Weihwasser tauchte, begleitet von einem verschämten Räuspern. Mutter kramte dann wie nebenbei Münzen hervor, die sie in den Opferstock warf, um vor einem Seitenaltar zwei kleine Kerzen anzuzünden, eine für ihren ältesten Sohn, der mit achtzehn verstorben war, eine für ihre Mutter. Ihr Gebet letzten Sommer erschien mir, als würde eine Regel gebrochen, nach der Glaubensdinge zwischen uns ausgespart blieben.

Ich schenke Champagner nach, lasse das Tablett mit den Brötchen herumgehen und setze mich auf den freien Stuhl neben meinen Bruder. Inzwischen hat Mutter ihn gebeten, das Fotoalbum aus dem Schrank zu holen, weil sie von unseren Wanderungen im Hochschwabgebirge in den Sechzigerjahren zu erzählen begonnen hat, einer Zeit, als wir noch vollzählig waren und an die ich einige Erinnerungen habe, die ich mit Geborgenheit verbinde. Mutter zeigt auf ein Bild, ich sitze als Dreijährige im Rucksack auf Vaters Rücken, sie selbst trägt ein Dirndl, unser älterer Bruder steht in kurzen Lederhosen mit Trägern und kariertem Hemd etwas abseits und blickt fragend in die Kamera. Mein Bruder und ich erzählen Geschichten aus der Zeit und lachen, weil sie sich so unterscheiden. Meine Brüder sind gemeinsam aufgewachsen, ich kam als unerwartete Nachzüglerin später dazu und wuchs, nach dem Tod des Ältesten und der frühen Heirat meines zweiten Bruders, alleine auf. Außer meiner Katze, den Wellensittichen und später dem Hund hatte ich niemanden, mit dem ich mich gegen die Schwermut meiner Eltern verbünden konnte.

5

Mutter liegt auf dem Sofa neben der Terrassentür, erschöpft von der Morgentoilette und vom kargen Frühstück, ein paar Schlucken Malzkaffee, zwei Löffel Haferbrei, und wartet auf Stuhlgang, damit sie ihren geblähten Bauch entlasten kann. Ich biete ihr eine leichte Massage an, die sie ablehnt, der Pfefferminztee, den sie schluckweise trinkt, würde ihr besser helfen. Seit ich mich erinnern kann, hat Mutter im Garten verschiedene Sorten Minze gepflanzt und die getrockneten Blätter, die ich ihr aufgebrüht habe, stammen aus ihrem kleinen Kräuterbeet, auf das sie so stolz ist.

Der Amtsarzt kommt, um zu beurteilen, ob Mutter Pflegegeld erhalten soll. Er ist anfangs zurückhaltend und wird im Verlauf gesprächiger, und es stellt sich heraus, dass wir gemeinsame Bekannte in Berlin haben, wohin ich alle zwei Jahre im November zum Kongress der deutschen Psychiater fahre. Ich wohne dann bei Freunden in Prenzlauer Berg, doch diesmal hätte ich, wie sich herausstellt, das Gästezimmer in ihrer Altbauwohnung gar nicht benutzen können, weil der Sohn des Amtsarztes seit einigen Wochen dort wohnt. Als er das erzählt, müssen wir lachen, auch Mutter, die froh ist, dass sich die Unterhaltung nicht mehr um ihre Gebrechen dreht, schmunzelt über den Zufall. Nachdem er wieder gegangen ist, meint sie, ich solle auf jeden Fall wie geplant auch dieses Jahr nach Berlin fahren. Allzulange würde sie es ohnehin nicht mehr schaffen. Ich setze mich neben sie und versuche sie abzulenken, schlage ihr vor, das höhenverstellbare Pflegebett, das wir bereits beim Einzug in die Wohnung erstanden haben, ins Wohnzimmer zu stellen. Sie könne dann den ganzen Tag bequem im Bett verbringen und die Aussicht ins Freie genießen. Mir ist unwohl bei dem Gedanken, dass jede Handlung, die über den Alltag hinausgeht, dem Tod den Weg bereiten wird. Mutter will nichts davon wissen, sie liegt lieber auf dem harten, niedrigen Sofa, von dem sie mittlerweile schwer aufsteht. Es braucht Zeit, sie soll selbst bestimmen, wann sie für den Umzug bereit ist. Das Gespräch mit dem Amtsarzt scheint Mutter vor Augen geführt zu haben, wie sehr sie inzwischen auf andere angewiesen ist. Sie kann nicht mehr ohne Unterstützung ins Badezimmer, kann sich nichts mehr zu essen zubereiten. Sie hat mir den Rücken zugedreht, liegt mit leicht angewinkelten Beinen auf der Seite, gibt zu verstehen, dass sie allein sein will, die Dinge mit sich selbst abmachen.

Draußen vor dem Fenster sehe ich auf die Bäume im Nachbarsgarten, das Laub hat sich gelb verfärbt, und muss an das Foto denken, das Mutter, mit einem strahlenden Lächeln im Gesicht, auf einer Bank im Garten der Großeltern zeigt. In den Armen wiegt sie ein kleines, in eine Decke gewickeltes Kind, am rechten unteren Rand ist das Datum notiert, eine Woche nach meiner Geburt, es ist Frühling, der alte Birnbaum trägt helle kleine Blätter. Ein paar Monate später habe ich laut Mutters Erzählungen das erste Mal »Mama« zu ihr gesagt und bald werde ich das letzte Mal »Mama« zu ihr sagen, zu einem Gesicht, das mich damals anlächelte und das ich jetzt noch immer zum Lächeln bringe, wenn ich ihr sage, wie gern ich sie habe oder dass sie gut aussieht, wenn wir mit der Morgentoilette fertig sind und sie für einige Augenblicke entspannt im Sofa lehnt und den Amseln, Meisen und Finken zusieht, wie sie am schwankenden Vogelhäuschen herumturnen.

6

28. Oktober. Todestag von Vater. Ich habe das Schmerzpflaster auf Mutters Rücken, das ich jeden dritten Tag
wechsle, mit dem heutigen Datum beschriftet. Wir sprechen über Vater, ich zünde eine Kerze an, stelle sie auf
das Fensterbrett, sie wird vierundzwanzig Stunden
brennen. Ich tue es, um die Familie, die sich auflöst, zusammenzuhalten und um etwas gegen meine Traurigkeit
zu tun. An Mutters Blick kann ich erahnen, wie sie sich
vorstellt, dass ich in ein paar Wochen auch für sie eine
Kerze entzünden werde. Mutter hat wieder öfter von
Vater gesprochen, von seinem Tod im Pflegeheim, wo er
die beiden letzten Jahre seines Lebens zugebracht hatte.
Ein paar Wochen vor seinem Tod versöhnten sich meine Eltern, nachdem sie sich viele Jahre nur aus der Ferne
gesehen hatten, weil Vater ihr nie verzeihen konnte, dass
sie ausgezogen war. Ihr Satz »Er soll nicht böse auf mich
sein, dass ich in der letzten Nacht nicht an seinem Bett
gesessen bin, bis er gehen konnte« hat mich erstaunt,
denn ich glaubte damals, sie entschied sich bewusst dafür, nach Hause zu gehen und ihn seinem Schicksal zu
überlassen.

Mutter wird nicht mehr fünfundneunzig Jahre alt

werden, so wie sie es bei ihrer Geburtstagsfeier letztes Jahr angekündigt hat. Damals meinte sie, hundert zu werden sei ihr dann doch zu mühsam, aber vier Jahre wolle sie, so es ihr vergönnt sei, noch auf dieser Welt verbringen. Es fiele ihr deutlich schwerer, sich über Neues zu freuen, und für die Zeiten, die jetzt auf ihre alte Welt zukommen würden, hätte sie wohl nicht mehr genügend Kraft. Sie habe viel gesehen, den Krieg überlebt, ihre Kinder großgezogen, einen Sohn und ihren Mann begraben. Mutter war im Lauf des Jahres bereits zwei Mal im Krankenhaus gewesen, das hat sie seelische Kraft gekostet. Zuerst wegen einer schweren Zuckererkrankung, die plötzlich entdeckt worden war, dann wegen eines Nabelbruchs, der operiert werden musste. Nachdem sie aus der Narkose erwacht war, hatte sie ungeheure Schmerzen, die von einem Wirbelbruch herrührten, den sie während der Lagerung auf dem Operationstisch erlitten hatte. Nach ihrer Rückkehr in die Wohnung hat ihr der Hausarzt das Schmerzpflaster verordnet. Bereits zwei Wochen später schöpfte sie wieder Zuversicht und konnte bald kleine Strecken selbstständig mit Hilfe des Rollators zurücklegen, was sie mir nach meiner Abreise bei unseren täglichen Telefonaten mit großem Stolz erzählte. Mich beruhigte die Kraft, die sie entwickelte, um wieder zu genesen, so konnte ich mich wieder meinem eigenen Leben zuwenden. Jetzt, nur ein paar Monate später, liegt vor ihr nicht mehr die Heilung, sondern das Ende des Leidens, von dem sie und ich noch nicht wissen, wie es verlaufen wird.

Mutter beginnt zu verstehen, dass manches unweigerlich das letzte Mal geschieht, und ich erkenne in ihren Augen ein Erstaunen, als würde sie die Welt auf eine Art inniger betrachten. Früher konnte sie Momente der Freude nur selten genießen. Es gab zwar Augenblicke des bewussten Innehaltens, an Tagen im Garten, im Schatten der Bäume, wenn sie im alten Liegestuhl saß, dessen ausgebleichte bunte Stoffbahnen schon bessere Tage gesehen hatten. Sie blickte dann hinauf in die sonnendurchfluteten Blätter des alten Apfelbaums, der im Herbst seine kleinen runzeligen Früchte tragen würde, und ließ das Buch, in dem sie gerade las, auf ihre Oberschenkel sinken. Doch meist war Mutter beschäftigt, konnte nicht ruhen, und wenn ich sie fragte, warum sie nicht zufrieden sein konnte, bevor eine Arbeit erledigt war, warum sie nicht der Müdigkeit nachgab und eine Pause einlegte, wusste sie nicht, wovon ich sprach. Jetzt in den letzten Tagen wendet sie sich den kleinen Dingen zu, die Zeit der Unrast ist vorbei, sie streift sanft und versonnen über die Haut ihrer schlanken Hände, wenn sie sich unbeobachtet fühlt, lobt den Geruch des Malzkaffees, den ich ihr am Morgen zubereite. Sie riecht daran, lässt den ersten Schluck der braunen Flüssigkeit lange im Mund, schmeckt der milchigen Bitterkeit nach, sieht zufrieden auf die Terrasse draußen und legt nach einer Weile den Kopf auf das Kissen. Vorsichtig löse ich die Tasse aus ihren Händen, bedacht, sie nicht zu erschrecken, sie ist eingeschlafen, ihr Gesichtsausdruck ist friedvoll.

7

Mutters Bauch wächst und wird langsam den Rest des Körpers dominieren, zuletzt auch ihren bisher ungetrübten Verstand. Sie nimmt wenig Nahrung zu sich, die sie oft nach wenigen Minuten als gelblich schaumige Brühe unter Anstrengung wieder heraufwürgt. Sie lehnt ab, als ich ihr vorschlage, eine Infusion zu verabreichen, weil sie weiß, wie brüchig ihre Venen inzwischen sind. Bereits die geringste Berührung mit der scharfen Nadel lässt die Wände der Blutgefäße zerreißen. In mir kommt das Gefühl auf, ich wäre schuld daran, wenn Mutter nicht genügend Flüssigkeit zu sich nimmt, was ihren Tod beschleunigen würde. Als Tochter bereitet mir die Situation Abscheu und Mühe, ich finde mich schwer zurecht in der Rolle der Ärztin, die im Kopf die Trinkmenge auflistet, sich die schlechten Werte der Nierenfunktion vorstellt, die Auswirkungen auf den Gesamtorganismus abwägt. Es gilt, alles medizinisch Sinnvolle zu unternehmen, um Mutters Leiden zu lindern, doch sehe ich ebenso ihr Bedürfnis nach Ruhe. Alles in mir sträubt sich dagegen, ihr Schmerzen zuzufügen. Sie zieht sich mehr und mehr aus der Welt zurück, schläft oft, und ich bin gezwungen, Entscheidungen zu treffen, ohne diese vorher mit ihr zu besprechen, wie die, ihr eine Spritze gegen den Brechreiz oder eine Tablette gegen die Angst zu geben, die sich nun häufiger einzuschleichen beginnt. Die nötigen Medikamente verschreibt der Hausarzt, der aber immer seltener vorbeikommt. Meine Befürchtung, Mutter könnte einen Darmverschluss oder eine Lungenembolie entwickeln, wächst. Solche Komplikationen würden mich dazu zwingen, sie ins Krankenhaus zu bringen, was sie unter keinen Umständen will. Dort könnte ich sie kaum vor der Geschäftigkeit des Betriebes und seinen hektischen Routinehandlungen bewahren. Mutter möchte zu Hause sterben, sie hat mich mehrfach darum gebeten. Wenn ich sie beim Waschen am Morgen unterstütze, hebe ich eine kleine Hautfalte an ihrem Unterarm von der Muskelfaszie und beobachte, wie lange sie benötigt, bis die Oberfläche sich wieder glättet, um den Bedarf an Flüssigkeit zu prüfen. Ich telefoniere mit zwei meiner engsten Freunde, beide Ärzte, sie betreuen täglich sterbende Patienten, haben große Erfahrung, die sie bereitwillig mit mir teilen. Meist gehe ich kurz auf die Terrasse oder in den Hausflur, um nicht in Anwesenheit von Mutter Details ihres sich verändernden Zustandes zu schildern. Sie sind die einzigen Personen, denen ich meine Sorgen und Befürchtungen ungeschönt mitteilen kann, meine Angst vor Komplikationen und meine Befürchtung, in dieser Situation nicht zu genügen. Sie hören an meiner Stimme, wie sehr mich die Situation an manchen Tagen belastet, wenn ich meine Dünnhäutigkeit nur mit Mühe überdecken kann.

In den Stunden, in denen Mutter tief schläft, kümmere ich mich um den Haushalt. Das Nötigste gehe ich rasch einkaufen, wie Gemüse, Milch und Käse für mich, Haferflocken und Tiefkühlspinat für Mutter, die einzigen Nahrungsmittel, auf die sie noch Lust hat. Mit schlechtem Gewissen verlasse ich die Wohnung, immer von der Sorge getrieben, Mutter könnte aufwachen und nach mir rufen. Nach der zurückgezogenen Routine in der kleinen Wohnung erdrückt mich die Stimmung im hell erleuchteten Einkaufszentrum mit Musikberieselung im Hintergrund und der Unmenge an Waren in den hohen Regalen. Die alten Frauen, die vor mir mit ihren großen, beinahe leeren Einkaufswagen an der Kasse stehen, erinnern mich an Mutter, die oft hier war, seit in der Altstadt alle kleinen Läden geschlossen wurden. Manchmal gehe ich rasch zur Apotheke, wo man mich zuvorkommend bedient, weil alle wissen, dass Mutter, die hier ihre Blutdruckmedikamente oder die Venensalbe holte, nicht mehr selbst in den Laden kommen wird. Die Apothekerin lässt Grüße ausrichten. Für die notwendigen Rezepte gehe ich zum Hausarzt, setze mich ins überfüllte Wartezimmer, höre den Menschen zu, wie sie mit der Sprechstundenhilfe über ihre Beschwerden sprechen, über ihren letzten Krankenhausaufenthalt oder über die vermutliche Todesursache von verstorbenen Bekannten.

Wenn ich dann aus dem Fenster des Wartezimmers blicke, schließe ich die Augen, und das Gebrabbel der wartenden Patienten rückt von mir ab. Der Wunsch nach einem frühen Schnee im Oktober, der alles in eine weiße weiche Decke kleiden soll, der alle Geräusche dämpfen und die Stille des Winters über die Welt stülpen möge, erfüllt mich. Schnee hat etwas Tröstliches, er verlangsamt, wenn er vom Himmel fällt, er hüllt die Landschaft in ein transparentes Leuchten, wenn er sein Tuch über alles breitet, die Kanten und Ecken schleift, seidenweich die Konturen verwischt. Erinnerungen an Spaziergänge mit Mutter stellen sich ein. Der erste Schnee fiel und wir streiften uns freudig Mäntel und Mützen über, holten die Stiefel aus dem Schrank und drängten hinaus ins weiße Gestöber, voller Erwartung, an etwas Numinosem teilzuhaben.

8

Mutter beginnt, von früher zu erzählen, und ich nutze die Gelegenheit, nach ihren Eltern und anderen Verwandten zu fragen. Ihre Stimmung ist abends meist besser. Wenn sie nicht von Brechanfällen geplagt wird, sitzt sie zurückgelehnt in ihren Kissen, wirkt gelöst. Wir sprechen nicht über das unvermeidliche Ende, obwohl wir beide daran denken. Nur diese eine gemeinsame Stunde noch. Es ist, als ob nichts uns trennen könnte. Mutter und ich waren bei meinen Besuchen oft lange beim Frühstück gesessen, um Erinnerungen an die Zeit auszutauschen, als Vater noch lebte, als ich ein kleines Mädchen war, »das Mensch«, wie ich von meinen Eltern genannt worden war. Es war über die Jahre zu einem wohligen Ritual geworden, unsere Vergangenheit heraufzubeschwören, und wir scheuten uns davor, das Gespräch zu unterbrechen, das uns in diesen Momenten so nah sein ließ.

Mutter erzählt mir von ihrem Vater, »Opa Piet«, wie er für mich und meinen Bruder hieß. Da sind die Geschichten von seinen Hasen im Garten, die sie als Kind gefüttert hatte, und von den Gänsen, mit denen er im nahen Main schwimmen gegangen war, von seinem Rückendurchschuss, den er in Verdun im Ersten Weltkrieg erlitten hatte, und davon, wie sich ihre Eltern in einem Lazarett kennengelernt hatten. Ihre Mutter war als Hilfsschwester der Krankenbaracke zugeteilt gewesen, in der er sich gerade darum bemühte, gestützt auf zwei Krücken, das Gehen wieder zu erlernen. Mutter versucht sich an die Einrichtung der Wohnküche ihrer Kindheit zu erinnern, wo in der Ecke ein Tisch für Lederwerkstücke bereitstand. Jede Woche musste sie als junges Mädchen die fertigen Gürtel und Taschen, die in Heimarbeit für die Lederfabrik in Offenbach angefertigt worden waren, zu einer Abgabestelle im Ort bringen, wobei sie einmal, durch ihre Schulkameraden abgelenkt, die Ware einfach an einer Hofeinfahrt stehen ließ, um kurz mit den anderen herumzutollen. Als sie zurückkam, war der Korb weg, das Geld für eine ganze Woche Arbeit verloren, wofür sie dann von ihrem Vater, der sonst nie handgreiflich geworden war, eine Tracht Prügel bekommen sollte.

Nach ein paar Schlucken Tee kommt Mutter auf die Zeit ihres Ankommens hier in der obersteirischen Kleinstadt zu sprechen. Sie hatte Vater, dem sie Briefe ins englische Kriegsgefangenenlager schrieb, nicht überzeugen können, im ausgebombten Frankfurt ein gemeinsames Leben aufzubauen. So kam sie, nach einer mehrwöchigen strapaziösen Reise, die sie wegen des unregelmäßigen Fahrplans zwischen den Besatzungszonen immer wieder unterbrechen musste, mit ihren Habseligkeiten in der Kleinstadt an, wo er sie, nachdem er sechs Wochen zuvor aus einem Repatriierungszentrum in Kärnten entlassen worden war, erwartete. Ihre Aussteuer war zum Teil gestohlen worden, teils hatte sie unterwegs Leintücher und Besteck auf dem Schwarzmarkt gegen Essbares eingetauscht. Bis sich meine Eltern eine eigene Wohnung leisten konnten, dauerte es zwei Jahre. Mutter sagt, sie hatte nicht mit den einfachen Bedingungen gerechnet, die sie hier vorfand. Sie hausten beengt mit der Schwester meines Vaters und deren Mann in einem Zimmer bei den Schwiegereltern, das durch Schränke in zwei Hälften geteilt worden war. Alle wuschen sich am Becken in der Küche oder in der Waschküche im Hinterhof, die Toiletten waren im Stiegenhaus im Halbstock untergebracht. Mutters erste Schwangerschaft fiel in diese Zeit, das Kind starb bei der Geburt. Viele Tausende waren als Flüchtlinge in der Stadt in Barackensiedlungen untergebracht, Zuwanderer aus dem Sudetenland oder aus anderen Teilen Europas, von wo sie als »Volksdeutsche« vertrieben worden waren. »Zugeraste«, nannte man sie hier, sie gehörten nicht richtig dazu, unterschieden sich durch die Sprache oder ihren protestantischen Glauben, wie Mutter auch.

Schon mindestens dreißig Jahre habe ich diese Schilderungen nicht mehr gehört. In meinen Ohren haben sie sich verändert, es ist, als ob Mutter tiefer eintauchen würde in ihre Vergangenheit, als stünden ihr Details, die sie vorher nie erwähnt hatte, deutlicher vor Augen. Ich frage nach, denn es könnte die letzte Gelegenheit dazu sein. Wer genau war der »Opa« väterlicherseits, der mir auf seinem alten Waffenrad das Fahrradfahren beigebracht hat und der im Bürgerkrieg aufseiten der Arbeiter beim Aufstand gegen Dollfuß dabei gewesen war? Ich stelle Mutter auch Fragen über meine demente Großmutter väterlicherseits, die zum Abschluss ihres Lebens mit ihrer Unruhe und ihren ständigen Fragen allen auf die Nerven ging und die schließlich im Altenheim starb. Es wäre ein Frevel, Mutters Erzählung zu unterbrechen. Es ist an mir, meinem Bruder bei Gelegenheit alles zu berichten.

9

Mutter sagt, sie habe geträumt, wie sie als junges Mädchen in einem Wollkleid und dicken Strumpfhosen an einem Teich nach dem Schlittschuhlaufen darauf wartet, von ihren Eltern abgeholt zu werden. Es sei bitter kalt gewesen und niemand sei gekommen. Sie habe mich nicht wecken wollen, denn ich könne ihr die Traurigkeit des bevorstehenden Abschieds nicht abnehmen. Bald sei sie es, die mich und meinen Bruder am Ufer des zugefrorenen Teichs warten lässt. Während ich mich neben sie setze, lege ich meine Hand auf ihren Arm, der auf der Bettdecke liegt, und verharre eine Weile still, bevor ich ihr auf ihren Wunsch Schwarztee zum Frühstück bereite.

Später versuche ich mit ihr zu besprechen, was sie in den nächsten Tagen zusätzlich an Unterstützung benötigen würde, denn weiterhin ohne Hilfe ihre Pflege zu übernehmen sei für mich schwierig. Mutter möchte dem Thema ausweichen, sie sagt, es sei für sie unerträglich, bald vollständig von anderen abhängig zu sein. Vor ein paar Tagen habe ich im Depot der ortsansässigen Werkskrankenkasse einen Leibstuhl geholt, weil ich für den Zeitpunkt vorsorgen wollte, wenn sie nicht mehr aus eigener Kraft die Toilette erreicht. Der Gang zur Krankenkasse brachte mich in eine mir von früher bekannte Welt, in ein stattliches Gebäude, das zusammen mit der Musikschule und dem Werkshotel Ende des neunzehnten Jahrhunderts erbaut worden war. Seit mehr als vierzig Jahren hatte ich es nicht betreten. Der muffige Geruch im Treppenhaus hinter der schweren alten Eingangstüre erinnerte mich an einen Termin hier als kleines Mädchen an der Hand meiner Mutter. Vater sollte wegen seiner Tuberkulose einige Monate in einer Lungenheilanstalt verbringen, wobei der Antrag vom Chefarzt genehmigt werden musste. Seit damals hat sich in den Räumen fast nichts verändert.

Wenn ich mit Mutter über den Leibstuhl zu sprechen versuche, fühle ich mich wie der Überbringer schlechter Nachrichten, den man bestraft. Ihr Tonfall wird ablehnend, entwertend, wenn sie sagt, das Ungetüm würde sie nie und nimmer benützen. Es ist ein unförmiges Möbel auf kleinen Rädern, unter dessen Sitzfläche, die aus einem mit blauem Plastik überzogenen Brett besteht, ein Nachttopf eingelassen ist, den man zum Entleeren herausziehen kann. Der Weg ins Badezimmer wird täglich mühsamer, selbst mit Unterstützung des Rollators. Das selbstständige Duschen entwickelt sich zu einer Qual, denn inzwischen ist Mutter bereits zu schwach, um ohne meine Hilfe stehen zu können. Sie will es noch einmal ohne diesen Stuhl versuchen. »So weit ist es noch nicht und so viel Zeit muss sein.« Ihr unverrückbarer Widerstand, den ich nur von seltenen Gelegenheiten kenne, bedeutet mir, sie gefälligst in Ruhe zu lassen. Früher konnte sie in misslichen Lagen scherzen, sie hatte eine Art Galgenhumor, der schwierige Situationen entschärfte, doch heute gelingt ihr das nicht. Dieser Humor kam letzte Woche zum Vorschein, als ich ihr zeigte, mit welchen Hebelgriffen ich sie beim Wechsel vom Bett auf einen Stuhl besser unterstützen konnte, wenn sie im richtigen Moment mithalf. Nach dem ersten Versuch schlug Mutter vor, die Halbdrehung zu erproben, solange sie noch einigermaßen bei Kräften sei, was wir dann auch taten, bis wir im Eifer der Wiederholungen fast miteinander tanzten. Ich begleitete die Bewegungen mit einem übertrieben ausgestreckten Arm, sie quittierte mit einem schelmischen Blick und neckisch zur Seite gedrehtem Gesicht, bis wir vor Lachen die Übung abbrechen mussten.

Mutter bittet mich inständig, vorübergehend noch auf die Hauskrankenpflege zu verzichten. Sie sagt, sie würde die wechselnden Gesichter, Stimmen und körperlichen Ausdünstungen der Frauen nicht ertragen, auch nicht die ruppige Art, mit der sie von manchen behandelt würde, als sei sie ein unartiges Kind. Im Spätsommer erzählte sie, wie grob ihr die Schwestern die Stützstrümpfe angelegt oder lautstark nach ihrem Stuhlgang gefragt hatten, als sei sie schwerhörig. Dafür ist sie nun einverstanden mit dem Umzug des Bettes ins Wohnzimmer und wir planen, ihn mit Hilfe meines Bruders am Abend auszuführen. Es erscheint mir wie ein Tauschhandel, auf den ich mich vorübergehend einlassen kann, und ich sehe Mutter an, wie froh sie ist, selbst den Zeitpunkt für Veränderungen bestimmen zu können.

10

Mutters Lippen, die Zunge, die Augen sind trockener geworden. Mit feuchten Tüchern, die ich in ihrer Nähe aufhänge, versuche ich Linderung zu verschaffen, mein Bruder hat versprochen, bei seinem nächsten Besuch einen Luftbefeuchter mitzubringen. Ihr Blick hat sich verändert, wirkt ferner. Noch am Vormittag, als ich sie fragte, ob sie ein Schmerzmittel brauche, sagte sie, sie wolle nicht durch die Wirkung der Medikamente betäubt werden, wolle mitbekommen, was in ihrem Umkreis geschieht. Der Tag war anstrengend für sie, weil sie oft erbrechen musste, nach einer Weile schläft sie erschöpft ein. Ich setze mich an den Küchentisch, versuche an einem Artikel für eine Zeitung zu arbeiten, dessen Abgabetermin näherrückt. Mein Blick fällt auf den Wochenkalender, dessen Blatt ich gewechselt habe, nachdem ich einige Tage lang vergessen hatte, es zu tun. Er zeigt ein leuchtend rotes Bild von Rainer Fetting mit dem Titel »Bügler VII«, das mich in seine innere Spannung verstrickt. Der menschliche Akt, der zu erkennen ist, wirkt durch die Auflösung der Farbkonturen an seiner Vorderseite verbrüht. Sein Anblick bereitet mir körperliches Unbehagen und ich vermeide es, die Figur zu fixieren, will nicht in diese Glut hineingezogen werden.

Meine Schulfreundin aus der Volksschule hat mich angerufen und mich zu einem Spaziergang eingeladen. Wir hatten seit dem ersten Schultag die Bank vorne am Katheder miteinander geteilt. Während des Gymnasiums hatten wir uns dann aus den Augen verloren, erst dreißig Jahre später sollten wir uns hier in dieser Kleinstadt wieder über den Weg laufen, um unsere Freundschaft fortzusetzen. Sie meinte, ich solle für das Wochenende meinen Bruder bitten, nach Mutter zu sehen, ich müsse ein paar Stunden hier raus, weg vom Sterben, sonst hätte ich nicht den Atem, bis zum Schluss durchzuhalten. Sie weiß, wovon sie redet, sie hat ihre Mutter und ihren Vater bis zu deren Tod eng begleitet, teils mit Hilfe rumänischer Krankenschwestern, die rund um die Uhr die Pflege übernommen hatten. Sie kümmerte sich neben ihrer Arbeit täglich um die Eltern, die Aufsicht über die Pflegerinnen und das kleine Haus, in dem wir früher, auf ihrem Stockbett verschanzt, Comics gelesen hatten oder im Garten auf die alten Obstbäume geklettert waren, um mit verschmierten Mündern und zerrissenen Strumpfhosen wieder herunterzukommen. Sie hat recht, ich versinke hier, mein Horizont beginnt sich zu verengen, mein Rückzug zeigt exzessive Züge, doch mir fehlt die Kraft, Ablösung zu organisieren. Eingebunden in Mutters Bedürfnisse, die den Tagesablauf bestimmen, in einen Rhythmus, der nicht meinem entspricht, wache ich beim geringsten Geräusch auf, bin nach einem leisen Husten, Räuspern, nach einem leichten Stöhnen, hellwach, so als ob ich gar nicht geschlafen hätte. Diese dauernde Anspannung laugt mich aus, ich fühle mich wie von einem Nebel umhüllt. Heute kann ich nicht weg hier, ich bin zu müde. Meine Freundin ist zunächst enttäuscht über die Absage, doch wir verabreden uns für den nächsten Tag.

11

2. November, Allerseelen. Mutter sagt, als ich zum Spaziergang zum Friedhof aufbreche, ich solle Vater und meinem älteren Bruder einen Gruß ausrichten, sie mögen sie doch endlich zu sich holen, das Sterben dauere ihr bereits zu lange. Ich schlendere mit meiner Freundin in das abendliche Meer von tausenden Grablichtern, so wie früher mit Mutter, wenn wir uns, in lange Wintermäntel gehüllt, zwischen den Marmorgrabsteinen und schmiedeeisernen Kreuzen hatten treiben lassen, umgeben vom Strom der Passanten, die mit murmelnden Stimmen ihre Schritte auf gefrorenen Kies setzten, in einer seltsamen Mischung aus Andacht und Erwartung. Die Menschen hielten dann am Fußende der Grabstätten inne, versuchten die verblichenen Namen auf den Inschriften zu lesen, tuschelten miteinander und deponierten Gestecke aus Tannenreisig und Trockenblumen, um der winterlichen Eintönigkeit etwas entgegenzusetzen, bevor sich eine hauchdünne Schneeschicht darüberbreiten würde. Auch heute umfängt mich wie damals dieser wohlige Schauer, dem eine Geborgenheit innewohnt, und ich kann das Flanieren in diesem Totenpark genießen, erfreue mich am Anblick der flackernden

Kerzen und Fackeln, der im milden Lichtschein erleuchteten Gesichter, lausche den Erzählungen meiner Freundin, die viele der alten Grabstätten und die Geschichten der hier bestatteten Familien kennt. Sie ist, nach einer beruflichen Laufbahn auswärts, wieder in ihre Geburtsstadt zurückgekehrt. Wenn ich bei Mutter zu Besuch war und wir abends noch stundenlang miteinander Karten spielten, dann fragte sie mich gelegentlich wie nebenbei, ob ich mir vorstellen könnte, in Österreich zu arbeiten, um dann fast im selben Atemzug zu bekräftigen, wie froh sie sei, dass ich mir in der Schweiz ein solides Leben aufgebaut habe. Doch hörte ich zur gleichen Zeit ihren Wunsch, ich möge wieder in ihre Nähe kommen. Ich sagte ihr mit gespieltem Ernst, dass ich froh sein könne, es geschafft zu haben, mich von ihr zu entfernen und nicht im Geringsten daran dachte, etwas zu ändern, worauf wir beide lachen mussten. Nach einer kurzen Weile pflegte Mutter dann noch zu sagen »Bleib in der Schweiz, man weiß nie, was kommt«.

Als ich nach dem Spaziergang die Wohnung betrete, sitzt Mutter im Bett und mein Bruder auf einem Stuhl neben ihr, der Fernseher läuft in voller Lautstärke. Die Situation befremdet mich. Als ich noch klein war, gab es in den ersten Jahren meines Aufwachsens in unserem Haushalt noch keinen Fernseher, die Nachbarn im Mietshaus, in dem wir wohnten, hatten im Hinterhof musiziert und gesungen, Karten gespielt oder im Garten bis zum Einbruch der Dämmerung geplaudert. Später zogen sich alle in ihre Wohnungen zurück, jede Familie saß allein vor dem Gerät, aus den Fenstern flimmerte nervöses graublaues Licht. Ich sehe seit mehr als zwanzig Jahren nicht mehr fern, nur gelegentlich bei Freunden ein Fußballspiel oder die Nachrichten. Selten gibt es Abende, an denen ich einen Film auf DVD abspiele, und dann kommt eine absurde Sehnsucht nach den Zeiten in mir auf, als ich abends mit meinen Eltern einen Spielfilm ansehen durfte. Es war ein friedlicher Moment, wenn wir uns im Wohnzimmer auf das Sofa setzten, das gemeinsame Sehen verband uns. Doch am Ende blieb ich allein inmitten meiner Familie zurück, ohne die Helden, die mutigen und schönen Männer und Frauen, in deren Leben sich die wahren Dramen abspielten, war zurück in meinem Leben als Kind einer Arbeiterfamilie in einer Kleinstadt in Österreich. Es erscheint mir trostlos, wenn sich Mutter jetzt mit Fernsehen aus den ihr verbleibenden Lebensstunden stiehlt.

12

Am Morgen macht Mutter Gymnastik im Bett. Ihr Bewegungsradius hat sich eingeschränkt, sie kreist ihre Hände, bewegt ihren Kopf auf dem Kissen hin und her, versucht ihre Beine anzuziehen. Seit jeher war sie darum bemüht, ihre Gelenkigkeit zu erhalten und nicht alle Wehwehchen der Medizin zu überlassen. Inzwischen merke ich selbst, wie sich mein Körper verändert, wie gewohnte Bewegungen sich eckiger anfühlen, die Knie oder die Hüften nicht mehr auf Anhieb den geschmeidigen Ablauf garantieren. Noch im letzten Sommer hatte ich die ersten äußerlichen Anzeichen des Älterwerdens nicht so ernst genommen, bis ich eines Abends über die trockene Haut meiner Unterarme strich, die unregelmäßig verteilten kleinen braunen Flecken wahrnahm und an die Altersmale der ehemaligen Nachbarin aus dem Unterstock denken musste. Als Kind hatte mich beeindruckt, wenn ihre bräunlich gesprenkelte Hand, von der ich kaum meinen Blick losreißen konnte, beim Viererschnapsen, zu dem Mutter gelegentlich eingeladen war, die Karten hielt. Es ist der schleichende Verlust des prallen Lebens, auf den man sich nicht vorbereiten kann, weil alles, was darüber erzählt wird, nicht aus dem eigenen Erleben kommt. In der letzten Zeit fallen mir immer wieder Mutters Warnungen ein. »Nimm genug Sonnencreme mit, damit Du keinen Sonnenbrand bekommst, das schadet dem Teint.« »Setz doch die Sonnenbrille auf, Krähenfüße machen ein Gesicht früh alt.« »Iss nicht so viel Süßes, Du sollst die Zähne noch im Grab mit Stolz tragen.« Lästige Kleinigkeiten für eine junge Frau Mitte zwanzig, die über die Unendlichkeit der Jugend verfügt. Ich habe keinen einzigen ihrer Ratschläge befolgt.

Diskret mit Verrichtungen in der Küche beschäftigt, warte ich, als würde ich von Mutters Streck- und Dehnbewegungen keine Notiz nehmen, bis sie wieder still liegt und nach mir ruft. Sie will mit dem Leibstuhl, den sie inzwischen akzeptiert hat, ins Bad geschoben werden und legt Wert darauf, am Waschbecken sitzend ihre Morgentoilette so weit als möglich selbstständig zu erledigen. Dann helfe ich ihr beim Anziehen, das haben wir inzwischen geübt, und sie widersetzt sich nicht groß. Sie möchte heute den Trainingsanzug und nicht das Nachthemd tragen. Nach dem Waschen bereite ich ihr Haferbrei zu, sie sagt, er würde ihrem Magen guttun, doch sie wird wieder Mühe mit der Verdauung haben. Diese letzten Geschmacksfreuden will ich ihr nicht nehmen, sie scheint die kleinsten Bissen mit Befriedigung im Mund zu behalten und zu kauen, mit Speichel zu tränken, bis sie die winzigen Portionen die Speiseröhre hinunterrutschen lässt. Haferbrei hat Mutter immer gern gegessen, er war für sie mit Heilung verbunden, und sie hat ihn manchmal gekocht, wenn sie sich nicht gut fühlte oder traurig war. Ich habe sie nicht gefragt, ob ihre Mutter für sie früher Haferbrei zubereitet hatte.

Am Vormittag kommt der junge evangelische Pfarrer zu Besuch, er hat erfahren, dass Mutter im Sterben liegt. Im letzten Jahr war sie gelegentlich sonntags in der Kirche, die um die Ecke liegt, und hatte ihn dort kennengelernt. Mutter erzählt ihm, sie würde jeden Tag zum Klang der Glocken beten, und er macht ihr den Vorschlag, doch im Anschluss an seinen Besuch gemeinsam zum Geläut das Vaterunser zu sprechen, er in der Kirche vor dem Altar und sie hier in ihrem Bett. Zunächst ist sie verdutzt und fragt ihn, ob er denn außerhalb der üblichen Zeiten läuten dürfe, worauf er schelmisch erwidert, wer denn hier nun der Pfarrer sei. Später sitzt Mutter ergriffen von dem durchdringenden, vielstimmigen Tönen, das durch die geöffnete Terrassentüre in die kleine Wohnung schallt, auf ihrem Bett und Tränen laufen über ihre Wangen, sie hält die Hände gefaltet, den Blick hinaus auf das gelbe Laub der Bäume und den darüberliegenden Himmel. Vor dem Besuch des Pfarrers hatte Mutter mich gebeten, ihre Konfirmationsurkunde aus dem Jahr 1935 in ihren Unterlagen zu suchen, was ich nicht ohne Verwunderung tat, denn ich hatte dieses Dokument noch nie gesehen. Mit einem Mal erzählte sie von ihrer Vorstellung, wir seien nichts weniger als Staubkörner im Universum, und wenn wir Glück hätten, bliebe ein Gran von der Energie, die wir auf Erden erschaffen hätten, zurück, so wie es auch noch die Energie derer gäbe, die uns vorausgegangen sind. Sie würde uns nach ihrem Tod begleiten und sie sei für mich und meinen Bruder da, auf eine andere Weise. Wenn ich in Not sei, solle ich sie rufen.

Vom Pfarrer hat Mutter ein Hinterglasbild geschenkt bekommen, eine moderne Christusdarstellung, ich klebe es an die Terrassenscheibe und räume alle anderen gerahmten Fotos von meinem Bruder, mir, den Enkelkindern und der Urenkelin weg, jetzt sind nur noch die Orchideen übrig, die sie seit Jahren hegt, sie blühen gerade. Durch das Christusbild fallen Sonnenstrahlen und werfen rote, blaue und gelbe Farbschlieren auf Mutters Bettdecke. Sie erinnern an die Farbspiele der Glasfenster auf den Steinböden in alten Kirchen, die ich auf Reisen fotografiert habe, fasziniert von der Unwirklichkeit dieser filigranen Erscheinungen, die manches Mal unerwartete neue Tönungen hervorbrachten, hingeworfen auf von unzähligen Schritten geglättete Steinoberflächen. Im Lauf der Jahre habe ich dutzende dieser Bilder gesammelt, die letzte Serie habe ich Mutter vor zwei Wochen gezeigt. Jetzt sieht sie das wechselnde Farbenspiel im Zimmer und lächelt, bedankt sich für die »Geistdecke«, mit der sie nun während des Schlafes in lichtere Sphären schweben würde.

13

Mutter will am Morgen ein Glas lauwarmes Wasser, um den Gaumen und die Zunge zu befeuchten. Ich wasche ihr das Gesicht, die Hände mit einem feuchten Lappen, anschließend döst sie eine Weile vor sich hin. Ich bereite mir Knäckebrot, Butter, Honig und Schwarztee mit Milch zum Frühstück, lese das Regionalblatt, auf das ich mich nach anfänglichen Widerständen wieder eingelassen habe, und verfolge die Berichte über die Ereignisse in dieser Gegend, mit denen ich in den letzten Jahrzehnten nur selten in Berührung kam. Manchmal, wenn mich der Hunger nach Information packt, lese ich im Internet in internationalen Zeitungen, um mitzubekommen, was in der Welt geschieht. Immer seltener ist mir danach zumute, eine Mail mit Freunden auszutauschen, denn was sollte ich ihnen schon berichten, es passiert einerseits viel, doch scheint die Zeit hier, von außen betrachtet, stehen geblieben. Dann folgt Mutters ausgedehnte Morgentoilette, die uns beide inzwischen viel Kraft kostet, anschließend verlangt sie meist nach einem Malzkaffee, um dann wieder weiterzuschlafen. In den Vormittagsstunden breitet sich eine Stille um uns aus, die ich nicht zu stören wage. Telefonieren kann ich kaum noch, die

Wohnung ist zu klein, Mutter kann mich überall hören. Jeder Kontakt nach außen erscheint mir künstlich, und es ist mir nicht möglich, am Telefon über Dinge zu sprechen, die mich und mein Leben jenseits dieser vier Wände betreffen. Dieses Leben ist aktuell zurückgestellt. Die Zukunft ist die Zeit nach Mutters Tod. Wie soll ich darüber reden, ohne Mutter zu verletzen? Auch habe ich kein Gefühl mehr für die normale Lautstärke, denn an manchen Tagen reden Mutter und ich nur leise miteinander, je nach ihrem Zustand und abhängig von ihrer Laune, die innerhalb eines Tages rasch wechseln kann. Das Klingeln des Telefons fühlt sich wie ein durch Mark und Bein dringender Lärm an. Die Aufforderung, den Hörer abzunehmen, ist physisch zu spüren, und auch wenn sich der Anrufer nur zaghaft melden will, ist er bereits mit dem Signal mitten im Raum. Ich fürchte mich vor jedem Anruf, und doch hebe ich jedes Mal ab, um die Isolation, die uns zu umschließen beginnt, zu durchbrechen und Mutter die Möglichkeit zu geben, mit Freunden zu sprechen. Wenn sie wach ist und ich ihr den Hörer reiche, nachdem ich mich durch einen Blick ihrer Bereitschaft versichert habe, bemüht sie sich, ein paar freundliche Sätze auszutauschen, doch meist winkt sie ab, und ich sage dem Anrufer, sie würde schlafen, es ginge ihr den Umständen entsprechend gut. Wir leben hier in Mutters Wohnung wie auf einem eigenen Planeten, abgeschottet von der Welt. Nur mein Bruder, ihre Haushaltshilfe Frau Gabriel und manchmal die engsten Freunde aus der Burggasse kommen noch zu Besuch. Auch Mutters Enkel, den sie früher als Tagesmutter einige Jahre gehütet hatte, und dessen Frau schauen auf dem Heimweg von der Arbeit herein und fragen, ob sie mich unterstützen könnten, worauf ich meist nichts erwidern kann, weil meine Tage hier aus einer Vielzahl von kleinsten Verrichtungen bestehen, die mir niemand abnehmen kann. Wenn mein Bruder abends kommt und leise die Eingangstür öffnet, löst er mich für eine Weile ab und ich kann meine Spaziergänge unternehmen. Geht es Mutter gut, sitzt sie im Bett und begrüßt ihn herzlich, stellt ihm Fragen zu seinem Tag, doch wenn sie zu schwach ist, nickt sie lediglich, um zu zeigen, dass sie seine Anwesenheit zur Kenntnis nimmt.

Wenn Mutters Freunde kommen, warte ich mit Tee und Kuchen auf, halte mich aber im Hintergrund. Mutter versucht ihnen Aufmerksamkeit zu schenken, doch meist döst sie nach einer Weile ein und erwacht erst, wenn die Besucher die Wohnung längst verlassen haben. Eine Nachbarin kommt jeden zweiten Tag an die Wohnungstür, wo ich sie vertröste, denn Mutter erträgt ihre Klagen über das Unglück ihres Sterbens nicht mehr. Mutter war mit ihr in den letzten Jahren fast jeden Sonntag in ein Restaurant zum Mittagessen spaziert. Sie hatte dann eine Begleiterin, bei der sie sich unterhaken konnte, wenn sie von Schwindel geplagt wurde, und im Gegenzug konnte sie ihrer Freundin, die fast erblindet war, bei Tisch behilflich sein. Sie schnitt das Fleisch oder filetierte den Fisch, wischte schnell, bevor es andere Gäste sahen, die verschüttete Sauce weg oder entfernte ein Salatblatt vom Tischtuch.

Die anderen Mitbewohnerinnen des kleinen Mietshauses haben sich zurückgezogen, keine hat mehr an Mutters Wohnungstüre geklopft. In den ersten Tagen nach Mutters Rückkehr aus dem Spital habe ich bemerkt, wie sie im Treppenhaus auswichen, was auch bei mir Unsicherheit auslöste. Diese eigentümliche Stimmung im Haus war nur erklärbar mit ihrer eigenen Angst vor Siechtum und Tod. Ihren Rückzug konnte ich wohl verstehen, doch wollte ich das bedrückende Schweigen brechen, fasste mir ein Herz und ging in den Gemeinschaftsraum, wo sie gerade Karten spielten. Ich erzählte ihnen, wie es um Mutter stand. Sie wünschten gute Besserung und wirkten erleichtert, als ich den Raum wieder verließ. Vor zwei Tagen läutete die Tochter einer Frau aus dem oberen Stock an der Wohnungstür und sagte, sie sei später an der Übernahme des Pflegebettes interessiert.

14

Mutter hat mir den Rücken zugedreht, sie will ihre Ruhe haben. Ihr Atem wird langsamer, sie schläft tief. Es ist zu früh, um ins Bett zu gehen, selbst wenn ich unter einer erdrückenden Müdigkeit leide. Ich setze mich an den Esstisch und lese weiter in den Zeitungen vom Morgen, doch kann ich mich kaum darauf konzentrieren. Das Wechselblatt des Wochenkalenders zeigt ein Bild mit dem Titel »Nachtblau« von Ernst Wilhelm Nay. Ein kühles, nüchternes Bild, ich habe es vorher noch nie gesehen, kannte auch den Maler nicht. Auf der Rückseite lese ich, dass seine Bilder unter den Nationalsozialisten als entartete Kunst eingestuft worden waren. Mutter hatte erzählt, dass sie in ihrer Schulzeit von den Geschmacklosigkeiten der modernen Kunst gehört hatte. Mit Bildbänden und auch Besuchen von Ausstellungen in Wien, Zürich, Basel, zu denen ich sie mitnahm, je nachdem, wo ich gerade wohnte, versuchte ich ihr die Malerei der Moderne zugänglich zu machen, doch Mutter reagierte oft mit negativen Kommentaren, so als hätte sich die Erziehung von damals bis heute erhalten.

Mein Bruder zieht sich in den letzten Tagen mehr und mehr von uns zurück. Er kommt später zu Besuch, geht früher, redet wenig und wirkt unnahbar. Er ruft an, er habe heute keine Zeit, das hat für mich zur Konsequenz, dass ich die Wohnung nicht für meinen üblichen Spaziergang, den ich so herbeisehne, verlassen kann. Er sagt, es sei an der Zeit, eine private Krankenschwester zu engagieren, er könne mein Zögern nicht verstehen. Wenn Mutter Hilfe von außen ablehnen würde, dürfe ich mich deswegen nicht für sie aufopfern, und legt den Hörer auf. Mutter bekommt von dem kurzen Telefongespräch nichts mit, ich gehe auf die Terrasse hinaus und atme tief durch, bleibe eine Weile, ohne mir etwas überzuziehen, bis ich vor Kälte schlottere. Ganz auf mich allein gestellt und ohne die Möglichkeit, regelmäßig nach draußen zu kommen und dem Sterben zu entfliehen, fürchte ich, die nächsten Wochen nicht durchzuhalten. Als Mutter etwas später aufwacht, erzähle ich ihr von einer Vermittlungsstelle für private Krankenpflegerinnen, die man zwar selbst bezahlen muss, dafür steht einem ein und dieselbe Pflegerin für längere Zeit zur Verfügung. Mutter reagiert unwillig und missbilligend, sie will keine fremden Menschen um sich, sieht die Notwendigkeit nicht. Im Moment gibt es kein Entkommen, ich kann hier nicht weg, kann nicht gegen Mutters Willen handeln, jeder Gedanke daran ist Verrat an ihrem Sterben.

Im Schein der tief heruntergezogenen Lampe, die ich mit einem Tuch verhängt habe, um Mutter nicht zu blenden und vom Schlaf abzuhalten, beobachte ich, wie sie zu mir herüberblinzelt, die Augenlider leicht geöffnet, vielleicht beobachtet sie mich, ich verzichte darauf, sie anzusprechen. Sie scheint im heiligen Land der Ruhe zu schweben, dessen Grenze ich nicht zu überschreiten wage, weil ich hoffe, dieser Zustand möge sie ohne Schmerzen in einem Kahn dahingleiten lassen, der sie langsam einer anderen Welt entgegenträgt.

Szenen von früher fallen mir ein. Am liebsten verbrachten Mutter und ich dunkle Winterabende beim Kartenspiel, und die Zeit floss kaum merklich dahin, ein Spiel nach dem anderen wurde angesagt, und noch eines, und noch ein letztes, begleitet von den immer gleichen Sprüchen, mit denen wir scherzhaft versuchten, einander von unseren vorhersehbaren Winkelzügen abzulenken. In den letzten Jahren sah ich den Bewegungen ihrer knochig krummen Finger beim Ordnen und Ablegen der Karten zu. Sie waren inzwischen langsamer und ungelenker geworden als in meiner Kindheit, und ich dachte, während ich Mutter beobachtete, sie würde vor mir sterben, so wie es das Leben und die Generationenabfolge vorsah.

Ich sitze über meinen Notizen, mache kleine Einträge zur Situation, will mich nicht vollkommen darin verlieren. Wenn ich nicht allzu müde bin, hole ich gelegentlich den Laptop hervor, um mich mit dem Konzept für eine Rehabilitationsklinik in den Bergen zu beschäftigen. Ich brauche einen Traum, dem ich nachhängen kann, der meine Phantasie beflügelt, mir Hoffnung gibt und den Willen, meine Visionen im Beruf umzusetzen. Der Rest des Raumes ist ins Dunkel getaucht, als würde das Licht meine Sphäre von der meiner Mutter trennen und doch eine behagliche Gleichzeitigkeit ermöglichen. Der Kreis der Wahrnehmung wird kleiner, das Sehen wird genauer, die Welt, die sich hinter den Beobachtungen auftut, wird tiefer und ist nicht mehr zu vergleichen mit der, die einem entgegentritt, wenn man im normalen Getriebe des alltäglichen Arbeitens und Erledigens steckt. Es ist ein Vorteil des Älterwerdens, wenn man sich mit dem Naheliegenden anfreundet, nicht damit hadert, sondern die Weite der Welt im Kleinen findet.

15

Die Falten an Mutters Oberschenkeln werden tiefer, die Brüste sind nur noch Hautlappen, was sie beim Waschen kommentiert. Sie betrauert den Verlust ihrer Weiblichkeit, was mich verwundert, weil alles zum Körper und zur Sexualität Gehörige zwischen uns meist eine ausgesparte Zone war. Weder hatte sie mich aufgeklärt, das hatte damals die Lehrerin im Biologieunterricht übernommen, noch hatte Mutter jemals einen unangestrengten Satz über Geschlechtliches verloren. Und jetzt diese Bemerkungen über ihre Brust, die ganz selbstverständlich daherkommen, als spräche sie zu sich selbst. Wenn es ihr angenehm ist, verwende ich etwas mehr Massagedruck beim Waschen und Eincremen, um die Durchblutung zu fördern und ihr ein angenehmes Wärmegefühl auf der Haut zu verschaffen. Das Bürsten der Haare überlässt sie inzwischen mir und kann die Berührung genießen, sie schließt die Augen, wird ganz weich und entspannt im Nacken, den ich ihr im Anschluss sanft mit Rosenöl einreibe. Als ich sieben oder acht Jahre alt war, gab es ein abendliches Ritual, bei dem ich mich auf ein Kissen zwischen Mutters Beine setzte. Sie kämmte meine langen Haare, versuchte unterschiedliche Frisuren mit Zöpfen, die sie mir flocht, über die wir dann, nachdem ich sie im Handspiegel betrachtet hatte, lauthals lachen mussten, weil ich aussah wie eine Hexe oder wie die Unschuld vom Land. Das zärtliche Ziehen an der Kopfhaut kann ich noch heute spüren.

Mutter bekommt von mir am Mittag einen feuchtwarmen Bauchwickel angelegt, die gestaute Luft kann so besser aus dem Darm entweichen, was ihr Erleichterung verschafft. Früher hatte sie sich bei Bauchschmerzen mit Schafgarbenwickeln kuriert und immer darauf geachtet, jederzeit genügend von den getrockneten Pflanzen in einem großen Einmachglas in der Küchenkredenz bereitzuhalten. Zusammen mit anderen Gläsern voll mit Pfefferminze, Wermut und Thymian, alles Kräuter, die sie in ihrem Gartenbeet zog, gehörten sie zur Hausapotheke und wurden bei verschiedenen Beschwerden eingesetzt. Ohrenschmerzen wurden mit frisch gehackten, in Honig angesetzten Zwiebeln, die sie in einem warmen Tuch auflegte, kuriert, Fieber hingegen vertrieb sie mit eiskalten Essigsocken. Jetzt versuche ich, Mutter mit derselben Sorgfalt und Geduld zu pflegen, wenn ich ihre Füße und Unterschenkel mit Lavendelöl massiere, vor allem nachmittags oder nachts, wenn das Liegen anstrengend wird und sie sich unter der Bettdecke unruhig zu bewegen beginnt.

Letzte Nacht hatte ich einen bewegten Traum, der weit in den Tag hineinreichte. Ich hatte mein Lager in einem Zelt auf einer Insel aufgeschlagen, im Hintergrund Berge, denen grüne Hügel vorgelagert waren.

Vor mir fiel das Gelände sanft zu einer kleinen Bucht ab, an deren Strand die Wellen eines graublauen Meeres schlugen. Den Tag verbrachte ich damit, zu Fuß die Umgebung zu erkunden, um abends am Feuer zu sitzen und einen Fisch zu braten. Als ich am Morgen erwachte, fühlte ich mich fremd in der Wohnung, und es dauerte eine Weile, bis ich mich wieder orientieren konnte. Ich fragte mich, warum es mir in meinem Leben selten gelungen ist, die Zeit genügsam zu verbringen, statt ständig mit etwas beschäftigt zu sein. Dann erinnerte ich mich an einen alten Grabstein, dessen altmodische Inschrift mich letztes Jahr auf einer Reise nach Südtirol in ihren Bann gezogen hatte. Darauf stand: »Es ist später als Du denkst.«

16

Mutter hat starke Schmerzen, und ich beginne mit einer kleinen Dosis Schmerzmittel subkutan, so wie ich es mit dem Hausarzt besprochen habe. Es fällt mir schwer, ihr die Spritze zu setzen, ich fühle mich unsicher, mir ist nicht wohl in meiner Haut und ich habe schwere Glieder, müde Beine, Kopfschmerzen, der Hals beginnt zu kratzen, ich befürchte krank zu werden. Trotz meiner Bemühungen, Gleichmut zu bewahren, überkommt mich manchmal ein Gefühl der Ausweglosigkeit. Allen guten Vorsätzen zum Trotz bin ich innerlich schnell aufgebracht, wenn etwas im Haushalt nicht funktioniert oder Mutter nachts öfter nach mir verlangt, weil sie Harndrang verspürt, aber nach aller Anstrengung, die es uns beide kostet, sie auf den Leibstuhl zu setzen, nur ein paar Tropfen Flüssigkeit den Boden der Plastikschüssel überziehen. In mir beginnt sich eine Wut aufzustauen, weil Mutter sich vehement dagegen wehrt, eine Pflegerin anzustellen, die mich entlasten könnte. Mutter sagte in schwierigen Situationen früher oft, »sie könne die Wände hochgehen«, drehte dann die Augen himmelwärts und gab einen Stoßseufzer von sich. Ich muss lachen, wenn ich daran denke.

Ich sollte für die sich anbahnende Erkältung dankbar sein, die mich müde und schlapp macht, denn in geschwächtem Zustand ertrage ich die Lage hier besser, und es kommt nicht so leicht das Gefühl auf, ich müsste ausbrechen. Der Tagesablauf kreist um die Aufrechterhaltung ihrer und inzwischen auch meiner eigenen Kräfte. Bislang konnte ich kurze Anspannungszustände kaschieren, konnte mich durch Wäschewaschen, Bodenwischen und Badezimmerputzen dermaßen zum Schwitzen bringen, dass ich kurzfristig alles andere hinter mir lassen konnte und mich danach ausgeglichen fühlte. Eine andere Art der Zerstreuung, die meist funktioniert, auch wenn ich müde bin, ist die Beschäftigung mit kleinen Zeichnungen, die ich mit schwarzer Tinte zu Papier bringe.

Während der Zeit am Gymnasium hatte ich, anstatt Hausaufgaben zu machen, begonnen, kleine Tuschzeichnungen anzufertigen, Miniaturen zunächst, mit dem alten Griffel, den ich in den Hinterlassenschaften meiner beiden Brüder gefunden hatte. Später benutzte ich Aquarellfarben, die auf meinem Schreibtisch bereitstanden. Wenn die Zusammensetzung des englischen Parlaments, die ich für die Schularbeit am nächsten Tag vorzubereiten hatte, nach der dritten Wiederholung langweilig zu werden drohte, erträumte ich mir malend Seen, sanfte Hügel in zahlreichen Grünschattierungen, von hohen weißen Wolkentürmen überragt. In der Volksschule hatte ich zunächst eine Abneigung gegen das Zeichnen gehabt, und so war es Mutter, die einige

Hausaufgaben in diesem Fach für mich anfertigte, wovon ich noch zwei Blätter besitze, den »Frühlingswald« und die »jungen Vögel auf einem Ast«. Es sind beides kindliche Zeichnungen, aber doch nicht naiv genug, um die Lehrerin zu täuschen, die mich zur Strafe nachsitzen ließ. Als Mutter in den letzten Jahren wieder zu zeichnen begann, entsprach es in der Art des Farbgebrauchs und der Strichführung ihrer Darstellungskunst von damals. Sie zeigte mir ein paar Arbeiten, und ich musste gerührt von den Erinnerungen an meine Schulzeit lachen, was Mutter zunächst missverstand, weil sie meinte, ich machte mich über ihre Künste lustig.

17

Mutter schläft. Eine ehemalige Nachbarin vertritt mich, sie sitzt im Lehnsessel und löst Kreuzworträtsel. Sie hat es mir vor zwei Tagen spontan vorgeschlagen, was ich dankend angenommen habe, nicht ohne Mutters skeptischen Blick zu bemerken, als sie das hörte. Sie hat dann weiter nichts dazu gesagt, und ich glaube, dass sie verstanden hat, wie schwer mir die letzten Tage, ohne Ablösung durch meinen Bruder, gefallen sind.

Es ist höchste Zeit, mit den Chefärzten zu telefonieren, um ihnen zu sagen, dass ich vor nächstem Frühling nicht zur Verfügung stehe, und das muss ich außerhalb von Mutters Hörweite erledigen. Es war mir unangenehm, dass sie gestern mitbekommen hat, wie ich einen Anruf von einer Klinik entgegennahm. Der Leiter fragte mich, ob ich zum Ärzterapport in drei Tagen kommen könnte, und ich sagte kurz angebunden, es sei nicht möglich, die Reise anzutreten, nicht jetzt. Zwei Welten prallen aufeinander, wenn ich am Telefon spreche. Ich höre, was das Gegenüber will, kann jedoch nicht sagen, dass ich erst kommen werde, wenn meine Mutter tot ist. Der Tod braucht Zeit, er duldet keine Eile, er duldet nichts anderes neben sich.

Ich fühle mich kränklich und steuere das Gasthaus in der Altstadt an, in dem ich manchmal einkehre, dort finde ich meist eine ruhige Ecke. Mein Kopf ist heiß und ich werde Husten bekommen, das schmerzhafte Kratzen im Kehlkopf lässt mich ahnen, wie zäh sich der Schleim in meinem Hals in den letzten Stunden festgesetzt hat. An einen Spaziergang ist nicht zu denken, obwohl ich mir gestern nichts sehnlicher gewünscht habe, als ein paar Schritte zu gehen, am Bach entlang, in der Au und dann noch weiter hinaus bis zum Sportflughafen.

In der Gaststube weit hinten ist mein Stammplatz, neben dem Fenster, wo man hinaus auf die Nebenstraße sehen kann, in der nur manchmal Fußgänger vorbeispazieren. Das Servierpersonal hier kennt mich bereits, ich bestelle immer dasselbe, einen großen Teller mit Frittatensuppe und eine Schüssel Endiviensalat mit lauwarmen Kartoffeln und Kernöl, nachher noch Kaffee. Inzwischen kann ich in Mutters Wohnung nicht mehr kochen. Der Geruch nach Essen füllt im Nu den Raum, und es ist eine Zumutung Mutter gegenüber, die selbst fast keine Nahrung mehr zu sich nehmen kann. Wir haben uns gestern über den Leichenschmaus unterhalten, sie hat unvermittelt mit dem Thema angefangen, hat sich zurückerinnert an Vaters Leichenmahl im Gasthof des Werkshotels und wollte nicht, dass ihre Verabschiedung am selben Ort stattfinden würde, außerdem meinte sie, das Gulasch sei im Gasthaus in der Altstadt, wo ich gerade sitze, besser. Das Werkshotel verbinde ich mit Orchesterkonzerten und Maturabällen, die ich ab sechzehn mit meinen Schulfreundinnen besuchen durfte, ich verbinde es aber auch mit der ehemaligen Arbeiterkantine, die Vater nach seiner Pensionierung noch besuchte und wohin ich ihn ein, zwei Mal begleitet hatte, um neben ihm an einem langen Tisch aus abgeschabten Tellern einen Eintopf mit Kartoffeln, Kohl und Wurststücken zu löffeln.

Ich habe Mutter versprochen, hier im Gasthof in der Altstadt noch einmal eine Kostprobe vom Gulasch zu bestellen, habe allerdings zurzeit einen Ekel vor Fleisch. Für sich selbst wünscht Mutter zum Leichenschmaus einen Teller Kartoffelsalat. Wenn sie ihn gegessen hätte, so sagt sie, würde sie gestärkt die Reise antreten, die nach ihrer Vorstellung einige Zeit in Anspruch nehmen wird. Zuerst noch ein paar Tage in der Nähe der Menschen und dann hinaus in die Weiten des Weltalls. Ich bin erstaunt darüber, wie sie von der Zeit nach ihrem Tod spricht. Das Hadern mit dem nahen Ende hat sich verändert, und Mutter scheint nicht mehr von den heftigen Ängsten gepeinigt zu werden wie noch vor zwei Wochen.

18

Mutter will nur ruhig liegen, will hinausschauen auf die Apfelbäume, deren hellbraune und rotgelbe Blätter im warmen nachmittäglichen Herbstlicht leuchten. Ich kann ihr an diesen langen stillen Tagen nicht anders beistehen, als ihr die Hand zu halten. Manchmal lese ich ihr morgens aus der Zeitung vor, abends aus den Märchenbüchern, die noch immer in Mutters Bücherregal stehen. Sie stammen aus unserer Kindheit, mit kolorierten Darstellungen der Schneekönigin, des Kalif Storch, Zwerg Nase, König Drosselbart und Rübezahl, die ich seit Jahrzehnten nicht mehr gesehen habe. Mit alter Vertrautheit blicken sie mich von den vergilbten, ausgefransten Seiten an. Gelegentlich schalte ich am Vormittag ein Hörspiel im Radio ein, so wie damals, als Mutter in der Küche am Herd hantierte und ich verträumt auf dem Sofa lag, beide ganz Ohr und weggetragen von den Geräuschen und Stimmen. Zwischendurch singe ich für sie Volksweisen aus unserem alten Liederbuch mit dem abgewetzten lindgrünen Stoffeinband, auf dem das stilisierte Bild zweier Vögel auf einem Engelswurzstrauch aufgeprägt ist. Mutter hat mir viele der Melodien beigebracht, andere habe ich in der Schule gelernt. Vater konnte nicht singen und so war er ein stiller Zuhörer gewesen, wenn wir am Abend ein paar Lieder zur Jahreszeit passend anstimmten. In den beiden Jahren vor der Matura haben wir zusammen in einem der Chöre im Ort gesungen, Mutter blieb dort Mitglied bis zu ihrem siebzigsten Geburtstag, doch irgendwann wollte der Leiter keine »alten Damen« mehr, die den Stimmkörper mit ihrem Vibrato zersetzen. Mutter war schweren Herzens ausgeschieden, konnte auch nicht mehr an den Ausflugsfahrten und Kegelabenden teilnehmen. Zunächst hatte ich ihren Rückzug in die Einsamkeit befürchtet, doch sie meldete sich mit einer Nachbarin bei einer Seniorenreisegesellschaft an. Die Welt mit Reisen alleine zu erkunden war ihr ein unüberwindbares Hindernis, denn sie besaß wenig Erfahrung darin. Vater hatte früher lediglich eine Bahnfahrt nach Frankfurt zu ihrer alten Freundin Ria geduldet und durch seine schlechte Laune, die er bei Mutters Reiseplänen an den Tag legte, weitere Alleingänge verhindert.

Am Abend ist Mutter mit dem Regeln ihrer Hinterlassenschaft beschäftigt. Sie bespricht mit mir und meinem Bruder, der seinen Boykott aufgegeben hat und wieder regelmäßig vorbeikommt, wem sie ihre Möbelstücke, die sie erst vor zwei Jahren erstanden hat, vermachen möchte, wer am ehesten den Tisch gebrauchen könnte, das Sofa, den Schrank. Mein Bruder und ich sitzen einträchtig an Mutters Bettkante, und sie bittet mich, ihre Schmuckschatulle aus dem Schlafzimmer zu holen, sie redet über das Begräbnis und den Spruch für die Todesanzeige, dessen Auswahl ihr schwerfällt. Sie ist aufgekratzt und redselig, die sonst drückende Schwäche scheint gewichen.

In diesen Momenten des Abschiednehmens frage ich mich, wer an meinem Totenbett sitzen wird. Ich habe keine Kinder. Mutter hat mich mit siebzehn zu einer Abtreibung gezwungen, nachdem ich trotz Verhütung von meinem ersten Freund schwanger geworden war. Es war für mich unabdingbar, die Matura zu erlangen, denn ich wollte weg aus dieser Kleinstadt, weg vom eingezwängten Leben meiner Eltern, das sich zwischen Werkshallen und Schrebergärten abspielte, doch nun drohte mir der Rauswurf aus der Schule. Nach dem Test, den ich mehrfach vorgenommen hatte und der stets positiv war, blieb mir nichts anderes übrig, als Mutter ins Vertrauen zu ziehen. Sie hörte mir zunächst schweigend zu und sagte dann, sie habe sich bereits gedacht, dass etwas mit mir nicht in Ordnung sei, weil ich in der letzten Zeit mehr gegessen hätte als sonst. Dann gab sie mir unerwartet eine schallende Ohrfeige und verließ die Wohnung, ohne mich noch eines weiteren Wortes zu würdigen. Ich blieb verstört zurück, hatte nicht den Mut, mit Vater zu reden, denn vor seinen Wutausbrüchen hatte ich am meisten Angst. In den Tagen darauf gab es ständig Krach zwischen meinen Eltern und mir, bis ich letztendlich zu meinem Bruder und dessen Familie zog. Mein Freund und ich versuchten in wiederholten Gesprächen mit unseren Eltern, uns für die Schwangerschaft einzusetzen, denn wir sahen beide eine Abtreibung als Fehler an, trotz der Angst, was aus uns und dem Kind werden würde, wenn wir dann in der Fabrik oder in einem Gasthaus unseren Lebensunterhalt selbst verdienen mussten.

Mutter sagte Jahre später, sie hätte mich davor bewahren wollen, mit »Kind und Kegel«, wie sie mehrmals betonte, zu Hause bleiben zu müssen, in Abhängigkeit eines Mannes, auf den möglicherweise kein Verlass gewesen wäre. Sie hatte befürchtet, ich würde nicht studieren und hätte eine düstere Zukunft vor mir, in einer Industriestadt am Ende der Siebzigerjahre, die von Arbeitslosigkeit geprägt war. Nachdem niemand uns unterstützte, ich nächtelang keinen Schlaf mehr fand und der Widerstand, der Zorn und das Schweigen beider Elternpaare immer unerträglicher wurden, meldete ich mich letztendlich zu einem Termin in der Frauenabteilung des Spitals an.

19

Mutters Gesicht ist regungslos. Sie scheint nicht zu träumen, reagiert nicht, wenn ich aus Versehen eine Tür zu laut schließe. Ein Mensch kann ohne Nahrung einige Wochen überleben, er benötigt vor allem Wasser, und dieses versuche ich Mutter in kleinen Schlucken anzubieten. Mutters Körper scheint zu schrumpfen, seit ihrem Geburtstag habe ich kein Foto von ihr gemacht, will den Verfall nicht mit Bildern dokumentieren. Mit ihrem Einverständnis habe ich heute zusätzlich wieder eine kleine Dosis Schmerzmittel unter die Haut gespritzt.

In der Früh war ich etwas hektisch bei der Morgentoilette, die Erkältung schwächt mich noch immer und mir war unwohl, die Anstrengung zu viel. Mutter hätte lieber mehr Zeit gehabt und hat dann, zurück im Bett, zu mir gesagt, ich sei sicherlich eine gute Ärztin, aber als Pflegerin hätte ich nicht allzu viel Erfahrung. Diese Bemerkung gibt mir das Gefühl, nicht zu genügen. Morgen werde ich die Wäsche langsamer gestalten, sie ist ein Höhepunkt des Tages, an dem Mutter ihren Körper begutachtet, Veränderungen wahrnimmt, sich mit dem Fortschreiten ihres Verschwindens auseinandersetzt, die

Beobachtungen benennt. Sie registriert die zunehmende Schlaffheit ihrer Oberarme, die Falten am Hals. Die Entspannung nach der Anstrengung der Körperpflege, wenn sie sich wieder in die Kissen zurücklehnen kann, wirkt auf mich wie die Zufriedenheit nach getaner Arbeit. Durch meine Eile habe ich ihr das heute versagt.

Noch immer »Nachtblau« von Nay, das Bild ist mir unangenehm, weswegen ich den Kalender ein paar Tage nicht beachtet habe. Die weiße Figur auf der linken Seite hat etwas von einem Geschwür. Das tiefe Rot auf der Gegenseite sieht aus wie die Andeutung einer Vulva. Ich habe mir den Kalender nicht ausgesucht, ich akzeptiere ihn als Gesellen, der mir grobe Orientierung für das Vergehen der Zeit bietet. Wäre ich diesem Bild in einem Museum begegnet, hätte ich meinen Rundgang fortgesetzt, ohne Notiz zu nehmen. Hier aber leben wir in einer Zwangsgemeinschaft. Ich wechsle das Blatt, freue mich über die mittelalterliche Darstellung des Heiligen Martin, der seinen Mantel mit dem Bettler teilt. Es erinnert mich an einen Aufenthalt mit Mutter und meiner Cousine in Assisi, wo wir an einem luftig warmen Frühlingstag die Kirche des Heiligen Franziskus besuchten.

Mutter sagt, sie hadere mit dem Sterben, sie habe sich das Ganze einfacher vorgestellt. Man könne nicht sterben, nur weil man es wolle, das habe sie inzwischen verstanden. Mutter war nie beim Sterben dabei, nicht bei ihrer eigenen Mutter, auch nicht bei ihrem Vater, der, zehn Jahre nachdem sie nach Österreich ausgewandert war, an einem Magendurchbruch verstarb. Ihr Schwiegervater hatte sich nachts, nach dem Besuch bei einer befreundeten Tischlerfamilie, wo er noch sein abendliches Bier getrunken hatte, mit seinem Lodenmantel ins Bett gelegt und war nicht mehr aufgewacht. Die Schwiegermutter fand man eines Morgens tot im Bett des Pflegeheimes. Ihr ältester Sohn starb mit achtzehn Jahren an einem Gehirntumor. Er kam nach einer Operation nicht mehr zu sich, und als Mutter, mit mir an der Hand, ihn im Krankenhaus besuchen wollte, war sein Bett leer.

20

Mutter hat den ganzen Vormittag verschlafen. Die Zeit vergeht langsam in ihrer Nähe. Es ist Mitte November, und ich bin seit einem Monat hier. Ich sitze am Tisch und sehe hinüber zu Mutters Bett vor dem großen Fenster. Am Morgen war draußen alles von glitzerndem Frost eingehüllt, eine dünne Eisschicht überzog das Wasser im flachen Tontopf, der sonst als Vogelbad dient. Die Sonne brach zaghaft durch den Nebel, abgefallene Blätter lagen festgefroren auf den Terrassensteinen, gesäumt von einem zarten Flaum aus kleinen Kristallen. Gestern Abend, als ich nach einem kurzen Regen noch aus dem Fenster gesehen hatte, sind Hundertschaften von Regenwürmern auf dem Asphalt vor dem Haus gekrochen, heute sind alle verschwunden. Der Schlossberg beugt seinen Rücken sanft und die Sonne wird trotz ihres tiefen Standes in den nächsten Wochen täglich über ihn hinwegrollen, um die Wohnung mit ihren Strahlen zu erhellen.

Mein Bruder kommt erst nach Einbruch der Dunkelheit, es ist dann zu spät, um noch ausgiebig durch Wald und Feld zu streifen. Ich muss versuchen, tagsüber für mehr Ablösung zu sorgen, doch ich bemerke meine Scheu davor, Freunde, die Mutter zwar nahestehen, mit ihrer Betreuung zu belasten. Es liegt ein Tabu in der Luft, als sei das Sterben etwas Privates, in das niemand außerhalb der Familie einbezogen werden soll. Wann immer ich Mutter in guter Obhut weiß und hinaus ins Freie kann, um zu gehen, bis ich meinen Körper wieder spüre, fällt eine große Last von mir. In den Wochen hier ist es immer wieder gelungen, meine Traurigkeit durch Gehen zu vertreiben. Es ist auch die Trauer um die eigene Kindheit, die mit Mutter unwiederbringlich verschwinden wird. Diese Zeit, in der sie mich behütet hat, in der ich ihr Kind, ihr »Weibi« war. Mutter hat oft mit Freude im Blick von ihrer kleinen Tochter erzählt, »ihr Mädel«, über das sie sich so gefreut hat, obwohl sie zunächst entsetzt gewesen war, wie sie sagte, so spät noch ein Kind zu erwarten.

Meine Spaziergänge orientieren sich an den Wegen meiner Kindheit und Jugend, an deren Kreuzungen die alten Gespenster hocken und mich mit ihrem Lächeln oder ihren Fratzen begrüßen, als hätten wir uns unlängst erst gesehen und als wüssten sie genauestens Bescheid darüber, was mich umtreibt, als wollten sie sich einmischen, um noch ihren Platz in meinem Leben zu behaupten. Manchmal gehe ich mit staunenden Augen, dann wieder mit dem Blick auf den Boden gerichtet, in Gedanken versunken, dann drängen sich die Gespenster dicht aneinander in mein Gedächtnis. Wenn ich nicht von ihnen erzählen würde, wären sie unweigerlich verloren, niemand würde sie mehr erkennen, sie im Vorbeigehen grüßen oder ihnen zurufen, sie sollten doch endlich verschwinden. Ich habe keine Kinder, denen ich von ihnen berichten kann und mit denen sie weiter ein Leben führen könnten, und meine Freunde interessieren sich nicht für sie, denn sie kennen diese Sorte Gespenster nicht, sie haben ihre eigenen. Mit dem Begehen der alten Wege ist mir auch eine Vertrautheit begegnet, ein Aufgenommensein in eine Landschaft, die schon immer so ausgesehen hat, mit all den Buchen und Linden, den Bergwiesen, den Fichten und Tannen, den Kirchen und Friedhöfen. Es sind Landschaften, die mich berühren, die jetzt in dieser Zeit etwas Tröstliches an sich haben. Der Geruch nach Vaters braunem Leinenrucksack, der im Kleiderschrank des Schlafzimmers meiner Eltern sein Dasein fristete, nachdem die Familienwanderungen im Gebirge schon Jahre zurücklagen, taucht mit einem Mal auf. Die Bergformationen, die mich als Kind bereits fasziniert hatten, erscheinen mir in den letzten Wochen noch lieblicher als in den dreißig Jahren zuvor. Für Augenblicke bin ich in meiner Vorstellung wieder das Mädchen mit den blonden Zöpfen und weißen Kniestrümpfen, das hier einmal zu Hause gewesen ist.

Ich möchte anwesend sein, wenn der Tod kommt. Ich möchte Mutters Hand halten, möchte ihr auf Wiedersehen sagen, ihr den letzten Dienst erweisen und ihr die Augen schließen. Bis jetzt bin ich dem Tod lediglich als Ärztin begegnet, kurz bevor oder nachdem er das Zimmer betreten hatte. Selten konnte ich dann länger anwesend sein, der Tagesablauf in der Klinik hatte es nicht zugelassen. Ich konnte nur die Aussichtslosigkeit im Kampf gegen ihn wahrnehmen, die Hilflosigkeit der Angehörigen, die oft bis zum Letzten nach medizinischen Maßnahmen verlangten und dabei vom leisen Hinausgehen der Seele nichts mitbekamen, bis sie dann überrascht und vorwurfsvoll auf den offenen Mund des zurückgebliebenen Leichnams blickten. Ein befreundeter Arzt hat erzählt, er würde den Umgang mit Sterbenden nicht missen wollen, denn manchen Menschen sei eine Weisheit zu eigen, wenn sie aufrechten Hauptes und gelassen durch das letzte Tor treten.

Wenn ich von meinen Spaziergängen zurückkomme, Mutter keine Schmerzen hat und friedvoll in ihrem Bett liegt, dann ist in der kleinen Wohnung alles licht und leicht. Die Minuten dehnen sich und doch erscheinen die vergehenden Stunden kurz, eine Zeit, die nirgends beginnt und nirgends endet. Ich kann dann einfach eine Weile lang dasitzen und nichts tun, fühle eine Gelassenheit dem Leben gegenüber und bin dankbar.

21

Mutter bemerkt meine innere Unruhe, fragt mich, ob ich nicht Lust hätte, an die frische Luft zu gehen, doch das kann ich nicht. Um die spürbare Spannung zwischen uns aufzulösen, schlage ich ihr vor, im Hintergrund Musik laufen zu lassen. Mutter hört gerne alte Schlager aus ihrer Jugend, Gassenhauer aus dem Krieg und den Jahren davor. Die Lieder der Comedian Harmonists oder von Zarah Leander summte sie früher oft mit, hatte teils den Wortlaut der Strophen im Kopf, so als hätte sie erst gestern »Veronika der Lenz ist da« oder »Ich weiß, es wird einmal ein Wunder geschehen« gesungen. Doch in den letzten Wochen liegt sie nur noch still da und hängt ihren Gedanken nach. Für mich waren diese Lieder untrennbar mit dem Zweiten Weltkrieg verbunden, der durch Mutters Erzählungen zu meinem Aufwachsen gehörte. Als ich einmal mit Mutter bei ihrer Jugendfreundin Ria in Fechenheim zu Besuch war, tauschten sie Geschichten von der Arbeit in der Telefonzentrale der Farbenfabrik aus. Darüber, wie sie bei Bombenangriffen vor lauter Angst mit den anderen Arbeitsdienstfrauen laut gesungen hatten, während sie die Stellung halten mussten, um die Warnsirene auszulösen, da der Rest der Belegschaft bereits in den Bunker flüchtete. Damals hatte sie Vater kennengelernt, der als junger Wehrmachtssoldat im selben Stadtteil als Funker seinen Dienst tat. Ich war sieben Jahre alt, und als Mutter und Ria die Geschichten von Hunger, von Hamsterfahrten aufs Land, von Bomben und Besatzungssoldaten aus ihrem Gedächtnis kramten, stellte ich mir vor, ich sei mittendrin im Sirenengeheul. Gestern sollte ich für Mutter »Lili Marleen« spielen, und mir war, als stünden wir beide vor der Kaserne und warteten auf Vater.

Manchmal will Mutter Opern hören, »Aida«, »Nabucco« oder »Madame Butterfly«, die sie mit ihrer Freundin in Wien, der Arena von Verona oder im Steinbruch von St. Margarethen gesehen hatte. Mutters Entdeckung der Opernwelt war an mir vorbeigegangen, und es ist ein neues Erlebnis, mit ihr Werke zu hören, die wir unabhängig voneinander in ganz verschiedenen Kontexten kennengelernt haben. Dieses gemeinsame Lauschen verbindet uns. Mutter liegt andächtig in ihren Kissen, den Oberkörper etwas erhöht. Sie möchte, wie im Publikum, eine angemessene Haltung einnehmen. Ich habe »Die Zauberflöte« eingeschaltet, bald wird Mutter ruhig einschlafen, und ich werde die Musik leiser drehen, damit sie bei den Fortissimi nicht aus dem Schlaf schreckt.

22

Es ist Jahre her, seit Mutter und ich das letzte Mal über das Kind gesprochen haben, das ich abgetrieben habe. Ich nenne es Rainer Maria, um beide Geschlechter zu berücksichtigen und um Namen aus unserer Familientradition zu verwenden. Lange habe ich nicht mehr so intensiv daran gedacht, nur manchmal hatte sich eine Zeitlang eine Wehmut bemerkbar gemacht, wenn ich davon hörte, eine Frau würde gebären. Heute wäre das Kind ein erwachsener Mensch und er oder sie hätte bereits selbst Familie. In den letzten Nächten lässt mich der Gedanke daran nicht schlafen. Ich schalte das Licht nochmals ein, hänge ein Tuch an die Rückseite der Tischlampe und stelle mir vor, wie ich mit meiner Tochter oder mit meinem Sohn gemeinsam in einen sommerlichen See springe.

Mutter entfernt sich mit jedem Tag, vielleicht ist es endgültig zu spät, um nochmals davon anzufangen. Sie hatte vor Jahren beteuert, dass sie, im Nachhinein betrachtet, anders entscheiden würde, dass sie alles tun würde, um mich und das Kind zu unterstützen. »Weißt Du, irgendwie wäre es möglich gewesen. Irgendwie hätten wir das geschafft.« Das musste wohl genügen. Sie hatte sich gerechtfertigt, aber bei mir entschuldigt hatte sie sich nicht.

Der evangelische Pfarrer kommt zu Besuch, er möchte mit Mutter, meinem Bruder und mir das letzte Abendmahl feiern, lässt uns gegenseitig unsere Hände halten und sagt, wir sollen alles verzeihen, all das, was wir uns je gegenseitig angetan haben. Für mich ist es der falsche Zeitpunkt, ich will über das Kind reden, kann mich noch nicht mit Mutter versöhnen. Ich kann nicht sagen, wie lange es her ist, seit ich mit innerer Beteiligung an einem Sakrament teilgenommen habe, möglicherweise zuletzt in Kindertagen. Trotzdem lasse ich, Mutter zuliebe, die Zeremonie über mich ergehen. Der Pfarrer meint beim Abschied, er wünsche Mutter Frieden und Gleichmut, und hält lange ihre Hand. In der kurzen Zeit ihrer Bekanntschaft hat sich eine Beziehung zwischen ihnen entwickelt. Er sagt, Mutter erinnere ihn an seine eigene Großmutter in Hessen, bei der er als Kind aufgewachsen war. Wer von beiden dem anderen mehr Beistand leistet, ist unklar. Wenn er Mutter von seinen Sorgen mit den Schülern erzählt, von der Einsamkeit, die ihn manchmal plagen würde, seit sich seine Verlobte von ihm getrennt habe, dann haben sich die Rollen verkehrt. Sie gibt ihm Trost mit auf den Weg, ein paar mütterliche Worte. Mutter bleibt, als er gegangen ist, in einer friedvollen Stimmung zurück. Sie versucht zu schlafen, wird aber unruhig und klagt über Schwindel, muss erbrechen, wieder und wieder, bitter riechenden Schleim, der Körper reagiert auf die Anstrengung, die es sie gekostet hat, sich ihre Schwäche vor dem jungen Geistlichen nicht anmerken zu lassen. Nachdem ich sie zur Nacht gebettet habe, bleibe ich mit einem Gefühl von Leere auf der Terrasse in der kalten Dunkelheit zurück.

23

Mutter hat in den letzten Tagen ein paar Löffel Haferbrei, wenige Schlucke dünne Spinatsuppe und winzige Mengen Malzkaffee zu sich genommen. Ich bemühe mich, in der Wohnung und besonders in Mutters Nähe Ordnung zu halten, alles sauber zu machen, die notwendigen zusätzlichen Hilfsmittel so zu drapieren, als würden sie wie selbstverständlich zur Einrichtung gehören, auch wenn sie hässlich sind und man sie eigentlich gar nicht als Dauergäste neben sich dulden möchte. Die Tabletten habe ich in einer Schachtel auf der Ablage bei den Büchern gelagert, die Schnabeltasse steht auf einem Kästchen neben Mutters Bett, ebenso die Papiertücher und die Nierentasse, falls Mutter erbrechen muss. Feuchtigkeitsstäbchen, das Fläschchen mit den Augentropfen und ein Waschlappen ergänzen die Ansammlung, die in Reichweite steht, alles soll seinen Platz haben, das ist Mutters Wunsch. Sie sagt, es solle nicht aussehen wie in einem »Lazarett«, auch nicht wie in einem Pflegeheim. Selbst hat sie immer Wert darauf gelegt, alles aufzuräumen, auch wenn sie krank war und alle Kraft dafür aufbringen musste, um sich auf den Beinen zu halten. Erst nach getaner Arbeit legte sie sich wieder aufs Sofa, zog die rostbraune Wolldecke, die sie seit Jahrzehnten begleitet, bis zu den Ohren hoch und döste. Mit gutem Gefühl konnte sie dann dem Tag ein oder zwei Stunden stehlen, es würde nicht auffallen, würde nicht geahndet. Wenn ungemeldeter Besuch kam oder der Arzt, war wieder alles ordentlich und bereit.

Die Nacht war kurz, ständig bin ich aus verworrenen Träumen hochgeschreckt, fühle mich benommen und habe nach dem Toilettengang mit Mutter eine Pause gebraucht und erst um acht Uhr mit der Körperpflege begonnen. Es drängt uns niemand, doch ist es wichtig, einen Rhythmus beizubehalten, für Mutter, für mich, sonst kommt ein Gefühl von Verwahrlosung auf. Meine Verzagtheit versuche ich vor Mutter zu verbergen, rede über ihren ehemaligen Nachbarn, dem ich am Vortag in der Altstadt begegnet bin, richte ihr Grüße von ihm aus, beginne ihren Bauch zu untersuchen, der prall ist. Der Darm arbeitet, ich kann ihn glucksen hören. Jeden Morgen lege ich das Stethoskop an die Bauchdecke, um die Verdauungsgeräusche zu prüfen, taste mit den Händen, ob die Flüssigkeit zwischen den Därmen zunimmt, alles mit routinierten Bewegungen. Professionelle ärztliche Handlungen, um Mutter und mir die Angst vor dem Ungewissen zu nehmen.

Mutter zu untersuchen hat mich früher mit Scheu erfüllt, doch als sie vor Jahren einmal schwach und angeschlagen mit Husten tagelang im Bett lag, der Hausarzt in den Ferien war und sie sich weigerte, einen fremden Doktor zu konsultieren, konnte ich durch das Abhören der Lunge die richtige Diagnose einer Pneumonie stellen, worauf Mutter nicht mehr so zurückhaltend war wie zu Beginn meiner Laufbahn. Sie trennte strikt zwischen Tochter und Ärztin, wobei sie der Berufsfrau viel zuzutrauen schien, was unser beider Umgang mit ihren später folgenden Erkrankungen erleichterte. Mutter konnte nicht verstehen, wie ich vom soliden Handwerk einer Allgemeinpraktikerin in das in ihren Augen unattraktive Fach der Psychiatrie wechseln konnte. »Willst Du Dein Leben nur mit Verrückten verbringen?«, war ihre erste Reaktion, nachdem ich ihr eröffnet hatte, dass ich eine Stelle als Assistenzärztin an einer psychiatrischen Klinik in der Schweiz annehmen würde.

Mutter ist nach meiner Untersuchung wieder eingeschlafen, ich bin müde, alle Glieder schmerzen, ich werde die Zeitung aus dem Briefkasten holen und mich nochmals aufs Bett legen, um Schlaf nachzuholen. Im Verlauf des Tages werde ich fiebrig. Die nächtlichen Schlafunterbrechungen vertrage ich zusehends schlechter, spüre ein Brennen in der Brust, das untrügliche Zeichen der Übermüdung. Der ganze Rumpf, der Kopf, die Gliedmaßen sind in Watte gepackt, alle Geräusche abgedämpft, die Ohren beschlagen, die Nasennebenhöhlen voll mit Schleim. Der Schmerz, die Trauer des langen Abschieds sind in diesem Zustand von mir abgerückt. Mutter hüstelt, ich gebe ihr einen Hustensirup mit einem kleinen Löffel und hoffe, sie nicht angesteckt zu haben, will nicht der Überbringer einer Krankheit sein, die ihr Sterben beschleunigt.

24

Mutter riecht nach Stuhl. Sie sitzt im Bett und sieht trotz
ihrer abnehmenden Kräfte erstaunlich gut aus. Die Falten um die Augen und den Mund scheinen sich zu glätten, obwohl sie durch den Schwund des Unterhautfet-
tes tiefer werden müssten. Ich bin erstaunt, wie träge
alles vor sich geht, der Abbau des Gewebes, das Aus-
setzen der Organe, das ich schon länger erwarte. Sie hat
die Zeitung aufgeschlagen, räuspert sich mehrmals, versucht, ihre Stimme zu finden, und beginnt ihren Traum
von letzter Nacht zu erzählen. Sie hätte sich mit ihrer
ehemaligen Nachbarin an einem Treffpunkt verabredet,
hielt zwei kleine Buben auf ihren Armen und wartete auf
den Reisebus, der sie abholen sollte für die Fahrt nach
Griechenland, wohin sie mit anderen gemeinsam aus-
wandern wollte. Zwei gepackte Koffer standen neben
ihr, sie sei nicht sicher gewesen, wie sie das Einsteigen in
den Bus bewerkstelligen sollte, doch war sie zuversicht-
lich, dass ihr jemand mit den Kindern helfen würde. Wie
selbstverständlich spricht sie von den Buben, so als ob
sie in ihrer Wahrnehmung real existieren würden. Mutter lächelt mich an. Der eine Knabe sei das Kind, das ich
damals mit siebzehn verloren hatte, der andere sei ihr

erstes Kind, das bei der Geburt gestorben war. Hellsichtig hat Mutter meine Wut und mein Hadern der letzten Tage wahrgenommen, und ich kann in diesem Moment nur ihre Selbstverständlichkeit akzeptieren, ihre Traumwelt, in der sie, ohne die Aussprache, die ich noch mit ihr suchen wollte, alles versöhnt. Ich setze mich neben sie, kann nichts sagen, wir schweigen beide.

Mutters Fürsorglichkeit, mit der sie mir ihre Zuneigung zeigt, kommt wieder zum Vorschein zwischen den Passagen der Ablehnung und des Rückzugs. Die kleinen Handlungen und beiläufigen Sätze lassen erkennen, wie sehr sie noch für mich sorgen möchte, wenn sie beim Märchenvorlesen meine Beine, die ich zu ihr aufs Bett gelegt habe, sorgsam zuzudecken versucht. Wenn sie aufwacht und etwas braucht, lächelt sie mich an und hat dann die Sorge, ob ich wohl Hausschuhe anhabe, damit ich keine kalten Füße bekomme, oder ob ich genügend essen würde, weil ihr nicht entgangen ist, dass ich mir selten etwas zubereite.

Es ist Abend, und das Notizbuch harrt seiner Anrufung. Es hat etwas Tröstliches an sich, wenn es geöffnet daliegt und die blaue Tintenschrift in sich aufnimmt, in ruhigen Zeilen, die gefüllt mit mäandrierender Schrift einen gleichförmigen Lauf simulieren. Es beruhigt mich, die Worte zu Papier zu bringen. Vor mir liegt ein langer Abend allein, Mutter ist bereits um halb acht eingeschlafen, nachdem sich endlich der Stuhlgang gelöst hat, auf den sie mehrere Tage gewartet hatte. Für gewöhnlich bleibt sie länger wach, um die Abendstunden, in denen es ihr körperlich besser geht, mit mir und meinem Bruder zu verbringen. Doch diese Momente werden seltener. Die abendliche Schmerzmitteldosis habe ich ihr früher als sonst verabreicht, denn ich mag ihr diese kantige Welt nicht zumuten, möchte auch nicht, dass sie in einen Entzug gleitet, der dann erst recht Schmerzen und Unruhe verursacht. Als sie mir eine gute Nacht wünschte, lehnte sie mit Tränen in den Augen in den Kissen. Die Tage mit mir seien traurig, aber auch schön. Dann fiel sie zufrieden in einen stillen Schlaf.

25

Mutter lässt sich von mir waschen und eincremen, die Intimzonen übernimmt sie selbst. Das ist gut so, so kann sie ihre Würde wahren und meinen Respekt behalten. Es ist der Bereich des Körpers, der Mutter gehört, aus dem ich vor fünfzig Jahren geboren wurde und den ich auch nicht antasten will, solange es nicht nötig ist. Der Verfall geht voran, an den Knien treten die Knochen stärker hervor, besonders wenn Mutter ihre Beine im Bett anwinkelt. Die Muskeln sind zurückgewichen und runden nicht mehr die Konturen unter der Haut ab. Die Unterschenkel glänzen weißlich, die bläuliche Verfärbung an den Füßen und Zehen, die in den letzten Jahren stärker wurde, ist verschwunden. Die Oberschenkel hängen wie schlappe Säcke an den Knochen, doch die Haut an deren Vorderseite ist im Liegen glatt und Mutter sagt, sie staune über ihre schlanken Beine, die sich doch sehen lassen könnten. In diesem Stolz auf ihre weiblichen Körperpartien, auf ihre Unterschenkel, auf die glatte Gesichtshaut, ist nichts Eitles, Eingebildetes zu finden, sondern eine Bewusstheit. Doch auf der anderen Seite war es auch Mutter, die mir im Umgang mit Körperlichkeit Zurückhaltung beigebracht hat, denn »Frau geizt mit ihren Reizen, betont sie nicht«. Mir schien es bereits als Mädchen als etwas Gefährliches, in kurzen Röcken mit hohen Absätzen und engen Pullovern herumzulaufen.

Beim Spaziergang zu meiner alten Volksschule im Redfeld überfällt mich plötzlich ein brennendes Gefühl in der Blase, und ich bin besorgt, dass ich mir eine der bei mir über Jahre üblichen Entzündungen eingefangen habe. Mein Bauch ist schmerzhaft aufgetrieben, auf der Toilette bemerke ich frisches Menstruationsblut, und das nach Jahren der Menopause. Zunächst denke ich an Krebs, doch das Blut hat mit Mutters Abschied zu tun, mit dem Abschied von meinem Kind und von mir selbst als Kind. Ich werde aufhören, Kind zu sein, weil ich und mein Bruder jetzt als Nächstes an der Reihe sind zu sterben. Die Abtreibung von damals, die mich in den letzten Tagen unerwartet quälend eingeholt hat, obwohl ich alles vergessen glaubte, die Nähe zu Mutter, ihr Sterben, meine Schwäche durch die Erkältung, mit einem Mal ist das alles körperlich sichtbar. Nach meiner eiligen Rückkehr in die Wohnung setze ich mich auf den Boden im Badezimmer. Das letzte Mal habe ich als Mädchen so hemmungslos geweint.

26

Mutter hat wieder den ganzen Vormittag verschlafen. Ich bin dazu übergegangen, ihr gleich nach dem Aufwachen eine Dosis Schmerzmittel zu verabreichen. Alle notwendigen Verrichtungen der Pflege sind für sie dann weniger strapaziös, was sie dankbar zur Kenntnis nimmt. Sie sieht zu mir herüber und fragt nach einer Weile kaum hörbar, ob ich gerade an meinem Manuskript arbeiten würde, was ich verneine. Wenn sie wolle, könne ich ihr aus dem Artikel vorlesen, an dem ich gerade arbeite. Es ginge darin um den Präsidenten der Deutschen Gesellschaft für Psychiatrie, der sich auf einer Gedenkveranstaltung im Vorjahr in Berlin für die Euthanasiemorde entschuldigt hatte. Mutter hört aufmerksam zu, wischt sich die Tränen aus den Augen, sagt, es sei gut, dass endlich darüber gesprochen und geschrieben würde. Sie hatte über den Tod ihrer Mutter kaum geredet, hatte ihn verdrängt, bis zu dem Zeitpunkt, als ich begann, über Großmutter zu recherchieren. Darüber habe ich später ein Buch geschrieben, und noch Monate nach dessen Erscheinen hatte Mutter das Gefühl, durch ihre Mithilfe während der Recherchen etwas Unrechtes getan zu haben. »Das hätte besser im Dunkeln bleiben sollen.« Wieder und wieder musste ich ihr in unseren Telefonaten versichern, dass es keine Schande sei, wenn man sich öffentlich dazu bekannte, dass Großmutter als Psychiatriepatientin im Nationalsozialismus ermordet worden war. Doch machte ich mir auch Vorwürfe, sie nach so vielen Jahren des Verdrängens mit dem Verlust ihrer Mutter konfrontiert zu haben. Vor zwei Tagen hat sich Mutter für das Buch bedankt, Großmutter würde auf diese Art nicht vergessen werden.

Auf unseren langen Autofahrten auf Hessens Landstraßen zu den psychiatrischen Kliniken, in denen Großmutter untergebracht gewesen war, hatten Mutter und ich uns über Euthanasie unterhalten, denn ich wollte wissen, wie viel sie damals im Krieg über die sogenannte »Aktion T4« gewusst hatte. Schließlich sprachen wir über die heutzutage in der Schweiz praktizierte Sterbehilfe. Ich sagte, als Ärztin würde ich einen assistierten Selbstmord nicht befürworten. Mutter pflichtete mir damals bei und fragte mich, wie man sich am besten das Leben nehmen könne, wenn man krank ist und den letzten Schritt selbst bestimmen will. Sie wollte es sich vorbehalten, dann, wenn es an der Zeit sei, aus freien Stücken aus dem Leben zu scheiden. Doch sie hat es nicht getan, konnte es nicht, für eine solche Entscheidung war sie nach meiner Ankunft bereits viel zu schwach gewesen.

27

Am Morgen sind Mutters Gelenke steifer. Sie tut sich schwer beim Drehen, beim Aufrichten, versucht so gut es geht, von ihrer Mühe abzulenken. Es ist nötig, die Bettwäsche und das Nachthemd zu wechseln, die Zahnprothese zu säubern, auch wenn Mutter der Ansicht ist, mit etwas Mundspülen sei es getan. Sie will sich nicht bewegen, will mir keine Arbeit machen, doch ihre Haltung erschwert alles, weil ich darauf beharren muss, sonst nimmt der Geruch nach Stuhl und Urin immer stärker von ihr Besitz. Erst nachdem wir mit der Morgentoilette fertig sind und erst nach einem Putzanfall in der Wohnung, mit dem ich meine angestaute Wut über Mutters Sturheit in Zaum halte, kann ich ruhig mit ihr reden und ihr sagen, dass es für uns beide einfacher wäre, wenn sie mich bei ihrer Körperpflege so gut wie möglich unterstützen würde. Mutter ist zunächst verwundert, doch dann lächelt sie und erzählt fast triumphierend von der Mühe, die sie mit mir manchmal hatte, wenn ich als Kind bockig war, sobald es darum ging, die Haare zu waschen, was öfter mit einem Geheul meinerseits endete. Sie bringt mich damit zum Schmunzeln, und Szenen von früher tauchen auf, wie ich, um nicht an den Zöpfen nass zu werden, mit Mutters weißer gerippter Badehaube in der Wanne sitze. Bei der Morgentoilette lasse ich mir inzwischen Zeit. Mutter registriert jede Beschleunigung, doch es ist schwierig, die Balance zu finden in einer Verlangsamung, die mir Zurückhaltung abverlangt, weil ich ein gewisses Tempo brauche, um gegen das Sterben, die eigene Bedrücktheit und Schwäche anzukämpfen.

Die Zeit in Mutters Nähe vergeht gleichmäßig, und es gibt stets etwas zu tun, ab und zu unterbrochen von seltenen Besuchen, die meiste Zeit bin ich mit ihr allein. Frau Gabriel, die am Vormittag vorbeikommt, meldet sich für einige Wochen ab, sie müsse zu ihrer Nichte nach Wien, um dort auf deren Kinder aufzupassen. Es ist vielleicht der letzte Abschied der beiden Frauen, die sich in den zurückliegenden sechs Jahren miteinander angefreundet haben. Zuerst hatte Mutter sich vehement gegen jemanden gewehrt, der ihr die Arbeiten, die inzwischen zu schwer für sie waren, abnehmen konnte. Beim Staubsaugen und Bodenwischen hatte sie sich wiederholt einen Nerv eingeklemmt oder sich beim Bügeln den Fuß verbrüht, als ihr das Eisen aus der Hand gefallen war. Erst nach einer schweren Grippe, am ganzen Körper geschwächt, seelisch angegriffen, nicht mehr in der Lage, selbst im Haushalt zuzupacken, habe ich Mutters Zustimmung bekommen und Frau Gabriel engagiert. Von da an gab es zu meiner Verwunderung nur Lob für deren Arbeit und ein ungeduldiges Warten auf den Mittwochmorgen, an dem sie »gemeinsam« ans Werk gingen, um einzukaufen und die Wohnung auf

Hochglanz zu bringen. Mit einem Mal war ich entlastet, konnte gelegentlich telefonisch bei Frau Gabriel nachfragen, wie es Mutter gehe oder ob sie rasch nach ihr sehen könne, denn sie wohnten in derselben Gasse. Die beiden Frauen haben nach und nach einiges miteinander unternommen, Mutter wurde mit einem Abonnement für die Konzertsaison beschenkt, und es war ein Vergnügen, am Telefon zu hören, wie sehr sie das Spiel des Kammerensembles im Rittersaal der Burg genoss. Es waren Momente der Zufriedenheit, wenn sie, eingetaucht in Musik, in Gesellschaft von Frau Gabriel und deren Mann, kostbare Stunden verbringen konnte.

Der Abschied jetzt erscheint mir eigenartig, als ob sie beide es nicht wahrhaben wollten, dass sie sich nie mehr sehen werden. Nachdem Frau Gabriel gegangen ist, wird Mutter unruhig, verlangt einmal Wasser, dann wieder Tee oder Suppe, nimmt aber nichts zu sich, benetzt nur kurz die Lippen. Es ist, als würde sie mich und sich selbst von ihrer Traurigkeit ablenken wollen. Mutter war nie gut darin gewesen, ihre Gefühle in einer adäquaten Art, die für das Gegenüber lesbar war, zuzulassen. Stets lag mehr hinter ihrer vermeintlichen Gelassenheit.

Mit einem leisen Piepston schaltet sich Mutters Mobiltelefon aus. Ich werde es nicht mehr aufladen. Mutter wird mir morgens keine SMS mehr schreiben und sie wird mich nicht mehr anrufen. Die Art, wie sie sich ernsthaft mit Dingen beschäftigen konnte, die für mich von Belang waren, schuf über die Zeit mit den täglichen Telefongesprächen eine Nähe zwischen uns, trotz der räumlichen Distanz. Ihren Rat habe ich immer geschätzt, auch wenn ich selbst oft anderer Ansicht war. In den letzten beiden Jahren haben wir jedoch vermehrt über das Wetter geredet, über Mutters Tagesplan oder über kleine Beschwerden, über ihren Kampf mit dem Älterwerden und das tägliche Überleben in Würde. Dieses Ringen hat sie zunehmend auf sich selbst zurückgeworfen. Mutter wurde auf eine Art distanzierter, sagte öfter »das wird schon gut« und »Du wirst das schon alles richtig machen«, um das Gespräch im Guten zu beenden, kein Spielverderber zu sein. Diese Reaktionen waren auch ein Schutz, nicht zu allem eine Meinung haben und über alles informiert sein zu müssen.

Mutter will zur Abwechslung Joghurt, sagt, sie habe Appetit darauf. Sie will sterben, aber sie will auch essen und nimmt das darauffolgende Druckgefühl in ihrem Bauch, unter dem sie dann unweigerlich leidet, in Kauf. Mir ist eng ums Herz, ich kann nichts entgegnen, will nicht klingen, als solle sie ganz damit aufhören, um uns beiden den langen Weg zu ersparen. Es kann noch Wochen so weitergehen, und ich werde diese Zeit mit Mutter durchstehen, auch wenn es mir an manchen Tagen unerträglich scheint.

28

Mutter sagt nach dem Aufwachen leise »Herrgott, warum hast Du mich verlassen«. Ich setze mich zu ihr an den Bettrand, welche Worte könnten das Leiden lindern, das einen am Ende des Lebens erreicht, wenn es keinen anderen Ausweg gibt, nur den sicheren Tod.

In den letzten Tagen und Nächten ging das Heraussetzen auf den Leibstuhl noch gut, doch jetzt ist Mutter zu schwach, kann sich kaum im Bett aufsetzen, ihr ist schwindlig. Ihr Körper ist schwer wie ein Zementsack, der sich nicht richtig greifen lässt. Ihr Verzagen nehme ich körperlich wahr, kann es als Schmerz unterhalb meines Brustbeins fühlen, als Enge im Hals, als Brennen neben den Zungenrändern, meine feuchten Augen kann ich kaum vor ihr verbergen.

Sie möchte meine Stimme hören, das würde sie beruhigen, ich solle doch das Märchen von gestern Abend wiederholen, sie habe im Dämmerschlaf, in den sie verfallen sei, nicht alles mitbekommen. »Das Mädchen mit den Schwefelhölzern«, die Geschichte vom armen Bettlermädchen in einer winterkalten Stadt, das Streichhölzer verkaufen soll und bei jedem Holz, das sie unerlaubterweise entzündet, um sich ein wenig zu wärmen, in eine Traumwelt eintaucht. Zuletzt entflieht es an der Hand ihrer geliebten verstorbenen Großmutter, die immer gut zu ihr war, in den Himmel. Am nächsten Morgen wird sie von Passanten erfroren gefunden, auf ihrem bleichen Gesicht ein Lächeln. Es ist eines von Mutters Lieblingsmärchen, sie hat es gestern ausgesucht, und beim Lesen konnte ich kaum meine erstickte Stimme verstecken, weil ich ganz vergessen hatte, dass es darin um einen Tod geht, der Tröstliches in sich trägt und der das Wiedersehen mit einem geliebten Menschen verspricht. Ich werde das Märchen Mutter noch einmal vortragen, langsam, mit kindlicher Andacht, und werde meine Tränen zurückhalten.

Es wird die Zeit kommen, in der ich Mutters Pflege körperlich nicht mehr gewachsen bin, deshalb trainiere ich jeden Tag, um meinen Rücken zu kräftigen und auch um mich zur inneren Disziplin zu zwingen, selbst wenn ich nach den Tagen mit Fieber noch leicht benommen bin und mich zu jeder Übung überwinden muss. Mutter mag sich heute kaum berühren lassen, es scheint schmerzhaft für sie zu sein. Sie spinnt sich in einen Kokon ein, einem Gemisch aus geistiger Abwesenheit, oberflächlichem Schlaf, diskreter Abwehr. Es bleibt manchmal nichts anderes übrig, als zugegen zu sein, so unaufdringlich wie möglich, leise und sanft, damit ich ihre Kreise, die sich enger um sie ziehen, nicht störe. Dieses ruhige Schweben sei für sie der angenehmste Zustand, sie fühle dann keine Schmerzen, keine schweren Gedanken würden sie plagen, Erinnerungen an ihre

Kindheit tauchten auf in diesen Sphären zwischen Tag und Nacht, zwischen Schlafen und Wachen. Sie habe ihre Mutter in der Küche hantieren sehen, als sie mich dabei beobachtete, wie ich Tee kochte. Mit halbem Bewusstsein sei sie hier in der Wohnung bei mir gewesen, doch auch im Haus ihrer Kindheit, dort habe ihre Mutter am Herd gesungen.

Mein Bruder und ich essen gemeinsam zu Abend und trinken Wein. Mutter möchte vom Wein probieren, den sie lange im Mund behält. Nach einer halben Stunde muss sie sich übergeben, kann selbst das Wasser nicht bei sich halten, das sie in kleinen Schlucken hinunterwürgt. Ich hadere mit meinem Leichtsinn, ihr vom Wein gegeben zu haben, muss ihr schließlich, nachdem mein Bruder gegangen ist und der Brechreiz nicht aufhören will, eine Spritze verabreichen. Ich fühle mich elend, Mutter liegt matt in den Kissen, die Anstrengung ist ihr ins Gesicht geschrieben. Es dauert eine Weile, bis sie wieder ruhig wird, ich setze mich neben sie, rede mit ihr, um sie von ihren Beschwerden abzulenken. Sie sagt, es falle ihr schwer, ihre beiden Kinder allein zu lassen. Obwohl wir bereits erwachsen wären, wolle sie für uns da sein. Inzwischen ist es Nacht, Mutters Atem ist oberflächlicher geworden, das Wasser beginnt in die Lungen zu steigen, weil sie sich kaum mehr bewegt, meist auf dem Rücken liegt. Sie fragt mich, ob sie jetzt langsam ersticken müsse, und ich helfe ihr, im Bett aufzusitzen, klopfe ihren Brustkorb mit den Fingern ab, um den Schleim zu lösen, lasse sie kräftig atmen, was sie nicht lange durchhält, weil die Anstrengung bald zu groß wird. Der Mond ist am Abnehmen, und vielleicht kann Mutter gegen Neumond leichter Abschied nehmen. Draußen vor dem Fenster zünde ich seit zwei Tagen bei Einbruch der Dunkelheit eine Kerze an, stelle sie in eine Glasvase, die als Windschutz dient. Sie beleuchtet die Hinterglasmalerei mit dem Christusbild und flackert mit friedlichem Schein die ganze Nacht. Mutter sagt, das Licht sei beruhigend, sie fühle sich nicht so allein, denn sie liege manchmal wach, wolle mich nicht wecken. Nachdem sie eingeschlafen ist, sitze ich am Tisch und betrachte ihre mageren, feingliedrigen Hände, die sie an die Wangen gelegt hat. Mir ist, als würde sie auch in Zukunft aufwachen, um anwesend zu sein, immer noch meine Mutter, und ich wäre dann noch immer ihre Tochter.

29

Mutters Gesicht ist bleich und eingefallen. Ich betrachte ihre Nasenflügel, die sich unmerklich heben und senken, ihre geschlossenen Lider, unter denen sich die Augäpfel langsam hin und her zu bewegen scheinen. Mutter träumt, vielleicht wandert sie durch die Landschaften ihrer Kindheit, einen stillen Fluss entlang.

Meine Spazierwege sind kürzer geworden, meist sind es Varianten durch den Buchenwald zum Schlossberg hinauf oder hinten an der Hauptschule vorbei zum Ufer der Mürz. Hier finde ich, von früher vertraut, viele herbstliche Cyclamen, dunkelgrünes niedriges Moos, Farne, zarte kleine Gräser und die riesigen Blätter, »die Blotschen«, die wir beim Pilzesuchen als Hüte verwendeten, um uns gegen den Regen zu schützen. In den Tagen um Allerheiligen war ich mehrmals auf dem Friedhof, jetzt mag ich nicht mehr dorthin. Es ist unerträglich, vor dem mit Efeu bewachsenen Stahlkreuz zu stehen und daran zu denken, dass Mutter bald dort liegen wird. Als Kind bin ich mit ihr stets durch Wälder und Felder gestreift, wir haben Kräuter gesammelt, Tannenzapfen oder Blumen, es fand sich immer etwas, das wir in unsere Rucksäcke oder Taschen stecken konnten. Zu Hause haben wir unsere Beute jeweils auf dem Tisch ausgelegt. Die Heidelbeeren, die auf einer frischen Omelette gut schmeckten, oder die trockenen Disteln und Gräser, die wir zu einem Strauß banden, der uns auf der Ablage unterhalb des Wandtelefons in den Winter begleitete. Ich bin Mutter dankbar für die Schule des Sehens auf diesen Wanderungen, die meine Wahrnehmung der Landschaft heute noch prägt, dankbar für all die Geschmäcker, die mich seit damals begleiten, sei es der des frischen Löwenzahnsalats im Frühling oder der gebratenen Schirmpilze im Herbst. In Zeiten, in denen ich aus der Welt zu fallen drohe, helfen sie mir, mich wieder in ihr zu Hause zu fühlen, wenn ich nach einem Streifzug durch die Wiesen ein paar Wildpflanzen in der Küche zubereite.

Zu Mittag koche ich Marillenknödel. Ich habe meinen Bruder eingeladen und die letzte Packung aus dem Gefrierfach geholt. Mutter hat die Knödel noch letzten Juni mit ihm gemeinsam zubereitet, er wollte das Rezept unter ihrer Anleitung ausprobieren, damit sie genauso schmeckten wie früher. Der Tisch ist sorgfältig gedeckt, Mutter sieht uns vom Bett aus zu. Wir loben ihre Kochkünste, erinnern uns an allerlei Gerichte, die sie in unserer Kindheit zubereitet hat. Zur Vorspeise gibt es Gemüsesuppe nach Mutters Anleitung. Während des Essens fällt sie bald in einen Schlaf, dem sie sich nun öfter und ohne Widerstand anvertrauen kann. Sie bemerkt nicht mehr, wie mein Bruder ihr sanft über die Hand streicht, bevor er geht.

Am Nachmittag sieht Mutter trotz aller Schwäche gut aus, doch der Verfall ist nicht zu übersehen, die Augen ziehen sich zurück, versinken in den Höhlen. Wenn die tiefe Sonne ihre Strahlen auf das Bett legt, das ich hinaufgekurbelt habe, um ihr den Blick nach draußen zu ermöglichen, sagt sie, sie genieße das wärmende Licht auf ihrem Körper, lächelt mir zu. Vor dem Fenster hat der goldene Herbst seine Blätter auf den Boden geworfen, ich habe einige gesammelt, gezackte Ahornblätter, wie ich sie als Kind nach Hause gebracht hatte, um sie zu trocknen. Das war zu Beginn der Schule, als sich für mich eine neue Welt eröffnete und ich mich aufmachte, das Leben unabhängig von Mutter zu erkunden. Am ersten Schultag sollte ich meine Freundin kennenlernen, die mich jetzt wieder begleitet. Sie wohnte damals beim Werkskanal, wo eine Schlackenseilbahn mit in der Luft schlenkernden grauen Stahlkübeln die Straße querte. Wenn ich sie besuchte, begab ich mich ans andere Ende der Welt, die mich damals einbettete. Diese Welt bestand aus dem Hinterhof unseres Mietshauses mit den Holzhütten an dessen Nordseite, Mutters Gemüsegarten am Weg zur Tischlerwerkstatt, wo sie jedes Jahr im Frühling ihr Gemüse anpflanzte, und endete an der Werkshalle mit dem Stahlhammer, dessen Schlag die Gläser in der Vitrine zum Klirren brachte. Das Beben des Fußbodens in unserer Wohnung wurde zum alltäglichen und nächtlichen Grundrhythmus, den ich bis heute in mir trage.

Abends löst mich mein Bruder ab, ich gehe in eines

der Konzerte aus dem Abonnement, das Mutter nicht mehr wahrnehmen kann. Sie sagt, ich solle ihr doch die Freude machen und an ihrer statt dort hingehen und ihre Bekannten grüßen. Es fällt mir leichter zu gehen, wenn Mutter darauf beharrt. Ich kleide mich dem Anlass entsprechend, nehme aus ihrem Schrank eine weiße Seidenbluse, die ich ihr vor Jahren geschenkt habe, und präsentiere Mutter, die mich mit einem Augenzwinkern betrachtet, meine Garderobe. Sie meint, ich könne wohl alles tragen und es würde gut aussehen, »selbst einen Kartoffelsack mit Gürtel«. Bei dieser Bemerkung muss ich schmunzeln, ich kenne den Spruch von früher und bin erstaunt, wie wach sie ist, ein wenig aufgekratzt sogar, als ob wir gemeinsam zum Konzertbesuch aufbrechen würden.

In einer mittleren Reihe links habe ich eine gute Sicht auf die Bühne, studiere die Gesichter der Musiker und entdecke drei ehemalige Mitschülerinnen aus dem Gymnasium, die bereits zur Schulzeit bei manchen Konzerten hier ihren Einsatz hatten. Als die Musik anhebt, schließe ich die Augen, bin eingetaucht in den Klang der Instrumente, der mich warm umfängt. Die Zeit dreht sich zurück, ich bin sechzehn und aufgeregt, abends mit einer Freundin im großen Saal des Werkshotels im Konzert zu sitzen, wir haben noch über einen Mitschüler getuschelt, der in der Reihe vor uns aufmerksam den Klängen lauscht und das erste Mal ein Sakko zur Jeans trägt. Seine lockigen braunen Haare fallen ihm auf die Schultern, er ist zwei Jahre älter als ich und wird mich in der Pause fragen, ob ich etwas trinken möchte. Zwei Wochen später wird mich Mutter schelten, weil ich mit ihm nach der Schule einen Spaziergang gemacht habe, sie wird einen Tag lang kein Wort mehr mit mir sprechen. Von meinem ersten Kuss erzähle ich ihr nichts.

Nach dem Konzert gehe ich nach vorn zur Orchesterbühne, dränge mich zwischen den Menschen hindurch, die langsam den Ausgängen zustreben, warte geduldig, bis ich endlich nahe genug bin, um eine meiner ehemaligen Mitschülerinnen rufen zu können. Sie sieht mich an und ist erstaunt, mich hier zu sehen, zieht ihre Nachbarin am Ärmel und deutet auf mich, beide kommen mir lachend entgegen. Wir verabreden uns an der Bar. Sie erzählen mir von ihren Kindern, ihrer Arbeit, und wir beteuern uns gegenseitig, wie wenig wir uns verändert hätten. Zunächst bin ich ganz bei ihnen, freue mich, erzähle, warum ich hier bin, schleichend aber fühle ich mich fremd in ihrer Gegenwart, möchte hier nicht länger sein, sondern bei Mutter, es drängt mich, den Heimweg anzutreten, ich muss zurück. Mutter könnte tot sein. Wir tauschen die Telefonnummern aus, und ich gehe eilig die große Empfangstreppe des Konzertsaals hinunter, schnappe mir an der Garderobe meinen Mantel, beginne zu laufen. Mutters Wohnung liegt fünf Minuten entfernt, es regnet, ich nehme mir nicht die Zeit, den Schirm aufzuspannen, und komme atemlos an. Vor der Wohnzimmertür halte ich inne, horche kurz. Leise trete ich ein, sehe meinen Bruder am Tisch sitzen, er korrigiert seine Schulhefte, dahinter liegt Mutter ruhig im Bett. Eine friedliche Stimmung erfüllt den Raum. Ich setze mich im Mantel zu ihm an den Tisch und versuche, meinen Atem zu kontrollieren.

30

Mutter redet am Morgen wirr. Sie ist unruhig, erkundigt sich nach ihrem verstorbenen Sohn. Wenn sie mir früher von ihm erzählte, erschien es mir oft, als ob er noch gar nicht lange tot sei. Er habe ihr im Haushalt geholfen und während seiner Tischlerlehre nützliche Kleinmöbel angefertigt, wie den Schemel, auf den sie gerne ihre Füße stellt. Er sei ein sanfter und liebenswürdiger Mensch gewesen.

Erst gestern, während des Konzerts, habe ich an meinen älteren Bruder gedacht, einer der Cellisten sah ihm ähnlich, mit dunklen gescheitelten Haaren, die beim Spiel locker in die Stirn hingen. Es war, als säße dort der junge Bursche mit dem nachdenklichen Blick, der mir von Bildern aus dem Familienalbum vertraut war. Als er starb, war ich vier Jahre alt, und ich kann mich an seine Stimme und an Ausflüge mit dem Fahrrad erinnern, auf die er mich im Kindersitz mitgenommen hatte. Bereits als Schulkind hatte ich oft Fotografien von ihm betrachtet, um herauszufinden, wer das war, an dessen Grab Mutter so lange verharrte und nicht mit mir sprach. Ich war dann ebenso in andächtiges Schweigen verfallen, weil ich sie nicht kränken wollte. Sein Tod war für mich als Kind abstrakt, ich dachte immer, er würde eines Tages wieder vor mir stehen und mich auf eine Runde auf seinem Drahtesel einladen.

Mutter nestelt an der Bettdecke, ruft leise nach ihm. Als ich ihr sage, er sei schon lange tot, sieht sie mich unter halb geöffneten Lidern verständnislos an. In der Hoffnung, es würde ihr helfen, gebe ich ihr zögernd eine Beruhigungstablette, was sie nach einigen Minuten entspannt. Die Decke ist ihr verrutscht, ich ziehe sie zurecht, lege meine Hand auf ihr Knie und betrachte ihr Gesicht. Ihren Mund umspielt ein zartes Lächeln. Die schnelle Wirkung der Tablette verblüfft mich, und gleichzeitig frage ich mich, ob es richtig ist, Mutter mit einem Medikament davon abzuhalten, ihren Sohn zu suchen. Vielleicht hätte sie ihn ja gefunden, wie er sie im Jenseits erwartet, ihr seine Hand reicht.

Draußen vor dem Fenster taumeln die letzten rostbraunen Laubblätter langsam zu Boden, niemand ist in der Gasse zu sehen, ich fühle in meiner Handfläche die Wärme von Mutters Körper. Ihre Stimme ist heute hauchdünn und höher als gewohnt, sie hat keine Kraft mehr, sich zu räuspern. Ich sehe zur Anrichte, der Kalender zeigt inzwischen Chagall »Die Blumen und der rote Zirkus«, ein Paar auf einem Pferd, ein musizierender Engel, Schaugestalten in einer Manege, unscharfe Blumentupfer. Chagalls Malerei ist mir fremd. Während ich Zuflucht suche im Anblick des musizierenden Engels, wünsche ich mir, er würde für Mutter spielen.

Nach einem langen Schlaf ist Mutter abends wieder ansprechbar, hat jedoch keine Kraft mehr, um sich von mir auf den Leibstuhl helfen zu lassen. Kein Aufrichten, kein Drehen, nichts ist ihr möglich. Ich telefoniere mit meinem Bruder, bitte ihn darum, rasch vorbeizukommen, ich bräuchte dringend seine Hilfe. Eine Bettschüssel habe ich noch nicht besorgt, denn mit einem so raschen Schwinden der Kräfte hatte ich nicht gerechnet und den Kauf auf die nächsten Tage verschoben. Diesmal wollte ich nicht so voreilig handeln wie beim Erwerb des Leibstuhls, der dann eine Zeitlang als Drohung in der Wohnung herumstand. Selbst Windeln habe ich keine zur Verfügung, um Mutters missliche Lage zu entschärfen. Nach dem ersten gescheiterten Versuch, sich abzustützen, weint Mutter verzweifelt, wütend. Mein Bruder kommt, er fragt nicht viel, packt an, und wir können Mutter aus dem Bett heben. Sie lässt es über sich ergehen, sagt nichts, und ich merke ihr an, welche Niederlage es für sie bedeutet, vor ihrem Sohn nackt und hinfällig zu sein. Mutter ist dem Tod einen weiteren Schritt näher gekommen.

Als wir wieder alleine sind, wasche ich Mutter das Gesicht mit einem feuchten warmen Lappen, sie hat kühle Hände, spürt sie nicht mehr richtig, sagt leise, sie habe ein taubes Gefühl. Den Strohhalm, den ich ihr an den Mund führe, kann sie mit ihren Fingern nicht mehr fassen, ist nicht im Stande, daran zu saugen. Mit dem Becher an ihren Lippen leere ich ihr langsam einen kleinen Schluck Wasser in den Mund. Sie lehnt sich zurück, und ich streiche ihr sanft über die weißen Strähnen und versuche ein Bild zu beschreiben, in das sie wie in einen Tagtraum eintauchen kann, erzähle von den sanften Wellen in einer Bucht, in die sie hinausschwimmt, von der türkisen Farbe des glasklaren Meeres, das kühl die Haut umfängt, frisch und angenehm, wenn sie mit leichten Bewegungen dahinpaddelt und zurückblickt ans Ufer, wo sonnenbeschienene weiße Häuser den Hafen säumen. Mutters Augenlider glätten sich, der Atem wird ruhiger, flacher, sie flüstert mir zu, wie schön es sei, sich im offenen Wasser zu bewegen, was mich dazu ermuntert weiterzureden, mich weiter einzulassen auf unser Traumbild. Auf einer Griechenlandreise gemeinsam mit meinen Eltern, ich war zehn Jahre alt, an einem Strand in der Nähe des Kanals von Korinth, Vater saß weiter hinten im Schatten einer Pinie, ist Mutter damals ins Meer hinausgeschwommen, während ich, die ich noch nicht schwimmen konnte, am Ufer bis zu den Knien im Wasser stehen blieb.

31

Mutter kann sich an die Episode von gestern nicht erinnern. Sie will sich im Handspiegel betrachten, hat darum gebeten, dass ich ihr den »Altweiberbart« entferne und bei der Gelegenheit auch einige der großen schwarzen Mitesser. Sie meint, es sei doch wichtig, bei der Aufbahrung gut auszusehen. Es ist befreiend, wenn sie ganz überraschend solche Wünsche hat und ihr Humor aufblitzt. Mutters frühere Belehrungen, die mir oft lästig waren, zielten darauf ab, wie sie sagte, »meine Chancen in der Gesellschaft zu erhöhen«, in der nach ihren althergebrachten Vorstellungen dezent zur Schau getragene Weiblichkeit ein Mittel des Aufstiegs war, denn »wer nix erheirat und nix ererbt, der bleibt en armer Deibel, bis er sterbt«. Es war ihr ein Graus, mir dabei zuzusehen, wie ich mit vierzehn die Haare kurz schneiden ließ und nur noch Hosen trug, ausgewaschene weite Pullover und alles andere, womit ich meine weiblichen Attribute verdecken konnte. Ich kam von meinen Streifzügen durch die Wälder mit aufgekratzten Beinen nach Hause, schnitt mir die Fingernägel kurz, sehr zu ihrem Missfallen. Mutter fasste das als Provokation auf.

Am Nachmittag hat Mutter Bauchschmerzen, und

nach Rücksprache mit meinen befreundeten Ärzten und dem Hausarzt habe ich die Dosis des Schmerzpflasters erhöht und ein Mittel zum Lösen der Darmkrämpfe verabreicht. Mit einer leichten Massage versuche ich Abhilfe für die quälenden Blähungen zu schaffen, wobei mich Mutter nur widerwillig gewähren lässt und fragt, ob ich keine wirkungsvollere Therapie zur Verfügung hätte. Den Unterton ertrage ich schwer und muss mich zusammennehmen, um nicht unfreundlich zu reagieren. Wir verstricken uns ohne Worte in einen Zweikampf, sie vermittelt mir das Gefühl, mit meiner Pflege ihren Bedürfnissen nicht gerecht zu werden. Als ich ihr einen nassen Waschlappen zur Erfrischung auf die Stirn legen will, frage ich sie, ob es ihr angenehm sei, und sie weist mich mit leiser, aber scharfer Stimme darauf hin, dass sie es nicht wissen könne, weil der Lappen kaum ihr Gesicht berührt habe. Mutter hat recht, ich habe zu früh gefragt. Trotzdem fühle ich mich wie damals in der Volksschulzeit, als ich ihr stolz eine Bastelei präsentierte und Mutter diese nur wortlos und mit einem abwertenden Blick würdigte. Oft wusste ich nicht, was ich anders hätte machen können, weil Mutter dazu nichts sagte, und so blieb ich dann mit meinem flauen Gefühl in der Magengrube allein.

Um unsere Spannungen zu mildern, in die wir in unserer Isolation unweigerlich zu geraten scheinen, habe ich für die nächsten Tage mehr Ablösung organisiert, sage Mutter, dass ab heute jeden Nachmittag eine der ehemaligen Nachbarinnen vorbeikommen wird, worauf sie nur stumm nickt und die Augen schließt. Ich telefoniere mit einer privaten Pflegehelferin, lade sie zu einem Gespräch ein, erkläre ihr die Situation, schildere die vehemente Abwehr meiner Mutter gegenüber fremden Personen. Sie lässt sich nicht davon beeindrucken, sagt, sie könne in den nächsten Tagen vorbeikommen, um sich vorzustellen und auch um zu sehen, ob sie mit Mutter arbeiten wolle. Ihre Aussage überrascht mich, Mutter kommt für ihre Betreuung eventuell nicht in Frage. Ihre Stimme und direkte Art empfinde ich auf Anhieb als wohltuend. Es löst sich ein Druck in mir, denn es geht mit einem Mal nicht mehr darum, ob Mutter jemanden akzeptiert, sondern sie selbst muss erst eine Prüfung bestehen, damit sich jemand ihrer annimmt. Dann telefoniere ich mit der Frau meines Neffen, die mir bereits angeboten hat, mich zu unterstützen, worauf ich jedoch bis jetzt verzichtet habe, weil sie mit ihrer Arbeit und der kleinen Tochter sehr eingespannt ist. Sie verspricht, abends vorbeizukommen, um mir bei der Körperpflege von Mutter zu helfen. Ich bin dankbar und erleichtert.

32

Mutter liegt mit offenem Mund da. Sie atmet schwer und muss den Kelch des Lebens bis zum letzten Tropfen austrinken. Sie kann sich nicht mehr aus eigener Kraft aus dieser Lage befreien. Ich werde sie auf die Seite betten, möchte ein Wundliegen verhindern, denn die Haut wird dünner und brüchiger. Mutter lebt in den letzten beiden Wochen nur noch von wenigen Schlucken Wasser. Sie ist zu schwach, um mitzuhelfen, wenn ich die Bettschüssel unter ihr Gesäß schiebe. Sie willigt schließlich verzagt ein, die Windeln zu verwenden, die ich inzwischen im Badezimmer bereithalte, um uns ein Debakel wie mit dem Wechsel vom Leibstuhl auf die Bettschüssel zu ersparen. Sie wollte so lange wie möglich nicht von mir in Windeln gewickelt werden. Ich sehe, wie sie um jede Freiheit kämpft, die ich ihr dann doch nehmen muss. Ihre Stimme ist kaum mehr zu hören, doch nach einem kräftigen Räuspern ist sie wieder da, wenn auch leiser als früher, die alte, vertraute Stimme, der unverkennbare Tonfall, den ich bald nicht mehr hören werde, weil sie immer weniger Kraft haben wird, den Schleim, der ihr im Hals steckt, abzuhusten.

Ein Traum in der Nacht hat mich eigenartig berührt

zurückgelassen, ein sehnsuchtsvoller Abschied von Mutter, auf einer gemeinsamen Reise, ständig im Wissen, dass es die letzte sein wird. Ich konnte sie gehen lassen, und als wir uns zum Abschied vor dem Bahnhofsportal trennten, stand ich lange mit zum Winken erhobenem Arm da, bis Mutters Silhouette in der Menge der Passanten verschwand. Genug des Leidens, genug des Abschieds, genug von dieser körperlichen Hülle, in die wir eingesperrt sind. Wenn einer von uns sich bewegt, muss der andere unweigerlich reagieren, nichts bleibt verborgen, selbst wenn wir schweigen. Mir wird eng in der Brust beim Anblick der zahlreichen Handtücher, die im Badezimmer zum Trocknen aufgehängt sind, ich kann die Cremetuben, Mundstäbchen, Öle, Waschlappen und die Brechschüssel nicht mehr ertragen. Die Grenze ist erreicht.

Das Hinterglasbild mit dem Jesus fällt bei einem Luftzug vom Fenster und springt in Stücke. Der Trost, den es Mutter bringt, wenn es von der Sonne oder von einer Kerze erleuchtet wird, ist durch nichts zu ersetzen. Mutters leiser trockener Kommentar »Siehst Du, der mag auch nicht mehr«, wobei sich ihr Mund zu einem angedeuteten Lächeln verzieht. Diese kurzen verbindenden Momente wird es bald nicht mehr geben. Die Sprache geht schrittweise verloren, vergessen, ich spreche oft den ganzen Tag mit niemandem, und wenn, dann leise als Begleitmusik zu Mutters Schlaf, in einem Monolog, dessen beruhigender Singsang aus einem anderen Raum zu kommen scheint. Ich werde das Bild zum Glaser bringen, es soll Mutter auch in ihren letzten Tagen begleiten.

Am Abend versuche ich, früher schlafen zu gehen, mache kaum noch Notizen, da mich das Schreiben zu lange wachhält. Zeitungen interessieren mich kaum noch, ich höre keine Nachrichten, lese keine Bücher mehr. Mein Kopf ist blockiert für jegliche Gedanken, die mit dem Hier und Jetzt nicht unmittelbar zu tun haben. Ich kann mich nur auf Praktisches, Alltägliches konzentrieren, das ich normalerweise in meinem Leben nebenbei erledige. Jetzt fordert es meine gesamte Aufmerksamkeit. Wenn ich all diese Symptome betrachte, wie bei einem Patienten, dann muss ich feststellen, dass ich in einem Erschöpfungszustand angekommen bin. Selbst die kleinen Erholungsphasen reichen nicht aus, weil mein Schlaf schlecht ist, essen kann ich nur wenig, ich habe an Gewicht verloren, merke es an den Hosen, die mir inzwischen zu weit geworden sind. Vielleicht geht mit Mutters Tod ein Teil meiner Energie von dieser Welt, unwiederbringlich.

33

Als Mutter aufwacht, erzählt sie leise, sie habe in der Nacht einen Druck auf der Brust verspürt. Eine dunkle Enge habe sie im Traum umklammert, die sich nach einer Zeit in ein gleißendes Licht auflöste. Auf die Frage, ob sie Angst habe, sagt sie, in der Helligkeit habe sie sich leicht und frei gefühlt wie noch nie. Nach einer Weile schläft sie wieder ein. Auf der Anrichte liegt ein Zettel mit den Uhrzeiten der Injektionen und Tablettengaben, damit ich in der Gleichförmigkeit der vergehenden Zeit die Übersicht nicht verliere und unbewusst zu große Zeitlücken zwischen den einzelnen Verabreichungen entstehen, denn ich habe Hemmungen, Mutter eine Spritze zu geben, während sie schläft. Es wird notwendig sein, mehr Schmerzmittel zu verabreichen, der Tumor scheint sich hungrig durch Mutters Eingeweide zu fressen. Wo beginnt die aktive Sterbehilfe und wo ist sie passiv, beeinflusst doch die kleinste Handlung den Sterbeprozess, jedes Geben oder Weglassen einer Schmerzspritze, einer Infusion oder einer Beruhigungstablette. Mit meinem Bruder kann ich diese Fragen nicht besprechen, er meint lediglich, ich müsse als Arzt tun, was ich für richtig befinde, und sonst solle ich den Hausarzt hinzuziehen. Die Telefonate mit meinen befreundeten Ärzten sind hilfreich, aber sie sind angewiesen auf meine Beobachtungen, denen ich manchmal nicht mehr recht traue. Die Situation erinnert mich an meine erste Stelle im Turnus, damals fühlte ich mich von den erfahrenen Kollegen alleingelassen mit den Entscheidungen über Leben und Tod, denn sie waren oft nicht erreichbar, wenn ich in der Notaufnahme einer vor Schmerzen schreienden jungen Frau zu helfen versuchte oder dem sich stumm krümmenden Alten.

Am Vormittag kommt eine befreundete Nachbarin, um mich abzulösen. Mutter wacht verschreckt auf und sieht mich starr an, hält sich verkrampft an der Bettdecke fest. Als ich ihr sage, dass ihre Freundin die nächsten zwei Stunden hier bei ihr bleiben würde, wirft Mutter ihren Kopf auf dem Kissen hin und her, bis ich die Frau, die noch nicht einmal das Zimmer betreten hat, verzagt am Arm nehme und ihr im Vorraum sage, es hätte wohl keinen Sinn, wenn sie bleiben würde. Wir sind beide überrascht von Mutters Reaktion, und später entschuldige ich mich telefonisch nochmals bei ihr. Sie ist verständnisvoll und sagt, sie habe Ähnliches mit ihrer eigenen Mutter kurz vor deren Tod erlebt, ich solle einen lieben Gruß ausrichten, es sei alles in Ordnung.

Nachdem Mutter wieder eingeschlafen ist, verkrieche ich mich im Keller, wo ich damit beginne, die Schränke zu sichten und leere Marmeladegläser in einen Papiersack zu räumen. Ich habe mit dem Entrümpeln begonnen, vor Mutters Tod. Sie selbst hat mich vor Tagen darum gebeten, ihre Kleider und Handtücher der Caritas zu bringen, doch ich habe ihr gesagt, dass im Moment alles so bleiben würde, wie es ist. Mutter hatte in den letzten Jahren angefangen, ihre Habe zu reduzieren, sie wollte meinem Bruder und mir nicht die Last aufbürden, hinter ihr aufräumen zu müssen, wie es damals nach Vaters Tod notwendig war, als wir uns durch Schränke voller Drähte, Schalter und Werkzeug wühlten, erstaunt über seine Sammelwut, mit der er alles angehäuft hatte. Man könne nie wissen, sagte er, ob es nicht für das eine oder andere Verwendung gäbe, wenn die Zeiten schlechter würden und es nichts mehr zu kaufen gäbe. Mutter hingegen erzählte uns bei jeder Gelegenheit, wovon sie sich unlängst wieder getrennt habe, seien es alte Kleidungsstücke oder die geflickten Leintücher ihrer Aussteuer. Die Auflistung der Gegenstände, die sie »entsorgt« hatte, scheint mir im Nachhinein ein Teil eines vorweggenommenen Abschiedes gewesen zu sein.

Als ich aus dem Keller in die Wohnung zurückkomme, bittet Mutter mich um ein Stofftaschentuch, das sie dann in ihrer Hand umklammert hält. So weit ich mich zurückerinnern kann, befand sich bei uns im Kleiderschrank ein Stapel gebügelter Taschentücher von Vater, den sie, nachdem sein Haushalt aufgelöst worden war, übernommen hatte. Eines davon trug sie stets in ihrer Handtasche.

Mutter ist dabei, in den Schlaf zu gleiten, und ich werde sie bewachen. Ihr Anblick rührt mich, die Unerbittlichkeit von vorhin ist verflogen. Dieses »Aus-der-Welt-

Gleiten« ist manchmal kein Gleiten, sondern ein Zerren, ein Winseln und Toben, ein innerliches Kreischen und Schlagen, das dann doch wieder in ein Schweben umzuschlagen scheint, in ein Fliegen und Träumen, eingebettet in Stille. Mutter hat mich in diese Welt gebracht, und nun geht sie und lässt mich hier zurück. Ich werde die Freude in ihren Augen vermissen, ein Strahlen, einfach weil es mich gibt. Ich sitze still neben ihr und sehe aus dem Fenster. Das Novemberlicht ist nun gegen Ende des Monats kurzatmig geworden, es hat an Blässe zugenommen, und die Blätter sind fast alle von den Bäumen gefallen. Der Nebel belagert jeden Morgen bis zur Mittagszeit das Tal und nachmittags kommt zaghaft ein bleichblauer Himmel hervor, für den ich dankbar bin. Wir wandern langsam auf das Licht am Ende des Weges zu. Bei Einbruch der Dunkelheit zünde ich eine Kerze an, die ich in Mutters Sichtweite platziere. Die Vorweihnachtszeit beginnt.

34

Mutter liegt still in ihren Kissen. Sie blickt hinüber zur brennenden Kerze, und ich kann nur ahnen, welchen Bildern sie nachhängt. Früher hatte das Hinleben auf den 24. Dezember etwas Anheimelndes, Ruhiges und Friedvolles, wenn Mutter und ich den Adventskranz aus Reisig fertigten, mit Zapfen, Disteln und Hagebuttenzweigen schmückten, die wir aus den umliegenden Wäldern mitgebracht hatten. Sogar zwischen meinen Eltern schien es eine Art Burgfrieden zu geben in dieser Zeit der Erwartung des Weihnachtsabends. Doch das Fest war dann meist voller Spannungen, nichts von Frieden, Erfüllung und Familie, das Gegenteil war der Fall, wenn Vater wieder einen über den Durst getrunken hatte und zu spät zum Abendessen auftauchte. Mutter versuchte, die Stimmung aufrechtzuerhalten, zündete feierlich die Kerzen am Baum an und sang mit uns Kindern »Leise rieselt der Schnee«. Ihre Angst, die mit jeder halben Stunde größer wurde, in der Vater nicht nach Hause kam, übertrug sich auf uns. Das waren Dinge, über die man damals außerhalb der eigenen vier Wände nicht sprach, auch mit den Schulfreundinnen nicht. Mutter sagte ohnehin nie zu jemandem ein Wort, es sei denn zu mir.

Ich habe den Baumschmuck in Mutters Keller gesucht, die Krippe mit den Figuren aus Ton, meinen Lieblingsengel, der mit gestreckten Armen ein hellblaues Spruchband mit der Aufschrift »Gloria in excelsis Deo« über seinem Haupt hochhält. Die Hoffnung, auf die alten Christbaumkugeln zu stoßen, die früher unsere Weihnachtsbäume zierten, war bald verflogen, nachdem ich alle Schachteln und Dosen aus Mutters alter Küchenkredenz durchgesehen hatte. Lediglich die Alraune habe ich entdeckt, die Mutter und ich vor vielen Jahren an den Ufern der Mürz gefunden hatten und die, bedeckt mit Rindenstücken und Moos, ab da als Unterschlupf für Josef, Maria, das Christuskind und den Esel dienen sollte.

Weihnachten war, auch nachdem ich von zu Hause ausgezogen war, eine Zeit, die mich schwermütig stimmte und die gleichzeitig die Verpflichtung mit sich brachte, Mutter, nachdem sie von Vater getrennt war, in meine Kreise miteinzubeziehen. Sie war am Heiligen Abend in meiner Studenten-WG dabei, wir verbrachten das Fest in einer nahen Diskothek, wohin sie uns dann neugierig begleitete, um zu sehen, womit sich die jungen Leute die Zeit vertrieben. Doch irgendwann sträubte ich mich gegen den stummen Aufruf von Mutter, nicht alleine sein zu wollen. Es war zu Beginn der Neunzigerjahre, ich war Ende zwanzig und das erste Mal in Paris, nachdem ich mein Studium beendet und die erste Stelle als Turnusärztin begonnen hatte, stolz darauf, endlich mein eigenes Geld zu verdienen. Mutter hatte insgeheim darauf gewartet, dass ich sie an den Festtagen besuchen würde, doch ich verlebte die Zeit in den Cafés und Museen der Stadt, zutiefst versunken in eine Liebe und die Niederschrift meines ersten Buches. Die kleine Pariser Wohnung, die uns zur Verfügung stand, war im obersten Stock eines alten Bürgerhauses gelegen, in meiner Erinnerung sehe ich den schwarzweiß gekachelten Boden der schmalen Küche, die hohen, schlecht schließenden Fenster, die Attrappe eines offenen Kamins mit einem Gasofen und den an den Rändern facettierten Spiegel darüber, in dem ich noch unser Spiegelbild erahnen kann, den kleinen Balkon vor dem Fenster mit der Sicht in die Rue Delambre. Im Flur stehen beige Wildlederschuhe mit Absatz, in denen ich mir damals, auf den rastlosen Streifzügen durch die unbekannte Stadt, Blasen gelaufen hatte. Es fiel mir nicht im Traum ein, bequemes Schuhwerk zu tragen, weil ich jung und schön sein wollte, und wir waren jung und schön, wie Hemingway und seine Frau im Buch »Paris, ein Fest fürs Leben«, das ich damals las. Am Heiligen Abend, ich hatte geplant einen weiteren Monat zu bleiben, musste Mutter ins Krankenhaus. Das schlechte Gewissen, nicht in ihrer Nähe zu sein, wog schwer, doch der Hunger nach Leben hielt mich davon ab, in den nächsten Zug nach Österreich zu steigen.

35

Mutter sagt zu meiner Verwunderung heiser: »Sie kann bleiben.«

Die neue Pflegerin hat sich vorgestellt und Mutter lächelte sogar, als sie ihr die Hand schüttelte. Die Körperpflege, bei der sie mir am Abend hilft, läuft ruhig und ohne Anstrengung ab, sie hat eine Begabung dafür, Menschen richtig anzufassen. Sie stört nicht, wenn sie den Raum betritt, sondern füllt ihn mit einer warmen Ruhe und unaufdringlichen Aufmerksamkeit. Mutter sieht nach dem Waschen zufrieden aus, doch ihr Atem geht schwer, mit schwachen Bewegungen versucht sie, die Decke zurückzustreifen, deren Gewicht sie stört. Ich habe ihr ein handbedrucktes Lavendelkissen auf das Kopfkissen gelegt, das sie sich unter die Wange schiebt und sagt, damit über violett leuchtende Felder im Süden gleiten zu wollen. Das Kissen habe ich vom Christkindlmarkt mitgebracht, auf den mich gestern meine Schulfreundin mitgenommen hat. Beim Abschied hat sie mir den Schlüssel zu ihrer Wohnung in die Hand gedrückt, das Gästezimmer sei bezogen und ich könne jederzeit kommen, auch mitten in der Nacht, wenn es so weit sei, denn ich würde vielleicht nicht mit der toten Mutter allein bleiben wollen. Zuerst war ich etwas verstört über die Direktheit, doch dann habe ich ihr einen Kuss auf die Wange gegeben und konnte gar nichts sagen, dankbar für ihr Vorausschauen auf eine Situation, die sie aus eigener Erfahrung kannte.

Um Mutter ist es stiller geworden, als würde sie sich unmerklich aus ihrem Körper zurückziehen. Selbst sanfte Berührungen scheint sie nicht wahrzunehmen, ich muss sie kräftig anpacken, um sie aus ihrem Dämmerzustand herauszuholen. Ich verzichte darauf, die Windel zu wechseln oder wenigstens nachzusehen, ob sie eingenässt hat, auch wenn es notwendig wäre. Sie verliert kaum noch Urin oder Stuhl, und die geringen Mengen werden nicht dazu beitragen, dass Mutter sich wundliegt. Ich störe ihre Ruhe nicht. Es gilt jetzt, diese kleine Welt hier mit allen Kräften aufrechtzuerhalten, ich kann nicht für später planen, der Gedanke an ein »danach« verbietet sich. Mutter soll behütet und beschützt sein.

36

Als ich Mutter zum Waschen aufwecke, erschrickt sie und weint, bis sie erkennt, wer ich bin. Dann hält sie meine Hand fest umklammert und will sie nicht mehr loslassen. Um sie nicht zu sehr dabei zu stören, sich immer weiter von der körperlichen Welt zu entfernen, versuche ich nur das Nötigste zu tun, doch meine Zurückhaltung scheint für die Pflegerin nicht akzeptabel. Sie kommt aus der Routine des Altenheims und ist es gewohnt, die Toilette effizient zu absolvieren. Sie erzählt mir vom Zeitdruck auf der Station, auf der sie zuletzt gearbeitet hat. Es liegt mir fern, ihre Arbeit zu kritisieren, doch frage ich mich, ob es notwendig ist, Mutters gesamten Körper einzucremen, was ich zaghaft thematisiere.

Mutters Geistesgegenwart überrascht mich angesichts ihres Zerfalls, denn nach der morgendlichen Verwirrtheit flüstert sie, sie wolle nicht, dass ich ihre Orchideen am Fenster mit Wasser versorge, sie hätten ihr in der Nacht erzählt, sie wollten mit ihr gehen. Dann betrachtet Mutter den Adventskranz mit der brennenden Kerze, der auf dem Tisch steht, und sagt kaum hörbar, dass sie mit dem Sterben doch gar nicht bis zum 1. Advent brauchen wollte. Bevor sie wieder die Augen schließt, sage ich ihr, ich würde für sie die Adventslieder singen, die wir früher gemeinsam gesungen haben, was sie mit einem Lächeln quittiert. Ihr Atem beginnt sich zu vertiefen, und ich sehe zu, wie sich der Brustkorb unter der Decke langsam hebt und senkt, beginne zu reden, obwohl Mutter inzwischen eingeschlafen ist, und erzähle ihr von der Angst, die ich habe, dass mich, wenn ich von hier wegfahren werde, eine Trauer überwältigen wird, von deren Ausmaß ich noch keine Ahnung habe. Dann erzähle ich von meinen Zukunftsplänen und darüber, was ich gerne in meinem Beruf noch erreichen würde, von den Arbeiten am neuen Buch, dessen erste Seiten ich ihr vorgelesen hatte. Nach einer Weile hole ich Mutters Fotoalben aus der Vitrine und beginne darin zu blättern, suche nach den Bildern, als sie noch eine junge, hübsche Frau gewesen war, und versuche nachzuerzählen, was ich aus den Schilderungen ihrer Kindheit und Jugend in Erinnerung behalten habe, halte gelegentlich inne, wenn ich unsicher bin.

Nach dem Verlust ihrer Mutter und den ersten Jahren hier hatte sich etwas in ihrem Aussehen geändert. Es wird mir deutlich auf einem Bild, das Mutter gemeinsam mit Vater Ende der Vierzigerjahre zeigt, sie wirkt aufgeschwemmt im Gesicht, hat einen karierten Rock an, dessen Saum schief über ihren Knien hängt, die Strickjacke, die über ihrem Busen spannt, ist aus grober Wolle gefertigt. Vielleicht ist sie mit dem ersten Kind schwanger. Als Mutter hierher in diese Gegend kam, redete sie die Sprache der ehemaligen Naziherren und passte nicht ins neue Bild der Nachkriegszeit, das keine Vergangenheit duldete. Sie hatte mir erzählt, dass Vater stolz auf seine junge Frau gewesen war und sie gehütet hatte wie seinen Augapfel, allen missgünstigen Blicken zum Trotz. Großvater unterstützte sie, wo er konnte, und unternahm Ausflüge mit seinen beiden Enkelbuben, doch die Großmutter und Vaters Schwester ließen Mutter spüren, dass sie keine von ihnen war. Vielleicht spielte es auch eine Rolle, dass Mutter nicht das Schicksal ertragen hatte müssen, das den Frauen hier während der russischen Besatzung widerfahren war, etwas, worüber niemand sprach. In den letzten zwanzig Jahren vermittelte Mutter den Eindruck, als wohnte sie gerne in diesem Ort, wirkte versöhnt mit ihrem Leben, das sie hier geführt hatte. Sie hat sich nie darüber beklagt, hierhergekommen zu sein, manchmal fragte sie, was wohl gewesen wäre, wenn sie in Frankfurt geblieben wäre, in einer Umgebung, wo sie Freundinnen hatte und wo sie auf dem Main gerudert war. Es gibt ein Foto aus dieser Zeit, sie sitzt mit einem Lachen in einem schmalen Boot, die Arme weit nach vorne gestreckt, die Hände umklammern die Enden der Ruder, der Rücken leicht gebeugt, die Knie angezogen, ihre schlanken Unterschenkel von der Sonne gebräunt, die Haare werden von einem breiten hellen Band aus der Stirn gehalten, ihre Augen leuchten verschmitzt.

Die Stunden verfließen während meines Erzählens, und ich rede mich in eine Trance, die den Schmerz des

Abschieds in eine wärmende Trauer umwandelt. Ich sitze an Mutters Bett, neben mir liegen auf dem Tisch die Fotoalben, mein Notizbuch. Daneben steht ein Krug mit Pfefferminztee, von dem ich immer wieder einen Schluck trinke, um den Geschmack der Kindheit auf der Zunge zu spüren. Als ich im Oktober hierherkam, dachte Mutter noch, sie könnte sich über die physischen Gesetze hinwegsetzen und rasch nach der Eröffnung der Diagnose eines unheilbaren Bauchspeicheldrüsenkrebses »ruhig entschlafen«, wie es auf Traueranzeigen heißt. Doch der Körper lässt sich nicht in die Ecke legen, wenn er das ganze Leben lang gekämpft hat, und Mutters Leben war über weite Strecken ein beharrlicher und zäher Kampf, sie wäre sonst nicht so lange bei Vater geblieben, »um die Familie zusammenzuhalten«, wie sie betonte. Mutter und ich haben früher beim Frühstück, oder im Garten unter dem Apfelbaum sitzend, oft über Vater gesprochen. Wir haben versucht, uns eine Vorstellung davon zu machen, woher seine Wut auf diese Welt gekommen war, und sprachen über seine Mutter, die mit Kindern und Mann überfordert war, über die Schläge, die er von seinem Vater bekommen hatte. Vaters Kriegszeit haben wir meist nur gestreift, er habe ihr kaum etwas über die Jahre in der Wehrmacht erzählt, die sechs Jahre, die sie im Krieg getrennt verbracht hatten. Ich bin mit Mutter noch im Sommer die Namen der Ortschaften seiner Stationierungen durchgegangen, die ich bei meinen Recherchen herausgefunden hatte, um damit den Fluss ihrer Erinnerungen anzuregen. Doch ich habe dabei kaum Neues erfahren, irgendwann habe ich meine Nachforschungen abgebrochen. Was er im Krieg erlebt und getan hatte, wird sein Geheimnis bleiben.

37

In der Nacht hat mich Mutter an den Händen gehalten und »ach Spatzl« zu mir gesagt. Heute Morgen ist ihr der Tod ins Gesicht geschrieben. Die Züge sind spitz geworden, die Backenknochen kantig, die Stirn ist glatt, das Kinn kommt deutlich zum Vorschein, die Augen liegen tief in den Höhlen. Wenn sie auf dem Rücken liegt, wölbt sich der Bauch hervor, doch Mutter lässt keine Schmerzen erkennen. Die Darmtätigkeit ist träge, manchmal kommt etwas Luft, wenig dunkler, stark riechender Urin. Ihre Finger sind spindeldürr, die rötliche Farbe ist daraus gewichen, sie sind bleich, fast transparent. Alles scheint zu schmelzen, sich zurückzuziehen, sich aufzulösen, und die Vergänglichkeit wird deutlich, auch weil ihr Wille gewichen ist und sie keine Kraft mehr hat, sich für etwas zu entscheiden. Die Füße sind über den deutlich sichtbaren Knochen wohlgeformt, die Zehen schlanker als noch vor ein paar Wochen, die Ödeme haben sich zurückgebildet, die in den Jahren davor an heißen Tagen das Gehen behindert hatten, wenn das Herz nicht richtig pumpen wollte, was Mutter bei der geringsten Steigung schnell den Atem versagen ließ. Der Prozess des Verschwindens scheint im Gleichgewicht, keine Wunden vom Liegen, die Unterschenkel zeigen keine Krampfadern mehr, die Arme und Beine ebenmäßig. Übrig bleibt der filigran wirkende Körper einer alten Frau, der die Falten und Runzeln ablegt und an Durchsichtigkeit gewinnt, die Schwere hinter sich lässt, in einer elfenbeinfarbenen Zeitlosigkeit. Es ist eigenartig wahrzunehmen, wie sich dieser Körper ohne sichtbares Zutun verändert. Mich schmerzt zu erkennen, dass es nicht mehr möglich ist, diesen Vorgang aufzuhalten, Nahrung in dieses welke Fleisch zu bringen, um es vor dem Verhungern, dem Verdursten, dem Verdorren zu bewahren. Wenn ich auf Mutters Körper blicke, sehe ich wieder Fotos von ihr in jungen Jahren, in einem adretten weißen Zweiteiler, den eleganten Strohhut schräg ins Gesicht gezogen, überlagert von den Bildern an der Leuchtwand des Röntgenbefundzimmers, die grauen Konturen vom Chaos in ihrer Bauchhöhle, das sich im Verlauf des körperlichen Verschwindens ebenso zurückgebildet haben wird, ausgehungert auch der Krebs.

Mutter hat eine weitere Stufe des Sterbens erreicht, sie hat von zehn Uhr morgens bis um sechs Uhr abends ununterbrochen geschlafen, ich konnte sie nicht mehr durch Ansprache oder den Versuch, sie auf die Seite zu drehen, wecken, sie reagierte nicht. Ob sie mich noch hört, kann ich nicht sagen. Ich habe für sie heute aus einem Impuls heraus norwegische Volksweisen in Moll gesungen, leise und getragen, Lieder, die ich gelernt habe, als ich dort zur Schule ging in einem Austauschjahr, in das sie mich damals mit Bedenken entließ. Mutter dachte, ich sei mit sechzehn noch zu jung dafür, doch sie hatte sich nicht an mich geklammert, auch wenn es ihr schwerfiel, mit Vater alleine zurückzubleiben. Als ich in der Maschine saß und unter mir das Flughafengebäude immer kleiner werden sah, stellte ich mir meine Eltern vor, wie sie still nebeneinander standen und hinaufblickten, bis der Punkt am Horizont verschwunden war. Als ich die Rollpisten aus den Augen verlor, wusste ich, dieses Jahr im Ausland würde für mich ein unumkehrbarer Schritt ins Erwachsenenleben werden. Ich stelle mir die Szene von damals vor, blicke zum Fenster hinaus und sehe den bleichblauen Himmel über den kahlen Bäumen, mir erscheint alles, was sich in der Welt draußen abspielt, unendlich weit weg. Ich sehe die Konturen von Mutters Körper unter der leichten weißen Überdecke. Ihr Atem ist unregelmäßig geworden, zunächst vier bis fünf Züge, dann eine Pause, ich zähle bis fünfundzwanzig, bis die nächste Atemfolge wieder einsetzt, das Herz schlägt unrund und schwach unter den Rippen, wenn ich meine Hand auf ihren Brustkorb lege, der Puls ist an den Handgelenken kaum spürbar. Mutters Winterschlaf hat begonnen.

Mein Bruder kommt, um bei Mutter zu wachen, und ich bin froh, die Wohnung, die nun ständig erfüllt ist von Mutters lauten Atemzügen, verlassen zu können. Er steht im Vorraum, und ich bemerke sein Zögern, einzutreten. Die Fürsorglichkeit, die er mir in der letzten Zeit angedeihen lässt, bezeugt eine tiefe Verbundenheit. Wir haben als Geschwister Ähnliches erlebt, das schwer beschrieben werden kann, Stimmungen, Töne und Gesten, die unsere Kindheiten begleitet haben, auch Gerüche, Lichteinfälle oder die Beschaffenheit eines Sofaüberzuges im Wohnzimmer, all das Teil eines Lebens, das uns als Bruder und Schwester gemeinsam gehörte. Wenn seine Eltern auch nicht meine Eltern gewesen sind, weil sie, bereits erschöpft und ermüdet von ihrem Weg, anders mit mir umgegangen sind, nachsichtiger mit dem kleinen Mädchen, so wissen wir beide ganz genau, wovon der andere spricht, wenn es um »damals« geht, um unser »Zuhause«, um unsere Eltern. Es gibt Dinge, die mein Bruder nicht in gleicher Weise mit Mutter geteilt hat, den Schrebergarten, in den ich sie oft begleitet habe, die Blumensträuße, die wir von den Wiesen mitbrachten, die Nachmittage, die wir mit dem Einkochen der Marillen und Zwetschken verbrachten, das Schwimmen im Freibad an den Sommermorgen in den Ferien, das Nähen von Röcken und Kleidern, die langen Nachmittage des gemeinsamen Kartenspiels.

Mutter liegt nach meiner Rückkehr mit halboffenen Augen in den Kissen, sie reagiert nicht, wenn ich sie anspreche. Ich sage mit erhobener Stimme »Mama, ich bin wieder da«, berühre sie sanft, streiche ihr über die Stirn, stelle den Luftbefeuchter näher an ihr Bett, aber ich halte mich zurück, will sie nicht herausholen aus ihrem hellblauen Schutzmantel, der sie in meiner Vorstellung umhüllt. Draußen auf der Terrasse blühen noch drei kleine Rosen in den Töpfen, zwei weiße und eine rosafarbene, eine ist ganz geöffnet und beginnt an den Blütenblatt-ränder braun zu werden, sie duftet zart mitten im Winter. Die Orchideen am Fenster welken, fünf Blüten hängen müde an zwei Stöcken. Der geschmückte Adventskranz steht tagsüber auf dem Terrassentisch, damit er nicht die Nadeln verliert, ich habe ihm auf seinem Teller ein Beet aus Moos und Zapfen zurechtgemacht, so wird er seinen dunklen Waldduft länger behalten und ihn abends im Zimmer auf dem Tisch in Mutters Nähe verbreiten.

38

Mutter hat die ganze Nacht geschlafen. Ich habe ihrem Atemziehen gelauscht, konnte keine Ruhe finden, habe mich gedreht und herumgewälzt. Bilder aus der Zeit meines Studiums sind aufgetaucht, von einer Ausfahrt mit einem alten Mercedescabriolet zu Ostern, gemeinsam mit Mutter und meinen inzwischen verstorbenen homosexuellen Freunden, die sie an ihrer eigenen Mütter statt gern in ihrer Mitte aufnahmen. Sie lobte deren Höflichkeit und verlieh der feiertäglichen Familieninszenierung durch ihren im Wind wehenden hellblauen Schal und das weißblau karierte Kostüm aus den Sechzigerjahren eine glaubwürdige Note. Schließlich bin ich in einen wenig erholsamen Schlaf gedriftet, aus dem ich mit schweren Gliedern erwache. Ich wecke Mutter nicht, möchte noch eine Weile den Morgen allein verbringen und vertreibe mir die Zeit damit, die Glasvitrine zu öffnen und Gegenstände herauszunehmen, die ich schon lange nicht mehr in Händen gehalten habe, wie das Porzellanosterei mit einem Frühlingsvers von Heine, den Mutter manchmal zitiert hatte. »Leise zieht durch mein Gemüt liebliches Geläute. Klinge kleines Frühlingslied, kling hinaus ins Weite«, eines der vielen Gedichte, die

Mutter auswendig konnte, Relikt eines Bildungskanons aus der Vorkriegszeit.

Mein Bruder kommt bereits am Vormittag und wir sitzen an Mutters Bett, erzählen von früher, und es ist, als würden wir uns für Mutter erinnern. Sie wird unruhig, nachdem er gegangen ist, und ich sage zu ihr, dass alles in Ordnung sei, ich würde bleiben. Es würde noch ein paar Tage dauern und dann würde es vollbracht sein. Ich halte ihre Hand, ganz zart, will sie nur mit einem Hauch meine Anwesenheit spüren lassen. Es ist ruhig in der kleinen Wohnung, bis auf Mutters Atemgeräusch, eine friedvolle Stimmung beginnt sich auszubreiten. In den nächsten Stunden werde ich alleine hier sein, und ich versuche, mich an die Kleider zu erinnern, die Mutter, mit der ihr eigenen Hingabe, über die Jahre für mich genäht hat. Das weiße Rosenkleid taucht in meinem Inneren auf, der grün und beige gestreifte Plisseerock, das langärmlige schwarzrote Dirndl und das bunte Strickkleid. Kaum hörbar beschreibe ich alles, vertieft in die Erinnerung an Szenen, die mir bei jedem Stück in den Sinn kommen, meine Stimme verbindet mich mit Mutter. Stechend drängt sich der Gedanke auf, dass es mit Mutters Tod auch um den Verlust des Ortes geht, an den ich, ohne mich rechtfertigen zu müssen, jederzeit zurückkehren konnte. Noch vor einem Jahr sagte Mutter, ich könne immer zu ihr kommen, falls ich meine Arbeit aufgeben würde, ihre kleine Rente würde für beide zum Leben langen, ich hätte sicher auch noch etwas Erspartes, sie würde mich in Ruhe an meinem Buch arbeiten lassen. Damals fand ich ihren Vorschlag absurd und war eigentümlich berührt, bedankte mich, machte noch einen Scherz, mit dem ich ihre Idee relativierte. Ich habe es erst jetzt verstanden: »Komm einfach nach Hause, hier hast Du immer Deinen Platz.«

Mutter gibt leise Töne von sich, ohne die Augen zu öffnen, ich lüfte die Decke, befeuchte ihre Lippen mit einem Stäbchen. Sie kann keine Bewegungen mehr selbstständig ausführen. Ich platziere vorsichtig ein Kissen zwischen ihren Knien, damit nicht Knochen auf Knochen zu liegen kommt, lege ihr einen nach Arnika duftenden Lappen auf die Stirn, stelle den Ventilator neben ihr Bett, damit sein Lufthauch, im Takt der langsamen Schwenkbewegungen, über Mutters Gesicht streichen kann, wie der Wind, der durch das geöffnete Eisenbahnfenster in die Haare bläst, was sie auf gemeinsamen Reisen immer genossen hatte. Es braucht nicht mehr viel, wenn das Leben sich zurückzieht und der Körper, als Überbleibsel einer irdischen Last, die Nachhut des Verschwindens bildet.

Spät abends kommt mein Bruder wieder, und nachdem er sich bei Mutter eingerichtet hat, stolpere ich durch die Dunkelheit auf einem unbeleuchteten Weg, im Drang auszuschreiten, die Lebendigkeit meines Körpers nicht verkümmern zu lassen. Als ich nach einer Stunde, verschwitzt von meinem Marsch, leise die Wohnung betrete, höre ich bereits im Vorraum das Atemziehen, das sich immer stärker zu verselbstständigen scheint und nichts gemein hat mit dem Atemholen meiner Mutter. Es klingt, als ob eine Maschine den Takt bestimmt, die unerbittlich weiterarbeitet, bis die letzte Reserve an Energie aufgebraucht ist. Mein Bruder und ich wechseln nur wenige Sätze, er wirkt müde, packt tapsig seine mitgebrachten Bücher ein, vielleicht ist er für eine Weile im Lehnsessel eingenickt. Es ist zehn Uhr abends, und die Szene gemahnt an den Schichtwechsel im Werk, wenn der neue Arbeitstrupp die Plätze bezieht, während sich der andere zur Heimfahrt bereitmacht. Ich setze mich an den Tisch, schlage mein Notizbuch auf, bin noch nicht müde, werde noch etwas schreiben, damit ich Ruhe finde. Manchmal sind es Stichworte zu den Ereignissen des Tages oder Ideen für das Buchprojekt, dazwischen kleine Zeichnungen und Skizzen. Ich versuche dem Geräusch, das aus Mutters halbgeöffnetem Mund dringt, nicht zu viel Aufmerksamkeit zu schenken, taste mit meinem Blick suchend im Zimmer umher. Das Bild des Kalenders »Venus mit dem Spiegel« von Velazquez will nicht so recht in den Raum hier passen. Ein weiblicher Akt liegt eingebettet in die starken Farben eines seidenglänzenden blauen Leintuchs und eines roten Vorhanges, die eine Wirkung von Sachlichkeit entfalten und ihn damit der Erotik entheben, als habe der Maler die nackte Frau zwischen Fahnen drapiert und sie damit ihrer sinnlichen Kraft beraubt. Der helle Rücken, in seiner bleichen Eleganz ästhetisch, wirkt tröstlich, gerade hier, im Umkreis der Vergänglichkeit. Doch durch den Spiegel, den ein kleiner Engel, am Bettrand sitzend, ihr entgegenhält, blickt mir nicht nur die junge

Frau entgegen, es ist zur Hälfte auch das dunkel über-
schattete Antlitz einer Greisin, das in die Tiefe der Zeit
verweist.

39

Zu Mittag beim Geläut der Kirchenglocken bete ich anstelle von Mutter laut das Vaterunser. Dann beginne ich ein Gedicht aus einer Anthologie vorzulesen, die ich ihr letztes Jahr geschenkt habe. Mutter hat aus Zeitungen und Illustrierten einige zusätzliche Zettel mit Versen ausgeschnitten und eingelegt, dazwischen das handgeschriebene Rezept für die Geburtstagstorte, die sie mir immer gebacken hatte. Als ich nach den ersten Zeilen innehalte, ist mit einem Mal jeder Laut zu viel, alle Ablenkung sinnentleert, und es ist die Stille zwischen den Atemzügen, die ihren Platz beansprucht, nicht mein Vortrag. Sie soll hinübergleiten, ich will sie nicht halten, binden, an die Geräusche der Welt, an die Stimmen der Lebenden. Vielleicht hört sie inzwischen andere Töne, Klänge, die mit dem Hier und Jetzt nichts zu tun haben. Wenn ich sie anfasse, dann ist da noch eine Wärme, das Leben in den schwächer werdenden Gliedmaßen, die warme Stirn.

Ich wasche Mutter gemeinsam mit der Pflegerin sehr behutsam. Wir betten sie vorsichtig, sie reagiert kaum mehr, wird nicht wach, wenn wir sie drehen und wickeln, in aller gebührenden Langsamkeit, mit leisen begleitenden Kommentaren zu den nächsten Handgriffen, um sie nicht zu erschrecken. Die Zahnprothesen setze ich nicht mehr ein, auch die Augentropfen träufle ich nur zögernd an die Ränder der geschlossenen Lider. Nach getaner Arbeit setze ich mich müde in den Lehnstuhl und spüre, wie die Anspannung in meinen Gliedern nachlässt, die Unsicherheit einer Zufriedenheit Platz macht, wenn ich auf Mutters Züge sehe. Im Schein der Kerze schreibe ich am Computer, den ich auf den Knien platziert habe, an Mutters Lebenslauf. Ich werde den Text dem jungen Pfarrer geben, wenn es dann so weit ist. Es werden einige Menschen zum Begräbnis kommen, mit denen sie nicht eng befreundet war und die sie nur aus der Ferne kannten, mit ihr im Chor gesungen, gemeinsam bei der Volkshilfe gearbeitet haben. Was kann ich über Mutter berichten, ohne etwas preiszugeben, das ihr unangenehm sein könnte? Von dem Selbstmordversuch mit Tabletten, in der Zeit, als ich in Graz studierte, hat Mutter niemandem erzählt, mit niemandem ihre Verzweiflung geteilt, die sie befiel, wenn es um Vater ging, seine nicht enden wollende Trunksucht. Sie sagte später, sie hätte keinen Ausweg mehr gesehen, weil sie wusste, Vater würde niemals einen Entzug machen. Sie hätte keine Kraft gehabt, sich von ihm zu trennen. Nachdem sie sich von der Tablettenvergiftung erholt hatte und man sie aus dem Krankenhaus wieder nach Hause entließ, holte ich sie zu mir in meine Studentenwohnung. Sie kehrte nicht mehr zu Vater zurück, begann als Aushilfskraft in der Altenbetreuung im Stundenlohn. Es bereitete ihr Freude und machte sie sichtlich stolz, endlich ihre Unabhängigkeit erlangt zu haben, auch wenn sie nicht viel verdiente und mit sechzig Jahren in einer Einzimmerwohnung mit Toilette auf dem Gang nicht gerade bequem wohnte. In der Zeit, die dann folgte, wurde unser Kontakt unbeschwerter, ich musste mir keine Sorgen mehr um sie machen, denn sie war oft mit ihren Chorkollegen und den neuen Nachbarn auf Reisen, holte nach, wie sie sagte, was sie über die Jahre versäumt zu haben glaubte, schrieb Ansichtskarten von Bergausflügen und vom Meer in Ägypten. Mir blieb die Sorge um Vater, dem ich in seiner ihm eigenen Sturheit kaum das Leben erleichtern konnte. Aber das ist eine andere Geschichte, sie liegt zurück in den Anfängen meiner Arbeit als Turnusärztin, als ich ihn übermüdet nach meinen Nachtdiensten besuchte, um seine Wohnung und Wäsche in Ordnung zu halten, was er oft nicht zulassen wollte. Nach Vaters Tod befiel mich ein Gefühl der Leere, ein Gefühl, »aus der Welt gefallen zu sein«, etwas, wovor ich mich fürchte, wenn dann auch Mutter gegangen ist.

Heute singe ich keine Adventslieder für Mutter, stattdessen laufen im Hintergrund kaum hörbar gregorianische Weihnachtschoräle, eine CD, die Mutter von mir geschenkt bekommen und die sie gerne gehört hat. Der bedächtige, erhabene Singsang erfüllt das Wohnzimmer, lenkt mich ab von Mutters Atemaussetzern, die mich unweigerlich zum Lauschen zwingen. Ich habe ein neues Schmerzpflaster auf Mutters Rücken geklebt und das

Datum darauf geschrieben. Sie träumt, die Augen zucken unter den Liedern, ihr Gesicht wirkt angespannt. Nah an ihrem Ohr flüstere ich, es gäbe keine bösen Geister im Raum, das Christusbild leuchte am Fenster und würde sie beschützen. Sie habe in ihrem Leben, soweit ich wüsste, nichts Böses getan, und wenn doch, dann sei es bereits gesühnt.

Vor einigen Tagen hat sie zu mir gesagt, ich käme ihr vor wie ein Spatz, der aus dem Nest gefallen ist. Doch ist es nicht vielmehr ihre eigene »Spatzhaftigkeit«, mit der sie selbst aus einem behüteten Nest fiel, weil sie so früh von ihrer Mutter Abschied nehmen musste? Ich werde ein wenig Weihrauch verbrennen, um sie damit einzuhüllen. Zur Weihnachtszeit haben wir früher auf dem Holzofen in der Küche die wohlriechenden Harzklumpen schmelzen lassen, und ich war fasziniert von den dichten kleinen Rauchwolken, die im Nu die Wohnung mit ihrem Duft erfüllten. Mutter hatte gemeint, das sei gegen die Geister des Winters, während der Raunächte müsse man auf der Hut sein. Vielleicht kann sie den Schutz brauchen, um gut über die Schwelle zu treten, die sie jetzt zu überschreiten noch nicht im Stande ist. So gerne würde ich ihr helfen, aber ich werde es nicht mit einer größeren Dosis Schmerzmittel tun, Mutter soll ohne Schmerzen, aber auch ohne starke Betäubung den letzten Weg gehen, wenn ich jetzt zum Medikament greifen würde, würde ich sie töten.

40

Mutters Augen sind gebrochen, die Lider stehen halb
offen. Seit fünf Uhr nachmittags hat sie begonnen, fast
pausenlos laut Atem zu ziehen, als ob ihr ein Kloß im
Hals steckte. Bei der Abendtoilette ist Mutters Körper steif. Stillschweigend kleide ich Mutter mit Hilfe
der Pflegerin in ein neues Nachthemd, um den scharfen
Uringeruch zu beseitigen. Es kostet mich Überwindung,
ich habe Angst, ihre Glieder würden bei der geringsten
Berührung auseinanderbrechen. Die Stirn ist kühl geworden, die Hände, die Füße, die Zehen, und bald wird
der ganze Körper kalt sein.

Heute ist Frau Gabriel wieder zurück, sie kommt
vorbei, nachdem mein Bruder gegangen ist, sie will in
ihrer zurückhaltenden und fürsorglichen Art nicht die
Familie stören. Während ich die beiden Frauen eine Weile alleine lasse und nach draußen gehe, um eine Runde
in der nächtlichen Stadt zu drehen, betrachte ich alles
mit dem wehmütigen Blick des Abschiedes, denn später
werde ich kaum noch Zeit in der Stadt meiner Kindheit
verbringen. Zurück in der Wohnung sagt Frau Gabriel,
als sie sich den Mantel im Vorraum überstreift, Mutter
würde diese Nacht nicht überleben. Es klingt eigenartig,

wenn sie ausspricht, was bereits spürbar ist. Sie sagt, sie würde vorbeikommen, wenn ich ihre Hilfe bräuchte, ich sollte mich melden, jederzeit. Nachdem sie die Türe hinter sich leise ins Schloss gezogen hat, setze ich mich neben Mutter und halte ihre Hand, ich beobachte den Atem, der schwer ist und jetzt immer wieder stockt. Das Sterben hat eingesetzt. Mutter ist weit weg. Ich habe ihren Lebenslauf vollendet, ungeschönt, liebevoll. Es war kein leichtes, kein fröhliches Leben, und ein Teil davon hat sich auf mich übertragen. Irgendwann im letzten Sommer, als wir abends auf der Terrasse ihrer Wohnung gesessen sind, hat Mutter gesagt »Es wird besser, wenn ich tot bin, dann bist Du frei«. Es wird nicht so sein. Ich halte ihre Hände, sie sind wärmer geworden, als ob der Tod noch einmal zurückgewichen wäre, doch es ist meine eigene Wärme, die sich auf Mutter übertragen hat. Ich werde schwer und müde. Ich werde mich kurz im Nebenzimmer ausstrecken, nur einen Moment. Bitte Mutter lass los.

Aufgewacht um halb vier am 1. Dezember – Mutter ist fortgereist für immer.

Am Morgen bevor mein Bruder kommt, um mit mir gemeinsam das Begräbnis vorzubereiten, wechsle ich das Kalenderblatt auf das erste Dezemberbild. Stillleben mit Obst und Hummer von Pieter de Ring. Mutters Proviant für unterwegs. Ein letztes Glas voll funkelndem, lichterfülltem Wein. Mit einer ausholenden Geste meiner rechten Hand proste ich ihr zu. Auf Dein Leben, Mama.

Verlagsgruppe Random House FSC® N001967

3. Auflage
Copyright © 2020 Luchterhand Literaturverlag, München,
in der Verlagsgruppe Random House GmbH,
Neumarkter Straße 28, 81673 München
Satz: Greiner & Reichel, Köln
Druck und Einband: Friedrich Pustet, Regensburg
Covergestaltung: buxdesign, München
Covermotiv: Plainpicture (Janklein; Joseph S. Giacalone)
Printed in Germany
ISBN 978-3-630-87506-4

www.luchterhand-literaturverlag.de